Alexander Stewart, James Logan

The Scotish Gaël
Or, Celtic manners, as preserved among the Highlanders: being an historical and descriptive account of the inhabitants, antiquities, and national peculiarities of Scotland. Vol. 2

ISBN/EAN: 9783337297978

Printed in Europe, USA, Canada, Australia, Japan

Cover: Foto ©ninafisch / pixelio.de

More available books at **www.hansebooks.com**

Alexander Stewart, James Logan

The Scotish Gaël

Or, Celtic manners, as preserved among the Highlanders: being an historical and descriptive account of the inhabitants, antiquities, and national peculiarities of Scotland. Vol. 2

THE SCOTTISH GAËL;

OR,

Celtic Manners.

VOL. II.

CONTENTS OF VOL. II.

CHAPTER I.
                                                                               Page

OF THE ARCHITECTURE OF THE CELTS   1

CHAPTER II.
OF ANIMALS, AND THE MANNER OF HUNTING   28

CHAPTER III.
OF THE PASTORAL STATE AND OF AGRICULTURE   55

CHAPTER IV.
OF THE FOOD OF THE CELTS—THEIR COOKERY, LIQUORS, MEDICINAL KNOWLEDGE, HEALTH, AND LONGEVITY   108

CHAPTER V.
OF THE SHIPPING, COMMERCE, MONEY, AND MANUFACTURES OF THE CELTS   185

CHAPTER VI.
POETRY AND MUSIC   217

CHAPTER VII.
RELIGION, MARRIAGE CEREMONIES, AND FUNERAL RITES   323

CHAPTER VIII.
OF THE KNOWLEDGE OF LETTERS AMONG THE CELTS   398

APPENDIX.
TABLE OF CLAN TARTANS   417
INDEX   425

List of Embellishments.

VOLUME II.

1.	Highland Bagpiper, dressed in full Costume, (coloured plate)	*Frontispiece.*
2.	Vignette in Title-page.	
3.	View of Dun-Troddan in Glenelg	*Page* 1
4.	Section of Mousa and Dun-Dornghil	17
5.	Do., showing the Galleries	17
6.	View of Dun-Dornghil in Strathmore	27
7.	Bas Relief of a Gallic Boar Hunt	28
8.	Horns of the Moose Deer	54
9.	Highlander employed at the Caserom	55
10.	Agricultural Implements	107
11.	Domestic Utensils	108
12.	Snuff Horn and its Appendages	184
13.	An Ancient Biorlin	185
14, 15.	British Coins	197, 198
16.	Funereal Urn and other Vessels	216
17.	Figures of Two Druids	217
18 to 21.	Specimens of Music	269
22.	Reeds of the Bagpipe	304
23.	The Royal Arms of Scotland (coloured plate)	305
24.	Harp of Queen Mary	322
25.	Stonehenge restored	323
26.	Plan of the Temple at Classerness in Lewis	397
27.	Obelisk, with Hieroglyphic Sculptures	398
28.	Mystical Figure	408
29.	Illuminated Capital, from a Gaelic MS.	415

"Dun-Troddan," in Glenelg.

CHAPTER I.

OF THE ARCHITECTURE OF THE CELTS.

In the art of castrametation, it has been shewn that the early Celts were by no means deficient. The state of society gave but little encouragement to the study of domestic architecture among these nations, and the simplicity of their lives did not require the conveniences afforded by this useful and ornamental science.

The little huts of the Gauls and the Britons were adapted to the wants of the people, but they were of too slight a construction to leave any very perceptible remains. The occupations of the pastoral life did not require the erection of permanent habitations: in perambulating a country, it is useless to bestow much labour on a building that must be soon abandoned. The freedom of a strolling life is congenial to untutored man. The Fenns, Tacitus says, sheltered themselves with the branches of trees, preferring this rude and cheerless state of existence to the painful occupations of agriculture, of constructing houses, and the continual trouble of defending their property.

Cæsar describes Britain as abounding in houses. Dio says the Caledonians lived in tents, meaning the simple booth of wattles, thatched with rushes, of which Strabo gives a particular description. The houses of the Britons, says he, are of a round form, constructed of poles and wattled work, with very high pointed roofs, the beams uniting at top. Diodorus says, for the most part they were covered with reeds or straw, materials of which the Carthaginians formed their tents.[a] We find that the houses of the Gauls and Britons were composed of wood, and the use of tiles and mortar being unknown, they were plastered with clay, or a sort of red earth, which was latterly procured in England. Vitruvius says, that in Gaul, Spain, and Lusitania, the houses were made of oak, shingles, and straw.[b] Certain reeds were used in Gaul as a covering for the houses; and, if well put on, Pliny says this sort of roof would last for ages, and it had this valuable property, besides, according to Aristotle, that it was not easily consumed by fire. A sort of stone was also applied to this purpose, and is at this day used under the name of Knappstein, or pierre de liais, on the continent. It is of a white colour, and is cut as easily as timber; and being sometimes very gaudy, the houses were called Pavonacea, from a supposed resemblance to peacocks' feathers.[c]

Wood is a material so convenient for architectural purposes, that it has been much employed even where necessity did not compel its adoption. Throughout Britain and

[a] Lib. xx. 3.   [b] Lib. ii. 1.
[c] Hist. Nat. Tome xii. p. 66, 4to ed. 1782.

Ireland many considerable edifices have been reared of timber in periods comparatively recent. In the ninth century, the houses in the Highlands of Scotland were usually of wattle work, and the residences of the chiefs were frequently built in the same manner. We find one Gillescop, in 1228, burning many wooden castles in Moray. Strong bulwarks were often constructed of apparently slight materials. Gir. Cambrensis relates, that in the reign of Hen. I., Arnulph de Montgomery founded a castle at l'embroke, the rampart of which was formed of osiers and turf. The chief residence of the kings of Wales was called the white Palace, from its appearance, having been built of wands with the bark peeled off. A sort of wattle work, or combination of twigs or prepared wood and earth or clay, was a common mode of building among the Gaël, both of Albin and Erin, and was known as "the Scotish fashion." Of this manner of building was that church erected in 652 by Finan, Bishop of Lindisfarne, composed wholly of sawn oak, covered with reeds.[d] *

The Scots were, indeed, the first native architects who invented the method of squaring timber, and applying it to large and public edifices.[e] In this way the first church at Iona was built, as well as numerous others, descriptions of which do not exist. In 1172, when St. Bernard describes a stone church in Ireland as a novelty, Henry II. was entertained at Dublin in a long wattle house, built, we are told, after the fashion of the country. William of Malmesbury speaks of a church in his time formed of rods

---

[d] Bede, Eccles. Hist. iii. c. 25.   [e] Pownall in Archaeologia, ix. iii.

* Up to the year 1746, Lochiel's residence at Achnacarry was a house curiously built of wattle work, said to have been both handsome and comfortable. It was burnt to the ground by the Government troops. The present castellated building is an exceedingly handsome and imposing structure. ED.

or wicker, and a MS. in the British Museum says that the religious edifices were all at first formed "ex virgatis torquatis."

Sir James Hall, in his learned and ingenious work on the origin of gothic architecture, which he believes is derived from the osier edifices, has shewn the progress of this beautiful style, and collected many curious facts, illustrative of the primitive manner of building, described by Bede as "in more Scotorum," of which a curious specimen exists at this day in the church of Grenestede, in the county of Essex. One thousand oaks from the mountains formed the hall of Crothar, an Irish chief, but none of the houses of Fingal were of wood, it is said, except Tifiormal, the great hall, where the bards met annually to repeat their compositions. By some accident it was burnt; and an ancient poet has left a curious catalogue of its furniture.‘

The Gaël have not relinquished the ancient mode of constructing houses. In many parts it is still common, but it is not so generally prevalent as formerly. Spelman, who lived in the middle of the sixteenth century, says wicker houses were the common habitations of the Irish. The Rapparee, in the time of King William III., lived in a hut, formed by means of a few branches of trees, one end being stuck in the ground, and the other resting on a mud wall or bank. The common people had also cabins, formed entirely of wattle work, with a coating of clay; and these rude hovels, which Sir W. Petty says could be built in three days, were held of the superior from May to May. In Jurah and other islands of the Hebudae, the cottages are still chiefly constructed of these fragile materials, and in many parts of the mainland of Scotland the same manner is followed. It is found comfortable for dwelling houses,

Mac Pherson, note on Ossian.

and is extremely well adapted for barns, and other edifices attached to farms.

The humble dwelling of the ancient tribes was called, in the British tongue, bod, or bwth, which signifies a cottage or dwelling. In Gaëlic, bothan is a cottage, and is particularly applied to the slight buildings raised for summer residence in the hills. These different Celtic words shew the origin of the English booth, and were applied to the simple dwelling which also received the names of tent and hut. The translators of Ossian render this word by different terms: "The hunter shall hear from his booth," "No hut receives me from the rain," &c.

If the residence of the Briton was on a plain, it was called Lann, from Lagen or Logan, an inclosed plain or low-lying place. If on an eminence, it was termed Dun, the origin of the Latin dunum, which terminates the names of so many Celtic towns. Durum indicated the position to be on the banks of a stream. Magus is apparently from magh, a plain, and Bona may be from bonn, round.*

Aiteach, a habitation, is derived from the Gaëlic ait, a place, whence the Greek αιδια, and the Latin aedes. Peillichd in Gaëlic, and peillic in Cornish, signify a hut made of earth and branches of trees.⁵ This term comes from feile, or peile, a skin or covering, which is the origin of the English fell, felt, and many others.† The Latin domus seems derived from domh, a dwelling.

It has been before observed that the roving life of the Celts did not require the erection of permanent habitations. The hill forts were known places of retreat in time of danger: on other occasions, the tribes formed their rude

---

* *Bona* rather seems to be from *bān*, fair, beautiful, Scottice *bonnie*. ED.

⁵ Armstrong and Pryce.

† From the Latin *pellis*, a skin, or hide. ED.

tents more for the purpose of temporary shelter than as fixed places of residence.

This was indeed in the most early ages, but long after they began to relish the sweets of a more civilized life, their dwellings remained rude and unimposing. The residences of the aboriginal British chiefs are described by Whitaker as formed of wood, the dwelling house and attendant offices forming a quadrangular court; he, however, notices the ruins of some stone buildings discovered at Manchester and Aldborough, of a square form, the walls being two yards broad and one deep, composed of three layers of common paving stone, on which were laid a tier of larger blocks, all cemented with clay.

The square form of these ruins certainly bears little indication of a British origin. The Celts adhered to the circular plan, at least while independent: on the subjugation of the Southern tribes they were induced to abandon their native manners, and imitate those of their conquerors, and their houses, we know from Tacitus, were then built after the models of the Romans.

Stone work is, however, no proof that ruins are not British. We are informed by the Welsh antiquaries that Morddal Gwr Gweilgi, mason to Ceraint ap Greidiawl, first taught the Britons to work in stone and mortar;[b] but the chronicles of that nation stretch too far into the regions of fable to receive unhesitating credence to all their relations. It would appear from Henry of Huntingdon,[i] that stone buildings were not very common in the Principality before the reign of Edward the First, but the natives were certainly able to construct such edifices.

In all parts of the island where stone was abundant, it may be safely presumed that the substructure of the primi-

---

[b] Roberts' Early Hist. of the Cumri.   [i] Book iv. 126.

tive hut was composed of it. Small circular vestigia are to be seen on the muirs in most parts of Scotland that are certainly the remains of the Celtic booths. They are sometimes in considerable numbers, and often appear within the area of fortifications.[k] A remarkable instance occurs in Cornwall, and is noticed in the "Beauties" for that county. The diameter of the ancient houses of the Caledonians is usually about nine yards, but some are considerably larger, and the door was invariably made to face the rising sun. In Glen Urquhart, near Lochness, these foundations are numerous, and one is observable called the Castle, which is much larger than any of the others. There is also one which has a double concentric wall, evidently intended to form separate apartments. Many similar remains are also to be seen in the neighbourhood of Fort George, or Ardnasœur.

The current tradition is, that these are the remains of the houses of the Picts. In Gaëlic they are denominated Larach tai[l] Draonich, the foundations of the houses of a Draoneach, which has led to the belief that they were the dwellings of Druids. This arises from the similarity of the term to that of Druinich, which signifies a Druid, but it is obvious that that order was not so numerous as to require so many houses. Some circular remains in the Isle of Sky and elsewhere, so small as only to be sufficient for the residence of a single individual, may have indeed been the houses of Druids,[m] and in Tai nan Druinish retain their proper name, but the true signification of Draoneach is a cultivator of the soil, a term which the inhabitants of the eastern parts of Scotland, where agriculture was first

---

[k] These places were called Longphorts, or camps, by the Irish, from long, a field tent.
[l] Or *taod*, i. e. *tai fhod*, rubbish of a house.   [m] Martin, p. 154.

practised, received from their neighbours in the Highlands, who continued a pastoral people.

Whether Draonaich be the origin of Cruithnaich, the name which the Irish gave to the Picts, it is certain that the latter people were distinguished from their brethren of the hills whom they termed the Scuit or Scaoit, from moving about with their flocks: and it is no less true that cultivators of the soil are to this day called Draonaich by the Gaël. It is a proof that the inhabitants of these houses employed themselves in cultivating the earth, and consequently erected edifices calculated for some duration, that in scarcely any instance are they unaccompanied by evident marks of surrounding cultivation.

Another curious group of these unobtrusive ruins is found in the parish of Dalmack, Aberdeenshire, and points out, as there appears every reason to believe, the site of Devana, the capital of the Taixali. A notice of this remarkable place was communicated to the Society of Scots Antiquaries, by the late Professor Stuart, of Marischal college, who describes the remains as amounting to some hundred individual circles, two or three feet high, and from twelve to twenty or thirty feet in diameter, scattered over a space of more than a mile in extent. The numbers of these observable in one place, evince that it must have been a settlement or permanent residence. Some care, it may be observed, is requisite to discriminate the site of a Celtic town, for many remains, presenting a similar appearance, may be referred to military encampments of more recent times.

The arrangement of the huts was made apparently without much design. The Germans, according to Tacitus, placed their houses in opposite rows, each having a certain clear space around it. In one of the bardic poems we are informed that twelve were the houses in the camp of

Fingal, and twelve were the fires in each house. This seems to prove that there was a settled order among the Gaël. The disposition of the booths or tents within the area of a fortification was probably left to a certain individual who acted as quarter-master: such an officer in the Highlands appears to have had a power of regulating the position of the vassals' huts. This member of their establishment was retained by most of the chiefs in the beginning of the last century, and he was entitled, among other perquisites, to the hides of all animals that were killed.

The royal palace of Wales was surrounded by lesser edifices, constituting the kitchen, dormitory, chapel, granary, storehouse, bakehouse, stable, and dog house. Whoever burnt or otherwise destroyed the palace, was obliged to pay one pound and eighty pence; and the fine for each of the other houses was a hundred and twenty pence, a total of £5 : 6s : 8d, or about £160 of our money.

In the Infancy of society, natural caverns are used as hiding places during war, and repositories for grain or other valuable articles. That the Britons availed themselves of such places of retreat there can be no reason to doubt, and that they improved the work of nature is evident from many curious remains. Several caves in the Western Islands, and throughout Britain, contain places for the purpose of cooking, seats hewn in the natural rock, &c.; and some are not only well lighted, but are divided into various apartments.

Subterraneous abodes seem to have been invariably selected for secretion by primitive nations. Josephus mentions them in Galilee, and during the Crusades the inhabitants retired to them for security. The Cimmerii lived in caverns underground, and the Germans, in winter, retreated to caves covered with dung, where they also deposited their grain." Even in the time of Kirchurus, they occasionally lived in such places, and there the gypseys of that country still pass their winters.

The singular caves at Hawthornden, near Edinburgh have at different periods afforded a safe and not uncomfortable retreat to the celebrated Alexander Ramsay, Dunbar, Haliburton, and others. A remarkable cave was discovered at Auxerre in 1735;° and in Picardy, a vast excavation in form of a St. Andrew's cross was laid open.ᴾ The subterranean works and caverns of the Britons may be seen near Blackheath and Crayford in Kent, at Royston, in Hertfordshire, in Essex, in Cornwall, near Guildford, at Nottingham, and in other parts. A curious place of this sort was recently discovered near Grantham, hewn out of the white stone rock, in the interior of which was found a hand mill, with wheat and barley of a black colour, and apparently mixed with ashes. The great cavern in Badenoch, where nine of the principal men of the Cumins were slain by Alexander Macpherson, commonly called the Revengeful, is thirty feet square and ten high. Curious subterraneous edifices are to be seen in many parts of Ireland, and generally within the area of fortifications. The side walls are usually formed of large stones pitched on end, the roof being covered with horizontal slabs. In many cases the roof is formed by several stones, each overlapping the other until a small space is left, which is covered by one of a larger size, thus forming a rude sort of arch. Some of these curious structures are of considerable dimensions, and are divided into different apartments or cells.ᑫ That some may have been places of

---

ⁿ Tacitus. Mela.   ° Le Beuf, Divers Ecrits, i. p. 290.
ᴾ Mem de l'Acad. des Inscriptions, ap. Pinkerton.
ᑫ A view and plan of a singular remain of this kind at Annaclough Mullach, Kilslevy, Armagh, is given in Archæologia.

sepulture is not improbable, but their general use was for the deposition of the grain and other valuable effects of the natives, and the occasional secretion of themselves in troublous times. It was a well known practice of the Celtic nations to construct such places as granaries, and Varro describes them as often very spacious and admirably adapted for the purpose.^r

In the north of Scotland numerous artificial caves are found, of a construction resembling those in Ireland. They are called Eird-houses in the Low Country, and are considered as the hiding places of the aborigines. They are sometimes of considerable extent, being long and narrow, but many, to render the size more commodious, have in subsequent periods been built up at the farther end. The sides are usually built of small stones, without cement, and the roof is composed of large thin stones resting on either side. The entrance to most of them appears now only a rude hole or opening, but some are more artificial. Near Tongue, in Sutherland, are some where the passage is formed by large stones inclined to and resting on each other.

The appearance of these Eird-houses on the exterior, when they are at all discernible, is that of a slight, green eminence, and except one is directed in his search, it would be difficult to discover them. In the parishes of Achindoer and Kildrummy, in Aberdeenshire, they are numerous. I have inspected several in these parts; but I confess I should not have looked for so many as the late Professor Stuart says had been discovered,—not less than forty or fifty! He justly observes, that perhaps so many in one place has never occurred. In all those which he visited nothing was found but wood ashes and charcoal, which

---

^r De Re Rust. 57.

with an aperture for the escape of smoke, may have been produced by recent occupants.

In the parish of Golspie, Sutherland, subterraneous buildings have been discovered, having a small oblique entry from the surface of about two and a half feet square, which after advancing three yards, widens to about three feet, and winds a few yards farther to an apartment of about twelve feet-square and nine high, covered above by large broad stones, terminating in one, formed like a millstone, having a hole in the centre, probably to emit smoke. From this cell a passage led to others, which are now inaccessible, from the fall of the superincumbent earth.

Rude as the common habitations of the ancient tribes were, and unimportant as the science of domestic architecture was deemed, the dwellings of the chief men were of a superior construction. Adomnan mentions castles as the residence of the Pictish kings, and many structures are undoubtedly of their era. The existence of palaces of these monarchs at Abernethy, in Perthshire, has been noticed by Mr. Small in a work devoted to an investigation of the subject.

The DUNS, properly so called, or those circular buildings in Scotland, constructed without any cement, and usually exhibiting double walls, to which this term is particularly appropriate, are objects of great antiquarian interest, and admirable specimens of Celtic architecture. These edifices have been scattered over Scotland in considerable numbers, but in most cases but very slight remains of their curious walls now exist.

It is asserted by the author of "Caledonia," that not one bears an appellation from the Pictish or British languages;[a] and that they are only found in the parts where

---

[a] Vol. i. p. 343.

the Scandinavians settled. Buildings similar in plan and internal arrangement, are indeed found in Orkney, Shetland, and in parts of Scotland where these people did reside; but why may not they have imitated the construction of the Celts? or taken possession of buildings erected before their arrival? The learned Mr. Grant, of Corimony, who devoted much attention to the examination of these antique structures, thus expresses himself concerning them: "That the Danes, or Norwegians, and the Gaël, were equally capable of building such edifices, there is no good reason to entertain any doubt; but that these towers were built by the native Gaël, and not by foreigners, appears to be in no small degree probable. They are of an uncommon construction, and different from any of those antique edifices to be seen in the islands possessed by the Danes."

A writer who is not inclined to concede much to the Celts, and who has certainly studied the national history with attention, however his prejudices may have misled him, thus observes: " It has been on all occasions found that there was a considerable resemblance in the manners, usages, warlike weapons, and monumental practices of the original British or Celtic inhabitants, and those of their early invaders, and there seems no ground for attempting a distinction in the structures which they erected for the purposes of defence."* Two queries may be proposed: the Norwegians invaded and subdued other countries; do we find them building any circular forts there? Are round towers found anywhere in Europe except in the regions inhabited by Gaël? If some of the Duns bear names which appear to indicate Norwegian or Danish founders, many others are distinguished by appellations

* Mac Culloch's Western Islands, i. 141.

decidedly Celtic. Those of Glenelg, without enumerating many others, have the appropriate names of Calman, Conal, Telve, and Troddan, that are purely Gaëlic, and were apparently imposed before the introduction of Christianity.

This remarkable assemblage of buildings, one of which, Caistell Troddan, being the most perfect, is represented in the preceding vignette, is, or rather was, to be seen in Glenbeg, a small valley, which terminates in Glenelg, in Inverness-shire. Within the extent of a mile four of these singular edifices were to be seen, displaying a mode of construction truly admirable.

The one alluded to is still upwards of thirty feet high, having, it is supposed, been originally somewhat more than forty,[a] and has a clear area of thirty feet diameter.[b] Two walls, each four feet in thickness, are built at four feet distance from each other. That in the interior is perpendicular, the outer one being inclined so as to meet the other near the top of the building. The interval between is divided by means of horizontal flat stones, inserted in both walls, into galleries. It was the opinion, according to the Rev. Donald Mac Leod, of some old men, that these passages had originally a spiral ascent, like some on the east coast, but they seem rather to have formed distinct flats or stories, as shewn in the section (C). At the junction of the walls, in the interior, is a row of large flat projecting stones, and about eight feet below was another similar range, destroyed by a military contractor.

There is no window or opening on the outside, except the door, which communicates with a small circular stone

---

[a] Dr. Mac Pherson found it thirty-four, and Gordon, who visited it about fifty years before, calls it thirty-three feet.

[b] The diameter of these buildings varies from seventeen to fifteen feet.

fabric, similar to what has been described. The windows, of which two are detached from the others, commence about thirteen feet from the ground. Six rows of the first are all one and a half feet wide; some are two and others three feet in height.

"The building of those edifices," says Mr. Grant, "must have been attended with immense labour and difficulty. The stones with which those structures are built, are many of them of great weight and size, and must have been brought from parts of the country at a great distance from the towers. No such stones are to be found in the whole extent of the valley where the towers stand. Stones of similar size, shape, and dimensions, it is said, are to be found near the summits of some of the high mountains which form one side of the valley. The great Mountain of Ben Nevis, near Fort William, is 1640 yards in height.* This mountain is not of a conical figure, terminating in a sharp point, like many others of the highest mountains in Scotland; the summit is a plain, exhibiting in abundance such stones as those with which the Glenelg towers are built. All the stones are flat-sided parallelograms; their edges are right lines, terminating in regular angles; they are capable of being closely joined, and built in such a manner as that the superincumbent stones are made to cover both ends of the immediately subjacent stones all round the building.

"Two of these towers still remain, though not whole or entire; the other two have been destroyed by unhallowed hands, and taken away to build the barracks of Bernera, standing at the bottom of the larger valley of Glenelg. These curious stones, laid with such admirable

* The actual height of Ben Nevis, according to the latest and corrected measurements, is 4406 feet or 1468·2 yards. ED.

skill, and collected with such wonderful industry by our remote ancestors, were to be confounded with common stones of irregular figures, to be hidden from the eye by cement and mortar, after the manner of more improved ages in the arts of architecture. Thus those curious monuments of antiquity were pulled asunder, and swept away, to gratify the mean avarice of servants in the pay of government. Disgraceful barbarity! It is to be hoped that the proprietor of those singular monuments of rude architecture, will in future pay particular attention to the preservation of their remains, which cannot but afford a delicious entertainment to the eye of curiosity."

These sentiments of a zealous and learned antiquary, must be congenial to every cultivated mind. It is unfortunately too often to be regretted that the interesting remains of ancient art fall into the hands of those who have no veneration for the works of antiquity, nor admiration of the ingenuity of former ages. Arthur's oven, that unique and curious specimen of ancient architecture, standing near the river Carron, was razed to the ground for the construction of a mill pond! This venerable monument, of which Stukely and Gordon give engravings, was of a circular form. The walls were bent over in the manner of a vault, without closing, a considerable aperture being left in the centre, which with an arched door and small window lighted the interior. It has been supposed a Roman temple erected to Terminus. Horsley thinks it a sepulchre, and Pinkerton believes it gave the hint for the erection of the Duns. It is certainly of the same character, and resembled some structures in Ireland that will be briefly noticed.

The following sections of two of these buildings, dun Dornghil, in Strathmore, parish of Durness, in Sutherland,

(A,) and the burg of Mousa, (B,) supposed of Norwegian construction, shew no further difference than a greater rudeness in the latter.

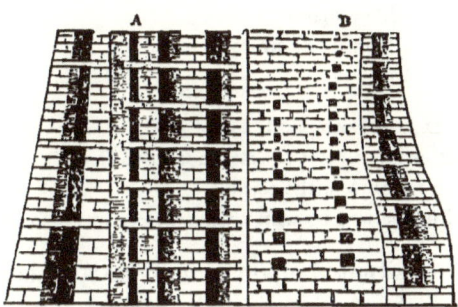

The stairs of these Duns were sometimes, as before observed, carried up in a rude winding form, as in that at Mousa; but the general plan appears to have been in the manner shewn by this section.

Dun Dornghil, erroneously called Dornadilla, is represented at the termination of this Chapter. It was, in the memory of man, about thirty feet high, but is now much dilapidated. Not a stone of this fabric "is moulded by a hammer, nor is there any fog or other material used to fill up the interstices among the stones; yet the stones are most artfully laid together, seem to exclude the air, and have been piled with great mathematical exactness."

The following verse concerning it, is repeated by the inhabitants.

> Dun Dornghil Mac Duiff
> Or an taobh ri meira don strha
> Sebcht mille o manir
> Er an rod a racha na fir do Gholen.*

TRANSLATION.

> The Dun of Dornghiall, son of Duff,
> Built on the side of the strath next to Rea,
> Seven miles from the ocean,
> And in the way by which the warriors travel to Caithness.▼

Castle Coul, situated upon a rock at the black water of Strathbeg, parish of Clyne, in the same county, is another remarkable edifice of similar construction. The walls are now only about eleven feet high; they are thirteen and a half feet thick at the base, and leave an area of twenty-seven feet clear. The stones are large and well joined, without any cement, and the building inclines inwards nine inches in three feet. In the middle of the wall, on each side of the entrance, which is three and a half feet in height by two and a half in width, is a small apartment, about six feet square and five feet high, that seems to have been intended for a guard room. Six feet from the base of the wall are the remains of another, which surrounded the dun.

---

* In a more correct orthography these lines will appear thus :—

> Dùn Dornghil Mac Dhuiff
> Air taobh na mara do'n t'srath;
> Seachd mile 'o mhanir,
> Air an ròd 'n racha' na fir do Ghallabh.

> The Dun of Dorngil, son of Duff;
> On the side next to the Sea of the Strath;
> Seven miles from Rea,
> On the way whereon men go to Caithness.
>   ED.

▼ Rev. A. Pope, in Archæologia, v.

This appears to have been for the purpose of forming, by means of large flag stones stretching to the castle walls, an additional security from assault. In this place it is said the cattle were kept during the night, and when the country was invaded.[x] The water of the river was carried by a ditch round the castle.

In the parish of Dunse, county of Berwick, is a ruin called Edwin's Hall, which is supposed to have been erected by the Picts, and will be seen from the description[y] to be of the same class as the Duns just described, only exhibiting an arrangement of three walls, with a mode of connecting the stones extremely ingenious and uncommon. Like all similar structures, it is situated on an eminence. Cockburn Law, the site of this fort, is 900 feet above the level of the sea. The circular walls, seven feet in thickness, are concentric, and the clear interior area is forty feet. The stones are chiefly a hard whinstone, and are fixed without any cement, but are attached to each other by alternate grooves and projections, or, in technical phrase, are dove-tailed.

In Ireland, from statements in a foregoing page, it might seem there were anciently no buildings of stone. Such observations are to be taken in a general sense, or with so much allowance, as will prevent the appearance of contradiction. The subterraneous structures already noticed were rude, but successful attempts in masonry: and although it is believed by some of the antiquaries of that country, that the Domliag, or stone house of St. Kianan, was the first of that kind, there is some reason to entertain another opinion. Many curious buildings are scattered throughout that interesting island, which, from their sin-

---

[x] Henderson's view of the Agriculture of the County.
[y] Traveller's Guide through Scotland.

gularity of style, and unknown appropriation, are in all probability of extreme antiquity. On the Skelig isle, off the coast of Kerry, are the remains of several cells, which are built of a circular form, and arched over. No cement whatever is used, but the stones are dove-tailed together in a very ingenious manner. On the island of Innis Mackellan, opposite Dunmore Head, and at Gallerus, are similar cells; and at Fane, all in the same county, are the ruins of another.[z] These buildings are perfectly impervious to water, and, consequently, were well calculated to resist the injuries of the weather for many ages.

The ROUND TOWERS, so numerous in Ireland, and which are spoken of by Giraldus Cambrensis as of great antiquity, even when he wrote, have attracted not merely the notice of the antiquary, but excited the admiration and curiosity of all who view them. Their singularity, and the mystery which envelops their origin and design, have drawn towards them much attention, and elicited many curious speculations on their apparent uses and probable era of construction.

It has been supposed that they served as edifices wherein to preserve the sacred fire of the Druids. It has been also said that they were places of residence and probation for devotees, who, by religious exercises and privations, gradually ascended from story to story, as they mortified the flesh and improved in holiness, secluding themselves from society, and acquiring a high reputation for superior devotion, and perhaps supernatural powers. This supposition, which may receive some countenance from what Tacitus relates of the Prophetess Veleda, that she did not permit herself to be seen, but lived in a *high tower*, having an

---

[z] Luckcombe's Tour. At Ithaca, a building resembling these still exists, supporting Grant's idea of the origin of the Gaël. Poems and Translations from the Gaëlic by Mr. Donald Mac Pherson.

attendant to communicate between her and all applicants,[a] and which does not appear to have struck any inquirers, is yet entirely conjectural. The preceding opinion is liable to the same objection, and is considered by Mr. Higgins as completely overthrown by the fact of the crucifixion, and other sculptures emblematical of Christianity, appearing on the walls. This is not a just conclusion, except it is first satisfactorily ascertained whether these figures are part of the original work. It certainly appears a strong argument in favour of the connexion of the towers with Christianity, that they are always in the vicinity of churches, and that those churches are invariably without steeples.[b] It is to be borne in mind, however, that Christian places of worship were founded on the sites of ancient temples;[c] and it is obvious that where one of those towers existed there was no necessity for building another steeple, its chief use being to hold the bells. That the towers were appropriated for this purpose seems clear, from their name of Cloghad, or bell tower. This appellation is decisive of their having been long so appropriated; but it has been asserted, without much reason, that their small diameter rendered them unfit for belfries. The height of these towers varies from about 60 feet to 130. The walls are usually about 3 feet in thickness, and the clear diameter about 10 feet.[d] They are built of stones about a foot square, neatly joined with very little cement. The inside is sometimes remarkably smooth, and the masonry is so good, that instances have occurred of their falling down and lying entire on the ground, like a huge cannon. Those in best repair are covered by a conical roof of stone, which has usually

---

[a] Annals iv.   [b] Archdall's Mon. Hist. 259, et seq., &c.
[c] The tower at Cashel is believed to be the oldest building on the rock.
[d] At Kineigh, a ruined church near Inniskeen, is a tower hexagonal to a certain height.

windows facing the cardinal points, and the inside generally shews the corbel stones on which the wooden floors of four to six different apartments rested. The door is commonly a considerable distance from the ground, sometimes 15 feet or more, and this is reckoned one of their most unaccountable peculiarities.

Assuming that these towers were erected after the introduction of Christianity, is it not probable that they were used as watch towers, whence the approach of an enemy could be descried at a great distance, and to which the ecclesiastics could speedily retreat with their relics and other valuable articles? The elevated entrance demonstrates that it was intended to be difficult of access, and is a well-known characteristic of the fortifications of other nations. A subterraneous passage between the cathedral of Cashel and its attendant tower corroborates the opinion that it was a place of retreat. Consistent with this use would be the position of an alarm bell, to ring on the advance of invading enemies, or the ferocious nations who had not learned to respect the persons of the clergy, or the rights of the church. In Scotland, and I believe also in Wales, the steeples of old churches have crenellated battlements, and other appearances of having been built with the prospect of having to sustain assaults; and the pages of history inform us that the sacred edifice did not always protect its inmates from the rage of a barbarous foe. In Scotland there still exist two round towers, in every respect like those in Ireland. They both stand in the territories of the ancient Picts; and Abernethy, where one of them is seen, was once the capital of their kingdom. The tower here is about seventy-four feet high, and has recently got a covering of lead. The stones of which it is built have been brought from the Lomond hills, five miles distant, and are carefully placed in regular courses, without much cement. The Rev. Andrew Small notices the tradition, that the stones were handed from one person to another, the edifice being finished in one day; to accomplish which, he calculates that 5,500 men were sufficient. It is clear to him "as a sunbeam," that this tower is the burying-place of the Pictish kings, and, on digging, an urn and eight or ten skulls, with other parts of the human body, and some bones of dogs were discovered. The tower at Brechin consists of sixty regular courses of hewn stone, of a fairer colour than the adjoining church. It is eighty-five feet high to the cornice, above which is a low roof of stone with four windows. It communicates with the ancient cathedral by a door, which, like that at Abernethy, is on the north side, but this may not be original. Both are forty-eight feet in outward circumference, which is, with a few exceptions, larger than those in Ireland.

The castles of Dunstaffnage, Inverlochy, and many others, are of undeniable antiquity. It is true that the remaining ruins do not display very perceptibly the marks of primitive architecture.* Buildings were successively repaired and renewed, until all traces of the original work were lost; but it would be quite unwarrantable to deny that the structures referred to in history, as standing on the sites of these buildings never existed. Both Picts and Caledonians were able to raise fabrics of sufficient grandeur and strength for the accommodation and security of their princes.

The Gaël do not adhere to the circular form in which their ancestors built their houses, but construct them of an oblong that sometimes stretches a considerable way. From the abundance of the material, they are usually of stone,

---

* Of Inverlochy Castle the oldest part is that called "Comyn's Tower," probably dating from the thirteenth or early part of the fourteenth century. ED.

built with much nicety, and are finished with or without the addition of mortar, according to circumstances. Turf and stone, in alternate layers, are much used, the first being laid in manner of herring-bone work. A sort of wall, formed of clay and straw, mixed together, called Achenhalrig, is prevalent in Banff and Morayshires. The interior arrangement is simple. Each end forms an apartment, the centre being occupied by wooden fixed beds, ambries or cup-boards, &c. These are termed in Scotish the but and ben ends, which are the Saxon words "be out" and "be in," applied to the common and better apartments.*

The cottages in Scotland are constructed without much trouble or expense, and are generally the work of the owners. An old corporal in Sutherland, who appears, from having seen a little of the world, to have acquired a taste for something better than the common sort of houses, being asked how he intended to build his dwelling, replied, that there should be one good room in it, should it cost two pounds! Few houses, except those of the chiefs and clergymen, had any upper floor, or any ceiling. In many parts of the Highlands there is a difficulty of procuring wood of sufficient length for couples or rafters. Cabers are rough boughs spread across the rafters; and for defence these were formerly interwoven, and the whole roof strongly wattled.

A usual covering for the houses in Scotland is feil or divot, i.e., turf cut thinly, and with much nicety, by a peculiar instrument called a flaughter spade.* This, when used alone, is laid in manner of slating, with the greatest care and the regularity of fishes' scales. The turf is gene-

* The Dutch have also buten and benen.

* Called in Gaelic *luir-chaibe*, the wooden-spade-mare. A curious name for the implement, having its origin in the fact that when using it the worker seems as if he *rode* upon it. ED.

rally covered with heath, a material so cheap and lasting, that it is surprising to find it not universally adopted. It can be used alone, and with timber of a very ordinary description. It also takes very little trouble to keep in repair; and, if the covering is well executed, it is equal to slates, and will last 100 years, if the timber do not give way. Many churches were formerly covered with heath, some within my own memory, the services from lands being often a certain quantity of it for this purpose. Its only disadvantage is being heavier than straw or rushes. Fern or rainneach is next to heath, but much inferior, and will not last above twelve or fifteen years. In Argyle the houses appear to be chiefly covered with it. A straw thatched roof is light, and has this advantage, that it is warmer in winter, and cooler in summer than the others.

The floors are commonly of clay or mortar, well hardened, but it is often partially laid with stones. The ben end in the houses of the better sort is sometimes floored with wood, and the ceiling is often of the same material. The windows are small, and few in number, and glass is an article with which they can easily dispense. The room is chiefly lighted by the chimney, and this, in the old-fashioned houses, where the fire occupied the middle of the apartment, was in the roof above it. In many Highland cottages it still retains this situation, a position which allows the inmates to get around it, an accommodation so desirable, that where the hearth is fixed, in accordance with the modern plan, at one end, a sufficient space is often reserved for seats between the wall and the fire. In the aboriginal huts the most convenient site for the fires was the middle of the dwelling. The Welsh had not altered its place in the time of Cambrensis, who informs us it occupied the centre of the round hall, and men, women, and children slept around it on rushes spread on the floor. Chimneys were alike unknown to the ancient and recent Gaël. At the present day, they have in many cases adopted the artificial funnel for carrying off the smoke; but a hole in the roof, above which there is sometimes a low chimney of wood or wicker work, is usually all that is thought necessary, and very inefficient it generally is. It has been observed by a recent traveller in these parts, that chimneys are a premature improvement, the cottages, while constructed on the old plan, and the inhabitants remaining in the same state, being sufficiently comfortable.

The houses of the Gauls were coated inside with an earth or clay, sometimes so varied, pure, and transparent, that it resembled painting.[f] The Britons preferred plainness in the decoration of their dwellings, white-washing the clay with chalk only.[g] The old Irish seem to have ornamented their wooden dwellings with rude paintings.

The furniture of the houses was more ample than might at first be supposed. When we find the arts of carpentry, pottery, &c., so well understood in remote ages, it must be evident that the dwellings of the Celts were not destitute of those articles which are subservient to domestic comfort. In this place, it will be sufficient to notice the general appearance of their habitations before proceeding to view, more particularly, their manner of living. As might be expected in those rude and martial people, the Celts had some singular and barbarous modes of ornamenting and furnishing their houses. They hung up the spoils of their enemies, with the skins and other parts of animals which they had killed, in the vestibules of their houses. The heads of the most noble of their enemies who fell in battle were cut off, and after being embalmed with oil of cedar, and other substances, they were carefully deposited in chests, and exhibited to strangers with much ostentation. They

[f] Tacitus.   [g] Strutt, from the same.

boasted with pride, that their fathers or themselves, although offered much money, would not accept it, nay, refused to part with them even for their weight in gold. The Caledonians were also accustomed to decapitate their enemies; but whether they preserved them to ornament their dwellings, we are not aware.

A poetical description is not indeed to be received as a faithful and unexaggerated picture, but it may tend to prove the existence of the arts of civilized life, among a people deemed by many little better than savage. The chamber of Everallin, the spouse of Ossian, was "covered with the down of birds, its doors were yellow with gold, and the side posts were of polished bone." We have found corroborative testimony that the ancient Gaël were able to form more ingenious ornaments than these, and an opportunity will shortly offer to investigate more particularly their acquirements in various arts.

CHAPTER II.

OF ANIMALS, AND THE MANNER OF HUNTING.

HUNTING is one of the principal occupations of mankind in a state of barbarism. With the exception of war, it is almost their sole pursuit, and the necessity of following it as a chief means of subsistence, overcomes the indolence which is so characteristic of uncivilized nations.

The Celtæ were celebrated hunters, and they pursued the game not only for the purpose of supplying themselves with food, but as an agreeable diversion, suited to their active and roaming dispositions. There was also an advantage in hunting, which, perhaps, had some influence in stimulating them to the pursuit: it lessened the number of ferocious animals with which their dense woods were filled, and to which their flocks were so much exposed, and this was urged as a strong reason by the Highlanders why they should be allowed to retain their arms. The produce of the chase continued to afford the Celts a plentiful supply of venison, when it had long ceased to be their chief dependence. The ancient Caledonians had numerous herds of domestic animals, and raised a scanty supply of corn. Their successors extended agriculture, but they preferred the hunting and shepherd state in which they remained until the sixteenth century, and continued both the practice and love of fowling and the chase until the disarming act altered their situation. Allan Mac Dougall, a modern bard,* regrets this change, in lines imitated in English by a literary friend:

> "Cha n'eil abhachd feadh na beann,
> Tha giomanich teann fo smachd ;
> Tha fear na croichde air chàll,
> Chaigh gach cilid a's mang as.
> Cha 'n' fhaighar ruagh-bhochd nan ält
> Le cū seang gachuir le strath ;
> An ciric gach cuis a bh' ann
> Feidirich na'n gäll sgach glaichd."

> "The cheerless hunter hangs his pensive head,
> No more the hills re-echo to his voice ;
> To meet the stately stag with mantle red,
> No more the fawn and bounding doe rejoice.
> No more is heard the deep-mouth'd hollow voice
> Of the lank greyhound that pursues the roe ;
> But, in exchange for all our former joys,
> Foul frowsy shepherds, whistling as they go,
> Are seen in every glen, O bitter sight of woe !"

* Better known as *Ailean Dall*, or "Blind Allan." He was in his latter days family Bard and Seanachie to Glengarry. Some of his poems have much merit, and a few of his songs are very popular throughout the Highlands. ED.

"Sealg is sugradh nan glean,"[*] a favourite air of the mountaineers, keeps alive the recollection of other times.

The Highlander scorned the shepherd life as an occupation, but none could be more attentive to the condition and pasturage of his flocks and herds. The care of looking after the cattle was assigned to the youth between boyhood and manhood: tending the goats and sheep was the peculiar duty of the girls. The Gaël thought it beneath them to spend their time in the servile occupation of a shepherd, but were by no means unwilling to assist their fair partners, recommending themselves to the good opinion of their mistress by an attention to her fleecy care.

The existence in Europe, at some remote period, of many animals that are no longer found in these regions, and of certain creatures whose species are now extinct, is well known. It is not intended to investigate the subject of the curious variety of fossil remains that have so often been discovered,—the deposits, perhaps, of an antediluvian world; but it is necessary to notice some of the animals that must have formerly inhabited these climates. Britain and its surrounding islands are found to have once contained an extensive and strange variety of the brute creation. The bones of a large sort of bear, of the hyæna, of the elephant, &c., have been discovered. The Welsh Triads notice the first as inhabiting the island before it became the permanent residence of human beings. Guillim says the bear was carried from Britain to Rome, but he does not give his authority for the assertion. It was very common in Spain, where the flesh was esteemed good food. The Beaver, an animal of which there will be occasion to speak in a succeeding page, long haunted the British rivers and lakes, and was only becoming rare in the time of Giraldus

---

[*] The ancient hunting and hilarity of the glen.

Cambrensis.* In the Welsh histories, this animal is called efaine, in Gaëlic it is named beathadach.

One of the most singular animals that formerly lived in these islands, is the MOOSE DEER, but the period of its existence has not been satisfactorily ascertained. Even the Irish legends, whose antiquity seems able to reach the probable era, do not appear to recognize these animals as inhabitants of Erin, where their remains are so frequently discovered. In a learned communication by Dr Hibbert, which I had the pleasure of hearing read at a meeting of the Society of Antiquaries of Scotland, it was maintained that they have not been so long extinct as is generally believed. On this occasion it was remarked, on what authority I cannot tell, that the Norwegians were anciently accustomed to pass from Orkney to the mainland of Scotland, to hunt the Rein deer! If this is true, the climate must be greatly altered. It is much too warm now for this hardy animal, which was formerly to be found plentifully in the Hyrcinian forest, in modern Germany, which they have long abandoned for colder regions.

Whether the moose deer were cut off by a general murrain, or were extirpated by the efforts of mankind, is matter of conjecture. The remains of some have been found, that bore the plain appearance of having received a deep wound, the apparent cause of death. The horns of this animal, that are frequently dug up in Ireland, in Scotland, and in the Isle of Man, are discovered sometimes alone, and at other times, several together, and they are not seldom attached to the skull. These enormous

* During the year 1875 an attempt was made to re-introduce the beaver into Scotland. The Marquis of Bute has at considerable trouble and expense procured three pairs, which have been let loose under the most favourable circumstances in the Island of Bute, where it is hoped they may thrive and multiply. Ed.

horns have measured two yards in length and nearly fifteen feet from tip to tip. The only species of animal resembling the moose deer, which is known now to exist, is that in America, which bears the same name. The ALCE of the continent, from the descriptions of the ancients, was a very singular animal. It was so extremely shy that it was very seldom taken or killed, and the greatest cunning was requisite to surprise it, for it could not be regularly hunted like other game. According to Pausanias, it was an animal between a camel and a stag:[b] it appears to have been the elk, the bones of which are often found in different parts of Britain. The Elk is mentioned in several poems of the ancient Bards. To this authority, however, the sceptical may object, as well as to a tradition but little known, that Lon dubh, a term now given to the blackbird, was originally the name of the moose deer, some of which Ossian appears to have seen.

WOLVES were anciently very numerous on the continent and in the British islands. The exaction of their heads as a tribute from the Britons, and the imposition of a certain number as a compensation for crimes, led to the extirpation of this fierce inhabitant of the forest. The wolf has been extinct in Scotland since 1697, when the last one was destroyed by the celebrated Sir Ewen Cameron, of Lochiel. The statutes by which the Barons were enjoined "to hunt and chase the wolfe and wolfe's whalps, four times a year, and as often as they see them;"[c] and "the Scherrif and Baillie to hunt them thrice in the year," with power to raise the country to their assistance,[d] prove how numerous they must have formerly been in the north, and evince the anxiety of the government to root out this formidable

[b] Lib. ix. 21. [c] Seventh Parliament, James I.
[d] First Parliament, James VI.

enemy to the Scotish farmer. These enactments, and a reward for the heads, hastened their extermination, since which the word fiadhchoin, literally wild dogs, has become obsolete. Malcolm Laing thought he had found a strong argument against the authenticity of Ossian's poems, in their silence respecting wolves; but the publication of the originals has overthrown this objection, raised from an ignorance of the Gaëlic language. In the first book of Fingal we find "the growling of wolves from their caverns;"[e] and in the poems of clan Uisnich[f] and Cuthon they are also alluded to. Faol, which occurs in ancient poems and various MSS., has long since fallen into disuse, but is preserved in the compound faoilteach, or faoltmhi, the wolf-month, which includes the last fortnight of winter and the first of spring.[g] Mada, a dog, and alluidh, ferocious, form the present name of a wolf among the Highlanders. Wolves are said to have remained in Ireland until the beginning of last century, the bog of Kilcrea being one of their latest and least accessible retreats. Derrick, in 1581, speaks of no other wild animal. Mr. Adams, an English gentleman, having been driven from his house with his family during the troubles in the seventeenth century, they were attacked, when in the woods, by wolves, and the whole party, to the number of fourteen, were destroyed.[h]

The Lupus cervarius, a hart or hind wolf, called by the Gauls Raphium, was found in their extensive forests, and several were exhibited at Rome by Pompey, as natural curiosities.[i] They were not the only remarkable animals

---

[e] Gadhair is fiadhchoin nam carn.
[f] S'air chuilen na fiadhchoin, stanza, 7, b. 3.
[g] Rep. on the Poems of Ossian, Appendix, p. 199.
[h] Ireland's Tragical Tyrannie, 4to. 1642.   [i] Pliny.

of the kind: there were a sort of very large and fierce creatures, called wolf dogs, being a cross from the two animals. Great herds of these roamed in the woods, and, what was most singular, a particular dog acted as a leader, all the others following and submitting to his direction. the whole pack observing an appearance of order.[j] They appear to have resembled the Irish wolf dog.

Foxes, called Madadh ruadh, red dogs, or Sionach, and Cat fiadhaich, WILD CATS, are still plentiful in Scotland, They are, indeed, much less numerous than heretofore, from the exertions of district foxhunters, but these gentlemen are not likely to obviate the necessity of their own diversions by exterminating the breed. The wild cat is extremely ferocious, and does much injury to the poultry. It would appear from royal licenses, that this animal was formerly common in England.

Boars were numerous in the primæval woods of Britain, where they ranged in natural wildness, and hunting them was a favourite amusement. The native domesticated breed has long been intermixed with others. In Sutherland, I believe, are still some remains of the indigenal stock, which was of small size. In Man they remained wild, or semi-domesticated, until lately, roaming without restraint in the woods and on the mountains. They were called purrs, and had all the flavour of the wild boar.[k] In the wastes of Germany these animals seem still to live in a state of nature. The ancient Gauls appear to have attempted their domestication, but Athenæus says they were allowed to remain during the night in the fields, and surpassed all others in size, strength, and swiftness, being little less dangerous than wolves.

---

[j] Pliny, vii. c. 40.
[k] Agric. Report. They were subjected to a particular tythe.

Deer, once so numerous in Scotland, are much reduced in number, and a chief cause assigned for their disappearance is the decay of the woods. In many parts, the mountains, that were formerly covered with red deer and roe, are no longer a retreat for them. The improvements in sheepfarming have driven them to the inaccessible parts of the Highlands. Their ancient haunts are now traversed by the shepherd and his dog, before whom they have fled to the distant heights, and it is in many parts now rare to meet with even a solitary straggler. This, however unpleasant to the sportsman, is, perhaps, less to be regretted by the farmer, who might have had his cornyard plundered by these animals, without being permitted to destroy them.

In the rugged mountains of Brae Mar numerous herds of red deer still find protection in the remains of the forest of Caledonia, where two or three hundred are sometimes seen together. It is supposed that upwards of three thousand are in the range of shooting-ground attached to Mar Lodge, a seat of the Earl of Fife, which is nearly a square of twenty miles. In the Rea forest, Sutherland, there are perhaps two thousand red deer, &c., and about two hundred fallow deer find comfortable shelter in two sequestered islands in Lochlomond.*

In the mountain of Arkel, in the forest of Dirimore, in Sutherland, there was a peculiar sort of deer, according to Sir Robert Gordon. They had all forked tails, three inches long, whereby they were easily known from any others. Bede informs us, that Ireland was celebrated for stag-hunting, but deer had become rare in that country

---

* There are many large deer forests in the Highlands. In the Black Mount, Kinloch-Leven and Benavric, Glenarkaig, and many other well-known forests are thousands of deer. Near Inverary the Duke of Argyle has recently prepared a forest calculated to hold some seven or eight thousand red deer. Ed.

about the beginning of the 16th century, and the roebuck is said to have been unknown.[1] There is a Gaëlic saying, S'fiach aon fhiadh 's Mhona' liath a dha dheug an Gäig, i. e., one deer in the gray mountain is worth a dozen in Gäig, or in the Grampians in general; an exaggeration, certainly, but meant to denote the superior size of the deer found in the gray ridge.

The CALEDONIAN OX is believed to have been peculiar to the north. The remains of this animal are frequently discovered deep underground, and it is remarkable that, in most cases, they are found without the horns.[m] The skull of one is preserved in the British Museum, from which the animal appears nearly allied to the European domestic ox, but of a larger size. At Craven, in Yorkshire, Chillingham park, in Durham, and Drumlanrig, in Scotland, breeds of these curious animals are yet preserved.* Numbers of .

---

[1] Riche's Description of Ireland.
[m] Cut off for drinking cups, or musical horns?

* Scott in his ballad of "Cadzow Castle" has some admirable verses descriptive of the old Caledonian breed of cattle.

> " Through the huge oaks of Evandale,
>   Whose limbs a thousand years have worn,
> What sullen roar comes down the gale,
>   And drowns the hunter's pealing horn?
>
> Mightiest of all the beasts of chase,
>   That roam in woody Caledon,
> Crashing the forest in his race,
>   The Mountain Bull comes thundering on.
>
> Fierce on the hunter's quivered band
>   He rolls his eyes of swarthy glow,
> Spurns, with black hoof and horn, the sand,
>   And tosses high his mane of snow.
>
> Aim'd well, the chieftain's lance has flown;
>   Struggling in blood the savage lies;
> His roar is sunk in hollow groan,—
>   Sound, merry huntsmen! sound the *pryse!*"

cattle must long have continued to live in a state of nature among the inaccessible woods and mountains. Gildas relates that in his time wild bulls were caught by means of strong nets.

The peculiar sort of wild cattle which the Triads relate were among the first living creatures in this island, are denominated Yohan-banog, oxen with high protuberances. They appear to have been buffaloes, the name of which in Gaëlic is bo-alluidh, or ferocious ox. Cæsar says that, in Germany, was a bull, from the forehead of which grew a straight horn!

SHEEP, Caoraich, like other animals, must have been originally wild, but the period when they were in this state in Scotland, is too remote to be ascertained. Donald Munro says, that in the Hebrides he saw sheep "feeding masterlesse, pertayning peculiarly to no man;" and in Orkney they are described by Brand as wild, but these assertions are inconsiderate, for although there may have been stray flocks, the sheep were formerly, from the small size of farms, more tame than they are now.

Lesley has the following spirited description of the animal:—

"In Caledonia olim frequens erat sylvestris bos, nunc vero rarior, qui, colorê candidissimo, jubam densam et demissam instar leonis gestat, truculentess ac ferus ab humano genere abhorrens, ut quæcunque homines vel manibus contrectârint, vel habitu perflaverint, ab iis multos post dies omnino abstinuerunt. Ad hoc tanta audacia huic bovi indita erat, ut non solum irritatus equites furenter prosterneret, sed ne tantillum lacessitus omnes promiscue homines coruibus ac ungulis peteril; ac canum, qui apud nos ferocissimi sunt, impetus plane contemneret, Ejus carnes cartilaginosae, sed saporis guavissimi. Erat is olim per illam vastissimam. Caledoniæ sylvam frequens, ad humana ingluvie jam assumptus tribus tantum locis est reliquus, Strivilingli, Cumbernaldiæ, et Kincarniæ.

Leslæus, Scotiæ Descriptio.

Much of this description is so applicable to our West "Highlanders" that they are probably a nearly allied breed. ED.

GOATS, Gabhair, have remained in a state of wildness almost until our own times.

The HARE was a native of Britain, and one of those animals used in divination. The religion of the Britons consequently forbade its use as food,[n] and it was only occasionally killed for the purpose of drawing auguries.[o] In the mountains of Sutherland, and other elevated situations, is found an Alpine hare, rather less than the common sort, a beautiful creature, white as snow in winter, and in summer marked with a few dark gray hairs on the back.

RABBITS, Coinean, appear to have been introduced to Britain,[p] probably from Celtiberia, where they were particularly numerous.[q] In most of the Western Isles they are yet unknown. Those of the smallest size are found in Isla; the largest are those of Man.[r]

POLECATS, WEASELS, and other animals of the same sort common to South Britain, are to be found in Scotland. Gordon gives a list of a variety of these creatures that were numerous in Sutherland.

A species of amphibious animal, apparently of the rat kind, called Beothach an' fheoir, is found in the eddies of the higher regions, always inhabiting the vicinity of the green patches around springs. When a horse feeds upon the grass that has been recently cropped by this animal, it swells, and in a short time dies, and the flesh is found blue as if it had been bruised or beaten. I believe this creature has not been hitherto described by naturalists.*

The tradition of St. Patrick having by his blessing

---

[n] Cæsar.   [o] Dio.
[p] Varro, iii. 12. ap. Whitaker.   [q] Pliny.   [r] Pennant.

* The animal referred to is probably the Water Rat or Water Vole— *Mus amphibius*—more nearly allied to the beavers, however, than to the rats. It is not uncommon in some parts of the Highlands. That it causes the death of horses in the manner stated is of course nonsense. ED.

saved Ireland from the annoyance of noxious reptiles, is well known, but has in later times been found to be not strictly according to fact. Some parts of Scotland, it appears, long remained free from rats. Badenoch is said to have been thus fortunate, and in Sutherland, Sir Robert Gordon says, there is not a rat will live, and if any are brought into it "they die presently, as soon as they smell the air of the country, and, which is strange, there are many in Caithness." It is certain, that before 1798 they were not known in that part of the country, but a ship being then stranded at Ceantradwell, in the parish of Clyne, a few rats got ashore and took refuge in a mill, where they increased, and soon overspread the country. Birt says he never heard of rats in the hills but at Coul na kyle, in Strathspey, to which they had been brought in 1723 from London, and were then thought a presage of good luck.

The Calf, a rock near the Isle of Man, was formerly celebrated for affording a supply of young puffins, esteemed a great delicacy; but a vessel unfortunately having been wrecked on it, the rats that got ashore soon exterminated these birds. In Man itself there are no foxes, moles, snakes, or toads; and magpies, frogs, partridges, and grouse were imported not perhaps more than one hundred years ago. A country may be happy in not possessing those noxious and unsightly creatures that annoy the inhabitants of other lands; but no calamity has happened to any place in these islands like what befel an unfortunate city of Gaul, where the inhabitants were actually forced to abandon it by a prodigious number of frogs. Nor have the number of rats been ever so formidable as they were to the poor German Baron, whose strong isolated tower could not preserve him from ultimately perishing by these disgusting animals.

The Britons had plenty of hens and geese.* Religion did not permit them to be used as food, but the people kept numbers of them about their dwellings. If their eggs were also prohibited, the Briton must have been influenced solely by superstition in keeping them around him. It does not appear from Pliny, who praises the German geese, that these people refused to eat them.† Those in the Highlands are half wild, occasionally resorting to the sea and lochs.

The CAPERCAILZIE, or cock of the wood, once found in tolerable plenty in the forests of Scotland, is now only seen on the most remote and inaccessible mountains, and so rarely is it met with, that it is supposed by some to have been extinct nearly a century. It is larger than the black cock, which is now also very rare.* The Ptarmigan, Grouse, and other game, are well known to be plentiful on the moors and mountains of Caledonia.

The EAGLE, Iolar, that majestic tenant of the craggy steeps, has been time immemorial the emblem of strength and independence. Its pinions were the badges of Celtic chieftainship, and were esteemed the most honourable reward by the adventurous sportsman. This noble bird is, however, extremely destructive to poultry, and even the young lambs are not secure from its audacious attacks. Two eagles had built their nest in the neighbourhood of a gentleman's house in Strathspey, and the quantities of game which they collected were truly astonishing. On the arrival of any visitors, however unexpected, the gentleman had only to despatch some one to the eagles' cyrie,

* Geadh, Gaëlic, a goose ; gnyz, Welch.
† He mentions the circumstance of a flock walking all the way from the territories of the Morini, (Terouenne,) to Rome, x. 22.
* The Capercailzie has again been introduced into certain suitable localities in Scotland, and is fast increasing in numbers. The Black Cock is quite a common game bird all over the Highlands. ED.

when an ample supply of hares, rabbits, muir fowl, partridges, ptarmigans, snipes, &c., were speedily procured.

The Scots, like the Germans, are fond of singing birds, and do not often kill them. The Nightingale, which has now forsaken the northern part of the island, is supposed to have once frequented the woods of Scotland. Its name in Gaëlic is beautifully expressive of the sweetness of its song, and the character of the bird. In Ros an ceol, the rose music, the melody is put for the melodist, the former being heard when the latter is unseen.

The DRUID-DUBH, erroneously called Lon-dubh, or mountain blackbird, I believe is peculiar to the Alpine regions of the Scotish highlands. It resembles in everything, except its colour, the blue bird of the Alps, mentioned by Bellonius and others. The female is larger than the common blackbird, and the feathers on the back are varied by a beautiful dark green gloss. The cock is distinguished by a snow white collar, or ring about three-quarters of an inch broad, round its neck, and above all birds for the loudness and clearness of its notes.

The CNAG, or Lair fligh, a bird like a parrot, which digs its nest with its beak in the trunks of trees, is thought peculiar to the county of Sutherland.*

The numerous sea birds found on the coasts of Scotland and the isles, that form so large a part of the subsistence of the inhabitants of some places, are caught with peculiar dexterity, and by the most adventurous methods, practised only by the hardy and experienced natives.

The Celtæ had a prejudice against fish, which probably arose from the veneration they paid to the waters. The

---

* The bird referred to is probably the Pine Grosbeak—*Loxia enucleator* of Linnæus—or it may be the Crossbill (*Loxia Curvirostra*). Both birds are rather uncommon, and more frequently met with in the northern counties than elsewhere. ED.

Gaël retained this antipathy, and notwithstanding the numerous lochs, rivers, and arms of the sea which intersect their country, the Highlanders have never paid much attention to angling or other methods of catching the finny tribe. Many of their lakes have never been stocked.*

The Gauls employed themselves very sedulously in hunting, and practised various methods to make sure of the game. The want of food is a strong incentive to the pursuit, which is not always one of pleasure, and however much attached a rude and spirited people may be to the activity and enterprise of the chase, we may believe with Tacitus, that during peace they usually resigned themselves to sleep and repasts.

Dogs were employed by the Gauls both in hunting and in war. The Celtic dogs were excellent in the chase, and those of the Britons were superior to all others. They were so much esteemed, that great numbers were exported not only to Gaul but to Italy, being highly valued by the Romans.[u] They excelled in swiftness, a quality for which all Celtic dogs were celebrated.[v] Those of the Belgæ, Segusi, and Sicambri, were next in value to the British.[w]

Vossius says, that the Latin catulus, a little dog, is a Gallic word. Lewis, in his history of Britain, derives the Roman cynegii, dog keepers, from the British ci, a dog. Ovid uses gallicus canis for a greyhound, and those now called beagles were denominated agassæos and vertragos.

The Scots dogs were celebrated all over Europe.[x] Their use in hunting rendered them inestimable to the tribes of

---

* A prejudice against fish is a characteristic of rude and uncivilized peoples. The Highlanders of the present day are as fond of fish as their neighbours, though there are some kinds of fish that they will not eat if they can help it, such as the skate, the eel, the flounder, and flat fish generally. ED.

[u] Strabo, iv. p. 200. [v] Arrian, f. 121. [w] Montfaucon.
[x] Symachus, ep. ii. 77. Ant. Pagi.

Caledonia, and produced a strong attachment between the hunter and his faithful companion, who was believed to accompany his master to the "airy hall" of his rest. A beautiful lamentation of Umad, an aged warrior, over Gorban, his hound, is preserved in the poem of "Manos," and it shews, in a strong light, the love of the Highlanders for hunting, and the regard which they have for their dogs, that this ancient composition is at the present day the most universally known among them.ʸ

The docility and attachment of the dog may have arisen from sharing its master's confidence, and receiving his continued attentions. Buffon ascribes these qualities in the Hottentot oxen to their enjoying the same bed and board as their owner, and experiencing his daily care. The Caledonians maintained great numbers of dogs, and the names of some of the most famous are still preserved.* Bran and

---

* In an old Ossianic ballad taken down from oral recitation by the editor a year or two ago, occur the names of five dogs celebrated among the Fingalians for their courage and speed.

Latha dhiunn a'n Gleann-a-Cheo,
  Deichnar—na bha beo dhe 'n Fheinn,—
Bha caogad chu a'n lamh gach fir,
  Scangshlios, Busdubh, Mollach, Torm a's Treun.

Be sid ainm mo chiulean con;
  Bu luath, laidir iad ri gaoith;
Bu ro mhath an siubhal air leirg,
  'Sair cholg feirg cha robh iad faoin!

A-hunting one day in the Glen of Mist,
  Of the Fingalian host were then alive,
Alas, but ten—the last of all the race!
  Of brawny deer hounds each of us led five.

Fifty good dogs in all, and mine were named
  Smooth skin, Black face, Mollach, Treun and *Torm*,
Fierce, with their bristles up! my gallant dogs
  That in their speed outstripped the howling storm.

ʸ Smith's Gallic Ant. p. 255.

Sgeolan were favourites of Fingal, and in Glenlyon, in Perthshire, is pointed out his conabhacan, or stake, to which his hounds were fastened. In the Isle of Sky is a stone which was used by Cathullin for the same purpose. The Irish greyhounds that were used for hunting the wolf, are described as having been bigger of limb and bone than a colt.[a]

The shepherd's dog I believe is peculiar to Scotland. The instinct of this animal is wonderful, and its services incalculable. It will bring the most numerous flock of sheep from the distant mountains, without other assistance, and without missing a single individual!

It is probable the Celts used horses in the chase, after they had been domesticated, but they may have often amused themselves in hunting the animals themselves; for in the northern counties of Europe they were formerly wild, and roamed about in large troops. Even in after ages these animals must have continued to enjoy a freedom approximating to wildness. This is still nearly

Seanghslios is smooth and small loined.
Busdubh is black muzzled.
Mollach is rough and hairy.
Torm is a mighty rushing river.
Treun is strong, mighty.
Appropriate enough names for favourite stag-hounds.
"Bran," an avalanche or landslip.
"Neart," Strength.
"Ciar," Brindled.
"Luath," Swift, are the names of dogs famous in Ossianic song.

In the, at least, equally genuine "Heroic Ballads," occur such dog-names as—

"Sear," a Splinter.
"Morbh," Surly.
"Ird" or "Inrd," the meaning of which it is difficult to tell.
"Gruailleach," Heavy browed, and others. ED.

[a] Campion.

the case in some parts of Scotland, and in the Isles of Orkney and Shetland. All, a Gallic term for a horse, is long gone into disuse, and is only preserved in cab-all, a tamed horse or mare.*

Besides the assistance of horses and dogs, the Gauls endeavoured to secure their prey by assisting the effect of their weapons with poison. With one sort, which Pliny calls venenum cervarium, they rubbed their arrows, in stag-hunting; limeum, or hartsbane, was used in the same way.[a] They also dipped the points of their weapons in the juice of hellebore, but in thus studying to render their shot effectual, they took care that the game should not be injured. They immediately cut the flesh from around the wound, and affirmed not only that the venison was uninjured, but that it was much improved, being rendered very tender.[b]

An antique sculpture, representing a boar hunt, was discovered in the province of Narbonne.[c] The animal appears of a very large size, and is attacked by two hunters on foot, each armed with a dart, or venabulum, about $3\frac{1}{2}$ feet long, which is held in the right hand, while in the left they carry a piece of cloth, which one of them is about to thrust down the throat of the animal, as it rushes open mouthed on its assailants. This forms the subject of the vignette to this Chapter, only it will be observed, that one of the figures, who is in the same attitude, is omitted. In the portfeuille of M. Lenoir, is a representation of a similar attack, by a single hunter, who, instead of the cloth, wraps his hand in his sagum.

The hunting of the boar was particularly famous among

---

* *Capull* or *Caball* is just the *Caballus* of the Latin, for which the Celt is indebted, as for so many other words, to the Romans. Ed.

[a] Lib. xxvii. 11. [b] Pliny, xxv. [c] Montfaucon.

the ancient Gaël. This perhaps arose from the peculiar address that was requisite in attacking so furious an animal; for we learn from Ossian, and other bards, that a warrior esteemed himself highly upon his address in spearing the boar, and one of their heads is represented to have been symbolical of particular prowess in hunting, being a trophy obtained at considerable peril.

HUNTING, among the ancient Scots, was an employment of the greatest importance. In the reign of Paganism it was connected with their mythology, for they believed that in the clouds they should enjoy, as a reward for their bravery, the pleasures of the chase in higher perfection than the earth could afford. According to Arrian, the Celts sacrificed to Diana the huntress. Whether the Gaël invoked Grianus or Baal to prosper their hunting expeditions, we are not certain, but to be accomplished in this exercise was the sure, the sole warrant for future renown and ability to govern. A young chief was obliged to evince his talent for conducting military operations by the leading of a great hunting incursion, a practice that long survived the last of the Fions.[d] The magnitude of the Highland expeditions against the wild tenants of the dense forests and rugged mountains was astonishing. Fingal, in an ancient poem, is said to have had 1000 hunters: succeeding chiefs have been accompanied by even a more numerous retinue. The heads of various and remote clans were accustomed to meet at certain times and in appointed places, attended by numbers of their followers, and commenced a rigorous campaign against all the inhabitants of the forest, which never failed in producing a most abundant slaughter: but fond as the Highlanders were of the chase, and useful as it was to their subsistence, they did not

[d] Martin.

pursue it to the neglect of more important avocations. "Though hunting," says their proverb, "be a good help, yet the chase is but a poor livelihood." The great hunting matches were the means of preserving a social intercourse between tribes who lived far distant from each other. It was a means also of bringing the chiefs and principal men of the country together, and enabled them to adjust differences, settle future proceedings, &c. They were at these meetings also able to arrange many things among themselves, which were of much more consequence than the ostensible object for which they were collected. A general hunting match has been the method by which the greatest enterprises have been suggested and matured, without a suspicion being excited beyond the mountains.

Huntings were often given in compliment to the visits of friends, and the vassals were summoned in suitable numbers. The chief would, of course, muster his clan by hereditary right, and they were besides specially bound to hunt with their superior, the Highland servitudes being hunting, hosting, watching, and warding. The gallantry of the ancient Caledonians led them to honour a stranger with the danger of the chase; in other words he was allowed to expose himself to the greatest hazard, and hence have the opportunity of gaining the most renown.

By the Welch laws of Griffith ap Conan, hunting was divided into three parts; helfa holet, hunting for the cry; helfa cyfarthfa, hunting for the bay, and helfa cyffredyn, common hunting, or that by which a person coming up to another who had killed an animal, could challenge the half.[e] The laws of the chase, according to Scotish Chronicles, were settled by Dornadilla, one of the kings or chiefs of the fabulous period of national history.

[e] Lewis.

Without any such intimation we are sufficiently convinced of the importance in which it was held by the Celts. Many superstitions were connected with hunting, from the belief that it formed part of the amusements of the blessed after death, and some curious fragments of bardic composition exist on the subject. In Scot's Discovery of Witchcraft, it is recommended to prevent hunters or their dogs from being ensnared by this foul art, that an oaken branch should be cleaved, over which they should all pass. It was a most ancient belief that the forest was infested with supernatural beings, who amused themselves at the expense of mankind.

A certain late writer has said that the Highlanders are naturally good marksmen. Their dexterity is produced solely by attention and practice; which has long rendered them famous for taking sure and steady aim. Nearly 200 years ago they are thus noticed: "In the first place stood Highlanders, commonly called Redshankes, with their plaides cast over their shoulders, having every one his bowe and arrows, with a broad slycing sworde by his syde: these are so good markesmen, that they will kill a deere in his speede, it being the chiefest part of their living, selling the skins by great quantities, and feeding on the flesh."[f]

A curious instance of the nicety of shooting occurred about seventy years ago. A poacher had long pursued his mode of life undetected, although the destruction of game was very great, and his habits well known; but this veteran protracted his fate by using the weapon of his ancestors, the noiseless bow and arrow, and he was perhaps the last who used it for the purpose. After his capture he vaunted of his skill in archery, and the Duke of Athol, pointing to

---

[f] His Majestie's passing through the Scots' armie, 1641.

a stag, desired him to shoot it through the off eye; on which the Highlander gave a particular whistle, the animal looked round, and immediately received an arrow in the intended spot.

Some interesting descriptions of Celtic huntings have been preserved. In the poem of "Fingal," three thousand hounds, that excelled in fleetness as in fierceness, were let loose, and each is represented as killing two deer; rather an exaggerated number, one should think.* In the poem of "Dermid" is a paragraph, describing the manner of hunting, which we regret has not been translated.⁵ Taylor, the water poet, celebrates this noble sport of the Highlanders in energetic verse.

> "Through heather, moss, 'mong frogs and bogs and fogs,
> 'Mongst craggy cliffs, and thunder-battered hills,
> Hares, hinds, bucks, roes, are chas'd by men and dogs,
> Where two hours' hunting fourscore fat deer kills.
> Lowland, your sports are low as is your seat :
> The Highland games and minds are high and great."

The Celtæ, we are informed by Pausanius, surrounded plains and mountains with their toils. In like manner, the Highlanders encompassed a hill or large tract of country, and, advancing on all sides with "hideous yells," they enclosed the animals in a small space, and cut them down with their broadswords so dexterously, as not to injure the hide. In other cases they arranged themselves, part on the plain, and the others along the declivity of the mountains, and with loud cries they advanced, drove the herds of deer and other animals towards the chief and his party, who

---

* In the "Ossianic" and other old Gaelic ballads, the number of dogs employed in the chase, and of stags and other wild animals is, as a rule, so grossly exaggerated as to be beyond all belief; nor is it easy to account for such constant and manifest exaggeration of numbers. ED.

⁵ Smith's Gallic Antiquities, p. 189.

were ready in a desirable spot to enjoy the sport. This resembles the Spanish batidas, where some hundred people collect and drive the game through a defile, where the king, with his attendants, in an arbour or hut, constructed of boughs, slaughter the animals as they pass.

King James V., having, in 1528, "made proclamation to all lords, barons, gentlemen, landward-men, and free-holders, to compear at Edinburgh, with a month's victual, to pass with the king to danton the thieves of Teviotdale, &c.; and also warned all gentlemen that had good dogs to bring them, that he might hunt in the said country; the Earl of Argyle, the Earl of Huntly, the Earl of Atholl, and all the rest of the Highlands, did, and brought their hounds with them, to hunt with the king." His Majesty, therefore, "past out of Edinburgh to the hunting with 12,000 men, and hounded and hawked all the country and bounds," and killed, as Lindsay heard, eighteen score harts. Next summer he went to hunt in Athol, accompanied by Queen Margaret and the Pope's ambassador, where he remained three days most nobly entertained by the Earl, and killed "thirty score of hart and hynd, with other small beasts, as roe, and roebuck, wolf and fox, and wild cats."[h]

The last expedition was accompanied with such extraordinary circumstances, that Lindsay's account of it must be interesting. "The Earl of Athole, hearing of the king's coming, made great provision for him in all things pertaining to a prince, that he was as well served and eased with all things necessary to his estate as he had been in his own palace of Edinburgh. For, I heard say, this noble Earl gart make a curious palace to the king, his mother, and the ambassador, where they were so honourably lodged as they

[h] Lindsay of Pitscottie, Hist. of Scotland, 225, ed. 1778.

had been in England, France, Italy, or Spain, concerning the time and equivalent for their hunting and pastime; which was builded in midst of a fair meadow, a palace of green timber, wound with green birks that were green both under and above, which was fashioned in four quarters, and in every quarter and nuke thereof a great round, as it had been a blockhouse, which was lofted and geisted the space of three house height; the floors laid with green scharets and spreats, medwarts, and flowers, that no man knew whereon he zied, but as he had been in a garden. Further, there were two great rounds on ilk side of the gate, and a great portculleis of tree, falling down with the manner of a barrace, with a drawbridge, and a great stank of water of sixteen foot deep, and thirty foot of breadth. And also this palace within was hung with fine tapestry and arrasses of silk, and lighted with fine glass windows in all airths; that this palace was as pleasantly decored with all necessaries pertaining to a prince as it had been his own royal palace at home. Further, this Earl gart make such provision for the king and his mother, that they had all manner of meats, drinks, and delicates that were to be gotten, at that time, in all Scotland, either in burgh or land, viz., all kind of drink, as ale, beer, wine, &c.; of meat, with flesshes, &c.; and also the stanks that were round about the palace, were full of all delicate fishes, as salmonds, trouts, pearches, pikes, eels, and all other kind of delicate fishes that could be gotten in fresh waters, and all ready for the banquet. Syne were there proper stewards, &c.; and the halls and chambers were prepared with costly bedding, vessel, and napry, according for a king; so that he wanted none of his orders more than he had been at home. The king remained in this wilderness at the hunting the space of three days and three nights, and his company, as I have shown. I heard men say it cost the Earl of Athole every day in expences a thousand pounds." All this sumptuous edifice was purposely consumed by fire on the king's departure!

Another old writer thus describes a great Highland hunting match.

"In the year 1563, the Earl of Athol, a prince of the blood royal, had, with much trouble and vast expences, a hunting match for the entertainment of our most illustrious and most gracious queen. Our people call this a royal hunting. I was then a young man, and was present on that occasion. Two thousand Highlanders, or wild Scotch, as you call them here, were employed to drive to the hunting ground all the deer from the woods and hills of Atholl, Badenoch, Mar, Murray, and the countries about. As these Highlanders use a light dress, and are very swift of foot, they went up and down so nimbly, that in less than two months' time they brought together 2000 red deer, besides roes and fallow deer. The queen, the great men, and others, were in a glen, when all the deer were brought before them. Believe me, the whole body of them moved forward in something like battle order. This sight still strikes me, and ever will, for they had a leader whom they followed close wherever he moved. This leader was a very fine stag, with a very high head. The sight delighted the queen very much, but she soon had occasion for fear. Upon the Earl's (who had been accustomed to such sights) addressing her thus, ' Do you observe that stag who is foremost of the herd ? There is danger from that stag, for if either fear or rage should force him from the ridge of that hill, let every one look to himself, for none of us will be out of the way of harm; for the rest will follow this one, and, having thrown us under foot, they will open a passage to this hill behind us. What happened a moment after confirmed this opinion: for the queen ordered one of the best dogs to be let loose on one of the deer: this the dog pursues, the leading stag was frighted, he flies by the same way he had come there, the rest rush after him, and break out where the thickest body of the Highlanders was. They had nothing for it but to throw themselves flat on the heath, and allow the deer to pass over them. It was told the queen that several of the Highlanders had been wounded, and that two or three had been killed outright; and the whole body had got off, had not the Highlanders, by their skill in hunting, fallen upon a stratagem to cut off the rear from the main body. It was of those that had been separated the queen's dogs and those of the nobility made slaughter. There were killed that day 360 deer, with 5 wolves, and some roes."[1]

When a single deer was wanted, the gamekeeper and a few assistants went to the hills, with a little oatmeal or other provision, and lay in wait for their prey, sometimes for several days and nights together. Stalking is the term applied to the pursuit of deer by individuals, and, as the animals are shy, incredible patience and exertion are necessary to secure the game. A deer stalker has walked two miles in deep water, and crawled a considerable distance on his belly, in order to approach the animals unobserved.

The forester was an important member of the clan, and enjoyed several perquisites. On the return of a young chief from his first public hunting, all his arms, clothing, and other articles were, by immemorial custom, given to the forester. Sir Robert Burnet, of Crathes, in Aberdeenshire, bears a Highlander as one of the supporters to his arms, his ancestors having been the king's foresters in the north.

It appears that HAWKING was a diversion of the ancient

[1] Barclay's contra Monarchomacus.

Britons. Helfa, hunting, signifies also hawking,[1] and Ossian, mentions "a hundred hawks with fluttering wing." By the laws of Hwyel Dha, the master of the hawks enjoyed his lands free, he sat the fourth man from the king, slept in the barn, and had a hand breadth of wax candles to feed his birds and light him to bed. He received a dried sheep, and was served with drink sufficient only to quench his thirst, lest his charge should be neglected. The hearts and lungs of all animals killed in the royal kitchen were allowed him to feed his birds, and he was obliged to have his horse always ready.

Rederch, King of the Strathclyde Welsh, included hawks, dogs, and swift hunters among his most valuable presents.*

---

[1] Lewis's Hist. Pliny describes hawking as practised by the Thracians, among whom the hawk and the hunter shared the prey.—Lib. x. c. 8.

* Stewart of Appin held certain lands in Duror and Glencoe in consideration of his having built Castle Stalker, or *Caisteal-an-Stalcaire*, the Falconers' Castle, for the accommodation of King James V., when he came to the West Highlands to enjoy his favourite sport of hawking. ED.

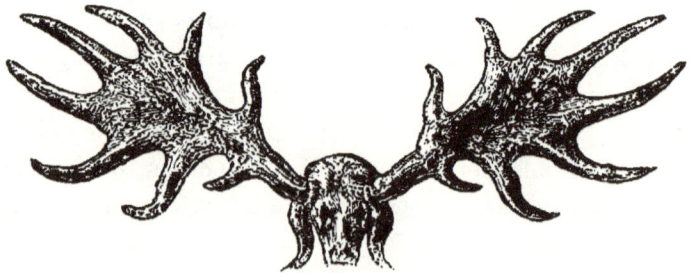

HORNS OF MOOSE DEER.

"Cas-Chrom."

CHAPTER III.

OF THE PASTORAL STATE AND OF AGRICULTURE.

The cattle of the Gauls, who were accounted affluent, were their chief riches, and some of them, according to Cæsar, lived entirely on their flesh and milk. The Celtic race were much attached to the pastoral life, for its freedom was suited to their state of refinement, and congenial to their independent spirit. The inhabitants of Britain, at the period of the first Roman descent, were for the most part in the pastoral state of society, and long after this epoch many of the tribes, like their remote ancestors, continued to pay almost exclusive attention to their flocks, contemning the servile and less advantageous task of cultivating the soil. Many parts of the island are adapted for grazing only, and those who inhabit the mountainous districts must continue to depend for subsistence on the produce of their herds.

Although the wealth of the Highlands has always consisted of cattle, the poets have not indulged in rapturous encomiums on the shepherd state, for this reason, that the education of the men was entirely military, the care of the flocks being left to the women and youth. Cæsar remarks the great numbers of cattle which were reared in Britain, and Solinus avers that Ireland was overstocked with them.[k] In Germany they were no less abundant, the inhabitants taking great delight in the number of their flocks, which, according to Tacitus, formed their only wealth. The animals were, however, but of small size, for they appear to have been indifferent to their appearance; whereas the Gauls took so much delight in them, that they thought they could never pay too dear for a beautiful ox.[l]

In the time of Severus, the people beyond Adrian's wall lived chiefly on the flesh and milk of their flocks, with what they procured by hunting. It is certain that at this early period the rude tribes of the north had domesticated numerous herds, it being customary for them to place cattle and sheep in the way of the Roman armies, to induce parties to straggle from the main body, and fall into their ambuscades.[m] A quarrel, concerning the bull of the heath of Golbun, forms the subject of an episode in the poem of "Fingal." Before the arrival of the Saxons, North Wales is said to have been chiefly appropriated for the pasturage of royal cattle, three herds of which consisted of 21,000 head.[n] The cattle and sheep of Scotland were anciently its chief resource; the numbers now raised for the supply of the English markets are immense, and it may with perfect truth be said of many of the Welsh, Irish, and Highland Scots, as it was of the ancient Gauls, that cattle are their only riches.

[k] C. 35.   [l] Bello Gall.   [m] Dio.   [n] Triad, 85.

The wild animals which inhabited the woods of Britain and Gaul, furnishing subsistence to the Celtic huntsmen, have been already described. The domestic animals can be here only briefly noticed. Those who are desirous of further information concerning the various improved breeds in the northern division of Britain, are referred to the Agricultural Reports, Transactions of the Highland Societies, the Statistical returns, and other similar works, for more detailed accounts.

There exists a belief that the inhabitants of Scotland had anciently domesticated a species of deer, and the tradition has received something like confirmation. A communication from H. Home Drummond, Esq., to the Wernerian Society of Edinburgh, describes a large stag's horn that was discovered in the great Blair Drummond moss, which had a piece of wood fitted into a circular perforation.º It is not improbable that these animals were tamed, as the rein deer are at present among the Laplanders.

The CALEDONIAN OX was considerably larger than that of the present day, as may be seen from the skulls, which are frequently discovered at great depths. At Drumlanrig, a seat of the Duke of Queensberry, herds of wild cattle of a white colour are still preserved. The Gaëlic bual, a buffalo, or any wild horned beast, seems bu-all, or bo alluidh, a wild ox. The breeds of Highland cattle and their qualities are well known.*

The GOAT, so useful a breed of animals in a mountainous country, is now much reduced in Scotland. In Inverness, Sutherland, Caithness, and other northern counties, there were formerly numerous flocks of goats, every farmer, about fifty years ago, having from twenty to one hundred. They wandered almost in unrestrained wildness in the moun-

---

º Letter read August, 1825.   * *Vide* note page 36.

tains, and their flesh was good meat, while, during summer, cheese was made either of the milk alone, or of a mixture with that of the cow. Their skins were an article of very early export, and in recent times could always fetch a shilling from the travelling chapman. In the Isles, a late visitor says they have almost disappeared. The goat is peculiarly fitted for a rugged country for it can pick up subsistence in places to which the more timid sheep cannot venture, and is able to defend itself against the fox, so destructive to the latter. It is curious to find that the deer will pasture freely with goats, but evince a strong dislike to sheep.

SHEEP formed a considerable part of the pastoral riches of the Celts. It would appear from what has been before observed, if we are to receive the doubtful testimony of D. Munro, that many were in a state of nature in his time, as they are said to have also continued until lately in the remote islands of Orkney and Shetland. There appears, however, in these assertions, an ignorance of grazing and sheep farming. Every mountain may be now found covered with sheep wild as deer, and to all appearance masterless, and where there were no foxes or other vermin to destroy them, the same was formerly observable; but each person's property was no doubt distinguished by the lug mark, or some other token. The flocks that range in freedom on the muirs, are collected four or five times in the course of the summer and autumn, and those gatherings exactly resemble the ancient hunt. The grazing range is surrounded silently as early in the day as possible, when a simultaneous cry of men and barking of dogs are set up, by which the timid animals are roused from all their haunts, and brought together in a narrow pass, where the fank or fold is erected. The native sheep were very different from the modern breed. The fleece was a sort of down, mixed with straight hairs of some length; the tail was short, slender, and tapering, and was thinly covered with long silvery hairs. They were remarkably tame, and very delicate, probably from the once invariable practice of housing them. The breeds of sheep have been so often crossed and intermixed, that the genuine native animal can scarcely be found. The original stock were small, and dun coloured, particularly in the face, but, notwithstanding their hardiness, and some good qualities, few now remain. It appears from Cambrensis, that in Ireland the sheep were chiefly black. Some of the old Scots' sheep still exist in Galloway, and a few may be found in different parts of the Highlands. A recent traveller seems to think them confined to the remote island of Hirta, or St. Kilda,[p] but they appear also to be found in Orkney and Shetland, and are supposed to have been originally brought from Norway. They were easily fed, their mutton was delicious, and their fleeces were soft, to procure which it has been said that the wool was pulled off, a practice, which, there is reason to believe, did not, at least within traditional knowledge, prevail among the Highlanders, who have an appropriate name for sheep shears, but none for common scissors. It is not long since both sheep and goats were committed to the entire management, and hence have been thought the exclusive property of the wife, being considered beneath the attention of a man, and so strong was this feeling that no man would condescend to assist at the sheep-shearing. The Highlands are admirably adapted for rearing sheep, the fragrant herbage of the hills producing most delicious mutton. Many ages since the inhabitants of various parts pursued with success the improvement of their stock. From before the middle of the sixteenth century, "all the districts of the

---

[p] M'Culloch. An epithet by which this island is designated: Irt na'n caoiraich feann, Hirta of the hairy sheep, is thought to indicate a peculiar breed.

shire of Aberdeen were distinguished for numerous flocks of sheep, which yielded fleeces of the finest wool."[q] Many Highland proprietors have of late turned their almost exclusive attention to sheep farming, and have followed their object with so much zeal, that whole districts have been depopulated, that they might be turned into extensive sheep walks! How far this may be ultimately of advantage to proprietors it is not easy to foresee, but its policy is certainly very objectionable. To force so great a number of the inhabitants to emigrate, and thus deprive the country of the services of a large proportion of the best part of the peasantry, is surely a serious national evil. Regiments can no longer be raised, in case of need, in those places where now are only to be seen the numerous flocks of the solitary shepherd. The piobrach may sound through the deserted glens, but no eager warriors will answer the summons; the last notes which pealed in many a valley were the plaintive strains of the expatriated clansmen—Cha till, cha till, cha till, sin tuile, " we return, we return, we return no more." The necessity for thus expelling the tenantry is doubtful, the President of the Board of Agriculture having proved by experiment, that the cheviot breed of sheep, so much esteemed by the farmer, could be introduced and thrive on the most bleak mountains, and a large proportion of the old inhabitants might be retained in their possessions.[r]

The sheep has always been associated with our ideas of the pastoral life, and, from its inoffensive nature and great usefulness, has ever been a favourite with the shepherd, and the theme of rural song, and it is to be remarked, that while cattle-lifting was not considered dishonourable, a sheep stealer among the Highlanders was held infamous. Although apparently a stupid animal, many curious proofs

[q] Heron's Hist. of Scotland, v. 15.   [r] Agric. Report.

of its strong instinct might be adduced. The attachment of sheep to the place of their nativity is remarkable. They have been known to traverse great distances for the purpose of revisiting the scenes of their youth and rejoining their progeny.*

SWINE, muic, were formerly numerous in the low country of Scotland, but the Highlanders appear to have paid little attention to them, allowing them to roam in a state of nature. The breed has been intermixed with others, and much improved in size, by the encouragement of the Highland Society, and the native animal, which was small, is extinct, except perhaps in the Isle of Man and in the wilds of Sutherland, where a few still remain. The Scots retain an antipathy to pork; whether derived from the ancient Celts, or the early Christians, is difficult to determine, and, although this aversion is disappearing, it is far from being eradicated. In the Agricultural Report for the county of Banff, it is stated that live swine have never yet been sold in any of the fairs of the north. Many places evince by their names that these animals must have been there found in considerable numbers. There is the Isle of Muc, Glen Muic, Mucross, &c.

Those who attended the cattle were, by the ancient Britons, called Cheangon, retainers, and Paruis, herdsmen, whence some tribes, it is thought, were named by the Romans, Cangi and Parisii. Goat herds were denominated Gabr and Gabrant, or Gabrantic.* The laws of Wales

---

* Out of a flock of some hundreds of two-year old wethers from the farm of Arybualan in Ardgour, sold at Falkirk some years ago, and taken by their purchaser to a farm in Perthshire, six or seven actually found their way back to Arybualan, their original home, before the end of the season. A glance at the map will show how wonderful must have been the instinct that guided them through so many intervening obstacles. ED.

* Whitaker, on authority of Ptolemy and Richard of Cirencester.

provided for the pasturage in common of all the cattle of one place. The Aoireannan of the Highlanders are the "keepers of cattle," and are a sort of farm servants who have the charge of cultivating a certain portion of land, and taking care of the cattle it supports. They are allowed grass for two milk cows and six sheep, and had also the tenth sheaf, with the privilege of raising as much potatoes as they chose. The slaves of the ancient Irish, or those purchased or carried off from England, Wales, or the continent, were employed in tending the flocks.[t] In the old practice of folding cattle on the farm lands, the herds shelter themselves in a little hut of poles and pliant twigs, and this, called Bothan tothair, is an exact model, on a small scale, of the ancient British hut.

The cattle of the Celts were usually secured in a strong inclosure connected with the camp or fort, as may be seen by inspecting the plans of the ancient strongholds. At other times they were placed in inclosures formed, according to Brehon regulations, by trenches and banks, strengthened by stakes or live hedges to guard against the attacks of wolves and other ravenous animals, as well as the attempts of hostile tribes. There is reason to believe that means were found to secure the cattle near the Duns, as at Castle Coul, before described. Pennant says the Boaghun was the Dun in which they were lodged. The Britons, according to Whitaker, had sheds, constructed of stone and wood, for this purpose, some of their ruins, 16 feet by 12, having been discovered at Manchester.

Pliny says there was no better pasture than the German fields.[u] The Gauls had very extensive fields of grass, and it was mostly natural; the only artificial sort known to them being trefoil: but the superior manner in which these

[t] Ware.   [u] Lib. xvi. 4.

people prepared their lands, and the judicious use of marle, must have rendered them abundantly fertile. Their cattle were objects of great pride, and in their anxiety to improve the breed they shewed themselves good farmers, and acquired the praise of others for their agricultural knowledge. It was remarked by Cato, and assented to by Pliny,[x] that the best means of deriving profit from a farm was to feed cattle well.

Since Scotland has become so destitute of wood, the pasture has materially suffered. The ground in the Straths, where the ancient woods have decayed, do not now yield a quarter of the grass it did when sheltered by the foliage, and the farmer is not able to outwinter his cattle as formerly: but the bare hills and flats are now abundantly stocked with sheep, the animal whose increase is said to have been the chief reason of the destruction of the young trees, and consequent deterioration of the pasture. Notwithstanding the care of the Highland farmer, he often loses great numbers of his cattle from want of food. The variable climate sometimes indeed reduces himself to want, but he frequently has his farm much overstocked, and the consequence, scarcity of provender in a severe winter, is certain, while to counteract the evil there are few means. In Strathdon, in Aberdeenshire, the people are accustomed to take heath tops for winter store with advantage; and when the cattle can be turned out they assist them to this food by clearing the snow from it.[y] *

In the early stages of Society, before land is regularly divided among the members of a tribe, the shepherds freely move from pasture to pasture as in the days of the

---

[x] Lib. xviii. 5.   [y] Stat. Account, xv. 463.

* A better system of farming, and more care and forethought in the management of stock now prevails, and one rarely hears now-a-days of any cattle dying for want of sufficient "wintering." ED.

patriarchs. The Suevi, the chief nation at one time in Germany, had no inclosure, but moved to new situations every year. Britain, says Gildas, abounds in hills that are very convenient for the alternate pasture of flocks and herds, which most certainly alludes to the ancient practice still preserved among the Scots Highlanders, and formerly a remarkable characteristic of the Irish, who maintained abundance of cattle. Spenser describes them as leading a wandering life, driving their herds continually with them, and feeding only on their milk and white meats, a practice which was called boolying.² This vagrant life, so like to that of the Scythians, seems to have given rise, as before observed, to the name of Scots, common to certain parts of the population of both countries. It has been long impossible for any among the civilized nations of Europe to pursue exactly this itinerant life, but in Scotland, where a large tract of mountainous country is annexed to a farm, the owner still continues to move his flocks in something resembling the ancient manner.

After the Irish rebellion, in 1641, several wandering clans, under the name of creaghs, or plunderers, overran the country with their numerous flocks, so much to the annoyance of the English settlers, that it was found necessary to restrain their perambulations by public authority." The Highlanders were till lately universally accustomed to move from the Bailte Geamhre, or winter towns, to the Arich, or breeding grounds, in the hills; every davoch, or tenpenny land, and even each farm, having a certain portion of mountain territory for this purpose.ᵇ

Page 37.
ᵃ Coll. reb. Hib. ii. p. 225. Beauford's Diss. on Irish Language.
ᵇ Grant's Thoughts on the Gaël. This intelligent writer believes the name of Argyle, anciently spelt Aregaël, and applied to a great proportion of the Highlands, signifies the breeding grounds of the Gaël.

Here the seisgach, or dry cattle, remained during the winter, if not too severe, while the others were brought down to the more sheltered homesteading in the glen. Spenser says, in Ireland each cantred maintained 400 cows in four herds kept apart. In Scotland, where their existed any right of common pasturage, the number of cattle which each individual was entitled to turn out was according to the number which he could fodder in winter on his own farm, and the proportions, in case of dispute, were settled by a form of law called an action of souming and rouming. The ancient practice, which is still fondly adhered to where practicable, is thus described by an intelligent proprietor of Sutherland. "The principal farmers, who reside in the straths, or valleys, along the banks of the streams, have extensive grazings in the mountains where the cattle are driven in the summer. Early in the spring a person, who has the name of Poindler, is sent to these hill pastures to prevent strange cattle from trespassing. and when the crop is sown and the peats cut, the guidwife and her maids, with some of the male part of the family occasionally, set out with the milk cows and goats, and take up their residence in the Shealing or Airie, which is a hut, or bothy, with one apartment, perhaps 12 feet square, for the purpose of eating and sleeping in, another of a similar size for the milk vessels, and, in general, there is a small fold to keep the calves apart from the cows. Here they employ themselves industriously in making butter and cheese, living on the produce of their flocks, some oatmeal, and a little whiskey, contented, happy, and healthy, dancing to the pipes or the melody of their own voices, and singing their old native songs, not only in the intervals of work, but in milking their flocks, who listen with pleasure and attention to the music, particularly to an air appropriate to the occupation, of which the animals even evince a fondness. Here they remain for about six weeks, the men occasionally returning to the homestead to collect their peats, and perform any other necessary work, when the pasture becoming exhausted, they all return to the farm, and leave the yeld, or young cattle and horses, to roam at freedom among the hills until the severity of winter drive them home. The practice was to rear a calf for every two cows, and after the family were served with the product of the dairy, there were twenty-four to thirty pounds of butter, and as much cheese from each cow."[c]

The temperature of the milk in churning is ascertained by the sound of the cream. When harsh, it indicates its being too cold, but when sufficiently warm, it is soft.

Rennet of a deer, lamb, or hare's stomach, are indifferently used by the Highlanders for coagulating the milk: sometimes the gizzards of fowls are applied for this purpose, and the stomach of a sow is said to be preferable to any other. The old practice was to convert the cream into butter, and the skimmed milk into cheese, but there is little sweet milk cheese now made. The old mode of curd cut into large pieces is therefore in a great measure given up. It is a very old custom in the Highlands to mix aromatic herbs with the rennet, a practice that has recently been recommended as a great improvement by some English writers, by whom it is thought a new discovery.

The ancient Celts had some singular methods of treating their cattle when ill, and superstitious observances to protect them from mischief. They were accustomed to take as much of limeum or belenium as could be laid on an arrow head, which was put in three measures of liquid and poured down the animal's throat. What disease this prescription was destined to cure does not appear, but the

[c] Agric. Report.

cattle were fastened to stakes until it had ceased to operate, for they often went mad from its effects. Samolus, march wort, or fenberry, which was gathered with peculiar ceremonies, was laid in the troughs where cattle drank, in order to save them from all diseases.[d]

The Highlanders, as may be supposed, have many superstitions regarding their cattle, and indulge in many absurd ceremonies, some of which may have at the same time originated in satisfactory experiment, and acknowledged efficacy of prescription. The manner in which the disease, or accident, called elf-shot, is successfully treated, has been before described. On new year's day it is a practice deemed salutary for the cattle, to burn before them the branches of juniper. It is common to the Highlanders and Irish to keep a large oval-shaped crystal, the virtue of which is, that water being poured on it and administered to the animals, they are *sained*, or preserved from many evils that would otherwise befal them.* Mountain-ash and honey-suckle, placed in the cowhouse on the second of May, we may be assured, has not been resorted to without undeniable experience of much good. Most of these superstitious customs have no doubt existed since the days of Paganism, their object being to counteract the designs of evil spirits. Witches, warlocks, and other "uncanny" persons, are now the chief objects of dread, and to baffle their diabolical efforts the farmer exerts his utmost skill and faith. Reginald Scot's "special charm to preserve all cattel from witchcraft," is doubtless a secret well worth knowing.

[d] Pliny, xxiv. c. 9.

* The Editor has seen several of these crystals. One very large, and reputed of wonderful efficacy, is in the possession of Charles Stewart, Esq., of Ardsheil. It is beautifully mounted in an eagle foot of silver; and there is a massive silver chain attached, by which it was carried about and suspended in the water afterwards to be drunk by the animal to be cured. ED.

While on the subject it may not be amiss to describe some of the methods by which the Highlanders endeavour to cure their cattle when diseased, and guard them from impending illness. To prevent the spreading of that direful disease called the blackquarter, the animal is taken to a house into which no cattle are ever after to enter, and there the heart is taken out while the creature is yet alive, and being hung up in the place where the other cattle are kept, it preserves them from death. A live trout, or frog, is put down the throat to cure what is called blood-grass. Murrain, or hastie, a complaint with which an animal is suddenly seized, becoming swelled, breathing hard, with water flowing from the eyes, and dying in a few hours, is treated in a peculiar manner. The disease is less frequent since the decay of the woods, but it appears in so malignant a form, for dogs who eat of the carcase are poisoned, that it is firmly believed to be the effect of supernatural agency. To defeat the sorceries, certain persons who have the power to do so are sent for, to raise the Needfire. Upon any small river or lake island,* a circular booth of stone or turf is erected, on which a couple, or rafter of birch-tree, is placed, and the roof covered over. In the centre is set a perpendicular post, fixed by a wooden pin to the couple, the lower end being placed in an oblong groove on the floor; and another pole is placed horizontally, between the upright post and the leg of the couple, into both which, the ends, being tapered, are inserted. This horizontal timber is called the auger, being provided with four short arms, or spokes, by which it can be turned round. As many men as can be collected are then set to work, having first divested themselves of

---

* The author doubtless meant to say " Upon any small island in a river or lake," &c. ED.

all kinds of metal, and two at a time continue to turn the pole by means of the levers, while others keep driving wedges under the upright post so as to press it against the auger, which by the friction soon becomes ignited. From this the Needfire is instantly procured, and all other fires being immediately quenched, those that are re-kindled both in dwelling-houses and offices are accounted sacred, and the cattle are successively made to smell them. This practice is believed to have arisen from the Baaltein, or holy fires of the Druids. Sometimes the diseased animal is brought, and held with its tongue pulled out, for about fifteen minutes, over a sooty turf fire, and the sods from the roof are at other times put in a pot with live coal and a quantity of good strong ale.

The Highland drovers, or those persons who are intrusted with the charge of bringing the cattle from the mountains to the southern markets, are a class of considerable importance, and their occupation is peculiar to their country. The drover was a man of integrity, for to his care was committed the property of others to a large amount. He conducted the cattle by easy stages across the country in tractways, which, whilst they were less circuitous than public roads, were softer for the feet of the animals, and he often rested at night in the open field with his herds. These trusty factors often come as far as Barnet, and even to London. In one of Sir Walter Scott's novels, the Chronicles of the Canongate I believe, is a spirited description of one of these Celts.

I am not aware of the rules which may have regulated the division of a cattle spoil, farther than that there was generally a mutual division, among the ancient Celts. The Highland practice, as before stated, was to give two thirds to the Chief, but whether any particular rights existed among the Gaël, as we find in other nations, does not appear. A constable was anciently entitled to all cattle without horns, horses unshod, and hogs taken in foraging, and the marshal received all spotted cattle.* If any one in the Highlands could claim horses without shoes he would have taken all. In a following chapter will be seen the perquisites which some individuals in Celtic society received when cattle were slaughtered.

The cattle of the Gaël were the temptation to mutual wars and unrelenting feuds, and they were the estimable reward of enterprising warriors. The herds often changed owners during the continuance of war. In 1626, we find the Governor of Ireland taking 4000 cows from the Burkes; and in 1587, Tyrone carries off 2000 cows, and a great number of garrons, &c., from Sir Arthur O'Neal. These were respectable creachs, and seem to justify the title which the Highlander claimed for the cattle lifters,—gentlemen drovers.

AGRICULTURE.

The Celtae, although much attached to the pastoral life, were not inattentive to the advantages of agriculture. The sterner tribes did not to be sure apply themselves with much assiduity to that or any other pursuit, save those of war and plunder; thinking with the Germans, of whom Tacitus speaks, that it was stupid to gain by their labour, what could be more quickly acquired by their blood, but in general they cultivated a greater or less proportion of ground.

The Belgic part of the population of Britain is described by Cæsar as practising agriculture to a considerable extent, while the Celts, or tribes of the interior, are represented as neglecting or remaining ignorant of this useful art,

* Edmonson's Heraldry.

paying exclusive attention to the pasturage of numerous flocks. This description has led to the belief that the cultivation of the soil was entirely confined to the Belgians, and even introduced by them, but the expression does not warrant this supposition. That the inland tribes were not ignorant of agriculture, but did raise corn, is certain. It may, at the same time, be readily admitted, that the local and commercial advantages of the inhabitants of the southern provinces stimulated them to greater diligence, but they were not the sole agriculturists in the island. The rich fields of corn which Cæsar found on the south and west coasts, a fortunate acquisition for the sustenance of his troops, most likely struck him as a peculiarity on observing the numerous herds and the limited crops in the interior. From the address of Bonduca to her army it is apparent that agriculture was not unknown to those tribes denominated Celtic, however limited the extent of their operations may have been.

It has been asserted, from the speech which Tacitus assigns to Galgacus, that the art of procuring sustenance by the culture of the ground was unknown to the Caledonians, but an attentive perusal of the passage will shew that this inference is not quite fair; the warrior only reminds his countrymen that, while free, they had no fields to cultivate for a master.[f] Dio Nicæus, who relates that the people north of Adrian's wall had no cultivated lands, but lived on the produce of their flocks, is also brought forward as authority on this subject, but his assertion cannot be unhesitatingly admitted. Strabo enumerates grain among the British exports, and it is well known that, shortly after the Romans had settled in the island, large quantities of corn were annually transported to the con-

Vita Agric. § 31.

tinent, for the supply not only of their friends, but the armies of the Romans. It is true that this increased industry in agricultural labour is attributed to Roman incitement, but as that people had not to teach the Celts how to improve their soil, but, on the contrary, found them enterprising agriculturists, the reasonable explanation of the fact is, that the Britons only availed themselves of the new opening for the sale of their grain. The same energy was exerted by the nations of the continent, Gauls, Germans, and Celtiberians; when subdued by the Roman arms, they found a profitable market for the produce of their fields, but these nations followed agriculture with success long before they became tributary to Rome.

Malmutius was a celebrated British legislator on agriculture. The laws of Moelmus, who is perhaps the same individual, are now believed to be lost.[g] The Welsh Chronicles celebrate Eltud, or Eltutus and others, as the authors of different improvements in the system of field labour.

The labourers of the ground were called by the ancient Highlanders, Draonaich, the genuine name, it is thought, of the Picts.[h] The people of the eastern coast, where agriculture could be pursued with success, were so designated by the western Gaël, and vestiges of the habitations of the Draonaich are found within the limits of the ancient Caledonia, proving the meaning of the appellation synonimous with Pict, and still retained by the Gaël. The sites of these houses are scarcely ever found without the visible marks of former cultivation on the adjoining heath.

Although the inhabitants of the plains, who devoted themselves to the cultivation of the ground, were called Draonaich, "yet a certain portion of the people residing

---

[g] Roberts.   [h] Grant's Thoughts on the Gaël.

among the Gaël of the mountains, were also known by the same denomination; of which important fact the most complete evidence remains to this day. The foundations of the houses of those who employed themselves in the cultivation of the soil are distinguished by the appellation Larach tai Draoneach, (the foundation of a house of a Draonaich or Pict.) These are very numerous in many parts of the country, and are, without exception, of a circular form, with the entrance to the house regularly fronting due east. In the neighbourhood of the place of residence of the writer of these sheets, within the bounds of the ancient Caledonian forest, there are cultivated fields; which further proves the fact, that the term Draonaich was not exclusively appropriated to the people inhabiting the more level country of Scotland, but was applied also to the cultivators of the soil in the mountainous parts of the country. Druim a Dhraonaich and Ach a Dhraonaich are fields well known in the western part of the valley of Urquhart, lying to the westward of Lochness; and still farther to the westward, in the adjacent valley of Strathglass, there is a cultivated field called An Draonache.* And even at this day the people who possess the arable lands in the bottom of the valley in the vicinity of Draonache, and who have been, for a long period of time, remarked to be more industrious than their neighbours, are called Draonaich Bhail na h amhn (the Draonaich of the River town,) which is a village situated by the side of the river Glass, running through the valley. When a man is observed employing himself in laborious exertion upon the soil, it is a common expression among the Highlanders, be'n Draoneach e, that is, he is truly a Draoneach. The Gaël of the mountains

* On Lochawe side is Inistrynich (*Innis Draoinich*) the island or lake side plain of the Draoinich, a name evidently of the same origin as the above. ED.

were divided into two classes, Arich and Draonaich. The first were the cattle breeders, and the other were the cultivators of the soil, and indeed comprehended all persons who practised an art. Accordingly in Ireland, Draoneach signifies an artist, and Draonachas, an artifice."

"The foundations of the houses of the Draonaich are so numerous in some parts of the Highlands, as to afford the most decisive evidence that the number of the cultivators of the soil must have been, in very ancient times, prior to the knowledge of the plough, very considerable."[1]

When mankind first associate together, and apply themselves to cultivate the earth, it is done by the joint labour of all the members of the community, who have an equal right to the crop that is produced, and will receive proportions of it according to their wants, but after a village has been some time settled, and the inhabitants advanced in civilization, this common property in the land is generally abolished. Each individual is considered entitled to the produce of his own labour, and as he continues to possess the same parcel of land, he is understood to have a certain right to it, and thus either by prescription, or allotment, the tracts under cultivation become distributed among all the members. In regulating these divisions, as in the management of the common property, the chief exercises his delegated power. The right he assumes of disposing of the public possessions is naturally acknowledged, and by retaining for himself an extent sufficient to support his rank, he acquires an additional authority, and subjects the different proprietors to the observance of certain conditions necessary for the general welfare. Such is the natural progress of mankind in the advance of civilization, but this tendency to an early division of the land is

---

[1] Grant's Thoughts on the Gaël, p. 280.

counteracted by various circumstances. Poverty, the rudeness of husbandry, the relationship of the members, and an adherence to ancient custom, with a strong impatience of anything like an infringement of their equal rights, combine to prevent a separation of interest. Under the patriarchal or clannish system of government, where the claims of consanguinity are so strong, mutual labour and assistance continue, and the practice of cultivating the land in common, once so universal in Scotland, where it still lingers among the Celtic inhabitants, is the ancient mode of conducting agricultural operations.

The Suevi, a powerful nation of Germany, who were distinguished for their attention to agriculture, pursued their rural occupations under the following regulations: the tribe consisted of 200,000 fighting men, and of these one half went yearly to the wars, where they served for twelve months, returning to take the place of the others, who, in like manner, took the field for the same period of service. The individuals seem to have had a certain quantity of land assigned to them, but no man was allowed to remain more than one year in the same place.[k] The Vaccæi, a nation of the higher Iberia, now Leon, every year divided their land, ploughing and tilling it in common. After harvest, they distributed the fruits in equal proportions, and it was death to steal or abstract anything from the husbandman.[l] The Germans, who raised corn only, and made no orchards, moved from land to land, and still assigning portions suitable to the number of persons, parcelled out the whole lands according to the condition and quality of each individual, every year changing and culti-

[k] Cæsar. This writer describes them as excellent agriculturists, yet he says they lived on milk and flesh. Is he inaccurate, or did these people, like some of the Scythians, raise corn to sell, and not to eat?

[l] Diodorus Siculus.

vating a fresh soil."[m] The partition of land did not preclude the existence of common holding among the members of a tribe or community, whose territorial possessions were, by public consent, reserved for themselves. All disputes concerning inheritances, and the limits of fields, were settled by the Druids."[n]

The practice of common holding still remains in the western isles of Scotland, and in many parts of the Highlands, and has not long been abolished in many districts. An act of Scots parliament, 1695, authorized the division of lands lying run rig, the term by which this common property was distinguished.[o] Under such a system it is not easy to regulate the proportions very nicely: there are generally more people living on lands so managed, than are taken into calculation, but, "absurd as the common field system is at this day, it was admirably suited to the circumstances of the times in which it originated; the plan having been conceived in wisdom, and executed with extraordinary accuracy."[p] One of its evils was, that sometimes none would commence work while any individual who ought to attend was absent, but this must have been in an ill regulated township. In the most western counties of England there is no common field. The lord lets off a portion of the common for two crops, when it is allowed to become pasture again.

When the land is cultivated in common, boundary lines scarcely appear necessary. The Suevi, Cæsar observes, had no inclosure: the Romans themselves appear to have had no other mark of separation than a statue of Terminus."[q] The old divisions of land were, when practicable,

---

[m] Tacitus. He says of one of their tribes, they laboured with more assiduity in agriculture than suited the laziness of other Germans.
[n] Cæsar.   [o] It was also called Rig and Rennal.
[p] Loudon's Agriculture, p. 504.   [q] Virgil's Georgics, iii. 212, &c.

regulated by natural boundaries, that were sometimes nicely determined by the point of a hill, whence the water was observed running to either side. It was also a most ancient custom, all over the Highlands, to build head dykes, or walls, that were erected where there appeared a natural demarcation between the green pasture and the barren heath. Within this dyke was the arable and meadow land of the farms, while beyond that line the cattle, horses, goats, and sheep, fed in common. In the Highlands are often seen the vestiges of inclosures that exhibit marks of great antiquity, concerning the original use of which the inhabitants have lost all knowledge; the ridges of stones, visible at a considerable distance, and displaying extended white lines along the brown heath, may, with propriety, be referred to this mode of laying out lands. Inclosures are often very improperly formed of the turf, or surface of the adjoining land. Galloway, or rickle dykes, are much esteemed in Dumbartonshire and other Highland districts. This fence is constructed of stones loosely piled up to the height of four or five feet, every tier being less in size, and at the top the stones are wide apart. The fabric seems too open and ill constructed to last long, but it is found to be durable. The stones being placed with the thickest end upwards, act in some degree like the key stones of an arch, and the wall opposes little resistance to the wind. This is an excellent protection against sheep, who will not venture to scale such an erection. According to the co-operative system, neighbouring proprietors joined in the erection of boundary or march walls. In 1577, we find the Deemsters of Man enforcing an ancient practice, that persons whose lands were contiguous should be at the mutual expense of forming the respective inclosures. By the Welsh laws the husbandman had a right to the second best of every three hogs, sheep, goats, geese, or hens, that trespassed on his corn. This enactment shews the care of that people to secure to every one the produce of his industry; it was afterwards modified: only one out of fifteen hogs, thirty sheep, goats, geese, &c., being awarded to the complainant, and if there were not so many animals, the compensation was made in money. For the encouragement of agriculculture no less than eighty-six laws were made by the Welsh. If any one obtained permission to lay dung on another man's lands, he was allowed the use of them for one year; and if the dung was in such quantity as required carts, the term was extended to three years. If the lands of another were cleared of wood, and rendered arable, the person who did so enjoyed their produce for five years, and a person who folded his cattle on another's field without objection, for one twelve months, was entitled to cultivate it four years after.

From the nature of society it is evident that farms or portions of land possessed and laboured by individuals must have been small. In other words, the land must have been subdivided, without a great disparity in the quantities of the different allotments. It was one of the earliest regulations of the Romans to assign every man two acres of land. The jugerum, or as much as could be ploughed in one day with a yoke of oxen, was reckoned a sufficient reward to a deserving officer, and to receive the half of a quartarius, or a pint of adoreum, a sort of fine red wheat, was esteemed an honourable testimony of public respect.[r]

[r] Pliny xviii. 3. Hence, by metonomy adorea, the quantity distributed came to signify honour, praise, &c. The first institution of Romulus was twelve wardens of corn fields, Ibid. 2; and it shews how important they considered the protection of agriculture, that when Carthage was taken, the only articles saved were twenty-eight books, which were written by Mago on that subject.

Steel-bow tenants in Scotland, received corn, straw, agricultural implements, &c., from the proprietor, on condition of their restoration at the end of the tack or agreement, and were bound to share the produce with the landlord. The old system of agriculture encouraged the residence of numerous labourers or cottars around the house of a farmer, who enjoyed their cottage, and a patch of ground as a vegetable garden, for which they paid small or no rent. In the Highlands, the malair, a person of the same order, was in the same condition. His sole dependance was not on the employment which the land on which he resided gave him, but he was bound to allow his services to the farmer in harvest and on other occasions. There were no day labourers in the Highlands. Their pride and sense of equality prevented them from working for a neighbour, although many toiled in the low country for very small reward. Improvements in Agriculture have led to the disappearance in many places of this class of peasantry, and it is long since the desire to increase the size of farms has destroyed the more equable division of land. Pliny says that large farms had been the ruin of the Roman provinces, and would eventually prove the ruin of the whole state.* How far they are to be considered national evils in these days, I am not prepared to state.* The country may be depopulated, and the numerical strength of a state may not be lessened, those who can no longer live as farmers taking up their residence in towns; in the Highlands, however, the ancient tenants who have been displaced, unable to gain a livelihood by their handi-

---

* Lib. xviii. 6.

* Whatever may be said to the contrary, there can be little doubt that everything that leads to the depopulation of a country is to be reckoned an evil. Much, of course, depends on the manner in which the depopulation is effected. ED.

craft, have for ever bidden farewell to their native soil, and sought an asylum in the wilds of America. A farm in Argyle, eighteen or twenty miles long, and three to four broad, is said, by Dr. Robertson, of Dalmenie, to be the largest in Britain. The sheep farm of Gallovie, in Badenoch, is about twelve miles long, and from eight to ten broad, which makes it at least ninety-six square miles, consequently sixteen square miles larger than that in Argyle. One at Balnagowan, in Sutherland, contains 37,000 acres. A Highland farm may be generally described as a certain part of a valley, stretching on either side of the burn or stream by which it is watered. To every possession, large and small, a share of arable, meadow, pasture, and muir land was allotted. The best part of the farm was distinguished as infield and outfield, the former being generally under crop, and in good state; the latter consisting of places not fit for tillage, but appropriated to pasture the cattle, and produce a little hay. Beyond this, and separated by the head dyke, was the common heath, extending to the summit of the mountains. Near the house was also the door land, which served for baiting the horse of a visitor at meal time, or such like. Crofters, or small farmers, had no outfield. In officiaries, which were generally an ancient barony, but sometimes a modern division of one to three or more square miles, the ground officer regulated the management of the farms, fixed boundaries, and settled disputes, in which he was assisted by the Birlaw or Boorlaw men, a sort of rural jury. The more ancient Gaëlic practice was, however, to refer the decision of the controversy to the oldest men of the clan, who determined according to the Clechda or traditional precedents, and their award was enforced by the chief. Several ancient terms, expressive of the extent of land, are still preserved. Davach is a common denomination, and is equivalent to four ploughs.[t] Many farms in Scotland retain the name, and a well known toast in Strathbogie is the forty-eight davach, alluding to the possessions of the Duke of Gordon in that district.

A Carucate is a term anciently in very general use, and is expressive of as much arable land as could be managed with one plough, and the beasts belonging thereto, in a year, with pasture, houses, &c., for the persons and cattle.[u]

An Oxgate was a certain extent of land, recognized in the later period of Scots' history. On the 11th of March, 1585, ""The lords fand that thirteen aikers sall be ane oxengate; and four oxengate of land sall be ane pound land of auld extent.''[x] The old extent was made about 1190, and remained in force until 1474.

The only mode of ascertaining the extent of arable land seems to be from the quantity of grain sown. The usual calculation is, that a boll of seed is required to an acre, hence land is let by this allowance, and by the number of cattle that it will maintain; but this valuation is not strictly correct, for if the land be good, a less quantity is used, and if bad, more is required; it is, however, a general guide for proprietors. Arable[y] land in Galloway, and most parts of the Highlands, is still reckoned by pence, farthings, and octos. The penny land is generally allowed to contain eight acres, consequently a farthing is two acres, and an octo is one, or a boll's sowing.

In Lochaber the land is reckoned by pence, farthings, and octos, but in Badenoch, and I believe in Strathspey, &c., it is reckoned in marks, eighty marks being equivalent to an octo, and eight octos making a davach. On the old

---

[t] Shaw.   [u] Preface to Doomsday Book.   [x] Harl. MS. 4628.

[y] Arable is derived from aratus, ploughed, a Latin word of Greek extract. Ar, in Gaëlic, is Agriculture, and in old Celtic was earth.

system, a quarter davach was reckoned a sufficient possession for a gentleman, and this quantity was generally attached to every baille or farm town. A good grazing quarter davach will support from twenty to thirty milk cows, and a proportion of yeld cattle and horses, yielding them sufficient fodder. The mountain skirting the Strath, and attached to the baille, was fed in common by the cattle of the davach, and was divided by water or land marks from the mountain of the next valley, but the people of as many as four or five davachs sometimes grazed in common, in the more distant summer sheilings or ruidhs. As many as eighty bothies might be seen on the plain of Altloy, in Drummin, in Badenoch, and the same on the plain of Killin, in Strath-Eric, a spot of itself worth a journey from London to see, about five miles above the celebrated Fall of Fyers.

Rents were obviously at first paid in kind, or by certain quantities of produce. This originating in early society, remained an unavoidable mode of payment in countries destitute of a sufficient quantity of coin to render the barter of commodities unnecessary. By the laws of Ina, in the end of the seventh century, a farm of ten hides or plough lands, paid ten casks of honey, three hundred loaves, twelve casks strong ale, thirty of small ale, two oxen, ten wethers, ten geese, twenty hens, ten cheeses, one cask of butter, five salmon, one hundred eels, and twenty pounds forage.[z]

In Scotland all sorts of domestic cattle and poultry, and the grain raised on the land, or proportions of meal, under the name of customs, were commonly rendered until late years, and still form the chief amount of rent in many places. Muir fowl, salmon, loads of peats and dry wood, &c., were by no means uncommon in rentals. Tenants were also formerly bound to indefinite servitudes or feudal

---

[z] Wilkins's Leges Saxonica, p. 25.

duties, under the name of arriage and carriage, or services used and wont, but by the act abolishing ward holdings, no services, except to mills, can be exacted that are not specially mentioned in leases or terms of agreement. The customary duties were certain days' work in seed time, hay and corn harvest, the leading or bringing home firing, &c., These services being often useless, from the non-residence of the proprietor, and money becoming more common, and being found a much more convenient medium of settlement, were often commuted for the legal coin. In the rental of the Bishoprick of Aberdeen, in the beginning of the seventeenth century, we see the gradual conversion of customs into money, and the improvement of society. As an instance, "The lands of Clovach, in the parochen of Kyldrymie, sett to Lumsden ffor £9 6s. 8d. One mart, twelve kidds, four geese, 3s. 4d. for bondage and services, 37s. 4d. for grassum, and 6s. 8d. of augmentation."[a]

The following enumeration of the different sorts of grain raised by the Celts, with accompanying observations, are perhaps more curious than important, but are not irrelevant to the subject now under consideration.

Corn, originally the natural production of the earth, was certainly cultivated by the Britons, before they were visited by the Roman legions. The Germans raised much oats. Barley, the most ancient food of mankind, had been long familiar to all the Celtæ,[b] and in Iberia they raised two crops of it in the year. That ancient historian Herodotus says, that the Egyptians neither used wheat nor barley, which were then common in other countries.[c] The wheat of the Gauls and Britons was light, and of a red colour,

Harl. MS. 4613.

Barley bread was anciently given to the Roman sword players, who were hence called Hordearii. Pliny xviii.

[c] Lib. ii. c. 36.

receiving the name of brance, breic, or brac, from its bright appearance.[d] It was also called by the Romans Sandalium, or more properly, it should seem, Scandalum, both terms being derived, according to Whitaker, from the red brogs of the Celtæ. Sandalium is indeed the Latin name of a shoe, but it does not appear to have been applied to those of the Celts, and the name of the wheat is variously written sandalum, scandalum, scadalam, &c. In some parts of Italy, Dalechamp observes, the word scandella is still in use.[e] This grain was peculiar to Gaul, and is celebrated by Pliny as of all others most neat and fair, yielding more bread by four pounds in every modius or bushel, husked and dried, than any other sort.[f] That called Arinca was also a native of Gaul, and made the sweetest bread.[g] The siligo, or white wheat, was chiefly raised in Gallia comata, among the Averni and Sequani; the Allobroges called it blancheen, as the modern French say Ble-blanche. In Aquitain much panicum was grown, a sort of wheat resembling millet, which last was the chief crop among the Sarmatæ.[h] The Thracian wheat was very good, being heavy, and ripening remarkably quick.[i] Our researches do not procure much information concerning the qualities of British grain in ancient times. It appears that Gwent Iscoed, a native appellation for part of Monmouthshire, was noted for abundance of wheat and honey; Dyfed, or Pembrokeshire, for barley and wine, while the staple of Carnarvon was barley alone.[j] One Coll ap Coll frewi, in the sixth century, is said to have introduced the culture of wheat and barley to the Welsh, oats having been the chief grain previously grown. Gildas says the Britons when at peace raised all sorts of grain in the greatest abundance.

[d] Whitaker. [e] Comment. ed. 1669, iii. p. 427. [f] Lib. xviii. 7, 10.
[g] Ibid. [h] Pliny. [i] Ibid. [j] Triad, 101.

In Scotland oats are the chief produce, and the chief food also, as all who have turned to the word in Johnson's Dictionary are aware. Great quantities of barley are likewise grown, but wheat, except in the southern and more champaign districts, is not very common.

From the marks of cultivation on the acclivity of mountains, and on the summits of hills, so generally observable in Scotland and in Ireland, it has been supposed that the population must have been considerably greater formerly than it is now. These appearances are of themselves no decisive proof of this, for the high grounds were evidently cultivated when the straths were obstructed by impervious woods.[k] The ancient farmers also preferred the security of the hill, to the risk which the haugh presented from the floods of autumn, an evil much to be dreaded in those moist climates, and they were, doubtless, careful to preserve the natural pasturage in the valleys, which no artificial means could supply on the hills. Another opinion is very prevalent. Where the marks of cultivation are found

---

[k] When the Caledonian forest was thick, its growth on the banks of rivers must have led to the formation of marshes. The plains on the sides of the Spey, which are still overflowed by the autumn floods, must have formerly been mere swamps. It is related of Michael Scot, Alexander Gordon, (Alastair Ruadh na Cairnich, probably Cairness,) and Mac Donald of Keppoch, that they had studied the black art in Italy, the end of the 15th century, and it is added that Mac Donald was the greatest proficient. He was accustomed to converse on the subjects with which his unhallowed learning had made him acquainted, with a female brownie called Glaslig, for whom it is believed he was more than a match.[*] One evening he asked her the most remote circumstance she remembered, when she replied that she recollected the time when the great Spey, the nurse of salmon, was a green marsh for sheep and lambs to feed on.

[*] Sir Ewen Cameron of Lochiel is also said to have had frequent encounters with the *Glaslig*, and to have always proved more than a match for her by means of his knowledge of the "Black Art," into the mysteries of which he was initiated by Keppoch. ED.

in Scotland, they are often considered the memorials of recent periods of scarcity, and the ravages of the civil wars, by which the proprietor becoming ruined, was obliged to abandon his farm; and it is argued that, in a short period of neglect the ground will become overspread with heath. It is true that this may be the case, but it is, from the ridges which remain, sufficiently apparent that those fields are recognised, and they may have been formed in very remote ages. There are many proofs in the pages of national history that the Scots were at an early period actively engaged in agriculture; they seem to have been equally celebrated as keepers of cattle and labourers of the ground, in both which occupations they are at present surpassed by no people. The Scots of Ireland were formerly noted for their assiduity in improving the land, for which they were much disliked by the less diligent natives.[k] On the submission of O'Neal, he solicited aid to assist him in expelling them, the manuring and fertilizing the ground appearing to be a chief cause of offence.[l]

In 1269, we find it recorded as a great calamity, that a frost in Scotland prevented ploughing from the 20th Nov. to the 2nd of February. In 1298, while the English were besieging Dirleton Castle, they were obliged to subsist on the peas and beans which they gathered in the fields,[m] and in 1336, a feud in Lothian laid one hundred ploughs idle.[n] Those facts, it must be allowed, relate to parts of the country that were not then Gaëlic, but they shew that agriculture was by no means neglected in distant ages. As the Highlanders, from their numbers of cattle,

---

[k] At a depth of five or six feet, a good soil for vegetation, formed into ridges, is often discovered. A plough was found in a deep bog near Donegal; and a hedge, and some wattles, were found standing at a depth of six feet.

[l] Derrick.   [m] W. Hemingford, i. 160.   [n] Fordun, xv. 31.

had it always in their power to supply themselves with corn in the Lowlands, and found it necessary to take grain in exchange for their flocks, it may in some measure account for the limited cultivation in "the rough bounds," for the Gaël were certainly not incompetent to raise grain, as far as the sterility of the mountains, and variable nature of the climate, would permit. Donald Munro, in 1549, describes Iona, Mull, and other islands of the west, as "fertil, and fruitful of corne."*

The Highlanders have been charged with laziness and mismanagement of their farms, from a stubborn adherence to old and erroneous practices; and their system of management is much censured by Southern farmers. There is, doubtless, some truth in this stigma; but when we consider the disadvantages of climate and soil, their conduct as agriculturists may be palliated. The husbandman can have little inducement to lay much of his land under culture, with a chance of his hopes being blasted, and his labour lost, by a rigorous season. If a severe frost should kill the seed before it has arisen; if a wet summer should prevent its ripening, or an early winter should destroy the crop, the loss will be easier borne the less it is. The farmer therefore risks but a limited quantity, sowing little more than he expects to want for use. If indolence exist, it is surely most excusable where there is no motive for exertion; and if the Highlanders mismanage their farms, few others would be found willing to undertake to make so much of them. It is believed by those best able to form a correct opinion, that it would be impossible to find any other people to inhabit the bleak mountains now possessed by the Scotish Gaël.° They may have old-fashioned

---

* On Icolmcille or Iona, wheat of the finest quality is raised, and is frequently ripe and ready for the sickle earlier than in the middle of England. ED.

° Rose of Aitnach, Agricultural View of Sutherland

notions, and awkward implements, but it is not always the case that novelties are improvements, or that the present generation are in all things wiser than their fathers. Birt acknowledged that "their methods were too well suited to their own circumstances, and those of the country, to be easily amended by those who undertook to deride them."

Gaul, says Mela, abounds in wheat and hay, and the lands of the Germanni, we otherwise know, were excellent for bearing grain. These nations well understood the art of fertilizing the earth, and it is an unequivocal proof of the ability of the Celtic farmers, and of their attention to agriculture, that they discovered the use of margam, or marl,[p] which they imparted to the Greeks and Romans.[q] The Hædui and Pictones of the continent made considerable use of lime to improve their grounds,[r] but margam, was in universal esteem. The obvious advantages of its application created an anxiety to discover new sorts, yet, according to Pliny, the various kinds were resolvable into two, as had been the case from the first, namely, the white fat marl, and the heavy reddish coloured rough sort, which was called capimarga, or accaunamarga. Both kinds would retain their strength in the ground for fifty years.[s]

The Britons possessed a superior knowledge of the various marls and their properties. Their chalky sort was the best, which retained its strength for eighty years, so that no man was ever known to marl his ground twice during his life.[s] That which the Greeks called Glischromargen, resembling fuller's earth, was used for grass land, and kept its vigour thirty years: the sort called Columbine, the Gauls termed Eglecopalam. The use of marl appears to have been forgotten for a long time in the south

[p] Marg, margu, marrow. Whitaker.   [q] Pliny, xvii. 6.
[r] Pliny, xvii. 8.   [s] Ibid. 7.

of Britain; one of the Lords Berkeley is said to have been the first who revived it.ᵗ

The people beyond the Po preferred ashes to other manure, raising fires for the purpose of producing it; but it was not used for all crops, and was never mixed with anything else.ᵘ The Ubians, a German nation, dug their lands three feet deep, a mode practised by no other people, and not equal to the application of marl, for the ground required to be broken up again in ten years.ˣ

Limestone is much used, but sea weed is the common manure in the isles and along the coast of the Highlands. The very objectionable mode of digging up the surface soil of the upper grounds, to mix with animal dung as a manure for the valleys, is visible in many places. The Highlanders convert their houses into good manure. As they are chiefly formed of turf, or foid, such frail tenements are only inhabited for a short number of years, and, when they are taken down, the materials, impregnated with smoke and soot, become a very useful compost. The method by which the inhabitants of St. Kilda prepare their annual manure, is singular, and apparently confined to that remote island. It is composed of the ashes of their fires, the dung of their cattle, &c., which accumulate on the floors of their houses during their long and dreary winter.*

The ancient method of conveying manure to the ground, general throughout Scotland, but now confined to the

---

ᵗ Berkeley MS.   ᵘ Pliny, xvii. 9.   ˣ Ibid. 8.

* The people of St. Kilda have vastly improved in all their social habits since our author's day. They now prepare the manure in a less objectionable manner, and while their crops are quite as good or better, their health is greatly improved. Their manner of preparing manure mentioned in the text was not only disgusting and unseemly in itself, but the direct and immediate cause of an infant mortality among them altogether unknown anywhere else in the kingdom. A form of lockjaw, known to the faculty as *Trismus nascentium* was so prevalent and fatal that *four out of every*

Highlands, was simple and expeditious. Two semi-circular creels, or, baskets, one and a half or two feet long, formed of strong wattle work, were suspended on each side of the horse, by means of ropes made of the pliant twigs of the birch or willow, and affixed to the clubbar, or saddle, which rests on the fleat, or summac, a sort of mat composed in general of straw and rushes interwoven. The bottom of the creels are attached to the side nearest the horse by twig hinges, so that it can be opened and closed, being fastened when full, by means of sticks which are slipped into nooses at either end of the basket. When the contents are to be discharged, the sticks of both baskets are simultaneously withdrawn, and the manure falls to the ground, but to do this properly requires peculiar address, for, should one side be discharged before the other, the apparatus is instantly overturned, to the great merriment of the other labourers. This method, apparently so awkward, is yet efficient, and is performed with celerity. Six loads of the Highland ponies are equal to a cart load, and the manure is more equally spread, and in much less time, than by carting.

The particular systems of agriculture, pursued by the ancient Celts and modern Gaël, are not very remarkable. They varied a little, according to the nature of the ground and other circumstances, the art being pursued with simplicity, but with considerable success. The Ubians, we have seen, dug their land three feet deep, which was more

---

five of the children born on the Island died between the eighth and twelfth days of their existence. That this dreadful mortality was caused by the filthy state of their homes, and the impure atmosphere within doors, is proved by the fact that since the objectionable way of manure making referred to by the author has ceased, the abnormal infant mortality of the island has altogether disappeared, their children now living and dying in about the same proportion to their numbers as in other places. ED.

than could be done by the plough; but we do not know how they disposed of the stones, where numerous, in clearing their fields. They may have accumulated them in certain places, as was the practice in Scotland, where the Draonaich collected them in numerous small heaps, leaving the intermediate spaces clear for cultivation. This is observable around all the sites of their dwellings, and differs from the later practice, which appears to have been occasioned by the operation of ploughing, the stones being thrown on each side, forming alternate ridges, with the clear land, and denominated rigs and baulks. The Welsh, Cambrensis informs us, used not to till during the year round, as in other places, but in March and April, once for oats, and in summer twice. For wheat, they only dug up the land once in winter. The Irish were formerly censured for their ill management, in having hay and corn harvest at the same time.[z] The unfavourable climate and sterility of the land are heavy disadvantages to the Highland agriculturist. From the mountainous nature of the country, he is obliged, in many parts, carefully to turn all the earth into one part, forming thereby an artificial bed, while the hollow on each side serves to carry off the water, which otherwise would wash down the scanty soil. The ridges are called in the Low country lazy beds, a name not very applicable, considering the labour necessary to raise and preserve them on the acclivity of steep hills. In such situations, no other plan of cultivation could possibly be adopted; the name, however, is often appropriate, when such beds are formed where the uniform depth of soil obviates any necessity for them. These spots of cultivation, scattered over a rugged hill, have a singular appearance.

The Highlander might certainly improve his methods

[z] Riche.

of cultivation, for in many things he is deficient. The ground cannot be very clean when it is tilled in the spring only, nor can it be very productive when not subjected to proper rotation of crops; but in objecting to the Celtic practices, it is right to bear in mind that in parts of the island, where natural obstacles did not check improvement, agriculture remained long in a state of great rudeness. Even in England, the farmers continued extremely ignorant, and, consequently, unsuccessful. In the reigns of Edward I. and II. they set beans by hand, and leazed the seed wheat from the ear itself, and in the time of Richard, they had not adopted the simple and efficient mode of improving pasture by penning the sheep progressively over the field, but gave themselves the trouble of carrying the dung in small quantities from a distant fold.

The harvest of the ancient Britons was by no means late. Cæsar, according to the calculation of Halley, arrived on the 26th of August, and the crop was almost all cut down, only one field, that had been later than usual, being observed standing. In the Highlands, where the climate is so disadvantageous, it seems unaccountable that the inhabitants should be partial to late sowing; they indeed give a reason, which may be allowed its weight, without however proving the system of management to be good: if the seed was put earlier in the ground, the Highland farmer alleges it would be smothered with weeds.*

That the Highlanders retain several old and ridiculous superstitions respecting their agricultural operations cannot be matter of surprise, when their more refined neighbours in the Low country, and the inhabitants of England, have

* Early planting and sowing is of late years the rule rather than the exception over all the Highlands. The consequence is, that crops of all kinds, if not heavier, are of a better quality and give less trouble in the season of ingathering than formerly. ED.

not relinquished equally absurd and unmeaning observances. In the most flourishing ages of Greece and Rome, the farmers were incredibly superstitious regarding the seasons, the influence of planets, the winds, &c.

The Highlanders think the moon ripens their corn as much as the sun does. This, like most popular beliefs, is founded on experience, although the effect is erroneously deduced. In clear and settled weather, when the moon is unclouded by night, as the sun is by day, the crop must obviously ripen well. A superstition, lately very prevalent, seems to have originated in the times of paganism. It was the custom throughout Scotland to leave a portion of land untilled, which was called, "the good man's croft," or "the old man's fold," a practice which the Elders of the Kirk in 1594, exerted their utmost influence to abolish,[a] without effect. This hallowed spot is believed to have been the place where the Druids invoked the divine blessing on the corn and cattle of the owner,[b] or where he himself sacrificed for an abundant crop.

In noticing the various implements used by the Celtic agriculturist, it will be seen that he possessed many ingenious articles that are generally supposed the invention of later ages. The PLOUGH was used by the Gauls in their agricultural operations, and was called Planarat, Plumarat, or more probably, as commentators have observed, Pflugradt.[c] The Celtic plough was very ingeniously constructed, for it was provided with two small wheels, and the shares were large and broad, turning up large turfs and casting a good furrow.[d] The practice was to make but two or three bouts and as many ridges, and one yoke of oxen were able to prepare forty acres of good land.[d]

[a] Arnott's History of Edinburgh.
[b] Rev. Mr. Johnstone, of Montquhiter.
[c] Pliny, xviii. 18 ed. Lugd. 1668.   [d] Ibid.

This seems to resemble the alternate ridges, which the old Scots formed, by their manner of ploughing, which received the descriptive appellation of rigs and baulks. The plough was very early in use among the Britons, if we could trust the relation of Geoffry of Monmouth, who says, Dunwallo, a prince who flourished 500 years before Christ, was a great encourager of agriculture, which he seems to have considered as an occupation connected with religion. A law assigned to him, enjoins the ploughs of husbandmen, and the temples of the gods, to be sanctuaries. Eltud, or Iltutus, improved agriculture, and taught the art of ploughing, until which time the land was dug with the spade and pickaxe in the Irish manner,[e] and no man was allowed to use a plough who could not make one. The ropes, or harness, were to be made of twisted willows; and it was not unusual for six or eight individuals to associate for the purpose of supplying themselves with this implement, and for their regulation many curious laws were enacted.[f] The old Irish plough was drawn by five or six horses yoked abreast, and five men were required to conduct the operation.[g] In the beginning of the seventeenth century, ten shillings annually were exacted for permitting the use of their "short ploughs," which were drawn by the horse's rump, a practice not altogether unknown among the Highlanders, among whom it was common to break a colt by tying a harrow to his tail. The Irish were so fond of this barbarous custom, that they petitioned the Deputy to be allowed to continue it without being taxed; but they were answered that the law was not so severe as in 1606, when a garron was the penalty for the first year's use of one plough in that manner, and for the second year two; and as the practice occasioned the loss of

[e] Triad. 56.   [f] Leges Wallicæ.   [g] Riche.

so many horses, it was necessary to abolish it.[h] The Irish are described by Spenser as "great plowers, and small spenders of corne."

In many places of Gaëlic Scotland, a small plough, called a ristle, is used, and employed to precede the larger sort. Its chief peculiarity is the culter, shaped like a sickle, to cut along the turf. In these parts deep ploughing is avoided, on account of the high winds to which they are subject, and which sometimes blow both seed and soil away.

The old Thraple plough is now seldom to be seen, except in the remote Highlands, or in the Orkneys. In Argyleshire, it continued to be used on some farms about twenty years ago, but was fast giving way to the more improved manufacture. In some places it was called the Rotheram plough, and was rude and simple in its construction, and awkward in its management. It was entirely composed of wood, with the exception of the culter and sock, and had but one stilt. It was drawn by four garrons or oxen, yoked abreast to a cross bar; which was fastened to the beam by thongs of raw hide or ropes of hair; and he who managed the stilt, held it close and firm to his right thigh, to protect which he had a sheep or other animal's skin wrapt around it. To keep the plough sufficiently deep in the earth, a person was required to press it down, while another performed the office of driver by placing himself between the two central animals, where he walked backwards,[i] protecting himself from falling by placing both arms over their necks. The mould-board was ribbed or furrowed, in order to break the land, and old people declare that the soil yielded better crops after being ploughed in this manner

---

[h] Des. cur. Hib. Ulster paid £870 of this tax.

[i] Gir. Camb. describes the Welsh ploughman, likewise, as walking backwards.

than it does by the modern practice. The supposition is, that by the old method the soil was more equally broken up.

That excellent instrument, the CASCROM, literally crooked foot, a kind of foot plough, which the Highlanders can manage with great dexterity, and which is too little known,[k] is still used in mountainous districts, and, from its excellent adaptation to the culture of steep and rugged hills, where a plough cannot be used, is not likely ever to be superseded by any improvement. With the same labour it will perform nearly double the work of a spade. It consists of a strong piece of wood, five to seven feet in length, bent between one and two feet from the lower end, which is shod with iron fixed to the wood by means of a socket. The iron part is five or six inches long, and about five inches broad. At the angle, a piece of wood projects about eight inches from the right side, and on this the foot is placed, by which the instrument is forced diagonally into the ground and pushed along, as may be seen from the vignette. By a jerk from the shaft, which acts as a powerful lever, eight or ten inches in breadth of the soil is raised from a depth of eight to twelve inches, according to circumstances, and dexterously thrown to the left side. Eight, ten, or a dozen of men are sometimes employed working with the cascrom. They arrange themselves in a line at the bottom of the hill, with their backs to the acclivity, and with surprising rapidity turn over the rough and scanty soil, forming, in their operations, an extended cut or trench, like a plough-furrow. This is repeated as they gradually ascend the hill backwards, and the land so laboured is very productive. One active man can turn more in a day with this instrument than four men with common spades. Munro

[k] Sir John Sinclair.

describes Tarnsay and other islands, in 1549, as "weil inhabit and manurit; bot all this fertill is delved with spaides, excepting sa meikell as ane horse-plough will teil, and zet they have maist abundance of beir and meikell of corne."

The Casdireach, or spade with a straight handle, is also in considerable use. The Manx have an implement similar to this, furnished with an iron spur for placing the foot upon; it is about four inches wide at the end, and well adapted for rough and stony ground. Serviceable spades are formed in the North, of fire-wood shovels, imported from Norway in exchange for meal, and afterwards shod with iron.

The spade used for carting or cutting turf for building or covering houses, &c., called also the divot, and the flaughter spade,* is a sort of breast plough, used by a person who presses his body with all his strength against it, forcing it before him, and nicely cutting off the grassy or short heathy surface of the ground. The labourer protects his thighs by a sheep's skin, or several folds of plaid, hung like an apron before him, and will cut nearly 1000 turfs per day. It may be noticed that in the Low country, the Highlanders are esteemed the best labourers at trenching or other hard agricultural work. The Gaulish method was to sow immediately after the plough, and cover the seed by means of harrows, after which the land required no more weeding. These harrows were furnished with iron teeth. In the Isle of Lewis there was formerly, if it does not still exist, a peculiar sort of harrow. It was small, and provided with wooden teeth in the first and second bars, to break the soil; in the third was fastened heath to smooth it, and a man dragged it along by means of a strong hair rope across his breast. Iron teeth are seldom used in the

* The *Lair-Chaibe*, or wooden-spade-mare, referred to in a former note. ED.

Highlands, because they bury the seed too deep in the earth, which wooden ones, from their lightness, do not.*

While the Romans reaped their corn with a sickle, the Gauls, whose fields were remarkably large, went to work in a more expeditious manner, and cut down their crops by means of a scythe, used by both hands, an implement for which we thus seem to be indebted to these people, who appear to have been more anxious to finish their labours as quickly as possible than desirous of executing their work nicely, for they did not cut close, but rather mowed down the tops.[k] They had also another ingenious method of cutting down their largest fields, which shews not a little perfection in the mechanical arts. A large machine, resembling a van, was constructed, in which the horse was yoked so as to push it before him. The sides were furnished with sharp teeth or knives, and this carriage being driven into the field, the ears of corn were cut off, and, at the same time, were thrown into the body of the car, which was made to receive them.[l] Giraldus says the Welsh reaped with an instrument like the blade of a knife, and a wooden handle at each end. In the Scillies, the corn is reaped with sickles, but it is all laid down regularly as it would be by a scythe.[m] The Britons were as regardless of the straw as the Gauls, reaping their corn by cutting off the ears only.

The harvest work in the Highlands is performed in a very creditable manner. The women are the chief reapers, and, in the words of Mr. Marshall, who drew up the Agricultural Report of the central Highlands, they cut it "low, level, and clean, to a degree I have never before observed."

---

* Wooden harrows with iron teeth are now in general use throughout the Highlands, wooden-toothed harrows being rarely, if ever, seen at the present day. In many districts harrows entirely of iron, both teeth and frame, are common. ED.

[k] Pliny, xviii. 28.   [l] Pliny, c. 30.   [m] Troutbeck.

Lint, also, which is said to be a late introduction to the Highlands, is allowed to be a well managed crop.* It is carefully weeded by the women on their hands and knees. In so variable and unpropitious a climate as that of the north of Scotland, much care was required in guarding the crop from injury when growing, and after it was reaped. In Sutherland and Caithness, the Highlanders had observed that if the hoar frost remained on the corn when the sunbeams of the morning first struck upon the crop, it became blighted; they were therefore accustomed to go to their fields before the sun arose, and with a rope made of heath, held by a person at each end, and pulled along the top of the corn, the frost was shaken off. The usual method of piling the corn in shocks, consisting of twelve sheaves, prevails in the Highlands, but in some of the Northern counties it was preserved in small round heaps resembling beehives, which were well thatched all round, and denominated bykes.[n] The sheaves are also in many parts, set up singly. It is usual to have the upper parts of the gables of barns formed of wattle work, so constructed as to throw off the rain and admit a thorough draft of air, a most judicious plan in a climate so wet. It would have been much to the advantage of the husbandmen of former years, in more favoured parts of the country, to have had similar buildings, for want of which they were obliged to keep the corn on the ground as long as they possibly could. In 1358, an inundation in Lothian swept away the sheaves that were laid out to dry at Christmas eve:[o] It is to dry hay and corn that the spacious and elegant barns of the Duke of Argyle were erected in Glenshira.

* Lint is not now grown in the Highlands. Cotton is now worn in its stead, and what linen fabrics are required can be bought cheaper in the south than they could possibly be made at home. ED.

[n] Pen. i. 202.   [o] Fordun. xv, 21.

The Britons laid up the corn in the ear, and preserved it in subterraneous caves or granaries,[p] a practice also of the Celtiberians. They deposited it in pits from which the damp and air was carefully excluded, and in these receptacles wheat so preserved remained fresh and good for fifty years, and millet for even more than 100.[q] The Thracians stored up their grain in similar vaults, and in the ear also, which Pliny recommends as the best method of preserving it.

Throughout Scotland, but especially in Highland districts, are found subterraneous buildings of rude but substantial formation. These are the eird or earth-houses before noticed, built of loose stones, and covered with large flags, which may have often served as the hiding-places of the natives, but were in most cases, there is every reason to believe, the places where the grain of the inhabitants was deposited for security. The remarkable number of earth-houses at Kildrummy has been referred to. All these subterraneous apartments are accompanied by a sort of square inclosure or space, level, and somewhat lower than the surrounding ground, and by noticing these places, one is often able to discover the caves; which, from examination, were evidently the storehouses of the ancient inhabitants. Many of the inclosures have been cleared out, and numbers of hand mill-stones have been invariably found. That these recesses were designed chiefly for the deposition of grain we may safely conclude from the known practice of the Celtic tribes, who were accustomed to take from their stores a requisite quantity of grain daily, spending their time in the woods hunting, or in warfare. The muirs of Achindoer and Kildrummie were eligible positions for the granaries of surrounding tribes, being warm and champaign, inclosed by

[p] Diod. v.   [q] Varro.

lofty ridges of hill, and, as it were, just within the mountains. They were not less favourably situated for cultivation; and to this day "Kildrummy oats" are esteemed before others in the Northern counties. To these plains the natives resorted for their daily supplies of corn, which they always ground for immediate use.

Those remarkable hollows on the borders of Wilt and Somerset shires, called Pen pits, are most singular remains of former ages. A space comprising more than 700 acres has been excavated into pits, in shape like an inverted cone; and various conjectures have been formed as to the purpose for which so numerous and close an assemblage was intended. As hand mill-stones have been found, I believe, in all that have been examined, and as the situation is so dry that no water has ever been known to stagnate in them, it appears probable that Pen pits were the storehouses of the aboriginal tribes who lived in that part of the country, and who in this place had their common granaries, whence they supplied themselves as occasion might require.

The most early method of separating the grain from the straw was by means of cattle, who, by repeatedly treading, effected the object. This was the mode in practice among the Jews in most ancient times, and the Romans either trampled their corn in the same manner, or pressed it with the tribula, a sort of dray made of rough board. The Gauls and Britons, however, used a Flail,[r] which performed the work much better, and in much less time. This implement was introduced in Italy about fifty years before Christ, but the Roman husbandmen, notwithstanding the encouragement given to agriculture, were inferior to the Gauls, for they continued to use their oxen in treading out their

[r] Whitaker.

grain, to whose assistance a roller, or heavy stone was added,[s] being the only improvement made on the old plan, and the awkward practice is retained to the present day.[t]

The inhabitants of Scotland continue to use the flail, where thrashing mills have not been erected, and where mills or farm houses are not provided with winnowing machines, the chaff is separated from the grain by sifting it in the open air, when the weather permits, or between the opposite doors of a barn, the draft of air carrying aside the lighter particles. Some of these buildings are constructed of an angular form, in order to catch the wind blowing from any point. The Waight, guil,[*] an implement for winnowing, is a sheep-skin, the wool being removed, of about one foot and a half in diameter, stretched on a hoop, like that on a drum head. In these the corn is exposed to the wind, and the chaff blown away, a light work, which the Highlanders commit to the women.

The most obvious, and consequently the first practised, method of reducing grain to flour, for the composition of bread, is by simple pounding. The Gauls had early arrived at the art of grinding their corn by a hand mill, which was also used by the Britons before they were visited by the Romans. This people, otherwise so greatly advanced in civilization and refinement, had not altogether discontinued the practice of bruising and pounding their grain, even in the time of Vespasian.[u] The hand mill is of great antiquity, as appears from many passages in the Scriptures. Pausanias ascribes its invention to Myleta, the son of Lelex. That of the British tribes was called Quern, and in Scotland, where its use is still by no means

---

[s] Colum. ii. 22.   [t] Blunt's Vestiges of Ancient manners, p. 209.
[*] Gaelic—*Guit.* Ed.
[u] Pliny.

rare, it retains the same name.[x] Grinding by the hand stone appears very awkward to those who are accustomed to good machinery, for it takes two women four hours to grind a bushel, and it is to this work which Barnaby Riche alludes, when he says that the women in the North of Ireland ground their corn "unhandsomely." The manner of preparing the grain for the quern was called Graddaning, a term which comes from grad, quick; but Jamieson derives it from the Norse word gratti, descriptive of the grit stone, of which the quern was made, whence are the Danish gryte, to grind; the English grits, German grout, Swedish groet, and Scots grots and crowdy. The process was thus conducted. A woman sitting down takes a handful of corn, which she holds by the stalks in her left hand. She then sets fire to the ears, and being provided with a stick in her right hand, she dexterously beats off the grain at the very instant when the husk is quite burnt, neither allowing the grain to be injured, nor striking before it is ready to fall. This practice is chiefly confined to the Western Islands and most remote districts of the main land. The usual method, in Badenoch and elsewhere, is this: the corn is switched out of the ear with a stick, fanned or separated from the chaff, and put in a Scots pot stuck in the fire, while a person keeps turning it with a wooden spatula, called speilag, in the same manner as coffee is roasted in some places. This manner of preparation is called araradh, often improperly written Eirerich.[*] "I have seen," says a gentleman from Laggan, "the corn cut, dried, ground, baked, and eaten in less than two hours." A labourer returning from his day's work carried home as much corn in the sheaf as he required for his supper and next day's provision.

[x] The quern is still used in the Scillies.
[*] Properly *Eararadh*. ED.

The water mill is believed to be an invention of the Romans, and communicated by them to the Britons; we, however, read that Coel, grandson of Caradoc ap Bran, first made "a mill, wheel with wheel." The Gaël of Albion were earlier acquainted with the nature of mill machinery than those of Erin, for about the year 220 Cormac Mac Art, King of Ireland, sent notice to carpenters from Albin to make for him a mill.[y] The horizontal mill, in Shetland called a tirl, and used in some parts of the Highlands, is a very simple piece of machinery.

There was usually a mill on each barony, and the Laird, to secure the multure or miller's fee, was solicitous to break the querns. The miller on every Lairdship had usually a croft for his support, besides the legal multures and sequels, i. e. the perquisites of the miller and his man. In Scots law, thirlage is the servitude by which lands are astricted to a particular mill, being bound to have their corn ground there on certain terms. The district or lands thus bound are termed the sucken, and the payments are the multure or quantity of grain or meal exacted by the heritor or his tacksman, and the sequels or those quantities given to the servants under the name of knaveship, bannock, and lock, or gowpen. In the Highlands the thirle is called sincam, and the multures are termed cis. The tenant paid a certain measure out of every boll to the chief, half that measure to the miller, and a quarter to the gille-mullin, or miller's man.

The Gauls refined or sifted the flour by sieves of horse hair, which were their own invention, and the Celtiberians improved on the discovery, by making two sorts, both formed of fine linen.[z]

The British tribes were sufficiently skilful to construct

---

[y] Keating.   [z] Pliny, xviii. 11.

cars of superior workmanship for war, and had evidently machines for the purposes of traffic, but it does not appear how far they made use of those conveyances in their agricultural operations. In Caledonia, the mountainous nature of the country almost precluded the use of wheel carriages. All work which could not be performed by manual labour was executed by horses, for which the farmer was obliged to keep considerably more than appeared to Lowland farmers compatible with good management. For this they are still condemned, but it is an overstocking which is unavoidable. In 1778, on a Highland farm, where one hundred and ten bolls of oats, and thirty-six of bear, were sown, there was not a wheel carriage of any description.[a] A waggon, or vehicle where the thill horse does not bear the weight, is well adapted for the Highlands, where it seems unknown. The old cart, the use of which is not yet entirely discontinued, was formed wholly of wood. The wheels were of ash or other hard wood, two feet and a half in diameter, and three inches in thickness, and were fixed to the axle, which moved with them, and the traces were fastened to a hoop of birch wood around the axle. Between the trams or thills a conical basket was placed, into which the fuel or manure was put, and, to unload the carriage, the driver had a method of oversetting and replacing it with great facility. The Irish car appears to be similar to this machine. In the Isle of Man, a sort of sledges are used, composed of two shafts, widening towards the end, but connected by five or six cross bars, and dragged along the ground. Oxen, it has been stated by a respectable author, are not worked in any part of the Highlands. The Welsh, by their ancient laws, were prohibited from using any other animal for the plough. A usual mode of con-

[a] Trans. of Highland Soc. i. 132.

veyance is by the crubban, a triangular machine formed of rods, and suspended across the horse's back on each side. It is well adapted for carrying peats, corn in sacks, hay, &c. A sort of stout creels, of a similar construction, are called Rechailich, and a tradition exists that the stones of which the bridge of Dee, near Aberdeen was built, about 1522, were conveyed by these means. A sort of saddle, called a Clubbar, formed of wood, has a deep notch in the top, for the purpose of holding a rope of straw, rushes, or heath, to which are fastened, on each side the horse, a basket or bag, made of straw, rushes, or floss, a sort of reed, and woven like a mat. They are of an oval shape, about three feet wide at bottom, and two and a half at top, being about one foot eight inches deep, and capable of containing half a boll of oats. They are called cazzies, or ceises, and are furnished with a handle or fettle at each end, by which they can be carried, and have two straw or other ropes to tie the mouth, when full. These simple and convenient articles are generally made during the winter nights: they will last two years, and their value in the Northern counties is perhaps fourpence or sixpence; but in Badenoch, where they were chiefly employed in carrying cheese and butter from the sheelings, they cost more. Highland garrons with these will travel through the most rugged paths, each fastened to the tail of the other, however many there may be, attended by one driver, and, when unloaded, the halter of the foremost is tied to the tail of the last, so that it is impossible for them to stray, as they can only move in a circle. This mode of fastening by the tail is thought an excellent method of breaking horses.

To conclude this chapter, it may be observed, that the state of the old Highland tenantry was far from being slavish or uncomfortable. Strangers seldom took farms, or indeed had the opportunity, for few were ever removed from their ancient possessions, to which they thought they had a sort of prescriptive right. The farm tenants of modern times have generally a cow on the common pasture, and one, or one and a half acres of land for vegetables, with the privilege of cutting grass on the bogs, for which they pay a rent of five or six pounds. The freedom of a pastoral and agricultural life is highly favourable to a military spirit, and it did not escape the observation of the ancients, that their best troops were raised in the country. The children born of husbandmen, says Cato, are the most valiant and hardy soldiers, and the most intrepid.[b] The late war evinced, in the case of the Highlanders, the truth of his remark.

[b] Pliny, xviii. 5.

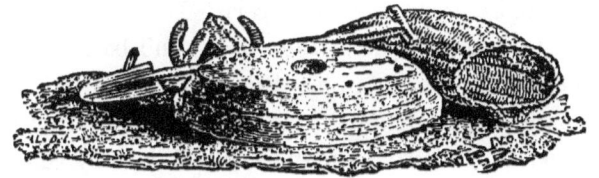

CHAPTER IV.

OF THE FOOD OF THE CELTS,—THEIR COOKERY, LIQUORS, MEDICINAL KNOWLEDGE, HEALTH, AND LONGEVITY.

THERE was no scarcity of food amongst the Celtæ, when they came under the observation of the more polished nations of Europe, and their good living must have materially assisted in producing the strong limbs and large stature for which they were so remarkable. The vegetable kingdom, unimproved by horticultural skill, and the wild herds of the forest, afford the means of subsistence to mankind in the first stage of civilization; but the nations of the west were not confined to these precarious supplies, having long before the commencement of our era, as may already appear, pastured numerous flocks of cattle, and cultivated, with success, extensive fields of corn. To this general observation the state of some of the remote and barbarous tribes will indeed be an exception. Strangers to the advantages of climate and intercourse with more refined nations, they continued in primitive rudeness, unaffected by commerce, and contented with their savage enjoyments; but the Gauls were far removed from that state in which human beings are under the necessity of appropriating the coarse fruits of the forest trees, or the wild herbs and roots of the field, for their chief subsistence. They were, as has been shewn, supplied with abundance of venison from their well-stocked forests, and other meat from their tame herds, and the plenty which filled the land was evinced by their well-supplied tables and continued feasting, which were the theme of even Roman commendation. The Aquitani were famed for their sumptuous and frequent entertainments,[a] and the Celtiberi were noted for being particularly nice and curious in their diet.[b]

Before manners have been changed by civilization, or mankind has emerged from a state of nature, the savage beings subsist on the coarse and undressed articles of food which they may be able to procure. The roots of the field, and the produce of the forest trees, supply a ready, though precarious, means of subsistence, and, consistent with the plan hitherto pursued, it will be inquired how far the ancient Celts depended on the wild productions of nature, or had supplied themselves with vegetables and fruit, improved by horticultural industry.

The Germans, according to Tacitus and Appian, lived chiefly on raw herbs and wild fruit, and some of the Britons, also, were accustomed to satisfy the cravings of hunger with the same unsavoury aliment; but this must have been in cases of necessity, and among the most barbarous of the tribes, for they certainly had, in general, ample supplies of other food. It is, besides, found that nations will continue the use of the hard fare which satisfied their fathers, when it is in their power to procure better provisions, as the

[a] Marcellinus. [b] Pliny.

Arcadians, who continued to eat acorns to the time that the Lacedemonians warred with them;[c] and the Celtiberia, who used, throughout all the country, to serve up roasted mast as a second course,[d] notwithstanding they had all sorts of flesh in plenty, and were not obliged to use this plain diet.[e] The Celts, although, as shall be shewn, they by no means disregarded good living, seemed to have considered temperance a virtue, being moderate, as Diodorus and Tacitus express themselves, in eating, banishing hunger by plain fare without curious dressing. This race have ever been noted for their contempt of delicacies, or aversion to epicurianism, and their ability to bear the privations of hunger and fatigue. It has been found that the Highlanders are, when surrounded with plenty, more sparing in their diet than others; and it is a fact, that they will continue a whole day at laborious field work, contenting themselves with only two meals of water brose, or a simple mixture of oatmeal and water. They will eat, says Mrs. Grant, with a keen appetite and sufficient discrimination; but were they to stop in any pursuit because it was meal time, growl over a bad dinner, or exult over a good one, the manly dignity of their character would be considered as fallen for ever. I have seen a piper from "the head of the Highlands," at a sumptuous dinner on St. Andrew's day, select, from the various choice dishes around him, plain boiled sheep's trotters in preference to anything else!

The ancient Celts held corpulence in so much abhorrence, that the young men had a girdle to determine their size, and if they were found to exceed its dimensions, they were subjected to a fine. A fat paunch has always been reckoned a great misfortune in the Highlands.

Health may be preserved with a much less quantity of food than is generally supposed; for repletion is more

[c] Pausanias, vii. 7.   [d] Pliny, xvi.   [e] Diodorus.

inimical to the system than a scanty meal. Martin justly observed, that if among the Highlanders there were no corpulent persons, none bore the appearance of starvation. The remark is still applicable; and although, from their hard living and frequent exposure to the severity of the weather, the appearance of old age is seen at a more early period of life than is the case with labourers in more favoured climes, yet they live equally long, if not longer, enjoy as good health, and perform as much work, and often of a great deal harder nature.[f]

The Caledonians, we learn from Dio, were obliged, when in the woods, to live on the fruits of the trees, and even on the leaves and roots of wild herbs; but game, the chief subsistence of an uncivilized peopled, formed their principal food, to which the vegetable kingdom formed an estimable accession. In the woods and valleys were found the natural productions, which diversified the simple meals of the Celtic nations, and the herbs and esculents which nature had spread before them, they were long satisfied to gather from the open fields, before they thought of cultivating them around their dwellings. The Britons, in distant ages, paid some attention to this useful pursuit, yet many, in Strabo's time,[g] were totally ignorant of horticulture. The vegetable garden of the ancient Celt, we may believe, was but scantily stored; the natural meadows in the vicinity of his humble dwelling, and the mountain wilds, afforded him a sufficient and not uninviting supply. In summer, the Gaël could vary his repasts by many sweet and wholesome productions of his native land; he could

[f] The alleged abstinence of some ancient nations is almost incredible. Pliny tells us the Sauromatæ took but one meal in three days! Lib. vii. 2.

[g] Lib. iv. p. 200.

gather subhans[h] in the glen and avrons[i] on the height; in the woods he could find various fruits and nutritious herbs—on the muirs he could pick the delicious blackberry, the aromatic aitnach, the luscious blaeberry, and many others.

A people occupied in pasturage could not fail to become acquainted with the value of different vegetables, either as human food, or sustenance for their herds. Turnips were served up at table in Gaul, and were given to the cattle in winter, a part of rural economy which we thus see is far from being an improvement of modern times.[j] A sort of wild carrot was known in almost every country. The kind called Daucus grew spontaneously in the woods of Gaul and Britain, and was known in Italy as the Gallic. Leeks, of which the Welsh are reputed to be so fond, were plentiful in the Principality in the fifth century. The old Irish made great use of water cresses, sorrel, and scurvy grass; and even shamrock is said to have been eaten by them. The poor of that country were often obliged to make such articles a chief part of their food. In 1673, they are represented as "feeding much on water cresses, parsnips, potatoes, and sea weed," and Sir William Petty describes them as using potatoes from August to May, a pennyworth of cakes serving an individual a week; to which, eggs and rancid butter were added by some; others, it is said, used a preparation of curdled milk and horse's blood, and those who lived near the sea gathered muscles,* cockles, and oysters, but flesh meat was seldom seen among the lower order.

[h] Strawberries, used in the Low Countries of Mar and Banff for raspberries.

[i] Otherwise oighreag, the cloudberry, rubus chamæmorus.

[j] Columella, ii. 10, p. 198, edit. 1595.

* The shell fish so called is now more properly spelled *mussel* to distinguish it from *muscle* of the animal frame. ED.

The ancient Gaël had a certain vegetable, of which about the size of a bean enabled them to resist, for some time, the effects of a want of either meat or drink.[k] The Highlanders, at this day, occasionally use an article that was in much esteem with their ancestors, and which, if not the above, seems to possess similar qualities. The root braonan,* which grows abundantly in the country, is delicious, and very nutritious when boiled. It is dug from November to April, and, when dried and ground, it makes good bread. Many, also, chew it like tobacco, and allege that it allays the sensation of hunger. Pennant confounds this with the cor-mheille,† or blue button, the root of which is only used as a tonic. The Scythians, according to Pliny, who, it must be confessed, was credulous, had two herbs which can hardly be classed among those used for food, although they appear to have answered as most valuable substitutes. One received its name from the people among whom it was found, or who discovered its properties, being called Scythica; the other was called Hyppici, and by keeping either in the mouth, the want of meat or drink was not felt for a considerable time.[l] A knowledge of these excellent articles would be of inestimable value to hungry wights in the civilized society of the present day.

Shunis, or Scots parsley, is much valued by the Highlanders, who use it both as food and medicine. The vegetables which they usually cultivated were cabbages, onions, carrots, beans, and pease. The kale yard, or garden for

---

[k] Dio.

* The *braonan*, earth-nut or pig-nut, is the *bunium* or *bulbocastanum* of botanists. When properly cleaned and allowed to lie by for some time it is a delicious morsel, not unlike liquorice root. ED.

† *Corr-mheille* or *carra-mheille* is wild liquorice or wood pease, *pisum sylvestre*. ED.

Pliny, xxv. 8.

the vegetable, Cole, was formerly an important adjunct to a cottage in the Lowlands, but since the introduction of potatoes, it is in less esteem. The Highlanders, about one hundred years ago, had in general an aversion to the productions of the kitchen garden. The Grants appear to have been the first among the clans who cultivated the above-noticed vegetable, and they are, at this day, often alluded to as "the soft kale-eating Grants." The old Highlanders were chiefly carnivorous and lactophagious, and even yet they are indifferent to the use of vegetables. The kale and cabbage which they require for planting, are purchased in the Low Country. Kale seems derived from the Latin, Caulis, a stalk or stem, but the original plant does not appear to be well-known.

The Celtæ paid great attention to the management of the dairy, the produce of which is necessarily a principal part of the subsistence of a pastoral people, and they were able to make butter, the nature of which was unknown to the Romans.[m] Pliny describes the churn as "longa vasa angusto foramine," but although a handle is not mentioned, the cream is said to have been shaken.[n] The name buyd ur, chief or excellent food, is believed to have arisen from its being confined to the use of the chiefs.[o] The better sort, who were thus distinguished from the poor, had so much that they sold of it,[p] and it is probable that the nobles received butter of their followers as a perquisite. In Gaëlic it is called Im.

The Irish are described as very "unmannerly in making their butter," and the process is certainly not likely to have been inviting when they thought it extremely unlucky ever to wash their milk vessels,[q] and by a practice of hiding

---

[m] Pliny, xxvii.   [n] Ibid.   [o] Whitaker.
[p] Dalechamp. Comment. on Pliny, xxviii. 9.   [q] Riche.

it in the bogs it was usually rancid. It would be unfair, however, to let it appear that the Irish alone were addicted to this filthy and superstitious practice, for in some parts of Scotland, I have been informed, the same prejudice exists, or did exist, which is humorously noticed in the "Cottagers of Glenburnie,"—"Do you not clean the churn before you put in the cream?" asked Mrs. Mason. "Na, na," returned Mrs. Mac Clarty, "that wadna be canny ye ken. Naebody hereabouts wad clean their kirn for ony consideration. I never heard o' sic a thing in a' my life." In some parts of the Highlands the gudewife takes the following method to procure fresh butter in winter. Salt butter being mixed with sweet milk, in the proportion of one pound to the chopin, or quart, of milk, is put through the same process as cream undergoes in a small churn : the butter, consequently, becomes sweet, and the milk turns salt. This is sometimes practised by the Irish also.

The Gauls made excellent cheeses : they were highly aromatic, and Pliny extols them as medicinal. The best of those at Rome were procured at Nismes, and two villages in the Gevaudan. They were excellent for present use, but were not made to be kept long. Pliny expresses his surprise that some nations, who thickened their milk into a pleasant curd and rich butter, should not make cheese,' an ignorance with which some of the Britons are charged by Strabo.[s] Càis is the proper Gaëlic name of cheese—cabog, the Scots kebbuck, seems to denote the shape. The process of making cheese in the Highlands has been before alluded to. There is one sort, of which some people are very fond, called càis tennal, or gathered

[r] The Germans used coagulated milk. Tac. de Mor. Germanorum.
[s] Lib. iv. p. 200.

curd, which is thus made:—the whey being pressed from the curd, it is put, without any salt, into a damp and dark place, where it is allowed to remain for fourteen or twenty days, when it is broken down, mixed with salt in the usual proportion, and put into the cheese press, becoming ripe for use in six or eight months. It is generally made of sweet milk, but cream is sometimes added when the salt is mixed with it. Cheese of goat and ewe milk is only used by the poorer people; the former yields scarce any cream,—the latter makes tolerable cheese, but white rancid butter. It was usually mixed with that of the cow, and the mixture produced the best of all cheese. Little goats' milk is now to be seen in the Highlands; and, since the establishment of large sheep farms, no ewes' milk at all.

A great accession to the supply of food is procured from the cultivation of the soil. Panick was much used in Aquitain, and formed part of the food of all the Celtae; the nations on the Euxine had no daintier meat than what was made of this grain; about the Po, they scarcely used any of it without a mixture of beans.[t] Barley gruel was in common use among the Gauls. In Germany, they cultivated oats, and lived much on gruel, or pottage, made of it, which they called abremouz.[u] The Japides, a Celtic nation in Pannonia, lived chiefly on oatmeal and millet. The Britons used the panick, which was first cultivated by the Gauls; and, in very ancient times, were accustomed to take as much grain from their storehouses as would serve them for a day, and having dried and bruised the grains, they made a sort of food for immediate use.[v] The Irish and ancient Caledonians pursued the same system, and among the remote Highlanders it still exists. They bring

---

[t] Pliny. The Sarmatians lived chiefly on potage, or gruel of millet, and used raw meal mixed with the milk of mares, and sometimes with the blood of the cattle.   [u] Ibid.   [v] Diod. v.

home at night as much corn in the ear as may be wanted at the time, and quickly convert it into meal in the manner described in page 103.

Eireirich, or araradh, is a term which the Highlanders apply both to the drying of corn in a pot, according to the old practice, and to the grain and bread so prepared. Giraldus Cambrensis says the Welsh lived on butter, cheese, &c., with plenty of flesh, but used very little bread. The Irish ate their flesh without bread, keeping what corn they had for their horses.^w An assertion that, in a wild part of Argyleshire, there was no bread, until some strangers arrived and taught the art of baking, is certainly untrue.^x The bread of the Gauls, who, according to Athenæus, used but little, was superior to that of the Romans, from the use of yeast in the kneading of the dough. Their knowledge of brewing enabled them to procure barm, which was a much better ingredient than honey or eggs, used by other nations. "When the Gallic and Celtiberian brewers steeped their wheat in water, and mashed it for their drink, they took the froth that collects at top, and used it instead of leaven, which was the reason that their bread was always lighter than any other."^y

Ovens must have been very early known to the Britons, from the discoveries of baked pottery; but if applied to the purposes of cooking, they were, probably, confined to the establishments of chiefs; nevertheless, the Celtæ excelled in preparing their bread, which Pliny attests was the best in the world. It was baked on stones placed around the fire, which the Romans denominated greidiol; and Whitaker says the inhabitants of Manchester retained this simple mode of preparing their bread until recent times. From this word is derived the Scotish girdle, a round piece

^w Campion.   ^x Birt.   ^y Pliny, xviii. 7.

of iron suspended over the fire, on which oat cakes are baked. Amongst the most rural of the Scots, the "cakes" are still "fired" in this manner, and are called bonnach claiche, or rather bonnach lichde, stone cakes.* The baking of this family, or household bread of the Scots, has not yet become a trade; every guidewife makes her own cakes, by which, as the agricultural reporter of the Isle of Man observes of the people of that interesting island, she is independent of the baker. There is no scarcity of bakers of wheaten bread, but oat cakes have not been sold, except, perhaps, in the lowest purlieus of Edinburgh, Glasgow Aberdeen, or other large and manufacturing cities.

Froissart gives us a curious account of the mode in which the Scots soldiers were anciently accustomed to convert their meal into cakes. Observing that neither knights nor squires took carriages into the field with them, he says, "Every man carries about the saddle of his horse a great flat plate, and he trusses behind him a wallet of meal, the purpose of which is this:—after a Scotish soldier has eaten flesh so long that he begins to loath it, he throws this plate into the fire, then moistens a little of his meal in water, and when the plate is heated he lays his paste upon it, and makes a little cake, which he eats to comfort his stomach. Hence it is not strange that the Scots should be able to make longer marches than other men."

The occupations of baking and brewing continued to be performed by women, even when the profession had become public.* The kings of Scotland had bakers and

---

* More frequently *bonnach-teintean*, a cake fired on the *hearth-stone*. It was sometimes kneaded on the hearth-stone, which was, of course, duly swept and washed for the operation. A cake thus made and fired, with good fresh butter and a slice of cheese, was a mouthful for a king! ED.

* When making bread became a trade at Rome, the chief bakers were women.—Pliny.

brewers,[a] who were, like most professors among the Celtic people, hereditary, and were in high estimation, holding lands in reward for their services.[b]

Little more can be said respecting the art of cookery, or the various dishes of the ancient Celts. The Germans ate their venison fresh,[c] the Gauls occasionally salted it. These latter also used great quantities of flesh sodden in water, or roasted on the coals or on spits.[c]* They had abundance of provisions, and were not indisposed to improve their food by culinary process, but it would appear they preferred plain joints, and feasted with more delight on such substantial fare as "the roast beef of old England," than on soups and hashes, so much esteemed by their French posterity. It appears from Varro, that they sent into Italy, sausages, hogs' puddings, gammons of bacon, and hams. The Celtic women carried pots of pudding into the bath, which they ate along with their children while they washed.[h]

The British tribes, who "were contented with plain and homely fare," were, probably, less expert in the art of cookery than those of the continent, and the people in the northern division of the island must have been still less versed in the science. The activity of their lives, and healthy, robust constitutions imparted a zest to their rough and scanty meals, which epicures wish for in vain. The heroes of Lacedemon lived on a certain black broth, so un-

---

[a] Baxter and Brewster, whence the family names.
[b] Caledonia, Robertson's Index, &c.   [c] Tac. de Mor. Germ.
[d] Strabo.   [e] Athenæus.
* The Scottish Gaëls held venison, and more especially the *fat* of venison, in high esteem. An old saying is—Geir féidh a muigh 'sa stigh, mar leighais sid thu, chaneil do leighais ann, that is, the fat of stags (applied) externally and internally; if that cure you not, your cure is not to be effected. ED.
[h] Plutarch, viii. 9.

savoury and coarse to those of more delicate taste, that a citizen of Sybaris, tasting it, said he ceased to wonder at the Spartan contempt for death, since they were obliged to live on such fare. The observation which was made to the tyrant Dionysius respecting it had more truth but less wit; "the dish wants the sauce," remarked the cook. "What sauce," asked he. "That of a good appetite," was the reply. The art of cookery, is, however, of more importance than might at first be supposed, and Drs. Hunter and Kitchener, Count Rumford, and others, have employed their talents in this useful science; but, although duly appreciated, it is by no means so highly esteemed as formerly. In the middle ages, the master cook, provost of the cooks, &c., were officers of dignity and emolument, and the king's larderer was often a clergyman of high rank. His Majesty's, cook is allowed, by the laws of honour and precedence the title of Esquire, now so much prostituted; but to return to the food of the ancient Celts. In Dio's account of the expedition of Severus, the food of the people beyond Adrian's wall is said to have been the milk and flesh of their flocks, what they procured by hunting, with the fruits of trees, and leaves and roots of herbs. The inhabitants of Thule lived chiefly on milk in summer, and on fruit in winter. The stature and strength of the ancient Caledonians indicate a sufficiency of food, yet they appear to have had some means of subsistence with which we are not sufficiently acquainted.

The Gauls are not entirely free from the imputation of cannibalism. Those who went into Greece with Brennus, according to Pausanias, drank the blood and ate the flesh of the best-conditioned infants at the breast.[i] The horrors of famine may be an excuse for so revolting a practice.

[i] Lib. x. c. 22.

Those who resisted the Cimbri and Teutones were reduced to the deplorable necessity of living on the bodies of the aged; and long afterwards, when besieged in Alesia, Critognatus, the commanding-general, advised his adherents to imitate their ancestors and do the same, rather than yield.[k]

The testimony of St. Jerome, representing the Scots or Attacots as cannibals, is well known. In this noted passage it is said, that when these people met with herds of cattle, sheep, and pigs, they were wont to select the most delicate parts of both the male and female keepers for their repasts. The correctness of this translation has been questioned, and the meaning asserted to be, merely that they preferred the rumps of the oxen, and udders of the cows, leaving untouched the other parts. I am afraid, however awkward the sentence may be, "pastorum nates, et feminarum papillas," cannot well be mistaken; but with deference to the Saint's authority, we may entertain some doubt of the prevalence of so horrible a practice. Diodorus had indeed said, that those nations who were towards the north, bordering upon Scythia, were so fierce and savage that they, according to report, ate men as the Britons who inhabited Iris did; and he is, unfortunately, not the sole authority for this shocking propensity of the ancient Irish. Strabo accuses them of a gluttonous indulgence in human flesh, and says they did not hesitate to eat their dead relations,[l] in which is he followed by Solinus, who represents them in a state of deplorable barbarity. Except we believe that those authors were misinformed, or exaggerated the vices of a people of whom so little was then known, it is to be feared the Irish, who claim the Attacots as a native tribe, must take them with this imputation, to which their

---

[k] Bello Gall. vii. 71.   [l] Lib. iv. p. 201.

ancestors, from concurring authorities, seem more certainly obnoxious than the Scots of Britain.

It will scarcely excite surprise that this idea of the cannibalism of the Celts should have prevailed among the ancients, concerning a people who were so distant, and reputed so barbarous, when we find that, so recently as the rebellion of 1745, the people of England really believed that the Highlanders were accustomed to eat children, a fact which is attested by several officers of the Scots army: Mr. Cameron, of Lochiel, on entering a house, was implored by a woman to spare her children; and on his assuring her, with some surprise at her alarm, that he had not the least intention of doing them any injury, she released them from a closet where they were concealed, telling them to come out, for the gentleman would not devour them! Mr. Halkston, of Rathillet, also, in inquiring where all the children were, as none could be seen, was told that they had been sent out of the way to prevent their falling into the hands of the Highlanders, who were believed to eat human flesh![m] Perhaps the good folks of England were at some loss to conceive how these Highlanders lived, they seemed to required so little food.[n] They did not, indeed, obtain very large rations during the progress of the rebellion, and it was well that their desires were moderate. When the Highlanders of former days took the field, they only provided themselves with a small bag of oatmeal: in 1745, they often had nothing else to carry them through their toilsome marches than a little of this, which they ate, mixed with water, morning and evening; but, to them, this rough fare was no privation. The ability of the Highlander to endure a long abstinence from

---

[m] Memoirs of the Chev. Johnstone, and remarks on ditto.
[n] It was said by the troops who so ineffectually pursued them, that "they lived by snuffing the wind."

food was remarkable; and the ancient Caledonian much excelled his posterity, for he could live many days concealed in the marshes, up to the neck in water, without sustenance; and in the woods he could live on the bark, roots, and leaves of trees. The Scots have always been an abstemious or rough-living people,—a quality excellent for soldiers. Cromwell complained that his troops were ruined, for "whom the Scots were too hard in respect of enduring the winter's difficulty."

The usual diet of the present Highlanders is milk and cream, cheese, butter, oat and barley cakes, and mutton or goat's flesh, with that excellent article, potatoes.* They also have meal of pease, which they usually buy unground, and which they use with milk in bread and puddings.º When at the Shealings in the summer months, their meals in general consist of curds and cream, or oatmeal and cream, mixed cold, and qualified by a glass of good whisky. In times of scarcity, which have frequently occurred in the Highlands, the inhabitants are under the necessity of bleeding their cattle in summer, and dividing the coagulated blood into square cakes, they boil it, and eat it with milk or whey.

Bruthuiste, or brose, a dish said to be of Greek derivation, is common all over Scotland. In the most simple preparation, it is merely meal and hot water mixed together; to which butter is added; but the proper way is to use the juice of cabbages or turnips in which meat has been boiled. The Irish, says Campion, "crammed" oatmeal and butter together. The Highlanders do the same still, forming it into rolls like sausages, called bodmear.

---

* Along the sea coast and in the Hebrides fish is largely used both in a fresh and salted state all the year round. ED.

º A mixture of bean and barley-meal used to be a favourite food in the south of Scotland.

Brochan is a similar preparation to oatmeal gruel, but the Gaël frequently add onions, and sometimes even pounded cheese. Easoch, or thin brochan, is eaten with bannocks, and was the sole winter diet of thousands of the Highlanders in the time of Martin.

Sughan is the suans or sowens of the Low Country, being the juice of "sids," or the siftings of oatmeal, after having been steeped in water until it has acquired a slight acidity. In the process of making sowens, a peculiar sieve is used in draining the liquid, which is thin and white, and, on being boiled, acquires a starchy consistency, in which state it is usually eaten with milk, and termed lagan by the Gaël; but many prefer it "knotted," or half boiled, with the addition of butter, a little sugar, or treacle. This is the preparation of which all in the Low Country partake on the morning of Yule day or Christmas. Cath-bhruish is sowens as thin as brochan—acidulated gruel, one of the most healthy preparations.

Libthe, or pottage, is the favourite preparation of oatmeal in Scotland. That it was much used in ancient times, appears from St. Jerome, who taunts Celestinus, a native, for gorging himself with Scots pottage."

Drammack, in Gaëlic Tiorman, is oatmeal and a little salt, sprinkled with cold water, and stirred with the hand until the whole is in a state of adherence. This is preferable to eating the meal dry, and is more agreeable than the fuarag or crowdy, which is a thinnish mixture of meal and any cold liquid. When milk is at hand, the crowdy, to save time, is preferred to drammack.

Potatoes have been a fortunate acquisition to the Highlanders. The various soups and other dishes of which they form a principal part, need not be enumerated; but

---

p Rev. Skene Keath, in Rep. of the Agriculture of Aberdeenshire.
q St. Hieron. on Jeremiah.

the practice of boiling and mashing them, and slicing them up the next morning, for the purpose of being toasted like bread, seems peculiar to the mountaineers.

Oon* froth is a quantity of milk or whey boiled, and then worked up by a stick having a cross part at the lower end. This substitute for more substantial fare was often used by the poor of the Western Isles; and Martin asserts that he saw those who had for months lived on whey thus prepared, climb the rugged mountains with as much agility as those who were better fed. Many curious anecdotes might be told of this pleasant but unsubstantial mess.

The people in the remote islands boiled dulce, a sea-weed, gathered from the rocks, and if able to add a little butter to it, it was esteemed a very excellent dish.

When cattle were slaughtered, the smith got the head, the quarter-master got the hides, and the piper was entitled to a certain share. This last person† was called ullaicher, literally, provider of both food and lodging. Droin-uinn, a rump, has been called the bard's portion from this circumstance:—when a person was helped to this part, he or she was obliged to compose a verse, or resign the nice morsel. A few of these rhymes would be a curious collection.

In dressing flesh-meat the old Gaël were probably contented with plain roasting and boiling, the latter being most usual. In the poem on the death of Carril, mircorra, a favourite dish with Fingal and Gaul, is mentioned. It was a choice collop, chopped small, and mixed with marrow and herb-seeds. The ancient manner of preparing their meat, after hunting, as preserved by tradition among the Highlanders, is curious. A pit, lined with smooth stones, was made, and near it a heap of smooth flat pebbles was

---

* More correctly *Omhan*. Ed.

† Not the piper, but the "quarter-master," is here meant. Ed.

placed. The stones and the pit were both well heated by burning heath, and part of the venison was then laid in the pit, and covered by the hot, loose stones; another piece was laid over that, and the same process repeated until the pit was full, when it was closed over with heath. To confirm this tradition, pits are shewn in various parts; and a passage in the poem of Fingal thus describes the preparations: "It was on Cromla's shaggy side that Dorglas had placed the deer, the early fortune of the chase, before the heroes left the hill. A hundred youths collect the heath; ten warriors wake the fire; three hundred chuse the polished stones. The feast is smoking wide."

The fires of the ancient Caledonians were formed of wood; and, at their feasts, a large trunk of an oak tree was reckoned an indispensable part of the entertainment; and so much attached were the people to the practice, that they viewed its disuse as a kind of sacrilege. The decay of the forests prevents the general use of wood; and peats, or turf, have long been the common fuel in the Highlands and in the North. The use of coal was early adopted in many parts, to which necessity alone seems to have led. Æneas Sylvius, afterwards Pope Pius II., says, the poor people in Scotland were obliged to burn black stone instead of wood.[r] At this day, crofters will go ten or fifteen miles for peat, in preference to coal, which might be had with less trouble and at as little expense. In digging turf, a particular spade is used, represented in the closing vignette of last chapter, which cuts it into regular squares of the form of a brick, the workmen either casting the peats as it is called, by cutting horizontally or perpendicularly. The latter, called pitting, was the ancient way

---

[r] Gough's Top. ii. 564. A coal mine was discovered in Ireland, concerning which there was no tradition. Hamilton's Letters on the Coast of Antrim.

of working mosses in the Highlands, and although, in some respects, objectionable, it is not so destructive to the bogs as running level, by which mosses have, in some cases, been rapidly exhausted. The Irish taught the inhabitants of Lismore and other islands the method of baking loose peat earth, which forms serviceable fuel. The cottages are always accompanied by the peat-stack, that is, the fuel neatly built up at the end of the house, a covering being formed of the surface parts of the moss or heath dug in large pieces. Great part of the summer is often consumed in casting and bringing from a distance the winter's stock of fuel, in which work the poor have the voluntary assistance of their neighbours.

The Celts used numbers of pots, pans, and spits for preparing their victuals; and thought game, killed by arrows dipt in the juice of hellebore, the flesh surrounding the wound being speedily cut away, became tender. The Britons, there is reason to believe, were less nice in their taste, and less attentive to their culinary arrangements. Among the rude tribes of the North, such an art received but very little attention. Their mode of roasting or baking, already described, was ingenious; but even in the time of Bruce the raw hide of the animal, stretched on four sticks, was used to form the bag in which the flesh was seethed. When Douglas and Murray retreated, after the celebrated inroad which they made on England, no less than three hundred of these awkward utensils, with a thousand wooden spits, were found in the camp which they had evacuated. The people of some parts of the Highlands, at a much later period, continued this custom. Birt tells us they had a wooden vessel, hollowed by the dirk, for the purpose of heating water, by means of hot pebbles thrown into it. The most ancient iron pot is seen in the vignette, with a high neck, and the sort at present in common use, which is not reckoned so good for boiling, is beside it.

In hunting, the flesh was occasionally eaten raw, after the blood was squeezed out; but the Irish were more accustomed to this barbarous food, and Campion remarks, that the flesh thus swallowed "was boyled in their stomaks with aqua vitæ, which they swill in after such a surfeite by quarts and pottles." They also, he says, bled their cattle, and baked the curdled blood spread with butter. A French writer, some centuries ago, describes Scotland as "pauvre en or, et en argent, mais fort bon en vivres;" and again, "assez des veaux et vaches, et par le moyen la chair est à bon compte."

The Caledonians, no doubt, preserved their meat by salt, which the surrounding ocean would supply, in the isles, the ashes of burnt sea ware was often used to preserve fowl and to mix in cheese; but they could save fish for many months without salt. In Gaul and Germany, salt was made by pouring sea-water upon burning wood. For this purpose the oak was generally preferred, the ashes of which alone was sometimes used. In certain parts, hazel was considered best for the purpose; but all salt so made, as might be expected, was very black. The Umbrians procured this article by boiling some sort of reeds and canes until the water was nearly evaporated. At Egelastæ, in Spain, there were mines whence salt was dug, which was reckoned medicinal.[*] No river in Germany possesses the qualities which are ascribed to one by Tacitus, who is either misunderstood or has been imposed upon by his informers. As the story is curious, it may be related: the Catti and Hermanduri quarrelled about the property of a river, the waters of which, on being poured over large fires of wood, produced salt, and they were, perhaps, the more irritable on the subject of their respective rights, in

[*] Pliny, xxxi. 7.

consequence of a belief that the stream and the neighbouring woods were near heaven. The war seemed to be one of extermination; for the Cattans, who were ultimately defeated, had taken a vow to devote the whole of their opponents—men, horses, and every article to be burnt or slain, in honour of Mars and Mercury.ᵗ There was also a controversy, fomented by the Romans, in the time of Marcellinus, between the Burgundians and Germans, concerning salt-pits.

The Britons procured salt from mines, and one of the ancient roads is called the salt way. Many curious observances, to be deduced from the Celts, were connected with this article, several of which still exist. The Manx will do nothing without carrying or interchanging salt; a beggar will even refuse alms if offered without it.ᵘ Camden says, that before the Irish put seed in the ground, the mistress sent salt into the field; and when a person entered on a public office, women in the street, and girls from windows, sprinkled them and their attendants with it. In parts of Scotland, a portion is put into the first of a cow's milk after calving, which is intended to prevent the person who receives it, if one of the "uncanny," from doing any harm to the cattle; and that it was an antidote to witchcraft, we learn from Reginald Scot, who assures us the devil cannot bear to take any in his meat, it being a sign of eternity. The Gorleg yr Halen, or prelude of the salt, is a tune which was first played, say the Welsh, when the salt-cellar was placed before Arthur and his celebrated knights,ʷ a fanciful origin, perhaps, of a more ancient ceremony. The Scots were anciently accustomed to salt beef in the hide.

The Celts are said to have had a dislike to the flesh of

Pliny, xxxi. 7.   ᵗ Tacitus' Annals, xiii.   ᵘ Waldron's History.
Stat. Account of Killearn, &c.   ʷ Pennant's Tour in Wales.

swine, which is supposed to have arisen from religious scruples. This aversion does exist, but it appears doubtful whether the antipathy is of ancient origin. The laws of Kenneth Mac Alpin contain some regulations respecting this animal; and from the Chartularies and other documents, it is apparent that very considerable numbers were formerly reared. The Gauls who inhabited Pesinus, a city of Galatia, could not bear to touch swine,[x] but the boar was a favourite object of pursuit with the Celtic huntsman,[y] and Strabo says, they used much pork, both fresh and salted.[z] In Spain, the inhabitants used to live on boar's flesh; but they believed that, to eat of the heads, drove men mad, and, therefore, effectually to guard against that calamity, they always burned them.[a] There was not, among the ancient Britons, a daintier dish than the chenerotis, a bird less than a goose.[b]

The Celtæ did not in general make use of fish as an article of food, from religious prejudices; for, as they adored the waters, it would appear they abstained from living on the inhabitants of that element. This abstinence, however, was not universally adhered to, for the Celtiberi caught scombri, or mackerel, from which they procured the celebrated garum,[c] and Athenæus says, the nations about the Po used both sea and river fish; while Solinus informs us, the people of the Hebudæ Islands lived on them; but the Caledonians are expressly noticed by Dio and Herodian as not eating the fish with which their seas and rivers abounded. The Irish "had little skill in catching fish" two centuries ago, a proof that they paid small attention to the pursuit; and the Highlanders appear to have been still

---

[x] Pausanius, vii. 17.
[y] Pork was much esteemed among the Scandinavians. Pink.
[z] Lib. iv. 19.   [a] Pliny, viii. 36.   [b] Pliny, xxii.
[c] Pliny, xxxi. The Scyths ate river fish.

more indifferent to it, and had a particular antipathy to eels and pike. From the abundance of land animals and the feathered race, this dislike to a species of food so excellent, and so bounteously provided by nature, in a country where the variable climate renders the harvest so uncertain, may have, in ancient times, produced little effect; but the continuance of so much indifference to so obvious a source of national profit is much to be regretted. The clergy were obliged to eat fish during their fasts, and necessity would, no doubt, compel the Celt to relinquish his ancient prejudice for a time, and might, ultimately, subdue his obstinacy; but as he had no motive ever to catch more than was sufficient for his wants, he was not likely to become very enterprising. The Dalriads, it must be observed, did not refuse to partake of fish; and in a copy of the poem of Darthula, in possession of the Highland Society, and of date 1238, their food is said to have consisted of fish and venison, but the Highlanders, notwithstanding the mention of fish in several old poems, certainly did never willingly make use of such food. It was matter of astonishment to an English resident among them a century ago, that the trout with which their streams were teeming remained entirely disregarded; but they retain a proverb which implies their contempt for fish-eaters, and the encouragement of government has not yet induced either the Scots, Welsh, or Irish, to enter with spirit into the fishing trade. "When we see a principle of religion itself exploded, producing consequences through so many centuries of change, we ought not to be surprised that the manners and customs of the same races of men should have continued for ages, so extremely analogous."[d] No great lines

[d] Caledonia, 1 p. 460. It is but just, however, to remark, that the English have not engaged with greater spirit into the fisheries than the Scots.

were formerly used in the west isles of Scotland; but cod, ling, and other large fish were angled for, and occasionally they were speared.

The Seal, Ron, may not have been considered as a fish by the Gaël, as it appears to have been eaten by them in most ancient times. The monks of Iona had artificial ponds of salt water, in which they were preserved,[e] and many of the Highlanders were accustomed in the last century to cure hams of them. Young seals are even at the present day eaten in some of the Orkney Islands.[f] Many dishes were formerly esteemed, that would now be thought intolerable. The monks of Dumfermline had a grant from Malcolm IV. of all the heads of a species of whale, called crespeis, that should be caught in Scotwattre, or the Firth of Forth, his Majesty reserving the tongues, as the most dainty part, for himself. In 1290, the ship that was sent to bring over the Maiden of Norway had the fish part of her provisions from Aberdeen, and, amongst other articles, were fifty pounds of whale.[g] Martin, whose curious work appeared in the beginning of last century, says the people of Tirey ate whales with certain roots. Seals and porpoises were common at English tables in the time of Richard II. At Uist they were regularly fished for in Martin's time; the steward and his officer had each a young one, as a perquisite, and the minister was allowed his choice of those caught. A poem in MacDonald's collection, of a date somewhat later, contains these lines:

> "Nuair a'ghabhd go tamh,
> Ann an cala port sheamh
> Cha b'fhallan bhom laimhs an ron."

In Aberdeenshire, a traveller of the last century observed, that "there was neither fine architecture nor garden-

---

[e] Adomnan, i. c. 41.   [f] Stat. Account. vii. 46.
[g] Mac Pherson's Annals of Commerce.

ing, but abundance of good cheer and good neighbourhood," the servants, during the summer, having so much salmon that they refused to eat of it oftener than twice a week.[h] In that part of the country a favourite winter dish is "stappit heads," or boiled haddocks, the heads being filled with a mixture of oatmeal, onions, and pepper. It is from the fishing villages on the coast of Kincardineshire, the adjoining county, that the much esteemed fish called Finan haddocks, from the name of a small port, are procured.[*] They are cut open when taken, and cured by being suspended for some time in the smoke of turf. In the isle of Sky, herrings were dried and preserved without salt, and if they were taken after the 10th of September, O. S., they would keep for eight months. About the Po, the inhabitants ate their fish either roasted or boiled, with vinegar, salt, and cummin, oil being too scarce for common use, but, had it been otherwise, they did not like it so well as their old sauce.

The Scots have but very recently divested themselves of many prejudices against certain fish, and those without scales are still disliked. "It was only at a late period that turbot was relished even in Fife, where fishing is so generally followed; and people advanced in life do not yet esteem it so much as the halibut, which is very commonly dignified with the name of turbot. There are living, or were very lately, in one of the coast towns, several poor people who were wont to derive great part of their subsistence from the turbots which the fishermen threw away on the beach, because nobody could be found to purchase them."[k]

HOSPITALITY was a virtue which the Celts carried to the

---

[h] Journey through Scotland, 1729.

[*] Findhorn, whence Finan or Finnon haddocks. ED.

[k] Tullis's ed. of Sibbald's Hist. of Fife.

extreme. They took the greatest delight in inviting strangers to their tables, before whom were always placed the fairest and best joints. The Celtiberi were famed for courteousness to strangers, from whatever place they came; and those who were so fortunate as to have it in their power to entertain guests, were esteemed the favourites of the gods.[l] In deeds of hospitality and social feasts, says Tacitus, no nation on earth was ever more liberal than the Germans.[m] The Gaulish chiefs had always a numerous retinue, who followed them to the war, and lived well at their expense.

Some curious instances of the delight which the Celts took in an ostentatious display of liberality are recorded. Ariamnes, a wealthy Galatian, formed a resolution of entertaining all his countrymen for a whole year, at his individual expense, and he proceeded in this manner. He divided the roads throughout the provinces into convenient day's journeys, and with reeds, poles, and willows, erected pavilions capable of containing three hundred persons or upwards, and having the preceding year employed numerous artificers to fabricate cauldrons, he placed them in these buildings, and kept them continually full of all sorts of flesh. Every day many bulls, swine, sheep, and other cattle were slain, and many measures of corn, and much barley meal ready kneaded, was procured; and all this was not confined to the inhabitants, but the servants were instructed to constrain all strangers to partake of the feast.[n] The riches of the Gauls enabled them to indulge in very

---

[l] Diodorus. Cæsar in like manner celebrates their hospitality, vi. 23.

[m] De Mor. Germ. This is a virtue of most unpolished nations. A poor woman in Norway refused any payment from some English travellers, observing, that "as long as the earth gives us corn, and the sea fish, no one shall have to say we have taken money of him." Boye's Tour in Norway. The Poles had Radogost, the god of hospitality, and the only one worshipped, in a covered temple, called Gontina.

[n] Athenæus, iv.

extravagant expenditure. Luernius, a king of the Arverni, to court popularity, was accustomed to throw silver and gold among the crowds who followed him as he drove through the fields. On one occasion he enclosed a space of twelve furlongs, in which he had constructed ponds filled with costly and delicious liquors. Stores of victuals, ready cooked, were also provided, sufficient for all who chose to partake of them, for many days.º It is not to be doubted but numbers availed themselves of this munificent treat, and the pleasure of the feast was heightened by the civilities of numerous attendants.

The manner in which the Germans received their guests was familiar and kind. To refuse admitting any person whatever, was held wicked and inhuman. Every one that came to a house was received and treated with lodging and repasts, as long and as liberally as the owner could possibly afford, and, when his whole stock was consumed, he took his guests to a new scene of hospitality, both proceeding to the next house, to which the formality of an invitation was unnecessary, and where they were received with the same frankness and joy, no difference being ever made between a stranger and an acquaintance, in dispensing the rites of hospitality. Upon the departure of a guest, if he asked any thing, it was cheerfully given. Favours were requested and bestowed with equal familiarity,ᴾ for in mutual gifts the Celts delighted, but neither claimed merit from what they gave, nor acknowledged any obligation for what they received. The Gauls, with singular delicacy, never asked the name of a stranger, what he was, or his business, until the entertainment was all over.ᑫ The guest of a Highland chief was not questioned as to his business until the expiration of a year, should he stop so long.ʳ There was a

º Ibid., from Posidonius.   Strabo also extols the Celtic feasts.
ᴾ Tac. de Mor. Germ.   ᑫ Diodorus.   ʳ Dr. Mac Pherson.

striking resemblance to these manners in the practice of hospitality among the Britons, who cherished this characteristic virtue of the Gauls as long as they were able to retain their primitive Celtic manners. Giraldus Cambrensis says of the Welsh, that when a stranger entered a house, water was immediately brought for him to wash his feet. If he did so, it was then known that he would stop some time, perhaps for the night, or longer, which diffused great joy throughout the family, and every entertainment which they could afford was provided for their guest.*

The Highlanders of Scotland formerly carried their hospitality to as great an extent as the ancient Celtæ; and even at this day the more sequestered inhabitants are prone to indulge in a habit of liberality, which, however honourable to their feelings, their limited means do not altogether justify. In past ages, it was uniformly a practice to leave their doors open during the night, as well as the day, that any traveller might be able to avail himself of shelter and entertainment. It was long considered infamous in a man of condition to have the door of his house ever shut, lest, as the bards expressed it, the stranger should come and behold his contracted soul. The gate of Fingal stood always open, and his hall was the stranger's home.† The Celts never closed the doors of their houses," but esteemed it the greatest happiness to have the opportunity of entertaining strangers.* In later times, it was the practice in Scotland, before closing the doors, to look out for strangers or wayfaring men, and it is still remembered in the traditions of the peasantry in many parts of the North, that the Laird

---

* Descripto Camb. c. 10.   † Smith's Gallic Antiquities.
" Agathias, i. p. 13, quoted by Ritson.
* In the Editor's boyhood, some years after the publication of this work, in the district of Morven, and in the opposite island of Mull, doors were never locked or barred, but at the most left on the *sneck* or latch. ED.

had his "latter meat table," daily spread for all who chose to partake of his liberality.

To their friends, the Gaël gave the protection of their roof, regardless of circumstances. To one who besought their hospitality, they performed the sacred duty, and were ready to fulfil their own saying, " I would give him a night's fare, although he had a man's head under his arm-pit."* An anecdote told of Mac Gregor, of Glenstræ, and young Lamond, of Cowal, is in point. The latter had killed the only son of Mac Gregor, and, when pursued, had rushed into the father's house to save his life, without knowing whose protection he had claimed. The old Laird, in ignorance of his loss, afforded him an asylum, fulfilled his pledge of protection when he knew him as the murderer of his son, and, to prevent the otherwise inevitable destruction of Lamond, he even aided his escape during the night.

For the following account of a worthy Highlander of the old School, I am indebted to Mr. Donald Mac Pherson, author of melodies from the Gaëlic. Donald Mac Donald, Esq., of Aberarder, of the house of Keppoch, father of Captain Mac Donald, of Moy, was remarkable for his hospitality, as well as for many other traits of eccentric virtue. Aberarder house is situated in one of the most romantic spots on earth, at the side of Loch Laggan, and is distant on one side four, and on the other six, miles from any house. In good weather, he used to seat himself on a green knoll, above the mansion, which commanded a view of the road, at least a mile each way, and when he discovered a traveller, he used to desire Mrs. Mac Donald immediately to prepare food, for that he had discovered a stranger, whose slow progress indicated the necessity of refreshment. Sometimes, it happened that the

* The Gaelic saying is, "Bheirin dha cuid oidhche ged robh ceann fir 'na achlais." Ed.

stranger passed without calling; on discovering which, he would exclaim, "Damn the scoundrel, I am sure he is a bad fellow at home." He was even known sometimes to follow a considerable distance with food, or to persuade the traveller to return and spend the night.

The unbounded hospitality of the Celtic chief was a favourite theme of the Bards, who continued, like their predecessors among the ancient Gauls, to fare well at their master's table, and enliven his banquets by adulatory effusions. In the compositions of this, latterly, servile body, the hero and the hospitable are almost the only persons whose praises are extolled, and it is remarkable that in Gaelic there is but one word for a landholder and a hospitable man. Cean uia' dai,* or the point to which all the roads of the strangers lead, was the epithet bestowed on the chief's house; and so uncommon was it for any to be otherwise spoken of, that the translator of Ossian declares, among all the poems he had ever met with, but one man was branded with the charge of inhospitality. He was described as the cloud which the strangers shun. Birt mentions a Laird to whose house he was going, who met him with an arcadian offering of milk and cream, carried before him by his servants."

But it was not the higher order only who were distinguished for the virtue of hospitality—the whole population was imbued with a spirit of disinterested kindness, which, according to their means, they cheerfully displayed. For this feeling the Scots are still remarkable. When Dr. Mac Culloch, who had fallen sick at Dollar, recovered so far as to be able to walk forth, "half the whole sex came

---

* Gaelic,—"Ceann-uidhe nan dàimh." Fing. i. 24. Dr. Clark renders it, "The delight of strangers." ED.

" Letters, ed. 1818, ii. 7. It was customary to offer milk to those passing a fold.

out of their houses when they saw the stranger gentleman crawling up the hill, to offer him seats and milk, and what not; and when I returned many years afterwards, I was received, not as one who had been a source of trouble, but as an old friend." The poorest cottager is ready to share his little provision with a stranger. On a hundred occasions I have partaken of their hospitality without being able to prevail on them to accept remuneration, which, in some cases, they have refused in a manner that shewed their feelings were hurt at the idea of selling their meat and drink. It is a common practice, not only where the Gaëlic prevails, but towards the Lowlands, to set before you milk, ale, bread and cheese, or whatever else they may have, unasked. Nor are they less willing to afford you the shelter of their roof, nay, will even give up the beds of the family for your use; and if you will listen to their kind solicitations, your day's march will be often shortened.*

The rites of hospitality were practised to a ruinous extent by the poor Islanders, who retained the virtue when its exercise was highly injurious to themselves. In the distant isle of Rona the clergyman who superintended the spiritual concerns of the inhabitants, was seldom able to reach these remote members of this flock; but when he could visit them, the poor people killed five sheep, being one for each family, and presented him with their skins neatly flayed and full of meal.ˣ The untutored, but generous islanders carried their charity to an imprudent length, for they bestowed so liberally the little they possessed that many unprincipled persons frequented the Hebrides for the

* Both on the mainland and in the islands things have of recent years changed much for the worse. "The Poor-laws," and the spread of sectarianism have together greatly changed the character of the people. They are less polite and less hospitable than formerly. ED.

ˣ Martin.

purpose of unworthily profiting by their indiscriminate bounty. Such improvidence, however well meant, brought on these simple people much inconvenience, and heightened the miseries of occasional want; and it was sometimes necessary for the chiefs to restrain so injurious a system of supposed charity, by enjoining their people to bestow their alms on natives or acknowledged objects only.[y] Those who subsisted on the bounty of others, in the Highlands, did not however appear as paupers. As the houses were never locked up, the poor entered freely, and, without begging, were supplied with present food, and perhaps something besides; and if in want of a lodging, a plaid was given them, in which they reposed themselves on the floor. The unprotected state of the houses proves the honesty of the people. Nothing was stolen, even by the poorest mendicants; and the altered state of society has not yet induced the inhabitants of many secluded districts to provide bolts for their doors. The number of persons in the Highlands who had no means of their own on which to subsist, was very considerable, but the statement in the Gartmore MS., where they are calculated at 57,000, is surely much exaggerated.[z] It is observable that, at the present day, the professional beggars are from the Lowlands.

The acts of the Scots parliament, ordering "that nane pass in the country an' ly on the king's lieges, or thig or sorn on them," but that "in all burrowes there sall be hostellaries, and provision for horse and man,—that all travelling men, on horse or foot, lodge in hostellaries, and that nane other receive them,"[a] were evidently framed to repress the practice of idle and dissolute people traversing the country, encouraged by the inconsiderate hospitality of the natives. In Ireland, statutes were passed for a similar purpose; but

[y] Ibid.   [z] Appendix to Birt's Letters, ed. 1818.   [a] Acts of James I.

such acts were anomalous and premature, in that country, for, while coigny and livery were prohibited, there were no inns, and it was treason to enter a house for refreshment, were it the dwelling of the traveller's own tenant![b]

When, like their ancestors on the continent, the stock of the Highlander was exhausted, he carried his visitor to the house of his neighbour, to whose care he was then resigned. "They never depart so long as any provision doth last; and when that is done, they go to the next, and so from one to one, until they make a round from neighbour to neighbour, still carrying the master of the former family with them to the next house." This was practised less than fifty years ago, and the custom is not entirely laid aside in the present day. It is only an idle people who could devote so much time to these protracted entertainments.

The practice of entertaining a stranger as long as he chose to stop, by a whole circle of friends, was zealously adhered to in Ireland, where its ancient name, coshering, is still in use, even in Dublin and other cities, and is applied in almost the original sense. The Irish gentlemen retain much of the hospitable disposition of the ancient chief, and the curious custom alluded to is thus described by a tourist of the last century. When strangers arrive at any of their houses, the relations of the family are informed of it, who immediately join the company. After you have received the attentions of your first host, you are invited to another family, where you are entertained with the same hospitality, and are successively conducted to the houses of others, until you have gone through the whole circle, if you are inclined to stop so long. The day of separation is the only one of grief and discontent.[c] The visits of the flaith, or chiefs, to the raths, for the redress of popular

[b] Spenser.   [c] Luckombe's Tour.

grievances, were the occasions of great feasts, the origin of coshering, among the ancient Gaël; but the chronicles of Ireland inform us that the fonnteach, or house for travellers, kept by a person denominated the bruigh, was supported at the public expense; and it is believed that every tribe had one of these establishments. In the British Museum is preserved a MS., in Gaëlic, which gives an account of six of these houses.[d]

It was said of O'Neil, in the language of the Bards, that "guests were in his house more numerous than trees in the forest." The Mac Swineys were anciently famous for hospitality. Near Clodach Castle, an old seat of theirs, a stone was set up by the high way, on which was an inscription, inviting all travellers to repair to the house of Edmund Mac Swiney for refreshment. One of the family overturned this stone, perhaps for very substantial reasons; but it was well remarked, that he who did so never afterwards prospered. Doctor Molloy relates that one of his ancestors, in the time of Elizabeth, entertained 960 men, at Christmas, in his house of Broghell.

The Forbes's, of Culloden, near Inverness, were celebrated for their extraordinary hospitality. Birt says, there was as much wine spilt there as would content a moderate family. "A hogshead was constantly on tap near the hall door, for the use of all comers; and it appears in the account-book of President Forbes, that for nine months' house keeping in his family, the wine alone cost a sum which, at the present price of that article, would amount to upwards of £2000 sterling.[e]

Among the Scots Highlanders, the chief gave a great entertainment after any successful expedition, to which all the

---

[d] Harl. Coll. 5280. Solinus, however, testifies against their hospitality, saying the country was rendered inhuman by their savage manners, iii. 6.

[e] Culloden Papers, p. xxii.

country round was invited. On an occasion like this, whole deer and beeves were roasted, and laid on boards or hurdles of rods placed on the rough trunks of trees, so arranged as to form an extended table, and the uisge beatha went round in plenteous libations. This was called the sliga crechin, from being drunk out of a shell. The pipers played during the feast, after which the women danced, and, when they retired, the harpers were introduced. There were also entertainments, some of which continued to be acted when Dr. Mac Pherson wrote; but if these little dramas were, as the Rev. Dr. Mac Leod says, chiefly selections from Ossian, they could scarcely deserve the epithet ludicrous, which the former applies to them. The funeral of any great personage was accompanied with profuse feasting, a custom, although conducted with less extravagance, not yet disused. At the burial of one of the Lords of the Isles, in Iona, nine hundred cows, valued at three marks each, were consumed.

At Highland entertainments, the chief sat at the upper end of the table, and the chieftains and principal men of the clan were ranged on each side, in order of precedence, the commons being at the bottom. The best dishes were, of course, served to those who occupied the honourable end.

The famous Lord Lovat was a striking example of a genuine chief of the old school. About 1725, when he was actively engaged in raising his company of the freceadin dhu, his manners, and the arrangement of his household, are thus described by a veteran who volunteered into his service.[f] His lordship got up between five and six o'clock, when both doors and windows were thrown open. Numbers of the vassals were about the house, and all were entertained at the chief's expense. The lairds sat towards the head of the table, and drank claret with their host; next to these were

---

[f] Mem. of Donald Mac Leod.

seated the duin uassals, who drank whisky punch; the
tenants who were beneath these were supplied with ale; and
at the bottom, and even outside, a multitude of the clan regaled themselves with bread and an onion, or, perhaps, a
little cheese and table beer. Lovat, addressing the second
class, would say, "Cousin, I told the servants to hand you
wine, but they tell me ye like punch best." To others,
"Gentlemen, there is what ye please at your service, but I
send you ale, as I know ye prefer it." It required good
management to make a limited income sufficient for so
liberal house-keeping, and some attention was necessary to
preserve the motley company in good humour.

In the laws of Hwyel Dha we find that two tables were
daily spread in the hall of the palace; the king, with ten
chief officers, occupying the one; the other being placed at
the lower end of the room, for the master of the household
and other three personages, empty spaces being left for such
as might, in consequence of misbehaviour, be dismissed
from the king's table. The whole were thus arranged:—
the king sat next the fire, and close to him the torch-
bearer, beside whom was placed the guest; next to him sat
the heir-apparent, then the master of the hawks, then the
foot holder, to be about the dish with him, and then the
physician, to be about the fire with him. Next to the fire,
on the other side, sat the chaplain, to bless the food and
chaunt the Lord's prayer,[g] the crier striking the pillar
above his head, to command silence. Beside him was placed
the judge of the court, and next to him the bard of presi-
dency, and the smith of the court sat on the end of the
form before the priest. The master of the household had
his station at the lower end of the hall, his left hand opposite the front door; and any of the guests whom he might

[g] The conclusion of the Highland chaplain's grace always contained a
hearty prayer for the prosperity of the chief.

desire were obliged to sit with him. The domestic bard sat on either side of the master of the household, and the master of the horse was to be near the fire with the king, while the chief huntsman was to be on the other side with the priest.

Giraldus Cambrensis gives the following description of his countrymen's meals:—The Welsh "remain fasting from morning to night, being employed through the whole day in managing their affairs; and in the evening they take a moderate supper. If, by any means, they are disappointed of a supper, or get only a very slight one, they wait with patience till the succeeding evening. In the evening, the whole family being assembled, they prepare their provisions according to their ability; in doing which, they study only to satisfy nature, not to provoke an appetite by the arts of cookery, sauces, or a variety of dishes. When supper is ready, a basket of vegetables is set before every three persons, and not before every two, as in other countries. A large dish, with meat of various kinds, and sometimes a mess of broth or pottage, is added. Their bread is made into thin and broad cakes, which are baked from day to day. They neither use tables, table-cloth, nor napkins. When strangers are present, the master and mistress of the house always serve them personally, and never taste anything until their guests have finished their repast, in order that, should there be any deficiency of provisions, it may fall to their share."

The old Highlanders had but two meals a day. "Taking a small bit of oatcake in the morning, and passing to the hunting or other business, they content themselves therewith until the evening."[b] In distant ages, they only took one repast in the day. Lòn, or daily meal, is the

---

[b] Chronicle, 1597.

only genuine native word. Breakfast, dinner, and supper are modern terms; but there is certainly diot (Greek Διαιτα) bheg, little meal, and diot mhor, great meal. Feill, cuirme, and fleagh, were the names applied to great feasts. The former was that which a chief gave to his vassals, and including the company as well as the entertainment, the term became used for a fair.[1] The Galloglach, who carried his master's armour, and was himself heavily armed, was allowed a biefier,[*] that is, a man's meat, or double allowance. The men servants were always allowed twice the quantity of food which the women received, an arrangement of which, says Martin, the females never complain, from a feeling consideration of the more severe labour of the men. When allowed meal instead of house board, the scalag received a stone, or seventeen pounds weight per week, the ban scalag, or maid-servant, being allowed only a peck, or about eight pounds.

It was, until lately, customary at festivals to burn a large trunk of a tree, which was termed the trunk of the feast. The common people looked on it as a sort of sacrilege to discontinue this ancient practice. On the first of November, it was an ancient Celtic practice to indulge in a sort of feast, which was called la mas ubhal, the day of the apple fruit, because, on that occasion, roasted apples were bruised and mixed in ale, milk, or, by those who could afford it, in wine.[J] This is the origin of lamb's wool!

An extract from the work of Barnaby Riche will give an idea of the coshering feasts of the Irish, and the viands with which the company were enlivened. Good bundles of straw, or, in summer, green rushes were laid on the floor, on which the guests sat down, another bundle

---

[1] Ross's Notes on Fingal.
[*] Properly *Biadh-fir*, a man's meal or sustenance. ED.
[J] Vallancey.

being shaken over their legs, on which were placed the dishes and meat. The rhymers sang, and the harpers played, whilst the company regaled upon beef, mutton, pork, hens, and rabbits, all put together in a great wooden dish. They had also oaten cakes, and good store of aqua vitæ, without which it was not to be termed a feast, and on Wednesday, Friday, and Saturday, when, according to their religion, they dare eat no meat, they substituted plenty of fish.

Derrick gives some other particulars of Irish banquets, which farther illustrate the manners of the people. Before they sat down, the priest blessed the whole party, and repeated his benediction before they rose from the table, after which, we are given to understand, they were well prepared for an assault on the English,—a favourite pastime. The seats were formed of straw or hay, plaited into mats or hassocks. They used wooden platters,[k] and "a foyner of three quarters of a yard long," for a knife. Milk was their common drink, but on great occasions the uisge beatha was handed about in basins. The bards and harpers were not brought in until the repast was finished.

We have some account of their mode of dining, at a more ancient period. Sir Richard Cristeed, who was appointed by Richard II. to introduce the four kings of Ireland to English customs, thus describes their manners at table, and his own conduct towards his pupils. "I observed, as they sat at table, that they made grimaces that did not seem to me graceful or becoming, and I resolved, in my own mind, to make them drop that custom. When they were seated at table, and the first dish served, they would make their minstrels and principal servants sit beside them, and eat from their plates and drink from their cups. They told me this was a praiseworthy custom of their

---

[k] Aisead, a platter, in Armoric aczyed, French assiette.

country, where everything was in common, but the bed. I permitted this to be done for three days; but, on the fourth, I ordered the tables to be laid and covered properly, placing the four kings at an upper table, the minstrels at another below, and the servants lower still. They looked at each other and refused to eat, saying I had deprived them of their old custom, in which they had been brought up." Having explained to them that it would be neither decent nor honourable to continue it, they good-humouredly gave it up. When they were afterwards knighted, and dined with his Majesty, notwithstanding their tutoring, and being "very richly dressed, suitable to their rank, they were much stared at by the lords and those present: not, indeed, without reason; for they were strange figures, and differently countenanced to the English, or other nations. We are naturally inclined," adds the knight, "to gaze at anything strange, and it was certainly, at that time, a great novelty to see four Irish kings."[1] The description of a coronation in Ulster, given by Campion, seems rather apocryphal. A white cow was killed by his Majesty, and immediately seethed whole. In the water of this carcase, he placed himself naked, and thus sitting, he and his people supped and ate the broth and flesh, without spoon or dish!

It is not digressing to observe, that knives and forks were not formerly in use among the Gaël. Indeed, the latter were introduced in England no earlier than the beginning of the 17th century, and they were not very generally used fifty years afterwards.[m] Martin, who visited the isles at the close of that century, says, the people of North Uist used a long stick for a fork, when eating the flesh of the seal, on account of its oiliness. The Highlanders, who carried knives and forks, politely cut the meat for the

---

[1] Froissart's Chronicles, vol. iv. c. 84.—Johnes's edition.
[m] Beckmann's History of Inventions.

ladies. The want of these utensils, so indispensable in modern society, is not felt by those who are unaccustomed to their use, nay, they are considered ridiculous assistants; so much are we under the influence of custom. Among the Arabs, there are no such articles as knives, forks, or spoons, but all sorts of victuals are taken up in the hands, a mode of feeding at which Europeans are extremely awkward: "Poor creatures!" exclaimed they, on observing some of our countrymen, who recently visited them, with so much difficulty taking up curdled milk in their hands, "they do not even know how to eat; they eat like camels!"

Diodorus and Athenæus give curious and not unpleasing pictures of the Celtic manner of conducting feasts. The former says, "at their meals, they sit upon the ground, on which wolves' or dogs' skins are spread; near at hand, are their fire-places, with many pots and spits, full of joints of meat, and they are served by young girls and boys," their feasts continuing until midnight.ⁿ No one touched anything until the master of the house, or chief person, had first tasted of all the dishes.º Among the Germans, every man sat by himself, on a particular seat, and at a separate table.ᵖ Strabo says, most of the Gauls took their meals sitting on rush beds or cushions. When a company could agree, they sat down to supper in a circle. In the middle sat he who was reckoned most worthy, either from his rank or valour, and next to him was placed the person who gave the entertainment. The others were arranged, each according to his rank. Behind the guests stood some who bore shields, a number of spearmen sat in a circle opposite to the others, and both took meat with their lords. The Celts offered their libations upon wooden tables, brought in, we are told, neat and clean, being raised a little above the

ⁿ Marcel.   º Herodotus, iv. ap. Montf.   ᵖ Tacitus.

ground, and covered with hay. It was the custom to put the bread, broken into many pieces, on the table, with flesh out of the cauldron, of all which the king or chief first tasted. Some would take up whole joints with both hands, and tear them in pieces with their teeth; but if the flesh were too tough, they cut it with a little knife, which was kept in a sheath, in a certain place near at hand. Boys served round the wine, both right and left, in earthen or silver pots. The company drank very leisurely, frequently tasting, but not taking more at a time than a glassful. After supper, they sometimes engaged in sword play, challenging each other to friendly combat, in which they only joined their extended hands and points of their swords, without injury, but sometimes they began to fight in earnest, wounding each other; in which case, they became irritated, and, if the others did not interfere, they fought till death. In former times, also, the strongest would take up the limbs of cattle, and, if challenged by any, they fought with swords until one was killed.ᵠ

In Celtiberia, the lights were brought in by boys, who cried out "vincamus;"ʳ and, speaking of lights, it may be noticed that the substitute for a candle among the Gaël, and Scots farmers generally, is a slip of the resinous fir wood, dug out of the mosses and dried. This is called Gius puil, or blair,* and is held beside the guid man during meals, by the younger branches of the family. It would seem that, anciently, the chiefs had servants for the purpose of holding their rude flambeaux; and a story is related of an Earl of Braidalbane showing some English friends these torch-bearers, in proof that he possessed much more valuable *chandeliers* than those of silver exhibited to him in

---

ᵠ Ritson, Mem. of the Celts, 211. waging war for meat and drink.
ʳ This seems what Athenæus calls Amm. Marc. xvi. 4.
* *Giubhas puill or blair.* ED.

the South. Old Gaëlic poems mention wax candles as in use. The Master of the Lights, an officer in the King of Wales' household, was obliged to hold a taper near the king's dish, when eating.

An ancient and common way among the Highlanders, of illuminating their dwellings, is this:—The quantity of gius required for the night is split in the morning from the roots, heaped near the peat-stack, and is placed on the Suäcan, and suspended at a convenient distance over the fire, to be thoroughly dried. At the close of the day's labour, the duine, literally the man, as the head of every family is emphatically called, takes his seat close by the head-stone of the fire, which is an oblong solid square, generally about three feet long, three feet high, and one and a half broad, placed at the back of the hearth. As soon as it is dark, the duine kindles the solus, or light, by putting a large burning coal on the top of the headstone, and laying some of the dry resinous slips upon it. This he continues to feed, by adding a fresh one or two; and such a light will illuminate a large apartment better than six good tallow candles.

The entertainment of James V. by the Earl of Athol, when on a hunting visit, as before noticed, was an extraordinary occasion; but as it is characteristic of the manners of the time, and as the various provisions are minutely detailed in the historian's quaint style, it is desirable to insert his account. "There were all kinds of drink, as ale, beer, wine, both white and claret, Malvasy, Muskadel, Hippocras, and Aquavitæ. Further, there was of meats, whitebread, mainbread, and gingerbread, with fleshes, beef, mutton, lamb, veal, venison, goose, grice, capon, coney, cran, swan, partridge, plover, duck, drake, brissel cock and pawnies, black cock and muirfowl, capercoilies; and also the stanks that were round about the palace were full of all delicate fishes, as salmonds, trouts, pearches, pikes, eels, and all other kind of delicate fishes that could be gotten in fresh waters; and all ready for the banquet. Syne were there proper stewards, cunning baxters, excellent cooks and pottingars, with confections and drugs for their desserts; and the halls and chambers were prepared with costly bedding, vessels and napery according for a king; so that he wanted none of his orders more than he had been at home in his own palace. The king remained in this wilderness the space of three days and three nights, and his company. I heard men say it cost the Earl of Athol, every day, in expenses, a thousand pounds. The ambassador of the Pope, seeing this banquet and triumph, which was made in a wilderness, where there was no town near by twenty miles, thought it a great marvel that such a thing should be in Scotland, and that there should be such honesty and policy in it, especially in the Highland, where there was but wood and wilderness. But most of all, this ambassador marvelled to see, when the king departed, and all his men took their leave, the Highlandmen set all this place in a fire, that the king and ambassador might see it. Then the ambassador said to the king, 'I marvel, sir, that you should thole yon fair place to be burnt that your Grace has been so well lodged in;' then the king answered and said, 'It is the use of our Highlandmen, though they be never so well lodged, to burn their lodging when they depart.'*

Water is the natural drink of mankind, but the art of rendering it pleasant, or increasing its strength by the addition of various ingredients, is found among people in the lowest scale of civilization. A very simple method of producing an agreeable beverage is by the admixture of other substances, and we find the Gauls steeping honey

---

* Pitscottie, p. 147, fol. ed.

combs in water, and the Celtiberi using drinks made of honey.

It here becomes necessary to say something of this article, the excellent succedaneum for sugar. "Of all the insect tribes, none have engrossed so much attention as bees. Their social habits, and indefatigable industry, must have excited the admiration" of mankind in the most early ages. Their delicious stores must have equally soon attracted attention. The Celtæ certainly employed themselves in the management of bees, their honey being in much request for mixture with different liquors, and Pliny observes, that the combs were largest among the Northern nations, noticing one found in Germany eight feet long, which, he says, was black inside. In Spain, which according to Diodorus, abounded in honey, it had a flavour of broom, from the great quantities of that shrub. In this country the people were accustomed, when the flowers became insufficient to afford the requisite supply for the bees, to remove with their hives to a more desirable situation, in the same manner that a pastoral people did with their flocks.'* The Britons kept considerable numbers of these useful insects. In Ireland the Brehon laws provided for their careful protection, and in the Isle of Man it is still a capital crime to steal them. Ireland was celebrated for swarms of bees, and abundance of honey, and the monks, in the fourth century, according to Ware, had an allowance of a certain quantity in the comb fresh from the hive.

The Celtic Britons kept their bees in a bascaud formed of willow plaited.ᵘ About fifty years ago one of these

ᵗ Pliny xi.8, xxi. 13.

* The same thing is done in some parts of Scotland at the present day. Those who keep bees in the neighbourhood of Paisley, Renfrew, &c., take them down for a month or six weeks every summer by rail and steamer to Bute, Arran, and the watering places on the Argyleshire coast. ED.

ᵘ Kauelh, in Welsh a large basket, is, in Cornish, a bee-hive.

was found in Lanishaw Moss, and about eighteen years since another was discovered, about six feet under ground, in Chat's Moss, both in Lancashire. This last was a cone of two yards and a half high, and one in diameter at bottom, and was divided into four floors or separate hives, to which were doors sufficiently large to admit one's hand. The whole was formed of unpeeled willows, and contained combs and complete bees. These were larger than the present species,ᵛ which may perhaps account for the great size of those combs noticed by Pliny.

Scotland was formerly called a land of milk and honey, but it hardly deserves the latter appellation in these days,* In most parts of the Highlands about fifty years ago, a farmer had two or three hives that remunerated him very well for the trouble attending the management. It is not so now, which is matter of surprise, the abundance of heath affording so plentiful a field for the collection of honey, at no expense; and it is well known that what is gathered from the heaths is much preferable to that which is extracted from garden flowers. The Highland Society of Scotland is, at this time, endeavouring to extend the culture of these useful insects throughout the country.ʷ That the Highlanders had anciently a liquor made from honey, appears from ancient allusion to it. It is probable that the beverage was similar to metheglin, or mead, called mil dheoch by the Gaël. This excellent liquid is made by

---

ᵛ Whitaker's Hist. of Manchester.

* Bees do not succeed on the West coast nor in the Hebrides, because of the wet, it is supposed. They do best in the midland counties. In the Highlands of Perthshire honey is plentiful, and of excellent quality. Ed.

ʷ Many superstitions formerly prevalent, still exist concerning bees. In Devonshire they are never paid for in money; never moved but on Good Friday; and, on occasion of a funeral, the hives are carefully turned round.—Brande's Pop. Ant. ii. 202. Ellis's ed. From Domesday book we find the Custos apium was a person of some note.

boiling honey and water in certain proportions, subjecting it to fermentation, and the Welsh, who have different ways of making it, and have used it from early times, derive its name from medyclyg, medicinal, and lyn, drink. The mead maker ranked the eleventh person in the household of the kings of Wales. The famed Athole brose is a mixture of whisky and honey, with a little oatmeal.

Milk, so easily procured by a pastoral people, is a common and excellent drink by itself, and affords, in its different states, a pleasant refreshment. The making of butter produces whey, a wholesome liquor, which some of the Highlanders, Buchanan says, boiled and kept in hogsheads under ground for several months, by which it was rendered a very agreeable beverage.[x] Sweet cream mixed with butter-milk is delicious. The Irish are said to be peculiarly fond of the latter, but they formerly used a great deal of other milk, whey, and broth.

The infusion of herbs in the formation of cordials must have been practised in the most early ages, and it is to be noted that the Gaëlic lusadh, drinking, is derived from lus, an herb, or plant. Boece says the old Scots were moderate drinkers, using chiefly infusions or mixtures of thyme, mint, anise, &c.

The Celtiberi, at their festivals, had a certain liquor in the composition of which no fewer than five score different herbs were employed, but no one appeared to know precisely the particular ingredients of this famous wassail, although every one understood that it required one hundred articles, if properly prepared, as its name implied. This name has not been preserved, but we are told the mixture was esteemed the most sweet and wholesome of drinks.[y] The people of the Scilly Islands are fond of

[x] Lib. i. It seems to be what Perlin calls "force laict."
[y] Pliny, xxv. 8.

distilling various flowers and herbs, to mix in their liquors, and they take special care to gather them at a certain age of the moon.^z

The art of making strong liquors seems to be one of the first acquirements of mankind; in all parts of the world, and in the rudest state of society, substances, or mixtures to produce intoxication have been discovered. Before wine became known to the Gauls they appropriated much of their corn for the production of an excellent beverage. The nations of Western Europe—Gauls, Germans, Celtiberians, and Britons made liquors of two sorts from grain steeped in water, which were denominated curmi and zythus, answering to the modern ale and beer.[a] Schœpflin thinks zythus was the British cyder,[b] in which he is evidently wrong. The Gaëlic suthan, juice, clearly shows its relationship to the ancient Celtic term. The Britons, Dioscorides says, drank the strong liquor called curmi, a word long retained by the Gaël in its original acceptation, being the curwi of the Welsh, which is their name for ale. Ol chni, I drink,* is the expression of a modern Highlander,[c] and it is not a little curious. Ol is ale, and el, in ancient German, signified water:[d] from which original term the alica, a drink of the Britons, apparently a sort of gruel or frumenty, and other names originated. The Highlanders substituted loin, or lain, provisions, for the ancient name of this liquor, not an inapt term for what is in modern times called "liquid bread."

---

[z] Troutbeck.

[a] The Egyptians made a similar liquor. Where vines would not grow, says Diodorus, Osiris, or Bacchus, taught the inhabitants to make drink from barley. Lib. i. 2, iv. i. In Illyricum, the liquor made from grain was called Sabaia. Marcellinus.

[b] Alsatia illust. p. 64.   [c] Sir J. Foulis, of Colintoun.

* *Tha mi G'ol*, I drink; *Olaidh mi*, I will drink; *Olam oirbh*, I drink to you. Ed.

[d] Cannegieteri Diss de Brittemburgo.

Corma appears to have been zythus made without the addition of honey.[e] Marcellinus mentions garaus as a drink of the Germans in the time of Valens,[f] and in Spain they used cœlia and ceri, or cervisia, which Whitaker tells us signify strong water. The Gauls drank the strongest ale with water, and the Celtiberi made it to keep for a considerable time.[g] Whether the Caledonians could make malt liquors so early as we find them in use by the south Britons, is not known, but curmi was drank in the third century, and was common in the sixth.[h]

The Picts are celebrated for possessing an art whereby they extracted a delicious drink from the tops and blossoms of heath, which it is believed was lost with their supposed extirpation. This is related by the national historians, and is preserved in popular tradition throughout Scotland; the story representing the secret as last remaining with a father and son, prisoners to Kenneth Mac Alpin, who were urged by the promise of liberty and liberal rewards, to impart their valuable knowledge to the Scots. The father, after long solicitation, expressed himself willing to accede to their proposals, on condition that his son should previously be put to death, which request being unsuspectingly complied with, the stern Pict told his enemies they might also put him to death, for he could never be prevailed on to disclose a secret known only to himself. The enraged Scots, as may be supposed, speedily sacrificed the obstinate captive. Many extensive tracts of Muir are observable that are level and free from stones, and they are believed to have been the fields cleared by the Picts for the cultivation of the heath, which they mowed down when in bloom. This shrub, I have been told, may, by a certain process, produce a good spirit, and a pleasant liquor is often made in

[e] Athenæus, iv.   [f] Lib. xxvii. i.   [g] Pliny, xiv. 22, xviii. 7.
[h] Scrip. Hist. August. p. 942, ap. Low's History of Scotland.

the Highlands chiefly from its flowers, but it differs from the ancient beverage, in having the additions of honey or sugar with other ingredients, whereas the heather ale of the Picts, it is thought, required nothing extraneous to bring it to perfection. In the Highlands it was an almost invariable practice, when brewing, to put a quantity of the green tops of heath in the mash tub, and when the plant is in bloom it adds much to the strength and flavour of the beer. The roots, also, will improve its qualities, for they are of a liquorice sweetness, but their astringency requires them to be used with caution.

Herb ale was a favourite "brewst" with the women of olden times. An ancient matron, whose grandmother had made it, has often descanted to me on its excellence, alleging that those who drank heartily of it became speckled in the face like a salmon. Being only a child when this was observed, she could not say what were the ingredients, but as her ancestors were natives of Buchan, where the descendants of the ancient Picts, according to Pinkerton, are to be found, the secret was not, perhaps, entirely lost.[1] I am assured by a native of the Highlands, that he could make beer, equal to the best malt liquor, from ingredients furnished entirely by the Scotish mountains.

Perlin describes the Scots as regaling themselves with "bierre, god alles, and alles." They were partial to malt liquor, and the old farmers used much more of it than their successors, and made it of a superior quality. Even the poorer sort brewed their own ale, sometimes using no other utensils than a common pot, and pail, or tub. Hops were unknown to the old Highlanders, and are not used by many even yet. The corr mheill root was, no doubt, an

---

[1] Augsburg beer, so much esteemed in Germany, is said to owe its excellence to aven's roots, geum urbanum, that are put into it.

excellent substitute,[j] but a common infusion was wormwood. A curious method of preserving yeast was used in the Isles. A rod of oak, which was to be cut before the middle of May, from four to eight inches long, and twisted round like a wyth, was boiled in the wort, and when dried was kept in a bundle of barley straw until wanted for use, when, being steeped in the liquor, it produced fermentation. Martin says he saw one that had served the purpose no less than thirty years.

Brewing devolved on the Celtic females, and the Saxons observed the same rule; it is only in recent times that the business has been done by men, malt liquor being formerly made and sold by the women. The "ale wife" was, at one time, synonymous in England with the keeper of a "pot house"—in Scotland the appellation is still expressive of the landlady of a "change house." A curious old Scots statute respecting "wemen wha brewis aill to be sauld," ordains "gif she makis evil aill, and is convict thereof, she sall pay an unlaw of aucht shillings, or she sall be put upon the cuckstule, and the aill sauld to be distribute to the pure folk."

Dr. Smith thinks the Caledonians had a drink formed by a fermentation of parts of the birch tree. It is well known that the birch furnishes the strongest and most pleasant of all British wines, but whether the old Highlanders knew this I cannot say; few of their descendants are aware of it, and, notwithstanding popular belief, there is reason to think the opinion that spirits were made of this tree, is not well grounded.

Whisky, so common in Scotland and Ireland, so much esteemed, and produced in such excellence, by the Celts of both countries, is well known, and the art of making it was

---

[j] Pennant says a fermented liquor was made of it.

probably possessed from an early period by the Gaël, who have so long been celebrated as distillers of the "mountain dew." It is, however, a matter of dispute with antiquaries whether it be a late invention or of ancient origin. Ware inclines to the former opinion, and Pinkerton says it became known perhaps three centuries ago.[k] Uisge-beatha is literally aqua vitæ, water of life; whisky is a corrupt pronunciation of the first part of the term. Trestarig is whisky three times distilled,[*] which is reckoned an excellent spirit, and uisge beatha baul is four times distilled, of which two spoonfuls is enough to drink at one time.[l] Whisky, illicitly distilled, is termed in Ireland potteen, and in Scotland pot dhu, that is, the small pot and the black pot, in allusion to the vessel in which the wash is boiled. The superior excellency of small still whisky is believed to be owing, in a great measure, to the regular coolness of the pipes, which is effected by introducing a small stream of water, which flows through the bothy where the spirit is made.

The Gauls were excessively fond of wine, which their own country did not, it is said, in early ages produce. It is evident from Possidonius, Strabo, and Martial, that the grape was cultivated by the Celts, but they do not appear to have understood how to make wine. The climate could not have been an obstacle to its manufacture, for the districts famed for the best varieties have long been the northern provinces of France.[m] The Celtiberians, according to Diodorus, also bought their wine, but Pliny mentions a vine called cocolobin, famed for a medicinal drink which

[k] Enquiry ii. 244. In 1599 it was a favourite beverage of the Irish.
[*] Gaelic, *Treastarriung*—thrice—drawn or distilled. ED.
[l] Martin.
[m] In 1808 there were nearly four millions of acres occupied in vineyards, and there are 1400 different wines in that country.

it afforded.[a] The berry called fionag, literally wine-berry, is produced in great abundance in the mountains of Scotland. It is about the size of a Zante currant, of the same colour, and equally juicy and sweet. It also bears the appellation dearcag fithich, crow-berry, but the above is the proper name, and from its being called wine-berry, it is clear that wine must, at some period, have been procured from it by the Gaël, unless we may suppose that that people came immediately from a grape-producing country into the Highlands of Scotland, and from the resemblance of the crow-berry to the grape, imposed that name upon it. I have no doubt, however, but good wine may be procured from it without the addition of sugar.

The Gauls imported large quantities of wine from other countries, and they are represented as drinking it with avidity as soon as they received it. The Roman merchants encouraged an intemperance by which they made immense profits, and supplied the Gauls with abundance of wine, both by the navigable rivers and land carriage. The trade was most lucrative; for so inordinately fond were they at one time of this excellent liquor, that they purchased it at any cost, and did not hesitate to give a boy in exchange for a hogshead.[o] They often drank it to such excess, that they continued, at times, "wrapt in wild and wandering cogitations," and even became stark mad; yet, perceiving these strange effects, they began to believe that the use of wine was highly improper, and Tully, in pleading for Fonteius, says, they had resolved to dilute it with water henceforth, because they thought it poison.[p] The Germans on the Rhine dealt largely in this article, and were equally remarkable for their intemperate use of it. They would continue drinking night and day, and the broils that con-

[a] Lib. xiv. 2.   [o] Diodorus, v.   [p] Amm. Mar. xv. 10.

stantly attended their debauches, commonly ended in maiming and slaughter. The Gauls in Asdrubal's service, having procured a large quantity of wine, made themselves raging drunk, when the army being attacked by the consul Cæcilius, was, in consequence, completely overthrown.[q] From the charge of debasing themselves in this way, the Nervians must be excluded, as the importation of wine into their territories was strictly prohibited. The Scythians are stigmatized as very intemperate, and gave rise to the saying of the Greeks, "let us drink like the Scyths," when they meant to indulge themselves immoderately.[r] A remark of one of their ambassadors, however, that the thirst of the Parthians increased as they deepened their potations,[s] does not countenance the charge of drunkenness. A favourite beverage of the rich Gauls was a mixture of wine and water, called dercoma; they also put salt, vinegar, and cumin in wine, ingredients which likewise formed a sauce for fish. Wine appears to have been very early known to the Highlanders, from its mention in old poems. It was formerly plentiful in Scotland, being chiefly procured from France, and was both good and cheap. Before the laws regulating the importation of Port affected that part of his Majesty's dominions,

————————"The free-born Scotsman stood,
Old was his mutton and his claret good ;
Drink Port ! the English legislator cried,
He drank the poison, and his spirit died."[t] *

The vessels out of which the Caledonians drank, were the corn or horn, the sliga or shell, and the fuach or cup.

[q] Diod. Fragment. xxxiii. Ritson.   [r] Herod. vi. 84.
[s] Pliny, xiv. 22.   [t] Home.
* This so-called epigram is generally quoted thus—
"Firm and erect the Caledonian stood,
Prime was his mutton and his claret good ;
Let him drink Port ! the English statesman cried—
He drank the poison, and his spirit died." ED.

Κεραθαι, the expression of Athenæus, translated, pour out the drink, is, literally, horn the liquor, the horn of animals being apparently the first articles converted into drinking-cups. Those used by the Highlanders are sometimes mounted with silver, or otherwise ornamented, and are usually formed of a portion of the horn, to which the ruder sort have a cork or wooden bottom. The chiefs were accustomed to use a whole horn, of large size, and richly ornamented, chiefly to be offered to visitors as a mark of respect, or as a trial of their abilities. It was the object to take off the contents at once; and if this was not done, the remainder in the horn, discovered the failure by the noise which it made in the sinuosities, on which the company immediately called out, corneigh, the horn cries; when the party was obliged to re-fill it, and drink celtic, i. e. according to the custom of the Celts." At Dunvegan, in Sky, the ancient seat of the chiefs of Macleod, is an ox-horn of this sort, finely mounted with silver, which was borne on the arm, and its mouth being brought over the elbow, the contents were drank off. The choicest liquors were served round in shells, whence the expressions to rejoice in the shell, and feast of shells. They were cockles, held with the thumb placed on the hinge part, and continued in use by the Highlanders until lately.* Whisky was filled out in a shell, at Mr. Mac Swein's, in the Isle of Cole, in 1773.ᵛ After the disuse of natural shells, some made of silver were retained. The Picts appear, from Adomnan, to have had drinking-glasses. The Highlanders

ᵘ Foulis, in Trans. of Scots Antiquaries, i. The hirlas horn of the Welsh appears to be a similar article.

* The favourite drinking shells were not those of the cockle, but of the scallop or escallop—the *Pecten Jacobœa* of conchologists. The hinge was frequently bound in silver with a projecting ridge to hold it by. They are sometimes still used. ED.

ᵛ Boswell's Journal of a Tour.

used wooden cups; but the usual article for ale was the maighder, a round vessel, with two handles, as represented in the vignette, by which it was carried to the head. The quach, so named from cu, round, is formed of different coloured pieces of wood, in manner of cooper's work, but the staves are joined together by mutual insertions, presenting a very pretty appearance, and they are, besides, often hooped with silver. Plenty of liquor was of great importance at festivals. Without this adjunct, as an author said of the Irish coshering, it could be no feast; the truth of which is proved by the term which the Highlanders apply to a great entertainment: they call it curme, the very word by which the strong liquor, at first confined to the household of a chief, is distinguished.

The bach-lamhal, or cup-bearer, was a high office among the Gael, and, like the steward of the household in Wales, tasted all liquors. The smith, among the latter, was entitled to a draught of every sort brought to the king's table. The truliad, or butler, who had the custody of the king's cellars, was the eleventh person in the royal establishment. When a guest sat down at the table of a Highland chief, he was first presented with a draught of uisge beatha out of the family cup or shell, and when he had finished this cordial, a horn, containing about a quart of ale, was given him, and if he was able to finish it, he was esteemed a good fellow."
Riche, in his Irish Hubbub, describes the manner of drinking among that people: One standing up and uncovering his head, took a full cup, and, with a grave countenance, gave the name of the party whose health was to be drank, and he who was pledged, took off his cap, kissed his fingers, and bowing himself "in signe of reverent acceptance," the leader took off his glass, and, turning the bottom up, gave

---

" Dr. Mac Pherson.

it "a phillip, to make it cry twango." The bumpers being re-filled, the person whose health had been drank repeated the same ceremony, and it went in like manner round the whole company, provided there were three uncovered until it had made the circuit of the table.

The love of intoxicating liquors is a vice which people in a low scale of civilization are prone to. The Gauls, who drank sparingly of their own beverages, indulged to excess in the produce of the Italian vintage. The Highlanders can enjoy a social glass as much as any persons; but although whisky is plentiful with them, habitual tippling is extremely rare, and there is a proverb which speaks their contempt of those who meet for the sake of drinking only. The renowned Fingal, who, by the bye, delivered his maxims in Triads, said, that one of the worst things which could happen to a man was to drink curmi in the morning. Measg, mixture, now pronounced meisg, signifies drunkenness, apparently from the stupifying effects of drinking *mixed* liquors. A gentleman assured me that in the parish of Lairg, in Ross-shire, where he was formerly resident, there was but one person addicted to drink; and a native of Laggan, Inverness-shire, knew but one individual in that part who was accustomed to intoxication: these characters indulged their depraved tastes in solitude, for they could find no associates. The Highlanders seldom met for a carousal, and when they did assemble they enjoyed themselves very heartily, the "lawing," or bill, being paid by a general contribution, for which a bonnet was passed around the company. If, however, the Highlanders seldom met to drink together, it must be confessed that when they did "forgather," they were inclined to prolong their stay, and would occasionally spend days and nights over the bottle. Donald Ross, an old man, full of amusing anecdotes of the gentlemen of Sutherland and the neighbouring counties, used to dwell with particular pleasure on those social treats. The laird of Assynt, on one occasion, having come down to Dunrobin, was accosted by the smith of the village, when just ready to mount his garron and set off. The smith being an old acquaintance, and the laird, like the late Mac Nab, and others of true Highland blood, thinking it no derogation from his dignity to accept the gobh's invitation to take deoch an doras, a draught at the door, or stirrup cup, for every glass had its significant appellation, and went into the house where the smith called for the largest jar or greybeard of whisky, a pitcher that held perhaps two gallons, meaning, without doubt, to shew the laird that when they parted, it should not be for want of liquor. "Well," said Donald, "they continued to sit and drink, and converse on various matters, and the more they talked, the more subjects for conversation arose, and it was the fourth day be-before the smith thought of his shop, or the laird, of Assynt."

It is customary at meetings of Highland Societies to accompany certain toasts with "Celtic honours," that are thus bestowed. The chief or chairman, standing up,* gives the toast, and with a slight wave of the hand, repeats three times, suas e, suas e, suas e, up with it, up with it, up with it, the whole company also standing, and joining him in three short huzzas. This is repeated, when he then pronounces the word nish, now, also three times, with peculiar emphasis, in which he is joined by the company, who dwell a considerable time on the last cheer. As the company sit down, the piper strikes up an appropriate tune.

* When a toast is given with the highest "Celtic honours," the company stand, each with one foot upon his chair, and the other on the edge of the table before him. Whether this is an ancient or a modern custom, in a large enthusiastic company it has a striking effect.   ED.

Everyone knows that the Scots are fond of snuff, and the figure of a Highlander is the almost invariable symbol of a snuff-shop. How they became so noted for their partiality to "sneeshin" is not easy to determine; it is a subject that has hitherto received little attention. There is a tradition, that when the Black Watch, now the 42nd regiment, first came to London, the men were so constantly calling to supply themselves with their favourite powder, that the dealers whose snuff had met with their patronage, adopted the figure of a Highlander to indicate their business. This may be very correct, but how came the inhabitants of the remote Highlands and Isles so speedily to bring into universal use an article that had been but recently introduced in England? Sir Walter Raleigh first brought tobacco here, about 1586, and we know that, like all innovations, it must have been some time before its use became common, even in the south; yet, in a poem by Mary Mac Leod, of the house of Dunvegan, addressed to John Mac Leod, brother to Sir Norman, and written about 1600, she thanks him for presenting her with a bra thombac, or tobacco millstone.

Now it is not at all probable that the Highlanders could have received their knowledge of this plant from the English, or that, in so short a time, they could have been, not only reconciled, but proverbially addicted to its use. The strong prejudice which the Gaël have to innovation of all kinds, even emanating from a less objectionable quarter than the Sassanach, forbids us to believe that their snuff was connected with Raleigh's discovery. The root cormhcille, or braonan, was chewed like tobacco by the old Highlanders, and may have been smoked or ground to snuff, but whatever the article was, it is certain that the Celts were accustomed to smoke, and their pipes have been frequently dug up both in Britain and Ireland. They were discovered, in considerable numbers, under ground, at Brannockstown, in the county of Kildare, in 1784, and a skeleton, found under an ancient barrow, had a pipe actually sticking between its teeth![x] Its form is much similar to those now in use, only of an oval or egg-shape. Herodotus says, the Scyths had certain herbs, which were thrown into the fire, and the smoke being inhaled by those sitting around, it affected them as wine did the Greeks. Strabo tells us, a certain religious sect among them smoked for recreation; and Mela and Solinus[y] plainly describe the smoke as being inhaled through tubes. The Highlanders appear to have adopted the tobacco introduced by Raleigh from a previous addiction to a native herb of similar pungency, and they are said to have formerly grown and prepared their own tobacco in a very judicious manner, drying it by the fire, and grinding both stem and leaf, making a snuff not unlike what is now termed Irish blackguard. They are so partial to snuff, that a supply of it is often a sufficient inducement for one to accompany a traveller across extensive tracts of mountain or muir.[*] The mull, as the neat spiral horn, represented in the preceding vignette, in which they carry their snuff, is called a constant companion, and they take much pride in ornamenting it. They usually carry it in the sporan, or purse, but it was formerly stuck before them in the belt,[z] and the snuff is taken by a "pen," either a quill or small spoon of tin, brass, or silver, attached to it by a chain of similar metal. The large ram's horn, with its

---

[x] Anthologia Hibernica, i. 352, where there is a print of it. The author picked up one, thrown out of a recent excavation at Primrose-hill, near London.

[y] C. xv. Brodigan on Tobacco, &c.

[*] In the Highlands snuff-taking is now much less common than smoking. Why it should ever have been otherwise may be wondered at. ED.

[z] Journey through Scotland, 1729.

appendages, as represented in the closing vignette, is for the banqueting table, and usually lies before the chief, who occasionally passes it to the company. This utensil is usually ornamented in a very costly manner with silver and precious stones, and sometimes both horns and part of the skull are retained. The hammer is to shake the snuff from the sides, the rake is to bring it within reach, the spike is to break it if pressed together, the hare's foot is to brush away any particles that may be dropped, and the pen is to convey the snuff to the nose. I cannot vouch for the truth of the assertion, that the large horn was formerly carried about the person.

The art of cookery and practice of medicine were formerly very intimately connected, and it is, perhaps, to be regretted, that they are now disjoined. Mankind, in a rude state of society, entertain a superstitious opinion of the healing powers of herbs; but their belief is not, in all cases, groundless. When the chief occupations of a people are the pasturage of tame and the hunting of wild beasts, or even when they are employed in agriculture, the vegetable kingdom, so constantly under their observation, is the wide field which nature spreads before them, whence they procure the simple remedies that are applied to their diseases and their wounds. Their materia medica is confined to roots and plants, and, from the experience of ages, they acquire a considerable knowledge of their sanative properties; the brute creation have even, sometimes, it is related, informed mankind of the medicinal virtues of certain plants; a crow is said to have led the Gauls to the discovery of the virtues of *coracion*.[a] It is easier to ascertain the properties of vegetables than those of minerals. From the vegetable kingdom are still procured many valuable specifics, and

[a] Aristotle.

the most ancient physicians prescribed no other remedies than what were derived from herbs.[b]

Untutored savages have been found to possess valuable secrets in the science of medicine, where the prescriptions were the natural produce of the earth, and administered almost without preparation: but, perhaps, the repute which has been, in some cases, attached to the application of simples, has arisen as much from their innocuous qualities as from their medicinal properties. People ignorant of more active medicines, will always esteem remedies which can be administered with safety, if not with a decided salutary effect.

The Gauls are represented by the ancients to have attained very old age, enjoying peculiarly good health and vigour. The Britons were particularly remarkable for their protracted lives. Plutarch says, some of them lived one hundred and twenty years, and the inhabitants of the Hyperborean Island are said to have lived until they were satiated with existence. Their mode of life was, doubtless, conducive to strength and longevity, but the Celts were not entirely exempt from disease: yet those which were common at Rome, were little known in Gaul or Spain.[d] The glacach, among the Highlanders, is a disease of a consumptive nature, affecting the chest and lungs. It is also called the Mac Donald's disease, because there are par-

[b] Pliny, xxvi. 1, 4. The virtues imputed to these prescriptions were so incredible, that, at last, a general scepticism arose, which paved the way for the new practice of Asclepiades; that, in its turn, became equally corrupted.—Ibid. The loss of that portion of Solomon's wisdom, contained in the treatise on every plant, "from the cedar-tree, that is in Lebanon, even unto the hyssop, that springeth out of the wall," is to be regretted equally by the physician and naturalist.

[d] Pliny, xxvi. 1. A sort of cancerous bubo is described as peculiar to Narbonne, which, without being accompanied by pain, carried its victim to the grave in three days. Ibid.

ticular tribes of that name, who are confidently believed to be able to cure it with their touch, accompanied by a certain form of words, means which are quite ineffectual if any fee is offered or accepted! From the simple and active lives of these people, they were subject to few diseases; and it is only since linen has come into general use, that rheumatism is said to have been known. In the large county of Sutherland, only one doctor can find sufficient employment.[e]

The practice of physic amongst uncivilized people is always accompanied by religious ceremonies, which have been assigned as the origin of all magic and incantations. The Druids were physicians as well as ministers of religion,[f] and, in certain diseases, their interposition with the gods was added to their physical applications, for the recovery of their patients. Sometimes it was thought necessary even to sacrifice a human victim for the removal of some desperate malady. As these priests were the chief depositaries of Celtic knowledge, which they preserved as part of their religious profession, it is probable that the other classes of the community paid less attention to a study that would have infringed on the peculiar privilege of the Druids; but this species of knowledge being, in a great measure, the result of experience, it could not remain entirely with that class, although the office of administering bodily relief may have been conceded to them from a belief in their superior sanctity and influence with the Deity.

In the Gaëlic poem of Oithona, we find a chief who had been a diligent student of Esculapius: "Can the hand of Gaul heal thee?" he asks; "I have searched for the herbs of the mountains, I have gathered them on the secret banks of their streams, my hand has closed the wound of the

[e] Agricultural Report.   [f] Bello Gallico.

brave."[g] Fingal is celebrated for his cuach fhinn, or medical cup, which is yet commemorated in Highland tradition.[h] Amongst the Celtic nations, Pliny celebrates the people of Spain as most curious in searching after simples; and some herbs, in great repute for their medicinal virtues, were peculiar to that country.[i] One of these was named cantabrica, from the territories of the Cantabri, where it grew. Vettonica, or betony, was not indeed peculiar to Celtiberia, but it received its name from the Vettones, one of the tribes of that country, who probably first discovered its salutary properties.[k]

The misletoe was esteemed a panacea, and was called by a name which signified all-heal. It was particularly celebrated for the cure of epilepsy, in which disease it is even yet sometimes applied.[l] Its wonderful properties, which need not be enumerated, were quite lost if it was allowed to touch the ground after being cut down.

An herb, called britannica, supposed to have been cochlearia, or spoon-wort, was celebrated for the cure of paralysis. The name seems to point to this country as its original soil; but although it was exported to the continent from Britain, Pliny says it was not very plentiful in this island, and confesses he does not know why it has received the name.[m] Its properties were first discovered to the Romans in the time of Cæsar Germannicus, when the army having drank the waters of a certain fountain in Germany, lost the use of their legs, and were otherwise much affected. On this occasion, the natives, who were well acquainted

---

[g] This is not, perhaps, a fair proof of the practice of surgery and medicine independent of the Druids; for tradition asserts, that the kings of Morven had, at this period, refused longer submission to that body.

[h] Smith's Gallic Antiquities.　　[i] Lib. xxv. 8.　　[k] Pliny, xvi. 9.

[l] Sir John Colbach, in 1720, published a Dissertation on the Misletoe, where he recommends it as a medicine excellent to subdue epilepsy and all other convulsive disorders.　　[m] Lib. xxv. 3, xxvii.

with the deleterious quality of the water, and of the value of this herb in counteracting its effects, instructed the Romans in its application.

Agaricum, a production resembling a mushroom, grew on most trees in Gaul, and was not only prescribed as a medicine, but became an article of export to Rome, where it was much esteemed as an ingredient in confections.ⁿ

Many very astonishing virtues were imputed to verbenacum or vervain. It was not applied solely to heal bodily infirmities, but was famed for removing mental disorders, having the power effectually to reconcile those who were at the deepest enmity, and by merely sprinkling the place where a party were to feast, it promoted hilarity and a good understanding among the company. These were, indeed, estimable qualities, especially as the Gauls are represented to have been extremely irritable, and prone to quarrel at their entertainments. This plant deserved the estimation in which it was held, for it was besides of much use in divination, and was gathered with the most superstitious observances. Those who were employed in the work, commenced their operations by drawing a circle around it, and slipping their left hand cautiously from under their cloak, as if afraid of being seen, plucked it up by the roots and threw it in the air. They finally made an oblation of honey to the earth, as an atonement for depriving it of so valuable an herb.º

The Romans retained the ancient and almost universal veneration entertained for verbenacum, imputing to it several wonderful virtues. When the heralds went on any embassy, they carried a bunch of it, pulled up for the purpose, from which circumstance they derived their name, Verbenarii.ᵖ The Greeks employed vervaine in the worship of their gods, and the Eastern magi paid the same

ⁿ Pliny, xvi. 9.   º Pliny, xxv. 9.   ᵖ Ibid. xxii. 2.

regard to it, affirming that it possessed many miraculous properties. The Druids, in their character of physicians, practised no greater deception than the priests of other nations.* They knew that this herb really possessed certain qualities, which the wisdom of succeeding ages has not disputed, (*e. g.*, for head-aches, wounds, &c.,) and if they disguised this knowledge by superstitious ceremonies, and pretended miracles, they only displayed what the credulous populace, who delight in the marvellous, were greatly pleased with, and thereby taught them to respect and venerate what they would not otherwise have valued. The shepherds in the North of France continue to gather vervaine, pronouncing certain words, the meaning of which is unknown perhaps even to themselves, and apply it, not only for the cure of several complaints, but believe that it can operate as a charm."

The Gauls seem to have believed that the potency of herbs were chiefly imparted by the mysterious ceremonies with which they were gathered and applied, an opinion that the Druids would naturally encourage. Those nations appear to have imputed to certain plants very wonderful and powerful virtues, and to have considered them as able to assist them in battle. Pliny, although sufficiently credulous, justly doubts their being able to fortify themselves by such means. "Where were those potent herbs among the Cimbri," he asks, "when they were so completely routed, that they yelled again?"[r] The supernatural powers which the Gauls ascribed to their medical applications were certainly ridiculous, but the articles which formed the pre-

---

* Up to a quite recent period vervain had an honoured place in the British Pharmacopœia, and is still held in repute among herbalists as a medicinal plant. Its botanical name *Verbena officinalis* speaks for itself. It is now, not very wisely, perhaps, utterly disregarded by the Faculty. ED.

[q] M. Latour ap. Phillip's Flora Historica. [r] xxvi. 4, 1.

scriptions, if not effectual in their operation, were naturally harmless. In general, they possessed some good quality, and, compared with the contemptible nostrums in credit among the Romans, they were respectable applications.

The Gaël do not appear to have been much tinctured with the belief in charms that prevailed among other people. Dr. Mac Culloch found no "superstitious remedies" among the people of the Isles, and amongst those to be noticed, few will appear to be such as deserve this term.* In an old Gaëlic poem, allusion is made to a ring used as a preservative from disease.—"I am astonished, from the virtue of his ring, how he should be in pain or torment." Need we be surprised, that "the savage Celt," as he is stigmatised, should have believed that this article possessed wonderful powers, when we find Sir Christopher Hatton, Lord Chancellor to Queen Elizabeth, giving her Majesty a ring to protect her from the plague!* The well-attested cure of Lady Baird, of Sauchtenhall, near Edinburgh, by the Lee penny, is on a par with the Chancellor's gift. This valuable penny was borrowed by the town of Newcastle, to protect it from the plague, and a bond was granted for its safe return.† In the Diary of El. Ashmore, 1681, we find, "I took a good dose of elixir, and hung three spiders about my neck, and they drove my ague away!" I believe some of the Highlanders still attach a deal of importance to unspoken water, which is brought from certain parts, and applied without uttering a single word. The veneration which the ancient Celtæ paid to water led

---

* The Highlanders are, and always were, much addicted to "superstitious remedies" in alleviation and cure of all their ailments. How the fact should have escaped the notice of Mac Culloch and of our author is not difficult to account for. The people are always adverse to talking of these matters, and to practising them openly. ED.

* Ellis's Letters on English History, iii.

† Murray's Guide to the Beauties of Scotland.

them to believe in the supernatural virtues of particular fountains and streams, in which their descendants continued long to bathe, in the faith of a cure, and this respect for wells was not relinquished by the Christian Scots!

Selago, or hedge hyssop, was reckoned by the ancient Celts excellent for all diseases of the eyes, the cure being produced by fumigation. It was gathered with singular ceremonies, of the same character as those observed in collecting other herbs; the person being clad in a white robe, with bare feet, &c.[u]

Samolus, which was procured with similar observances, was chiefly employed as a preservative of cattle from every disease, but all its virtues seemed to depend on the due performance of the formalities with which it was pulled. Those who were employed in this office were enjoined to do it fasting; they were not on any account to look aside, or turn their eyes from the herb, &c.[w]

The Celtic nard was valued at Rome as only inferior in quality to the Indian, and a pound of it was sold for thirteen denarii, something more than eight shillings sterling. It was much used by physicians, and was employed in the manufacture of a certain wine, greatly esteemed by the Romans, but whether the composition of this beverage was learned from the Gauls does not appear.[x] The nard was plucked up by the roots, which were carefully washed; it was then steeped in wine, dried in the sun, and made up into little bundles wrapt in paper, for sale.[y]

Exacon, a sort of centaury found in Gaul, was esteemed very useful in several distempers.[z] The virtue of ischæmon, or mylet, in staunching blood, was discovered by the Thracians. The scithica, which received its name from

[u] Pliny, xxiv. 9. [w] Pliny, xxiv. 9. [x] Ibid. xvi. [y] Ibid. xii. 12.
[z] Ibid. xxv. 6.

the Scyths, besides its use among that people, as a preventative of hunger and thirst, was applied to the healing of wounds, for which it was much esteemed, even in Rome.[a]

We know very little of ancient Celtic pharmacy. The juices of herbs were usually extracted by bruising or boiling. Sometimes the plants were dried in the shade, at other times in the sun, and these operations were accompanied with many superstitions and nice observances. The leaves, the roots, and the stems of verbenacum, were each carefully and separately dried before use in a place shaded from the rays of the sun.[b] The Gauls extracted the juice of hellebore, a poison with which they rubbed the points of their arrows, and which had the property of making the venison sweet and tender.[c] Limeum, called also belenium, was another poisonous extract, which, besides several other uses, was administered with salutary effect in a draught to cattle.

Xenicum, also a poison, killed with such celerity, that it was necessary for the hunter when he had struck his game, to run up quickly and cut the flesh from around the wound, to prevent the matter from spreading. An antidote to xenicum was oakbark, or a leaf which they called coracion.

There can be no doubt but the Celtæ were skilled in the treatment of wounds, the reduction of fractures, &c. The state of almost constant warfare in which they unhappily lived, afforded but too much practice to the surgeon. Sir Richard Hoare, in a barrow which he opened, near Stonehenge, found a skeleton, the skull of which had a piece, about five inches broad, so neatly cut off, that he thought it could

---

[a] Ibid. xxvi. 14, xxvii. 1.   [b] Ibid. xxv. 9.
[c] Aulus Gellius, xvii. 15. Pliny, xxv.

only have been done by means of a saw. Severe wounds, that must have been long healed, are often perceptible on the mouldering remains of the Celtic warrior.

The physician was hereditary, like other professions, and one was generally found in the retinue of a chief, where he held a situation of some distinction. In Ireland, the surgeon and the priest were placed beside each other at table, the chief perhaps considering the person who took care of his body on a near equality with him who attended to his spiritual welfare, or, it may be more likely, that when the professions were separated, the priest was assigned the place which the Druid had occupied.

The kings of Scotland, from the most early period, had physicians in their establishment, who enjoyed lands as the reward of their services. Amongst the Highlanders, the rights of the physician were secured by royal grant. In 1609, King James granted to Fergus Mac Beth the office of principal physician of the Isles, with the lands of Ballenabe and Tarbet.[d] The Scots always paid great veneration to the profession, but they made it a rule to abstain from physic as much as possible, relying much on a system of abstinence for effecting a cure. A mutilated treatise on physic, and another on anatomy, were in the hands of Dr. Smith; and one on medicine, written in the end of the thirteenth, or beginning of the fourteenth century, was in possession of the late Mr. Astle. The Doctor says, there were in Mull, until lately, a succession of doctors, who wrote a chest full of Gaëlic MSS., on subjects connected with their profession, which were purchased by the Duke of Chandos.

Their prescriptions were from necessity chiefly confined to simple preparations of herbs, to which the inhabitants

---

[d] Mac Farlane's MS. Gilcolm is said to signify "son of the physician."

of the Isles and the coasts of the mainland added certain sea weeds. A clergyman in the north of England writes to Dr. Fosbrooke,* "I have often regretted that our village herbalists are fallen so much into disrepute. There are some plants have qualities which are disallowed or neglected by botanists; and these qualities, brought into action by an old crony, will sometimes cure a disease that has been given up by her betters as irremediable." He instances a decoction of plantain and salad oil, successfully applied by these rural doctors for the bite of an adder, &c. A good constitution is more in favour of a patient, perhaps, than any power in the application, which, if it does not possitively assist recovery, it is not likely to check. The herb, or herbary, was a spot in gardens, anciently devoted to the rearing of medicinal plants.

We have a curious account of one of the self-taught Highland doctors in the work of Martin, who wrote 125 years ago, and attests the cure of a gentlewoman of his acquaintance, who was believed to be within but a few hours of her last, by this person, who only applied a simple plant. Neil Beaton was a native of Sky, and his renown was not only spread over the Islands, but extended far and wide throughout the Western parts of the main land. He extracted the juices of roots and plants by a process peculiar to himself, at little or no charge, and had so nice a discernment, that he could discover their nature by the colour of the flower. He treated medical works with contempt, from observing that their methods had often failed when his had succeeded. Martin says he examined him, and, with great simplicity, declares his belief that he worked by no supernatural assistance, but formed his system of treatment chiefly from a consideration of the

* Traditions and Recollections.

constitution of his patient.[f] In Ireland, the O'Calinanes were so very famous for their skill, that it gave rise to a proverb. In that country, willow herb, lythrum salicaria, is a celebrated medical plant.

A few recipes of acknowledged efficacy will impart an idea of the state of medical science among these people. The tops of nettles, chopped small, and mixed with the whites of eggs, applied to the forehead; or erica baccifera, boiled for a little in water, and applied warm to the crown of the head, procures sleep. Spirewort, cut very small, and applied in the shell of the limpet to the temples, removes tooth-ache. A similar application, sufficiently strong to raise a blister, cures sciatica and other complaints. The infusion of wild garlic is drank for the stone. Fern, mixed with the whites of eggs, dispels bloodshot from the eyes, Wild sage, chewed, and put into the ears of cows or sheep, certainly restores sight. The broth of a lamb, in which the herb shunuish has been boiled, is reckoned good for consumption. The liver of a seal, dried, pulverized, and drank with milk or whisky, is a good remedy for fluxes. Linarich, a green coloured sea weed, is applied to the temples and forehead, to dry up defluxions, and for the cure of megrim: it is also applied to burns. I am not sure if the following practice was peculiar to the Highlanders. At the birth of a child, the nurse took a stick of green ash, and putting one end in the fire, while it was burning, she received in a spoon the juice which oozed from the other end, which she gave to the infant as its first food.[g] In the Island of Gigay, nettles were used to staunch bleeding, but the most esteemed article for this purpose is the bolga-beite, a round sort of fungus, that when it dies becomes

---

[f] Western Islands, p. 198. Dr. Mac Culloch says dyspepsia was the prevailing disease.

[g] Lightfoot.

full of a light powder, of a brownish colour, which, being exposed to the wind, flies off like smoke. In cases of fracture, a poultice of barley meal and white of eggs must be immediately applied; the part then surrounded by small splinters of wood, tightly wrapt up, and not to be untied for several days. An ointment of St. John's wort, bettonica, and golden rod, all cut and mixed in butter or grease, with which they cure wounds in general, is then applied, and in this manner they treat the most compound fracture with tolerable success. When the feet were benumbed, the West Highlanders used to scarify their heels. When they were hot and galled with hard walking, they were bathed in warm water, wherein red moss had been put. The leaves of alder, applied to the feet, when inflamed by travel, was a prescription in other parts.

A singular but effectual method of inducing perspiration was anciently practised by the inhabitants of the Hebudæ. A large fire was made on the earthen floor, and when it was properly heated, the fire was removed, and a heap of straw spread over the place, upon which was poured a quantity of water. The patient then lay down upon it, and was quickly in a profuse sweat. In more recent times, they adopted another equally efficacious means. The patient's shirt was boiled, and put on wet, and as warm as could be borne.[h] To cure jaundice, the patient laid bare his back, for the inspection of the doctor, who, without any previous intimation, gently, but quickly, passed a hot iron along the vertebræ. Others suddenly dashed a pail of cold water on the naked body. In both cases the cure was produced, or attempted, by the fright which the patient receives.

Having thus described the manner of living among the

[h] Martin, p. 189.

Highlanders, exhibiting the activity and freedom of their lives, and showing the supply of food which their situation affords, with the means which they adopt to counteract disease or accident, the inference must be, that these people are both healthy and long lived. Such, indeed, is the case, most of them attaining extreme old age, without suffering from any of the maladies which are the scourges of the luxurious and inactive.

Martin, himself a native of the Hebrides, whom it has been found necessary so often to quote, in his very curious and particular account of these islands, and their inhabitants, mentions several instances of protracted existence, some of which came under his own observation. Gilour Mac Crain, an inhabitant of Jurah, he says, kept 180 Christmases, in his own house, and notices a woman in Scarba, who reached the patriarchal age of 140 years, and a person in South Uist, who had but lately died at 138. In more recent times we find Flora Mac Donald, who died in Lewis in 1810, with full possession of her faculties, at the age of 120, and Margaret Innes, who died in Sky in 1814, aged 127. In 1817, Hugh Cameron, called Eobhan na Pillie, died at Lawers in Braidalban, in his 112th year; and one Elizabeth Murray died at Auchenfauld, in Perthshire, when she had reached 116. Peter Gairden, who has been before alluded to, a native of Mar, was a sturdy old Highlander when he died at the advanced age of 132. This veteran, whose portrait has been engraved, continued to wear his native garb, in this and other particulars resembling Alexander Campbell, alias Ibhorach, who lived in Glencalvie, in Ross-shire, and was born in 1699. This "ancient of days" died at the age of 117, retaining his vigour of body and mind to the last, and enjoying his favourite amusement of roaming about the glens. A walk of eleven miles, to visit his clergyman, was a recreation, and shortly before his death he went to Tain, a distance of twenty-six miles in one day. He trod with a firm step, and uniformly dressed in the kilt and short hose, leaving his breast and neck exposed to the blast, however cold. Poor Ibherach, after living so long, was indebted for support to the generosity of his friends. About a year before his death, in 1816, he received from Lord Ashburton a shilling for every year of his life, with something additional for whisky, to moisten his venerable clay, and cheer his spirits in the evening of life. This sum outlasted Campbell, and helped his clansfolk to perform the last offices with becoming decency and respect to the hoary veteran. In August, 1827, John Mac Donald, a native of Glen Tinisdale, in Sky, died at Edinburgh, aged 107. It was too memorable a circumstance to forget, that early one morning he supplied two females, as he supposed, with water from a fountain, which individuals were Flora Macdonald and Prince Charles Stewart in disguise. This man was very temperate and regular, and never had an hour's illness in his life. On new year's day, 1825, he joined in a reel with his sons, grandsons, and great-grandsons.

The public prints have for many years past occasionally recorded the deaths of Highlanders, whose remarkable old age may have entitled them to notice, but who obtained a place in the obituary chiefly from the circumstance of their having been concerned in the last unfortunate struggle, and being supposed at the time the only survivors of those engaged in that affair. Successive communications have hitherto proved the supposition erroneous, and afforded a proof of the general longevity of the Gaël. It is represented, that when his Majesty was in Edinburgh, John Grant, aged 110, was presented to him as one who had fought against the Royal forces in 1745, when, addressing his Sovereign, he observed, that although "he might not rank among the oldest friends of his throne, he was entitled to say that he was the last of his enemies."*

* The great age ascribed to the individuals above mentioned must be taken *cum grano*. Such exaggerations are common where no exact and authentic records are kept. It is now admitted on all hands that very few, *if any*, well authenticated instances of any one's having actually reached a hundred years are in existence. ED.

An Ancient "Birlinn."

CHAPTER V.

OF THE SHIPPING, COMMERCE, MONEY, AND MANUFACTURES OF THE CELTS.

It has been said that no art is so primitive as navigation, nations in the rudest state of existence being found to possess sufficient ingenuity to form vessels capable of bearing them on the surface of the waters. The Gauls, in the most distant ages, appear to have had ships wherein they transported themselves to other countries, as those who, escaping after the battle of Thermopylæ, passed into Asia.*

A canoe, formed by hollowing the trunk of a tree, seems the first attempt at ship-building. Hannibal, in passing the Rhone, bought all the small boats of the natives, a great number being there at the time attending the fairs of the sea; he also, as Polybius informs us, made so many vessels of hollow logs of trees, that every man strove to

* Pausanias, i. 4.

cross the river by one for himself. Lord Kames, however, thinks that beams and planks were first used in the construction of vessels, an opinion that is scarcely tenable.

The remains of log canoes have been discovered under ground in Scotland, evincing a very remote but unknown antiquity. In the Lochermoss, near Kilblain, one was found that measured eight feet eight inches in length, the cavity being six feet seven; the breadth was two feet, and the depth eleven inches: it had evidently been hollowed by fire, and at one end were seen the remains of three pegs for the oars or paddles. In the same moss, in 1736, another was found which measured seven feet in length, and contained a paddle. The Welsh Triads celebrate Corfinawr, a bard, as the first who made a ship for the Cumri, and the account which Athenæus gives of the mainmast of King Hiero's great ship having been procured from the mountains of Britain is, no doubt, equally true.[b]

Coit, an obsolete term for a tree, is the name which the Highlanders apply to the simple vessel formed of a hollow log. It was also called amar, literally a trough, both appellations being in use by the Irish and Scots. When Dr. Mac Pherson wrote, about fifty years since, a few were still to be seen in some of the Western Isles. We are told by Pliny that the German rovers, who formed their boats in this way, made them sometimes sufficiently large to carry thirty men.[c] Long is also Gaëlic for a ship; and Pryce, in his Cornish British Archæology, says it is the British log.

This first essay at ship-carpentry was succeeded by a frame of wicker, covered with hides, a sort of vessel used by the Iberians,[d] Veneti, &c. They were also used by the British tribes in the most early ages, from whom Cæsar learned their manner of construction, and by this means

[b] Campbell's History of the Admirals.   [c] Lib. xvi. 40.
[d] Strabo. Virgil.

conveyed his army across the river Sicoris. Lucan, referring to this circumstance, describes them

> "The bending willow into barks they twine,
> Then line the work with spoils of slaughtered kine:
> Such are the floats Venetian fishers know,
> Where in dull marshes stands the settling Po;
> On such to neighbouring Gaul, allur'd by gain,
> The bolder Britons cross the swelling main."[n]

The Saxons, also, we learn from Sidonius Appollinaris, crossed to Britain in these apparently frail barks, in which our ancestors fearlessly ventured on the most stormy seas. The Britons went a distance of six days' sail in them to Mictis, when pursuing the trade in tin. Saints Dubslane, Machecu, and Manslunum, left Ireland in one, and after having been seven days at sea, they landed in Cornwall, a very fortunate voyage, considering that they took neither oars nor sails with them.[o] Saint Cormac also made a voyage from Orkney to Iona, in a similar vessel, but he appears to have had less faith than the others, for he provided himself with oars.[p] Wicker boats continued in use by the inhabitants of Scotland, Ireland, and Wales long after they were able to construct vessels of stronger materials. Dr. Mac Pherson says it was not above thirty years since such a boat was employed in the Isle of Sky. In some parts of Ireland they are still to be found, and in Wales they are more common. One Robert Leeth, who made a survey of Ireland, in 1572, states, in his expenses, "item for a lethere boat, with three men and a gyde, to serche the said greate ryvere of Mayore."[q]

The Gaëlic name for this boat is curach—in Cumraëg, it is called cwm, and corracle. The Spanish curo, applied to small vessels used on rivers, is evidently a relic of the

[n] Lib. iv. v. 130.   [o] Marianus Scotus.
[p] Adomnan.   [q] MS. in Brit. Mus.

primitive language. In this wide spread tongue, barc, which Pelletier acknowledges to be genuine Celtic,[r] is a general name for shipping, and is to be found, with little alteration, in most European languages. In the English, Armoric, French, German, Swedish, and Danish, the sound is similar—the Dutch have boork, and the Spanish have barca.

The curachs must have been strongly built, and often of a large size: there is a tradition that the one in which Columba made his voyages was forty feet in length, but from its dimensions preserved in an earthen mound at Iona, it appears to have been sixty-four feet. The curach, in which the above three holy men performed their voyage, was composed of 3½ ox hides.[s] One of the heroes of Morven, in Dr. Smith's Gallic Antiquities,[*] says, "my father wove a barc of the branches of trees." It is well known that the British tribes excelled in the formation of wicker work. The modern corracles in Carmarthenshire are only five feet and a half long, by four broad, forming an oval shape.[t] The hides are pitched, and they are furnished with a seat, the men being accustomed to paddle with one hand, and fish with the other; they are so small and slight, that, when brought ashore, the owners carry them home on their backs.

It appears from Eumenius and Cæsar, that, on the descent of the latter, the South Britons had not one vessel of war,[u] their shipping consisting solely, according to antiquaries, of the small skin covered boats, the reason of which appears to be that their navy was lost in the defeat of the Veneti, to whose assistance it had been sent; and to

---

[r] Dict. de la Langue Bretonne.   [s] Mathæus Westmon.
[*] These "Antiquities" are now looked upon by Celtic scholars with a suspicion closely akin to that which "Ossian" himself is regarded. Ed.
[t] Tour in Wales, 1775.   [u] Paneg. ii. Huet du Commerce.

encourage the subdued tribes to improve their navy, the Romans held out considerable advantages. Certain rewards were offered to those who would fit out vessels capable of containing 10,000 modii of corn.[x] Although it is, perhaps, impossible to ascertain when the Britons acquired the art of building vessels of timber, it must have been known very anciently. The Caledonians had certainly numerous fleets in distant ages, and it is evident that they were not all curachs. The long and perilous voyages which they made to Scandinavia and other parts, are celebrated in bardic lore. Their skill and dexterity in working their vessels, and the intrepidity with which they encountered the storms of a Northern ocean, are celebrated in a description so striking, that it is to be regretted the translator of Ossian did not meet with the poem. Those adventurous warriors, like the Ligurians described by Diodorus, made long voyages in their skiffs, daring the most tempestuous seas, and guiding their course by the reul;[y] yet some of their vessels must have been stoutly built, and of a goodly size. The Gaëlic biorlin, the term for a ship or boat, is said, by some etymologists, learned in that language, to signify the deep or still water log, showing its original application to a rude float; but it appears, with much more reason, to be a corruption of barlin, the top of the waters, and in some parts the word is still so pronounced.[*] We know less of the form of these ships, and the manner in which they were built, than of those used by some nations

---

[x] Cod. Theod. v. 1. 13. Campbell, in his Naval History, however, says, the Romans confined themselves to the use of the curach.

[y] Guiding star, from ruith, course, and iul, star.

[*] *Biorlinn* or *birlinn* has nothing to do with *burlinn* or *bairlinn*, except that the final syllable is common to both words.

Bior is anything sharp-pointed of wood; *linn* or *linne* is the sea or sea-pool. *Birlinn* then is the sharp-pointed wood of the sea, *i.e.*, a boat. ED.

on the continent, a description of which may not be uninteresting or unconnected with the subject. The ships of the Suiones were so built, that either end became the prow as circumstances might require, and they were consequently impelled in any direction without the trouble of being put about. They had no sails, and the oars were not fixed, but the rowers plied in all parts of the ship, changing their position from place to place as they were led to alter their course.[p] The Veneti, we learn from Cæsar, had a great navy, and excelled in nautical science; their ships, with which the Roman fleet had an engagement, this accomplished writer considered superior to his own galleys. They were entirely formed of oak, very strongly put together, their bottoms were flat for the purpose of clearing shallows, and the prow and stern were high to resist the waves. The benches of the rowers were a foot in width, and were fixed with inch-thick iron bolts. The cables were of iron chain, and the sails were of skins and of soft leather.[q] The Gauls, in general, however, manufactured canvas for sails.[r] Stones, sand-bags, &c., were first used for anchors; they were afterwards made of wood, and the invention of the double fluc is ascribed to Anacharsis, the celebrated Scyth.[s] From the figures on ancient monuments in the West Isles, and a sculpture at Iona, the prow and stern of the Caledonian ships were equally high. A single mast placed midship sustained a square sail, as represented in the vignette at the commencement of this chapter,[t] and the flag was borne on a mast fixed at the prow.

[p] Tac. de Mor. Germ.   [q] Bello Gall. iii. 8, 13.
[r] Vol. i. p. 268. Some of the vessels on the Po had sails of rushes.—Pliny. The Spaniards made cables and other tackling of genista, or broom.—Ibid. xix. 2.
[s] Beloe on Herod.
[t] The distant vessel is modern, but the anachronism will be pardoned.

The cordage was formed of thongs. There were anciently a number of galleys, of twenty oars, in the Hebrides, the service for many lands being to provide and maintain a certain number; hence the longfad, or lymphad, in the arms of the Campbells and others. In the twelfth century, Somerled's fleet amounted to fifty-three sail, but they were afterwards augmented to 160, which enabled him to shake off the Danish yoke, and contend with Malcolm IV.

Hailes relates, on the authority of Mathew of Westminster, that, in 1249, a large vessel was built at Inverness. The ship that was discovered in the ancient bed of the river Rother, and exhibited in London some years ago, is believed to have been one of those used by the Saxon rovers. This singular hulk was clinker-built, long and narrow, in the form of a barge or canal boat, and was caulked with a vegetable substance said to be moss. We find that the people of Picardy bruised certain reeds, with which they filled the seams of their vessels, and for this purpose it had no equal."

In a manuscript account of Dumfriesshire, written more than a century ago, is an account of a ship, or part of one, dug up at Stranraer, in a place to which the tide had long ceased to flow; nay, the remains lay under a spot of ground that, from time immemorial, had been a cabbage-garden. In this instance, the planks were fastened with copper nails, in a manner very different from that in use now, or at the period of the discovery." As the greater part of this vessel, which appears to have been of a considerable size, remains undisturbed, it is to be hoped that an opportunity may hereafter occur of making more accurate observations.

---

u Pliny, xvi. 36.

v Trans. of the Society of Antiquaries of Scotland, 1828, p. 52.

As there was an incentive to battle among the Highlanders, there was also an incentive to seamen, or stimulating address to the crews of the Biorlins.* One of these curious poems, the composition of Alexander Mac Donald, and recited to animate the crew of the *Lord* of Clan Ronald, is a work of considerable merit, and an analysis and a few quotations, for which I am indebted to a literary friend, whose favours I have before had to acknowledge, will show its character.

It commences with a benediction thus:—"Now the ship of Clan Ronald is launched, I fervently implore God's blessing upon her, on the chief, and on his crew; a crew unmatched in bravery and courage: And, O God! render thou the breath of the sky propitious, that it may urge us over the waters uninjured to a safe haven. Almighty Father, who hast, by thy word, called forth from nought the ocean and the winds, bless our lank bark, and our stout heroes all, and take them under thy protecting power. Do thou, O Son! bless our anchor, our sails, our shrouds, and our helm, our tackling, yard, blocks, and mast, and be our pilot o'er the waves! Our stays and haulyards keep sound. Preserve us from all dangers free. Let the Holy Ghost be around us, who knows every harbour under the sun. We submit ourselves to his protection."

The benediction on their arms then follows:—"May God bless our swords—our keen, blue, Spanish blades, our heavy coats of mail, proof against the soft edge of an ill-tempered weapon, our cuirasses and bossy shields. Bless all our armour, offensive and defensive; the bows of bright and polished yew, that we bravely bend in the strife; our birchin arrows, that will not splinter, and the badger's

---

* Called Prosnachadh fairge.

rough spoil that contains them; and whatever other warlike stores are now on board of Mac Donald's bark."[x]

Addressing the crew, the bard says:—"Be not deterred by womanish softness from acting like the hardy and the bold. As long as the sides of our biorlin are unrent, as long as four boards of her keep together, as long as she can swim under your feet, be not appalled by the angry ocean. The pride of the sea will submit to the brave. If thy foe on land finds thy courage increase with thy danger, he will the more readily yield. 'Tis even so with the great deep; its fury will yield to the efforts of the fearless and the bold."

Address to the Rowers, or the Prosnachadh Uimrai:— "That you may urge on the long, dark, brown vessel, man the tough, long, polished oars; keep time, strike quick, and deeply wound the heaving billows, and make the surges fly like sparkling showers of living flame. Send her, swift as an eagle, o'er the deep vales and mountains of the sea. O, stretch, bend, and pull the straight sons of the forest! And see how the stout conquerors of the ocean bend their muscular forms like one man! Behold their hairy, sinewy arms! See how they twist their oars in the bosom of the deep! Now the pilot's song inspires them with fresh vigour —see how they urge the swift courser of the ocean, snorting o'er the fluid plain! Lo! how her prow cuts the roaring

---

[x] The Gaëlic liturgy, composed by John Kerswell, afterwards Bishop of Argyle, 1566, contains the form of blessing a ship when going to sea. The steersman says, "Let us bless our ship," the crew responding "God, the Father, bless her!" Repeating his request, they rejoin, "Jesus Christ bless her!" and, to the same observation, the third time, "The Holy Ghost bless her!" The steersman then asks them what they fear, if God, the Father, be with them, &c.; to which they reply, "We do not fear anything." They did not, however, altogether rely on the assistance of the Trinity, for they were careful to suspend a he-goat from the mast, to insure a favourable wind.

waves! Her strong sides creak amidst the dark heaving deep, while the sons of the forest, wielded by the strong arms of the crew, impel her against the storm. These are the fearless, unwearied, unbending rowers, whose oars can shut the very throat of the whirlpool."ʸ

As soon as the sixteen rowers were seated at their oars, and ready to row the vessel into the fair wind, Callum Garbh, Mac Ronald of the ocean, the fore oar's man, sung the Ioram, which consists of fifteen stanzas.

Having got into the fair wind, they hoist their sails, and Clan Ronald orders his officers to appoint every man to his station, the bard addressing each separately respecting his particular duty, in which great nautical knowledge is displayed. The steersman is first addressed; next the man who manages the main sheet, then he at the jib sheet, then the pilot, then a person who is called Fear Calpa na Tairne, then the describer of the waters, or the man on the outlook, and next the thrower out of the water. There were also two who assisted in a storm or when needful, and four who were in reserve, lest any of the others should be disabled, or, as the bard expresses it, "lest the sea in its fury should pull any of them overboard."

Everything being now prepared, and every man at his post, they set sail at sunrise from Lochainart, in South Uist, on St. Bridget's day, and the voyage, which proved rough, is described in the most picturesque and poetic strains. They had scarcely "stretched the well-shaped yards to the tall masts of sound red pine, and fastened the sails and rigging through loops of iron," than a storm arose, and "the awful world of waters drew on its rough mantle of thick darkness, swelling into mountains, and sinking into glens; the dreadful monsters of the deep ex-

---

ʸ Probably alluding to the Coire bhreacain, a remarkable whirlpool between the Isles of Jurah and Scarba.

press their terror by their terrible bellowing and roaring. By the agitation of the waters, and by the blows of our sharp prow, their brains are scattered on every wave—the sea is red with the gore of its inhabitants, and our ship is damaged by coming in contact with the monsters of the ocean. 'Twas deafening and maddening to listen to the roaring of the monsters, and the awful voice of the demons of the deep." As night approached, the storm increased, accompanied by thunder and lightning, "until the ocean beheld our invincible spirit with admiration, and hushed his fury into peace. But there was not a mast unbent, yard unsnapped, or sail unrent. Half her planks were sprung, and all her carcase was loosened, and groaned with distress. It was at the cross of the Strait of Isla, that the ocean made peace with us, and dismissed this host of winds to the upper regions of the air, leaving the waters smooth as a polished mirror. We returned thanks to the King of Kings for having delivered the good Clan Ronald from the fearful death that had threatened him. We then laid her mast along the deck, and stretched out on each side the smooth polished oars, made from the good red pine, cut by Mac Varas, in the Isle of Funen.* We rowed with strong arms, as if one man moved all the oars, until we came to port near Carric Fergus. We cast anchor, took food, and the cup went unsparingly round, before we laid ourselves down for rest.†

The art of ship building was brought to great perfection in Scotland, and this subject may be concluded with an account of a ship of a remarkably large size, built by King James IV., which consumed so much timber, that she

---

* The Island of *St. Finan* in Lochsheil.

† Mac Donald's very fine poem of "The blessing of Clan Ranald's Birlinn" has been very fairly translated into English verse by Pattison. Professor Blackie has also attempted it with some success. Ed.

is said to have wasted the woods of Fife. This vessel was one hundred and twenty feet long, and thirty-six feet wide within the sides, which are said to have been no less than ten feet thick! "This great ship cumbered Scotland to get her to sea." She was provided with 300 mariners, 120 artillerymen, and 1000 men of war, and cost £30,000, " If any man," says Pitscottie, " believe that this description be not of verity, let him pass to the gate of Tillibardine, and there afore the same, ye will see the length and breadth of her, planted with hawthorn by the wright who helped to make her."*

Before the precious metals are adopted as the medium of exchange, commercial transactions are simply the barter of different commodities. Cattle is the property which most uncivilized people possess, and which they can part with to others, and it consequently becomes a standard of value among primitive nations. The armour of Diomede, Homer tells us, cost only nine oxen, while that of Glaucus cost a hundred. From this commodity, which regulated the traffic and indicated the wealth of the Celts until a late period, is derived the name which the Romans gave to their coined money. Pecunia is deduced by Varro from pecus, a flock, pointing to the time when domestic animals were the only means by which all other necessaries were procured. The inconvenience of this sort of traffic becoming much felt on the advance of civilization, it naturally led to the adoption of precious metal, as a more convenient article to exchange for whatever might be wanted. Gold, silver, brass, and iron, are therefore adopted as money, and are bought and sold in a state of roughness, by weight. The system of trading by the exchange of commodities may, however, continue long among a rude people. The inhabitants

---

* Chronicles, p. 108, fol. ed.

of the Silures, or rather Cassiterides, we are told, adhered to their old customs, and refused to buy or sell for money, continuing the primitive method of exchange. It was for the convenience of this trade of barter that fairs were anciently instituted. In Ireland they were denominated aonachs, and one was held near Wexford, much celebrated by the native historians, who assert its existence in an era of improbable antiquity. In that country, and in Scotland, the want of coined money long rendered an exchange of goods the only means of supplying reciprocal wants.

Tacitus, speaking of the Germans, says, silver and gold the gods had denied them, whether in mercy or wrath he could not venture to say. They formerly disregarded these metals, although they had silver vessels, but when he wrote, the Romans having made them acquainted with its use and value, they had learned to receive money. Tacitus informs us, that those on the frontiers of Germany placed most value on coins that bore the impress of a chariot with two horses.

"In Britain, I hear," says Cicero, writing to Trebatius, "is neither gold nor silver." Iron appears to have been so scarce and valuable, that it was adopted for money, and passed by weight. With this and copper, the subdued tribes paid the imposts which the Romans exacted.[a] The iron money of the Britons was in the form of rings,[b] but the description has not enabled antiquaries to agree concerning their precise shape and size. In Oudendorp's edition of Cæsar's works,[c] it is supposed that they resembled the money of the Chinese, who perforate their coin for the convenience of carrying them on a string, as here represented;

[a] Huet, Hist. du Commerce, p. 204.
[b] Cæsar. Herodian.
[c] Vol. i. p. 224, ed. 1737.

but quantities, amounting to some horse loads of iron pieces, of the other form, have been found in Cornwall, that very probably once passed for coin.[d] In a barrow that was opened in the parish of Kirk-patrick-fleming, in Dumfriesshire, a stone chest was discovered, which contained an urn and several iron rings, about the size of a half-crown, and much corroded. Those singular articles, called Kimmeridge coal money, are believed to have been used in place of coin. It is not improbable that their appearance would lead to the conclusion that they were rather employed in some game, the indentations with which they are marked varying in number. At all events they are not perforated like the ring money.[e][*]

The rudest of the Britons soon acquired a knowledge of the value of more precious metals than iron. In 198 we find Lupus purchasing peace of the Meatæ, by paying them a large sum of money, and long before this time it would appear coins and medals, composed of tin and lead, rudely formed, were current among the Southern tribes. The coins of the Britons bear the impression of the heads of their princes, with various figures on the reverse, either symbolical, or representing articles, the uses of which are now unknown; but the figure of a horse, the mystical symbol of Ceredwen or Ceres, as here shewn, is frequently introduced.

[d] Lhuyd, in a Letter to Mr. Tomkins.

[e] The opening of the Deveril Barrow by Mr. Miles, contains some observations on these articles.

[*] The so-called coal money of Kimmeridge Bay in Dorsetshire is now supposed to have been models or moulds in an early Phœnician pottery work in the Isle of Purbeck, and on the opposite mainland. ED.

The British coins usually present the inscription Tascio, concerning which there has been so much conjecture. It has, with much appearance of reason, been said to be the native appellation of the nobles, being the same as the Gaëlic toshich, which signifies chief, and hence it meant no more than the Rex of modern coin. It is to be noticed, however, that tasgaidh, in Gaëlic, is the treasury, and taisg. is to hoard or treasure up; hence Dr. Pettingall thinks it signified the tascia, the tax or tribute paid to the Romans, who, on their establishment, prohibited the native princes from coining. In this opinion he seems borne out by others, who trace tax from task, and that from tasgia; but Pegge[f] believes it is the name of the Mint-master, who was a Gaul.

It is observable that "not any coin bearing the head of a Welsh prince, or which can in any respect be supposed to have issued from the mint of a prince of that country, is known to be extant."[g] Ceiniog, or denarios, is the only coin that has a name in Welsh.[h] The Gaëlic bonn is applied to coin, and signifies anything round, and of a portable size, whence probably the English bun. The Caledonians had no coins for nearly 1000 years after Cæsar.[i] The Irish appear long to have remained destitute of money. Campion says there was no coin in any great lord's house. The ancient money of Man was formed of leather.

Of the commerce of the Celts, and of the state of the arts, both necessary and ornamental, it is proper in this place to take notice. The spirit of enterprise which this people displayed, when, after their subjugation to the Romans, their manners became altered, and their mercantile advantages were discovered, was no less remarkable than

[f] On the coins of Cunobeline.
[g] Introduction to the Beauties of England and Wales, p. 313.
[h] Robarts' Early History of the Cumri.   [i] Dr. Mac Pherson.

their warlike propensities. Cæsar bears testimony to the industry of the Gauls, their ingenuity and success in imitating anything manufactured by others; and Diodorus, who praises the diligence of the women in their household matters and attention to their personal appearance, extols the acute understanding and aptitude to learn, so conspicuous in the race. They supplied their conquerors with various articles, which were found both useful and ornamental in the refined society of Italy; and the Romans, who never hesitated to copy the barbarians in anything really worthy of imitation, derived from the Gauls the knowledge of many useful inventions. The policy of the Romans, however, appears from Tacitus to have restricted the advantages of commerce to the Hermandures, and the stern Nervians prohibited the pursuit altogether, from an apprehension that it was subversive of their pristine valour and hardihood, and inimical to their independence.

The Celts were reputed very affluent,[j] and their riches consisted of gold and cattle, articles easily moved about.[k] There were no silver, but numerous gold mines in Gaul, and this precious metal was often found without the labour of mining, being washed down by the rivers. It was so plentiful, that both sexes covered themselves with ornaments of it—rings on their fingers, bracelets on their arms and wrists, massy chains, pure and beaten, about their necks, and heavy croslets upon their breasts.[l] The better sort were accustomed to scatter great quantities of gold in their temples and sacred places, on which no one ever laid a sacrilegious hand, except the Romans, to whom it is said the riches of these fanes offered the great temptation for hostilities. When Claudius Cæsar rode triumph for the

[j] Tacitus' Annuals. Agrippa asks the Jews if they were "richer than the Gauls."

[k] Polybius, ii.   [l] Diodorus.

conquest of Britain, he had with him a crown of gold weighing nine pounds, presented by Gallia comata.[m] Spain paid annually 20,000 pounds of gold, and one mine yielded of silver 100,000 pounds yearly.[n]

The above enumeration of ornaments shows that the Celts not only possessed the precious metals in abundance, but were excellent artificers. The gold, whether procured from the rivers or by mining, in which the Aquitani were particularly skilful,[o] was melted in a furnace, and subjected to the process of refining, and the articles fabricated were finished with great care and ingenuity.

The prevailing use of brass in the formation of weapons of war has been noticed. This metal is sooner discovered and easier wrought than iron, and in ancient times it was more valuable than gold. It was a favourite metal with the Celts, and was held in particular esteem by the Pythagoreans, a sect whose doctrines were analogous to those of the Druids. The ancients appear to have been in possession of a method of indurating brass by a process now unknown, their alloy being found different from that which is at present used. Aristotle assigns to Lydus, the Scyth, the invention of the art of melting and tempering brass.[p] The Britons imported this metal, and in smelting it they used a considerable quantity of lead. In Ireland some weapons were found formed of brass, containing a proportion of gold. Copper, in its pure state, was also a metal in much esteem by the Celts, and was particularly abundant in Aquitain.

Lead was procured with difficulty from the mines of Gaul and Iberia, but was easily found in Britain, where it was indeed so abundant, that there was an express law among the natives, prohibiting more than a certain quantity from being dug up.

[m] Pliny, xxxiii. 3.   [n] Gibbon, i. c, 7.   [o] Bello Gall. iii. 22.
[p] Pliny, vii. 56.

Britain, says Strabo and others, produces corn, cattle, gold, silver, and iron; besides which were exported wicker work, copper, tin, lime, pearls, skins, slaves, and dogs, excelling all others, and much used by the Gauls in war. The Romans, we are told, laid no heavy duties on British exports or imports. In Strabo's time they made more of the customs, small as they were, than they could raise by the exaction of tribute.

Tin is the metal for the production of which ancient Britain is most celebrated. It is erroneously supposed that no other country then produced this metal, an opinion which in the second Chapter of the preceding volume has been proved untenable. It is remarkable that Polybius, speaking of the Spanish tin, and alluding to Britain in the same sentence, says nothing of this metal, for which it is said to have acquired so much celebrity. The Britons, according to Diodorus, dug the tin in the promontory of Balerium, or Cornwall, and melted and refined it with much care and labour. They beat it into square pieces, like a die, and carried it in carts to an island called Ictis, which was only insulated at high water; whence the merchants, by whom it was bought, transported it to Gaul in boats covered with skins, and carried it on horses' backs to the Rhone, a distance of thirty days' journey.

The Briton, like his continental ancestor, was no doubt long unacquainted with the art of working metals, the knowledge of which is forced on barbarians by the necessity of fabricating arms for their protection; but it may be presumed that instruments of stone continued in occasional use among the Celts after the discovery of so useful an art as forging brass or iron, and until these materials became sufficiently plentiful to admit of general adoption. Arms of brass or copper were more easily formed than those of iron, of which besides the Britons had but little. The uses of this metal, and the art of rendering it malleable, are not easily discovered, and it is believed that it was only a short time previous to the first arrival of the Romans that mines of iron ore had been opened and imperfectly worked, on a very limited scale.

That the ancient Caledonians were acquainted with the manufacture of iron appears from the testimony of historians. "The hundred hammers of the furnace" are alluded to in a Bardic composition, and a simile is drawn from the art—"Fire pours from contending arms as a stream of metal from the furnace."° The uniform tradition is, that the Gaël anciently made their own iron, in corroboration of which, heaps of iron dross are found in many places among the mountains that are confidently believed to be the remains of their foundries.ᵖ There is still to be seen in Glenturret a shieling, called Renna Cardich, the smith's dwelling, with the ruins of several houses, and heaps of ashes, with other indications of an iron manufactory. Old poems mention it as a work where the metal, of which swords and other arms were made some miles lower in the valley, was prepared.ᵠ In Sutherland also are distinct marks of the smelting and working of iron with fires of wood.ʳ Peats were the usual fuel, and they are yet in general use. The smith's fire is made of turf, first half burned, and then soaked in water, by which process it is hardened and made sufficiently solid to stand the heat to which it is subjected. In muirs, deep narrow pits are frequently to be seen, where it is said the peats were thus prepared, but the practice at present is to dig holes three or four feet deep, in the form of a bowl or basin, which are filled with peats that are set fire to, and extinguished when sufficiently charred, by being covered with turf. Charred peat is still used in Germany,

---

° Report on the Poems of Ossian, Appendix, p. 245.
ᵖ Agric. Report of Argyle, &c.   ᵠ Newte's Tour.   ʳ Sir Robert Gordon, &c.

and it answers all the purposes of smelting, welding, &c. The Rev. Mr. Macqueen, of Kilmuir, describes, from traditional record, the famed Luno, the son of Leven, who made the swords of Fingal and his heroes, as a wild savage, going on one leg, with a staff in his hand, notwithstanding which he was remarkably fleet, and clad in a mantle of black hide, with an apron of similar materials. He was no inapt personification of Vulcan. Cæsar represents the Gauls as perfectly skilled in the manufacture of iron,* but the Celtiberi must be allowed to carry the palm in this art. Their method of purifying and tempering the iron was by burying it under ground until the weaker and less useful part was consumed by rust, when the remainder was found much improved both in strength and solidity.* Of this they made their weapons, and their swords were celebrated even among the Romans, for they cut so keenly, that neither shield, helmet, nor bone could withstand them. The worth of Spanish blades has been acknowledged in later ages, and they were always preferred by the Highlanders. The plates and chains of iron with which the Caledonians and Picts ornamented themselves, satisfactorily prove their knowledge of the manufacture.

In 1719, a bushel of those implements called celts, each inclosed in a mould, were found at Brough, on the Humber; and at Skirlaugh a large quantity of celts, spear heads, blades, &c., were found, along with several cubes of the same metal, and some masses evidently fitting into the neck of the moulds in which the celts were cast. The whole was wrapped in coarse strong linen, and inclosed in a case of wood.† On Easterly moor, twelve miles north-west of

* Lib. vii. 21.

* It is a fact that if the blade of an ordinary pocket knife is stuck into the ground and allowed to remain there for some time, its temper is greatly improved. ED.

† Poulson's Beverlac, p. 5.

York, in 1735, there were found one hundred celts of copper, with some pieces of rough metal and much cinders. The colony celebrated in Irish history under the name of Danans, carried from Britain a large brass vessel, or cauldron.[u]

It would appear, from some ancient poems, that the Highlanders had metal mirrors.[v] The reader who is curious has been referred to works containing plates and descriptions of the remarkable variety of ornaments in use among the British tribes. The discoveries in Ireland are often so singular, that an antiquary is at a loss to determine the era to which they belong. Articles of solid gold and silver, and of elegant and unique workmanship, are so often found, as to incline us to doubt the truth of those accounts which represent the people as formerly in a state of barbarity. Among other things, crowns of gold are not unusual! These relics are often dug from considerable depths, and it seems impossible either to account for their numbers, or for their deposition in such places. The distractions with which that unhappy island has ever been disturbed, may have induced the petty kings and nobles in their adversity to bury their diadems and other valuables,[w] but still we are surprised at the existence of so many.

The Irish regal crown was called asion from assian, plates, it being composed of folds or ribs. At the Tain bo, an event that occurred eight years before Christ, Maud, the queen of Connaught, rode in an open chariot, four others being at a distance to keep off the crowd, and prevent the dust from staining her golden asion.[x] It was by his dia-

[u] Trans. of Highland Society, i. 334.
[v] Keating. O'Conner. Nen. Brit.
[w] Sir Henry Radcliff writes, in 1576, that on a report that all pewter and brass vessels were to be taken from the Irish, they immediately buried and concealed them. [x] Harris, ed. of Ware.

dem of gold, according to Mariannus Scotus, that Brian Boroimh was discovered after the battle of Clontarf.

Some of the articles which formed the exports of the ancient Britons have been noticed in a preceding page. Insignificant as their commerce may have been, they nevertheless carried on a regular trade with the continent, and the produce of the interior was conveyed in cars along the tractways that extended throughout the island. The fourteenth Triad commemorates Beli as a constructor of roads from the southern shores even to the extremity of Caithness, at the same time affording protection to those found on them.[y] The Watling street, running from Chester to Dover, appears to have been called by the Britons, Gwyddelin sarn, the road of the Irish.[z] The trade of slaves seems to have been common in Britain; but who the miserable beings disposed of were, does not clearly appear, for slavery was unknown among the Celts. Some Gauls are indeed said to have been so fond of Roman wine, that they bartered children for it, and the Germans sold buffoons as slaves,[a] but the bondmen must have been those captured in war. The Irish resorted to Bristol for the purchase of slaves.

The exportation of skins was a branch of commerce in both islands from the most remote times, and it is believed that Scotland was long unable to part with anything else. From the abundance of game great quantities were formerly disposed of; and in Ireland, at the close of the seventeenth century, we find the revenue was chiefly derived from hides.[b]

In the fabrication of many of the articles described, other implements must have been employed. Those formed of

---

[y] Roberts' Early Hist. of the Cumri.   [z] Hoveden, p. 432.
[a] Amm. Mar. xxix.   [b] State of Ireland, 1673.

stone could only have been moulded into shape by patient exertion, but other means must have been employed to bring the metal weapons to an edge. The Celts must have possessed whetstones, not only to sharpen their swords, daggers, spears, scythes, &c., but the razors with which they shaved the lower part of their face. The Romans had long made use, for this purpose, of stones procured from the island of Crete and other places, which could not be used without oil; but about the period of their first visit to Britain, they discovered that the Gauls used a sort which they called passernices, that they were much superior to the others, could be used with water, and were to be procured in Italy. The hones used by the Roman barbers were procured in Hispania citeriore, and required only to be moistened with spittle.[c] British whetstones three inches and upwards in length, some much worn and others apparently unused, have been found in various places. They are often discovered in barrows, and are sometimes accompanied by those implements, in the manufacture of which they were necessary.

The Gauls, who were noted for always having plenty of pots and pans for dressing their meat, invented the art of tinning these utensils and all others formed of brass and appropriated for domestic purposes, and the Bituriges, or people of Bourges, were most celebrated for this work, which was commonly called incoctilia.[d] It is probable that they covered other articles with tin as an ornament. The Romans, who repaid nations for the loss of liberty by the encouragement which their luxury and voluptuousness gave to the exertion of the manufacturer and artisan, could not fail to estimate the value of covering their copper and brazen utensils with a substance so innocuous, nor overlook the

[c] Pliny, xxxvi. 22.   [d] Ibid. xxxiv. 17.

beauty which could, by such a process, be imparted in many different ways. The Gauls, on their part, were not insensible to the advantages to be derived from a prosecution of the art, and began about half a century after Christ, to silver and gild over the harness of horses, and particularly to decorate all kinds of chariots in that way. The people of Alise, a town of the Mundubii, in Burgundy, were the most celebrated artificers in this line, and the Roman extravagance led them, in a very short time, to distribute their ornaments in the most lavish expenditure.

It is curious to find that the Gauls were the inventors of soap. Their solicitude to preserve the yellow colour of their hair, or to deepen its tone, led to the invention of an article used in washing their bodies, composed "ex sevo et cinere." This was much used in Germany, chiefly by the men; it was either solid or liquid, and the best was made of the ashes of beech wood and goat's suet.[e]

The utensils and furniture of the Celtic dwellings were suited to the wants of the hardy inmates, but these articles were not, however, by any means so inartificial as might be supposed. Polybius does not lead us to think very highly of the acquirements of the Gallic nations who lived in Italy, when he says they dwelt in villages without inclosure, and had no furniture, but lay on the ground, living also on flesh, and making no profession but those of war and tillage, their wealth consisting of gold and cattle. That the Celts did not sleep on the ground, but on beds of grass or straw, he elsewhere informs us, and also says they slept on mattresses.[f] In this he is borne out by other authors, who affirm that they were the inventors of flock beds, a manufacture which they taught the Romans. They were usually made from the refuse of the wool after dyeing; a superior

[e] Pliny, xxviii. 12.   [f] Lib. xi.

sort was formed of the Cadurcian flax, but all the different kinds retained their original Celtic names.ᵍ

The Britons spread the skins which they wore during the day, under them at night, and this practice of sleeping on skins continued until very lately among the common people of Germany.ʰ The Celtiberians made their mattresses of the herb genista, a sort of broom, peculiar to that country.

The Highland practice of sleeping on heath nicely put together on the ground, with the green tops uppermost, was reckoned very conducive to health. Reposing on a bed of this sort, " restored the strength of the sinews troubled before, and that so evidently, that they who at evening go to rest sore and weary, rise in the morning whole and able." The Gaël, to whom it was matter of indifference whether they reposed on the heath as it grew on the hill, or stretched on it when prepared in their cottage, were so strongly prejudiced against anything tending to effeminacy, that, according to the chronicle from which the preceding quotation is made, " if they travelled to any other country they rejected the feather beds and bedding of their host, wrapping themselves in their own plaids, and so taking their rest, careful indeed lest that barbarous delicacy of the mainland, as they term it, should corrupt their natural and country hardness." The heather bed was certainly well adapted for the camp, both from the expedition with which it could be prepared, and the excellence of the materials. Sir John Dalrymple remarks, that this mode of preparing their beds, was " an art which, as the beds were both soft and dry, preserved their health in the field when other soldiers lost theirs."ⁱ The Highlanders naturally viewed the introduction of luxury and refinement as calcu-

---

ᵍ Pliny, xix. i.   ʰ Cluverius.   ⁱ Memoirs of Great Britain, pt. ii. p. 53.

lated to sap their independence, and they were not long in observing that the members of the Freiceadan dubh, or black watch, became less hardy than their other countrymen. Whatever may be said as to the ultimate advantage of *civilizing* the Highlanders, it must be allowed that the old chiefs acted wisely in discouraging the premature introduction of conveniences and improvements, the want of which was not felt, and the adoption of which could only be partial. The inconsiderate countenance of innovation could only produce discomfort and dissatisfaction throughout the Highlands. "The happiness of Highlanders," says Sacheveral, the historian of Man, "consists not in having much, but in coveting little." Simplicity of life was not confined to the vassals, but extended to the houses and tables of the greatest chiefs, who equalled their retainers in manly qualifications and hardiness of frame. O'Neal, who vaunted that he would rather be O'Neal of Ulster than Philip of Spain, sat on a green bank under a bush in his greatest majesty.[j]

Adverting to the ancient Celts, Pausanias bears a reluctant testimony to their ingenuity, and the avowal of a Greek can be easily appreciated. Brennus, says he, was not unskilled in the art of war, but, for a barbarian, sufficiently acute, and he tells us that his troops constructed bridges over the rivers, compelling the nearest inhabitants to rebuild them, when they were destroyed by the Greeks.[k] The Gauls appear to have made greater progress in civilization than the Germans, who longer retained their stern and unyielding dispositions. Tacitus dwells with pleasure on the docility and capacity of the Britons, who so cheerfully received the instructions and followed the precepts of his father-in-law, who did not hesitate to declare them superior in intellectual ability to the continental Celts.

[j] Riche, p. 9.   [k] Lib. x. c. 20.

The Briton was, no doubt, at one time in a state of cheerless barbarism, ignorant of the arts of the first necessity; but his natural ingenuity enabled him rapidly to attain a state of comparative civilization and comfort, not only providing for his own wants, but exporting his surplus productions to other nations. Their abilities recommended them to the Emperor Constantius, who, in 296, carried a great number of British artificers to the continent, where they were employed to adorn his favourite city Autun.[1]

The art of the potter must be known to a people occupied in pasturage, who require vessels to contain the milk of their flocks; but although the ancient Britons were not unacquainted with the manufacture, but certainly made urns and other vessels of forms not inelegant, and ornamented sometimes with considerable taste, they appear to have been unable to supply themselves without other assistance; earthenware being one of the commodities they received in their barter with others. Perhaps those vessels imported were superior to the native workmanship—the sepulchres disclose many varieties of urns and other vases. Adomnan says the Picts used vessels of glass for drinking, and it is recorded of St. Patrick that he used a chalice of this material. We also find that Rederch, king of Strathclyde, possessed gold, precious stones, &c., and a cup made by Guielandus, of the town of Sigenius. Turgot says of Queen Margaret that she caused the king, Malcolm, in 1093, to be served in dishes silvered and gilt. The ingeniously-formed and prettily-ornamented wooden and horn vessels of the Gaël have been noticed in a preceding page.

Saguntum, in Spain, was famous for the manufacture of earthenware cups,[m] but Gauls, Lusitanians, and Celtiberians were accustomed to use vessels of wax.[n] The Celts some-

[1] Eumenius Peneg. viii.   [m] Pliny, xxxv. 12.   [n] Strabo, p. 107.

times used cups made of the skulls of their enemies, and ornamented with gold.º The Scyths were also accustomed to use these cups, and among the Isedones it was the skulls of their relations that were so appropriated. The old Irish are accused of a similar practice, but there may be a misapprehension of the term, for skull was formerly applied to a drinking cup.ᵖ It seems originally to have signified any capacious vessel, and is, in the present day, applied by the fishermen in the north to a sort of basket. The Thracians used wooden platters and cups of the same materials, and also of horn, according to the manner of the Getes.ᵠ In Gaul there were a sort of vases for travellers to carry their wine, made of yew tree, which, in Pliny's time, had lost their repute from the poisonous nature of the wood, by which some had lost their lives.ʳ

The Britons had some vessels of amber, and it was believed by the ancients that it distilled from the trees in Great Britain.ˢ This curious substance, which was called glessum,ᵗ was gathered in the territories of the Suevi, who were the only people who dealt in it, and who carried on a considerable trade in it, taking it by the way of Pannonia to Rome. The women in the villages around the Po wore collars of it, as a preventative of the goitre.ᵘ Lapis specularis was originally found in Celtiberia, and formed an article of export to Rome.ᵛ It appears to have been the glass of the ancients, and different from Mica.ʷ

The British pearls were anciently very famous. The hope of obtaining a rich booty of them is said to have been a chief motive for the Roman invasion, and when Cæsar

---

º Silius, xiii. v. 482. Livy.
ᵖ Jamieson's Scots' Etymol. Dictionary.   ᵠ Diod. Fragmenta, xxi. § 4.
ʳ Lib. xvi. c. 10.   ˢ Sotacus, in Pliny, xxxvii. 2.
ᵗ Pliny, xxxvii. 3. The Scyths called it searium, as one would say, "ecoulement du pays des sacs."—Note on ditto, xii. 202, ed. 1783.
ᵘ Pliny ut sup.   ᵛ Ibid. xlvi. 22.
ʷ Note on Pliny, xii. p. 76, ed. 1782.

returned to Rome, he dedicated a military ornament, embellished with British pearls, to Venus. Tacitus and Marcellinus, however, do not speak highly of their value. Pearls are found in many rivers in Scotland, but they are said to be more rare than formerly. In 1120, Nicholas, an English ecclesiastic writing to the Bishop of St. Andrews, begs a number of pearls, particularly four large ones, and if the Bishop had them not, he requests him to procure them from the king, who had, he knew, an abundant store.[x] Sir Thomas Menzies, of Cults, procured a famous pearl in the water of Kellie, in Aberdeenshire, which, having been informed was of great value, he went to London and presented it to the king, who rewarded him with twelve chaldrons of grain and the customs of Aberdeen for life.[y]*

The Gauls formed precious stones into ornaments for their persons, and even sometimes employed them for hatchets and other implements. They were soon taught by their conquerors the value of such articles, and when they discovered how advantageously they could dispose of such articles, they established a prosperous trade, and began to impose on their credulous customers many articles of little value as wonderful productions.[z] The old Highlanders set precious stones in their rings,[a] and, in treating of their costume, many of their other ornaments have been noticed. The most ingenious and beautiful article that has, perhaps, ever been discovered in these islands, is that supposed to have been the handle of a dagger, richly embellished with innumerable minute gold pins, described and engraved in Sir Richard Hoare's splendid work on ancient Wiltshire.

[x] Hailes's Annals, i. 58.
[y] Survey of the city of Aberdeen, 1685. This pearl was reported to have been placed in the crown.
* Pearls of considerable value are still found in the large fresh water mussels of many of our Scottish rivers. ED.
[z] Pliny, xxxvii. 11. [a] D. Smith, in Trans. High. Soc. i. 340.

That the Celts, and particularly the Britons, were able to construct very ingenious works in carpentry, is evinced by their chariots and agricultural implements. On some of the coins of Cunobeline, struck between the first and second Roman invasion, seats or chairs, with backs, four feet, &c., are distinctly represented. The Irish are said to have been anciently much celebrated for their skill in working of wood, great quantities of which they exported.

The Celtic artisans were hereditary, like all other professions. Much has been said in favour of and against this system; if it is calculated to prevent improvement, which is not apparent, it must be remembered that Celtic civilization was long stationary, and there was no stimulus to invention. An Englishman was astonished to find that every employment passed by descent, not excepting the Rhimer. "Every profession," says Riche of the Irish, "hath his particular decorum—their virtue is, they will do nothing but what their fathers have done before them." The case was the same with the Scotish Gaël.

The Britons were particularly ingenious in the manufacture of osier utensils, or basket work, which they executed so neatly, that it became an article in much demand at Rome, to which large quantities were exported. In a Gaulish monument, discovered in Blois, in 1710, a female figure is seated in a chair of wicker or straw plaited,[e] with a high back, similar to those I have seen for sale in Dublin.

The Highlanders are naturally ingenious, and of a mechanical turn of mind. It has been stated that they make their own agricultural and other implements; they also carry their simple but useful manufactures to fairs for sale, by which they are able to procure those articles which their own country does not produce. Besides the exportation of cattle and wool, with much kelp, the manufacture of which

[e] Montf. x. pl. 136.

is a late introduction, hames of hair, and sometimes of twisted thongs of raw hides, brakings, and collars for horses and oxen, made of straw, waights, caises, sumacs or fleats, &c.; sacks formed of skin, tartan cloth, kersey, blankets, carpets, and woollen yarn, and the produce of their dairy, are all disposed of, and carried occasionally in some quantities out of the country. The short wood in the glens is worked into various useful articles, and disposed of in the low country. In the month of August there is a timber market held in Aberdeen for several days, which is of ancient origin, and to which the Highlanders bring ladders, harrows, tubs, pails, and many other articles; those who have nothing else, bringing rods of hazel and other young wood, with sackfuls of aitnach or juniper and other mountain berries. There is a market somewhat similar in Edinburgh. It seems with reference to this, that a proclamation, 11th of August, 1564, commands that in Aberdeen, Banff, Elgin, Inverness, Forres, and Nairn, " nane sell timber but in open market."

The wooden locks of the Highlanders are so ingeniously contrived by notches, made at unequal distances, that it is impossible to open them but with the wooden key that belongs to them.

In the former volume, when treating of costume, the abilities of the Highland dyers and weavers were noticed with some attention, and several of the excellent colouring substances produced in the country were enumerated. It is matter of much regret that the adaptation of the Highlands for the establishment and successful pursuit of manufactures is so unaccountably overlooked, for it is evident that they could be carried on to much national advantage. The Scotish mountains afford an abundant supply of various articles, capable of imparting the most beautiful dyes, and which can be procured without trouble, and at the least possible expense. A command of water for any machinery is in most places at all times to be found, and the cheapness of living would keep wages very low. It is surprising that Highland proprietors have paid so little attention to so obvious a means of enriching themselves. With how much advantage could the carpet manufacture, for instance, be carried on, where the wool is always at hand, as well as the materials for dyeing it. Mr. Cuthbert Gordon, before mentioned, declared that he had made a discovery which would lead to the incalculable benefit of Scotland, but as he unfortunately did not meet with sufficient encouragement to mature his plans, which I believe related to dye stuffs, the valuable secret was never communicated to his countrymen. There can be no doubt but that the Highland weavers, who indeed, as it is, occasionally make carpets of great beauty of design and goodness of fabric, if properly encouraged, would soon rival, if not much surpass, the manufacturers of Kidderminster.

The vessels represented underneath are selected from various discoveries, as specimens of the earthenware manufactures of the ancient Celtic tribes of Britain, and must be allowed to be not altogether deficient either in beauty of form or ornament. That in the centre is the most usual form of the funereal urn.

FUNERAL URNS.

Two Druids.

CHAPTER VI.

POETRY AND MUSIC.

THE estimation in which poetry was held by the ancients is well known. It is the original vehicle in which the knowledge of past events is carried down to posterity, and the medium through which laws are at first promulgated. Legislation and religion are at first intimately connected, and poetry is the excellent auxiliary of both. Hesiod and other Greek poets lived ages before Pherecides, who, according to Pliny, was the first who wrote in prose, and the compositions of Homer were preserved in detached pieces by oral tradition, long before they were collected and embodied in the regular form which they now present.

In the first stages of civilization the characters of priest and legislator are combined, whence arises the connection of poetry with the first institutions of society, for the ministers of religion are both poets and musicians, and the service of their gods and precepts of morality are equally rendered in verse. Before the era of written record, the Greeks preserved their laws in traditionary rhymes, the same word in their language signifying a law and a song.[*] The statutes of this people continued long to remain in oral record, before it was permitted to reduce them to writing. The progress of civilization softened the reluctance, so strong in that enlightened race, especially among the Spartans, to commit to the preservation of letters, the laws which were inculcated in popular verse, but when inscribed on tablets in the public streets, the poetic form was rigidly adhered to.

This veneration for oral record strongly pervaded the Celtic race, and it regulated society among the Gaël of Albin, while their ancient institutions remained entire. The principle does indeed exist to this day in the British kingdom, where the common law of the land is a certain unwritten but recognised code, emanating according to the opinion of the best antiquaries, from the Druidical system of legislation. The well-known practice by which the Recorder of London is obliged to make his report to the King by word of mouth, is, with every appearance of probability, referable to the same institution.

The chief object aimed at in poetic composition being the assistance of recollection, no pains were spared to improve the memory. The Pythagoreans, a sect resembling the Celtic Druids, exercised their memory with the greatest

[*] Walker's Irish Bards, who quotes Wood on the genius of Homer.

care and diligence, the first thing they did in the morning being to call to mind whatever they had done the preceding day, from morn to night, and if time permitted, they were accustomed to recount the actions of the day previous, the third, the fourth, and even farther.[b] In no shape could the traditions of an illiterate people be preserved so effectually as in verse, which in ancient composition was very simple, a character applicable to the early poetry of all nations. The song of Moses consists of a certain number of words in every sentence, an arrangement eminently conducive to the mental retention of the subject.

The Celtic poetry is remarkably forcible, and from its peculiar construction is easily remembered, and it was an object of great solicitude to teach the rising generations the traditions of their fathers. It was not only a national care, but was esteemed a sacred duty in parents to make their children perfectly acquainted with the ancient poems. The expression of an American chief, in a parallel state of civilization with the old Highlanders, is here applicable:—"While I was yet young, my father taught me the traditions and laws of the nation, day by day and night by night." Columba is said to have retained the Celtic practice at Iona, and delivered his precepts in verse; it would even appear that in Ireland, historical relations were not written in prose before the twelfth century.[c]

The influence of poetry over the nations of antiquity is evinced by many signal instances. Tyrtæus, by chaunting his verses, so inspirited the Lacedemonians, that they turned the tide of prosperity and came off victorious. The Celtic bards stimulated their hearers to war, or subdued them to peace by the mere recitation of their poems. With this race the gift of poesy was highly honoured:

[b] Diodorus, Fragmenta. Valesii, vi. § 36, 37.
Walker's Irish Bards.

"the mouths of song" were a sacred order. When Ovid, in his banishment, wrote poems in the Getic language, the admiring people crowned him with laurel, and conferred on him many honours and immunities.[d]

The ceremonials of Pagan theology were conducted in verse, the meaning of the poems being wrapt up in allegory and mysticism. It is probable we have not lost much that would have been useful if known, from this secresy, which rather appears to have been intended to keep the vulgar in awe than to preserve information of past transactions or knowledge of useful arts,[e]—the historical records were not concealed from those who could study and understand them. The priests of antiquity were national historiographers. Josephus' Antiquities of the Jewish nation were published from the sacred books, and in the stories of Greek and Roman theology, relating the adventures of persons, deified in subsequent times, we have only fragments of vague and traditional, but in most cases, if divested of fable, real history. The old poems of the Germans, according to Tacitus, were their only registers. The songs of the bards are represented as consisting chiefly of hymns to their gods, and poems in praise of their ancestors, but in these were contained their national annals, for the origin of all nations is connected in their fabulous history with that of their gods. The Celtic bards were members of the priesthood, and no class of society among the ancients have been more celebrated. Whether we consider the influence which they possessed, their learning or poetic genius, they are one of the most interesting orders of antiquity, and worthy of our entire admiration.

[d] Clark.

[e] The Orphic verses are believed to have been the very hymns sung by the initiated in the Eleusinian mysteries. "He that has been initiated in the mysteries of Eleusis, or has read the poems called Orphic, will know what I mean." Pausanias, i. 36.

The favourite songs of the bards are said to have been those celebrating the renown of their ancestors. The praises of great men were accompanied with a sort of religious feeling. It was not only useful to the living to extol the virtues of former heroes as an excitement to their imitation, but was reckoned extremely pleasing to the deceased—it was indeed thought the means of assisting the spirit to a state of happiness, and became consequently a religious duty. But even where this superstition has no influence, an elegy on a deceased friend continues to gratify the human mind, and the example of virtue seldom fails to inspire youth with a generous spirit of emulation. Eginhart celebrates Charlemagne for committing to writing and to memory the songs on the wars and heroic virtues of his predecessors, and Asser bestows similar praise on the great Alfred. With how much effect the Celtic bards pursued the practice of inflaming their hearers with a spirit of freedom is universally acknowledged. So influential were they, that national enterprises were directed and controlled by them; and the Roman policy, so cruelly carried into effect by Suetonius in Anglesea, was imitated by Edward the First in his sanguinary wars with the Cumri. Even Queen Elizabeth thought it necessary to enact some laws to restrain and discourage the bards both of Ireland and Wales.

The Bardic compositions, commemorating the worth and exploits of heroes who had successively figured in the different states, were a sort of national annals which served the double purpose of preserving the memory of past transactions, and of stimulating the youth to an imitation of their virtuous ancestors. The lives of the upright Celtic statesmen and heroes were handed down to posterity, and exhibited as illustrious examples for the youth to follow. Their virtues were detailed in verse so forcible, and national calamities were pourtrayed in language so affecting, that the hearers were excited to the most daring heroism. On occasion of an embassy from the Romans to Attila, two bards recited to him a poem celebrating his victories, and so powerfully were the audience affected, that whilst the young men exulted in rapture, the old shed tears of regret that their vigour was gone.[f] The effusions of Nelan, a bard of Erin, more powerful than the wise council of the Christian primate, stimulated to precipitate rebellion Lord Thomas Geraldine, in the reign of Henry VIII. The sublime strains in which the virtues of the chiefs of Morven are celebrated continued to animate the Gaël until the decline of bardism and subversion of their institutions, and they still remain, even in translation, specimens of most admirable composition. Diodorus informs us, that the bards had power to prevent an engagement, even when the spears were levelled for immediate action. This strong influence was probably increased by their religious character, in which they were able to determine when it was expedient to fight, in reference to which, the Irish tell us the shaking "the chain of silence" was the signal to prevent or to put a stop to the battle.

The practice of animating troops by the chaunting of heroic poems is of most ancient origin. Tyrtæus, the Lacedemonian, who flourished 680 years before our era, composed five books of war verses, some fragments of which it is believed yet remain. Tacitus speaks of the old poems of the Germans, some of which related to the origin of the people, and the collection continued to increase, for it was the duty of the priests or bards to commemorate events, to celebrate the virtues and denounce the vices of successive heroes. One poem, celebrating the worth of Arminius, a hero famous for his struggles for freedom, was composed in the days of Tacitus.[g]

[f] Priscus, quoted in Robertson's Charles V.   [g] Annals.

It was not only in actual war, and previous to an engagement, that the bards rehearsed their spirit-stirring compositions; each chief was constantly attended by a number of these poets, who entertained him at his meals, and roused his own and his followers' courage by their powerful recitations. The liberal manner in which this order was provided for, shows how indispensable their services were reckoned. and, in return for so much respect, the bards were most assiduous to please their patrons, and blazon their renown. The profession, even in recent times, was by no means one of easy acquirement. It was indeed hereditary, but a long course of study, and a life of continual practice, were necessary for proper qualification and due success. In a publication, by Cambray, member of the Celtic Academy at Paris, it is said that Druidic learning comprised 60,000 verses, which those of the first class were obliged to get by heart.[h] The Irish bard, according to Walker, was obliged to study for twelve years, before he was admitted to the order, the Ollamh, perfecting himself by a probation of three years devoted to each of the four principal branches of poetry. Campion says they spent sixteen or twenty years at their education, and talked Latin like a vulgar language. "I have seene them," says he, "where they kept schoole, ten in some one chamber, groveling upon couches of straw, their bookes at their noses, themselves lying flat prostrate." This refers to a comparatively late period, but it shows that their requirements were not superficial, and that a common education was by no means sufficient for an aspirant to poetical fame.[i] When a student was admitted to the profession of bardism, he was honoured with the degree of ollamh, or doctor, and received an hono-

[h] Mac Arthur's Observations on Ossian's Poems.
[i] The last Filean school was kept in Tipperary, in the time of Charles I., by Boethius Mac Eagan.

rary cup, called barred. In 192 the lawful price of the clothing of an ollamh, and of an anra, or second poet, in Ireland, was fixed at five milch cows. Concovar Mac Nessa, King of Ulster, is represented in Irish history as establishing seven gradations in the order of Fileas,[j] which is said to have originally combined in one person the offices of seanachaidh and breitheamh. These were the Fochlucan, who was obliged to repeat, if asked, thirty tales; the Macfuirmidh, who had to repeat forty; the Doss, who repeated fifty; the Canaith, whose name seems derived from Canadh, to sing; the Cli, the Anstruth, so called from an, good, and sruth, knowing; and lastly the Ollamh, who required to store his memory with seven times fifty stories. An account of their various duties, real or supposed, may be seen in Walker's History of the Bards. The Irish authorities are extremely questionable, but it appears from other proofs that the different provinces of the profession were committed to separate individuals. The Scots of both countries had originally their Ferlaoi, or hymnists; the Ferdan, who sang the praises of the good and valiant; and the Seanachaidh, or Seanachies, to whom were submitted the registration of events and preservation of family history, but on the declension of the system, the offices were often necessarily held by one person.

The Caledonian bards officiated as a sort of aides-de-camp to the chief, communicating his orders to the chieftains and their followers, an office that tends to confirm my explanation of the beum sgiath, or striking of the shield. When Fingal retires to view the battle, "three bards attend to bear his words to the chiefs." Each chief appears to have had a favourite or principal bard, similar to the Welsh domestic bard, who closely attended the person of his master. The

[j] Walker's Irish Bards.

bards animated the troops in battle, and amused them by their songs during the hours of darkness—"song on song deceived as was wont the night." Nor was this part of their duty confined to the field; they solaced their master after the fatigues of the day, and composed his mind for rest by their moral and entertaining recitations. The bard was an important member of the Comhairlich, or councillors presiding over and directing in his professional character their deliberations. "Though it was every man's duty to fill the ear of his chief with useful truths, it was more particularly the duty of the Filea, for to such only do princes lend an ear." Some curious particulars of their duties may be found in Ossian. When a bard brings a challenge to battle from Torlath, he refused to raise the song himself, or listen to the bards of Cuthullin, who had invited him to partake of their cheer, but as he withdrew, he sings an extempore poem, which, in mystical language, alludes to the slaughter that is to ensue. "The meteors of death are there," says he, as he looks towards the hill, "the grey watery forms of ghosts." This must be considered a coronach in anticipation over the Gaël, who were to fall, and it is curious that Cuthullin's bard joins in it.

An important part of the bardic duty was the preservation of the genealogies and descent of the chiefs and the tribe, which were solemnly repeated at marriages, baptisms, and burials. The last purpose for which they were retained by the Highlanders was, to preserve a faithful history of their respective clans.

Lachlan Mac Neil, mhic Lachlan, mhic Neil, mhic Donald, mhic Lachlan, mhic Neil more, mhic Lachlan, mhic Donald, of the surname of Mac Mhuirich declared,[k] that according to the best of his knowledge, he is the eighteenth

[k] Before Roderick Mac Leod, J. P., and in presence of six clergymen and gentlemen.

in descent from Mhuireach, whose posterity had officiated as bards to Clan-Rannald, and that they had, as the salary of their office, the farm of Staoiligary, and four pennies of Drimisdale, during fifteen generations. That the sixteenth lost the four pennies, but the seventeenth retained the farm of Staoiligary for nineteen years. Then there was a right given to them over these lands as long as there should be any of the posterity of Mhuireach to preserve and continue the genealogy and history of the Mac Donalds, on condition that the bard, failing of male issue, should educate his brother's son or representative, in order to preserve their title to the lands, and it was in pursuance of this custom that his father had been taught to read and write history and poetry by Donald Mac Neil, mhic Donald his father's brother. This last of the race, who, according to Doctor Mac Pherson, was "a man of some letters, and had, like his ancestors, received his education in Ireland, and knew Latin tolerably well,"[1] was bard, genealogist, and seanachaidh.

From their antiquarian knowledge, the bards were called seanachaidh, from sean, old, a title synonymous with the Welsh, arvydd vardd, an officer who latterly was of national appointment, and whose heraldic duties were recognised by the English College of Arms. They attended at the birth, marriage, and death of all persons of high descent, and the marwnod, or elegy, which they composed on the latter occasion "was required to contain, truly, and at length, the genealogy and descent of the deceased from eight immediate ancestors—to notice the several collateral branches of the family, and to commemorate the surviving wife or husband. These he registered in his books, and delivered a true copy of them to the heir, &c., and it was produced the day after the funeral, when all the principal branches of the family and their friends were assembled

Letter to Dr. Blair.

together in the great hall of the mansion, and then recited with an audible voice."[m] He also made a visitation called the bard's circuit, once every three years, to all the gentlemen's houses, where he registered and corrected their armorial bearings. Many of their books still exist, distinguished by the name of the bard or the house whose honours it records, and some of their award of arms are of so late a date as 1703. One of the Triads commemorates the three golden robed heralds, Caswallon, son of Beli, &c. The bard had a stipend paid out of every plough land, and the chief was called "King of the Bards."

Much has been done to restore the order of bards in the Principality, or at least to encourage the effusions of Cumraeg poesy and music, and many meritorious individuals have met with flattering encouragement. I believe the kings of Great Britain have always maintained a Welsh minstrel. In the laws of Hwyel Dha, it is said that at an entertainment the bard ought to commence singing in praise of God, and then in praise of the king, and the fine for insulting him is six cows, and one hundred and twenty silver pennies, his value being estimated at one hundred and twenty-six cows. He was assigned a place at table suitable to his rank.[n] In the reign of Harald Harfager, the bards, or scalds, sat next to the king. The Aois dana of the Gaël, mentioned in the end of the seventeenth century, who appear to have been a certain class of bards, sat in the sreath or circle, among the chiefs, and took precedence of the ollamh or doctor, the title which was bestowed on completion of the bardic studies. Their persons, houses, and villages, were sacred.[o] A respect for the bards continued after the introduction of Christianity, the precepts they inculcated being unobjectionable, and the early missionaries appear to have

[m] Preface to the History of Cardiganshire.   [n] See p. 144.
[o] Armstrong.

held them in considerable esteem. Columba had a particular regard for them, and actually became their advocate at the celebrated council at Drumceat, in 580, mediating successfully between those of Ireland and the King, who threatened their extirpation, for their insolence had become insupportable, and they at last insisted on receiving the royal buckle and pin of gold, too audacious a demand to be unhesitatingly complied with. The honours which were heaped on this body made them forget themselves. Their arrogance in Wales arose to such a height, that in the time of Griffyth ap Cynan, it was necessary to control them from asking the king's horse, greyhound, or hawk.

No event in the annals of literature has excited so much wonder and curiosity as the publication of those ancient Gaëlic poems, usually distinguished as Ossianic, from the name of that most distinguished of the Caledonian bards. To those unacquainted with the state of society in the Highlands of Scotland, and lamentable until lately was the ignorance concerning that part of the kingdom, the existence of traditional poetry of such antiquity appeared impossible, and scepticism, confirmed by the unaccountable reserve of the translator, bestowed on him an honour, and imputed to him a merit, of which he was by no means worthy—that of being the author of the poems in question. Public opinion was indeed divided as to the authenticity of Ossian's poems, but the general belief at first was, that they were an impudent forgery, and the talents of many learned individuals were exerted to expose the imposture. Their writings, as might be expected, had for some time great weight, while the only satisfactory answer to their objections was not returned. The regret of the admirers of this sublime bard, and vindicators of his poems, was at last relieved by the publication of the originals, by that truly patriotic body the Highland Society. A reference to these most interesting relics might be sufficient, but, consistent with the design of this work, I shall endeavour to display the manners by which their preservation was effected—manners which no longer exist in Europe, and which, after a continuance from the earliest dawn of record, expired with the system of social government, which received its mortal blow in the Act of 1748.

The history of the Celts, their laws, and usages, were preserved in their poems, which were their only registers. It has been shewn that traditional verse was the only medium by which the early Greeks transmitted their most important statutes, and the memory of past transactions, and that it was by no means a "feeble instrument" is very evident. The oral registers of the Germans were ancient in the days of Tacitus, and in spite of the fluctuations and reverses of that people, they were not forgotten even in the eighth century. The Lusitani had poems, which they maintained were two thousand years old.

When we consider that the preservation of these national annals was entrusted to the Druidical order, and was a point of the utmost public solicitude, and when we consider that the vanity of individuals, whose own exploits, or those of their ancestors were celebrated, was flattered by the record of their fame, we perceive strong motives acting in aid of the preservation of these singular historical monuments. It is not to be forgotten also, that this personal feeling pervaded the whole nation, for if the memory of a chief was consecrated to fame in the impressive strains of the bards, his followers, from the ties of consanguinity, felt closely interested in the glory of their clansman. That the Celts preferred oral record to that of writing may be regretted, since to this prejudice the loss of much information, which would probably have been highly curious and instructive, is to be attributed; but as both the principles and practice of the Druids were hostile to literature, we can only pursue the investigation of the peculiar system which they chose to follow, and allowing the above causes their united effect, added to this other powerful one, that the chief amusement, both public and private, was the recitation of their poems, much of our wonder at the long preservation of bardic compositions must cease.

Many of those who believe it impossible for poems or prose relations to be preserved for any length of time without being committed to writing, do not advert to the ancient state of society. To instruct the youth in the traditional knowledge of their country was then a branch of the most careful education, and that knowledge was couched in verse. If a noviciate in Druidism spent twenty years in getting by heart the knowledge necessary for his profession, some idea may be formed of the amount of learning which the sons of the better classes found it necessary to acquire. The choicest pieces of ancient poetry have come down to us in the same manner as Ossian's productions. The poems of Homer were preserved in detached parts, called Rhapsodies, as, the battle at the ships, the Death of Dolon, &c., long before they assumed their present form; and the Athenians found it necessary to offer rewards to those who could furnish the most authentic fragments of the Iliad or Odyssey, before they were able to produce the works as they now appear.[a] Even since the Christian era, the ability to repeat traditional poetry was reckoned a qualification not unbefitting the highest princes. Charlemagne is praised for his talents this way, and he had made a large collection of most ancient poems, which in barbarous style related the actions of the first kings.[b]

That poems of great antiquity existed at the period when Ossian sung, is evident from the frequent allusion he

[a] Ælian.   [b] Eginhart.

makes to "the songs of old," and bards of other years. "Thou shalt endure, said the *bard of ancient days*, after the moss of time shall grow in Temora; after the blast of years shall roar in Selma."ᵖ The Tain-bo, or cattle spoil of Cualgne, commemorating an event that occurred 1838 years ago, is believed to be the oldest poem in the Gaëlic language. The Albanach Duan, a poem of the time of Malcolm III., 1056, which is an indisputed relic, must have been composed from poems much anterior to its own age, and this is admitted by those who have been most noted for their scepticism as to Celtic literature.ᵩ

The lengthened discussions on the authenticity of the poems ascribed to the Caledonian bard, relieve me, in a great measure, from the task of advocating at length their antiquity. "The poems of Ossian," says Gibbon, "according to every hypothesis, were composed by a native Caledonian." The era of that Caledonian was the end of the third century. When accounts of Mac Pherson's publication of these poems and the controversies which it engendered had reached the Highlands, the natives were equally surprised at the doubts concerning their genuineness, at the scanty collection which had been made, and their imperfect translation. Finding so much interest excited, they were not a little displeased that more justice was not done to the memory of their venerated poet.ʳ "There is

---

ᵖ Smith's Gallic Antiquities. ᵩ Pinkerton, &c.

ʳ Ewen Mac Pherson, aged 73, who made a declaration in 1800, that he accompanied the translator to several of the Isles, relates the following anecdote of his travelling companion. Having met with Mac Codrum, a descendant of a race of bards, he asked him "a beheil dad agad air an Fhein?" This question, it would appear from the incorrectness or inelegance of the Gaëlic, could bear another construction, viz.: Are the Fingalians indebted to you? of which Mac Codrum, being a man of humour, took advantage, and answered, that "really if they owed him anything, the bonds and obligations were lost, and he believed any

infinitely more," says Mac Donald, of Killepheder, in his deposition, "to be found among us, than what Mac Pherson is said to have translated of the works of Ossian; and that to many persons who never saw that man, who never heard of his name, and who are totally ignorant of the English language." The Rev. Donald Mac Leod, of Glenelg, writes thus to Dr. Blair, in 1764. "Mac Pherson took too little time to be able to have collected the whole of them; for as the works of Ossian are dispersed all over the Highlands, there is not a clan through whose lands you travel, but you will find some one of these poems among them, which is not to be met with anywhere else."

The knowledge of these poems was not confined to the Highlands. From the history of King Robert Bruce, written by Barbour, Archdeacon of Aberdeen, about 1380, we find that they were well known in the Lowlands. In the third book we are informed, that when the Lord of Lorn saw that his troops durst not follow the enemy, he was "rychtangry in his hert," and said

>   ———— "methink Marthokys son,
> Rycht as Gaul Mac Morn was won,
> To haif fra Fingal his menzie,
> Rycht swa all hys fra us has he."

Boethius[*] calls the King of Morven, concerning whom fabulous stories were sung, Fynnan filius Cœli; and Gawin Douglas speaks of Gow Mac Morn and Fyn Mac Coul,—

> "My foir grand syr hecht Fyn Makoull,
> That dang the deil and gart him yowl."[†]

Fingal and Ossian are mentioned in Mac Geoghagan's Ireland, 1627. A MS. in the British Museum, noticed by

attempt to recover them at the present day would be unavailing;" which sally of Mac Codrum's wit offended Mac Pherson, who cut short the conversation and proceeded towards Benbecula.

[*] Lib. vii.   [†] Evergreen, p. 259.

Pinkerton, also alludes to them;[u] and Buchannan, in his History of the Buchannans and other clans, mentions " rude rhimes on Fin M'Coel."

All this indisputably shews that the poems now before the world were formerly well known throughout Scotland and Ireland; and it must be declared, that however much we are indebted to Mr. Mac Pherson, the obligation must be shared with others; for besides the partial translations of Jerome Stone and Mr. Hill, who published portions of these poems some time before Mac Pherson, a large collection of them were made long previous by Dr. Smith, of Campbelltown, which he afterwards gave to the public, under the title of "Gallic Antiquities." This gentleman was a native of Glenurchy, and heard an old man called Doncha rioch Mac Nicol, who was famous for his knowledge of traditional lore, repeat many of the Ossianic poems. The Fletchers of Glenforsa were also famous for their recitation. Mr. Mac Donald, a priest in Moidart, knew a whole poem that had escaped the research of Mac Pherson; and "Cath Benedin," the Rev. Donald Mac Leod says, was recovered after the collection was published, and he thinks it superior to any of the others. A Mr. Mac Diarmid, of Weem, in Perthshire, got Ossian's Addresses to the Sun, as they appear in Carthon and Carricthura about 1770, from the repetition of an old man in Glenlyon, who had learned them in his youth from people in the same glen. It may be here observed that this beautiful address was particularly pointed out as a glaring forgery!

Captain John Mac Donald, of Thurso, who was formerly of Breakish, in Sky, and furnished Mac Pherson with some of the pieces in his collection, declared at the age of seventy-eight, on the 12th of March, 1805, that when a

---

[u] Ayscough's Cat. 4817.

boy of twelve, or fifteen, he could repeat from one to two hundred poems, which he learned from an old man of about eighty, who used to sing them to his father at night when he went to bed, and in spring and winter before he got up. Niel Mac Mhuireach repeated to the Rev. Mr. Mac Niel the whole of the poem of Clan Usnoch, called by Mac Pherson, Darthula. Malcolm Mac Pherson, in Portree, Isle of Sky, son of Dougal Mac Pherson, who had been tenant in Benfuter, in Trotternish, and was an eminent bard, declared on oath before two justices of the peace, that his brother, who died in 1780, recited four days and four nights to Mac Pherson.

What has been said, it is hoped, will shew that there was nothing to render the preservation of poems for so many centuries impossible; nay, that under such circumstances they could scarcely be lost, and convince the sceptical that such poems have been fortunately saved from oblivion, and brought down to our times in great purity.

Nothing has yet been said of Gaëlic MSS. which Dr. Johnson and many others believed could not be found except of modern date.

The Highland Society has now in its possession various MS. versions of Ossian's poems, of different ages, the oldest of which the late Mr. Astle, keeper of the records in the Tower, a competent judge, pronounced to be of the ninth century. This, to be sure, does not reach the period when the bard flourished, but it disproves the assertions of those who maintained that there never were any written poems. I think Dr. Mac Pherson speaks very reasonably, when he says, "we have among us many ancient MSS. of detached pieces of Ossian's works, and these may have been copied from MSS. still more ancient." A tradition is noticed by Dr. Smith, that Mac Alpin took down all Ossian's poems as he repeated them; and another tradition, which need not be repeated, informs us of the cause of their destruction. The Scots, as may be seen in another part of the work, were very early acquainted with the use of letters, and were distinguished throughout Europe for their learning.

A few of the depositions of those persons examined on the subject will prove more satisfactorily that MSS. did exist, and shew the means by which the interesting and beautiful compositions of the Gaëlic bards were preserved, more satisfactorily than any argument of mine, while it will, at the same time, elucidate the former state of that celebrated order.

Hugh Mac Donald, of Killepheder, in South Uist, before-mentioned, says, in his testimony as translated, that the last bard of the Mac Donald family, "was John Mac Codrum, who had lands and maintainence from Sir James Mac Donald, and from his brother and immediate successor, the late Lord Mac Donald. John Mac Codrum's predecessor was Duncan Mac Ruari, who possessed, as bard and by inheritance, the lands in the district of Trotternish, in Sky, called Ach na' m'Bard, (the bard's field,) and his descendants, as well as the collateral branches of his family, are to this very day called Clann 'a Bhaird." He observes, that the bards of Clan Rannald held their lands on the express condition of transmitting in writing the history and poetry connected with the family: and continues, "there is still extant a poem composed by one of them, Niel Mor Mac Mhuirich, to the Mac Donalds, immediately before the battle of Gariach, called the Prosnachadh cath Gariach. As a proof of the estimation in which the bards were held, I need only mention, that when the chief of the Mac Leods dismissed Mac gilli Riabhich, his family bard, Mac Donald received him hospitably, and gave him lands on the farm of Kilmorey, in Trotternish, which retain to this day the name of "Baile gilli Riabhich."

Mac Mhuireach, part of whose testimony is given in p. 225, remembered well, that works of Ossian, written on parchment, were in the custody of his father, as received from his predecessors, some in the form of books, and some loose and separate, which contained the works of other bards besides those of Ossian. He affirmed that the leabhar dearg, or red book, was long in his father's possession, and was received from his predecessors. It was of paper, and contained a good deal of the history of the clans, written by different hands. He remembered well that Clan Rannald made his father give up the red book to James Mac Pherson, from Badenach. Several parchments, he believed, were taken away by the Rev. Alexander Mac Donald and his son Ronald, but he saw others cut up by the tailors for measures.' He having no longer any lands, and not being taught to read, he set no value on them. This declaration he signed before Roderick Mac Leod, J. P., in presence of six other clergymen and gentlemen. Dr. Mac Pherson knew the last of these bards, who had been in the service of the Lords of the Isles before they entered that of Clan Rannald. He was a man of some letters, understood Latin, and, like his ancestors, received his education in Ireland. He travelled through the country about 1735, and read as well as repeated poems from a MS.

Malcolm Mac Pherson, in Portree, gave to the translator of Ossian a 4to volume about 1½ inch thick, containing the works of that bard, which he had procured at Loch Carron when an apprentice. Lord Kames, in his Sketches of Man, mentions four books of Fingal that Mac Pherson got in Sky. Mrs. Fraser, of Culbokie, had a MS. volume

---

' The Rev. Angus Mac Niel, of South Uist, said in 1763, that Clan Rannald told him a volume was carried to Ireland by some worthless person. Ewan Mac Pherson attested the delivery of the above volume to the translator, which appears also to have been lost.

of Ossian's poems, that was written by Peter Mac Donell, chaplain to Lord Mac Donell, of Glengary, about the time of the Restoration, as well as others which her son carried to Canada. It is said that Dr. Watson, author of the Lives of Fletcher and Gordon, discovered at Rome a MS. of these poems, which had been brought away after the rebellion in 1715.[w] A MS. once in the Scots' college at Douay, much of it written before 1515, by a Mr. Farquharson, contained all the pieces given by Mac Pherson, besides many more. Mr. Farquharson left another similar collection at Bræ-Mar before he went to Douay, which was unfortunately destroyed, but he thought it would be easy to make another collection. "He was not sensible of the rapid, the incredible, the total change which had taken place in the Highlands of Scotland."[x] "Thirty or forty years back," say the authors of the Report on the Poems of Ossian, in 1803, "the number of persons who could recite tales and poetry, and could write Gaëlic, was very much greater than at the present time." Since 1745 the amusement of listening to recitation is scarcely known.

It was usual for the young women of a baile, or hamlet, which consisted of from four to twenty families, to carry their work to the houses of each other's parents alternately. In these societies oral learning was attained without interrupting industry, and the pleasure of instructing and receiving knowledge was mutual. The matron, visited on one evening, perhaps excelled in genealogy, while another was well versed in general history; one may have been an adept at poetry, and another an able critic, &c. The Highlander, after his daily occupations, hastened to join the society of the young women, where he met his beloved, or had the pleasure, in her absence, of repeating the last sonnet he had

[w] Literary Journal, i. p. 458.
[x] Letter from Bishop Cameron to Sir John Sinclair on the subject.

composed in her praise, for which he either received applause or encountered disapprobation. With us, fools will publish what impartial criticism may condemn; but with the Highlanders it was otherwise, " what could not be published in the above societies could not be published at all: they were to them what the press is to us; a song that was learned by a few out of mere compliment to its author was soon forgotten. It may be readily supposed that local circumstances sometimes gave a temporary existence to very indifferent compositions, but their popularity being confined to the districts where the subjects of them were best known, with those subjects they generally expired. I have spoken in the past tense," continues the writer, " because, within a few years, the manners of my countrymen have suffered a total revolution, very little to the advantage of the present race, who are neither so hospitable, so learned, nor so pious as the generation they have succeeded."[y]

What has been a very great means to preserve the Ossianic poems is this, that the greatest number of them have particular tunes to which they are sung, the music of which is soft and simple. Duan Dearmot, an elegy on the death of a celebrated warrior so called, is held in much esteem among the Campbells, who trace their descent from that hero. In Lord Rea's country is a tribe of this name, and the following anecdote of an old member is here appropriate. The Rev. Alexander Pope having got this veteran to sing the poem, he commenced his performance by reverently taking off his bonnet; but, says the writer, " I caused him to stop, and would put on his bonnet; he made some excuses; however, as soon as he began, he again took off his bonnet.—I rose and put it on—he took it off—I put it on; at last, as he was like to swear most horribly, he

[y] Notes on the superstitions of the Highlanders, by Mr. Donald Mac Pherson, 1824.

would sing no more unless I allowed him to be uncovered. I gave him his freedom, and so he sung with great spirit. I then asked him the reason; he told me it was out of regard to the memory of that hero. I asked him if he thought that the spirit of that hero was present; he said not, but thought it well became them who were descended from him to honour his memory."*

Of the music adapted to these poems, a specimen furnished by the Rev. John Cameron, of Halkirk, in Caithness, from the recitation of a very old man in his parish, is given by Sir John Sinclair, in his excellent dissertation prefixed to the Highland Society's edition of Ossian. One of superior merit is given in the musical part of this work, and several others of undoubted antiquity are noticed.

That Fingal fought and Ossian sung there can be no rational doubt. The names of places all over the Highlands testify the existence of such persons, and the manners described in the poems suit no other period in history but that of the ancient and unmixed Celts.ᵃ When General Wade, in the operation of forming the military roads, had to remove Clachan Ossian, or the monumental stone of this revered bard, about four score indignant Highlanders, in becoming solemnity, carried off his bones, with pipes playing, and deposited them within a circle of large stones on the summit of a sequestered rock, in the wilds of western Glen Amon, where they are not likely evermore to be disturbed. That the Highlanders are disposed to receive anything alluding to those remote times as productions of Ossian is false, and can only be advanced by those who know nothing of their poetical judgment; succeeding bards

* Letter to the Rev. Alexander Nicholson, of Thurso, 1763.

ᵃ Mr. Rosing, the Danish consul, in reply to a letter from Sir John Sinclair, finds Ossian's recitals corroborated by Suhme's History of Denmark.

followed their great predecessor as a model, but never approached the sublimity of "the voice of Cona." Many have studied his works, and a most successful imitator was Ailen Mac Ruari. A modern bard in Glendochy, in Perthshire, and another in Glendovan, Argyle, after laborious attempts to catch the poetic fire of this prince of Celtic poets, gave up the pursuit.[b] The nearest approach was made by M'Intyre, whose works display true poetic feeling. The Highlanders can, however, detect the true Ossianic from other poetry, by its peculiar excellence, simplicity of construction, and grandeur of imagery. There were several Ossians in the profession of bardism, who flourished in times subsequent, but none ever rivalled their predecessor.[c] Nor do the Highlanders swallow the poetic descriptions as strictly natural. They can well discriminate between hyperbole and plain narration, as in the instance of Civa dona, where the description is allowed by the most enthusiastic to be ideal. In matters of history, Doctor Mac Pherson admits that the bardic accounts are not altogether to be depended upon; but it is a fact that curious discoveries have been made in consequence of songs. Treasure buried for centuries has been recovered, and the poem of Cath Gabhra, commemorating the interment of Conan, a king, under a stone, inscribed in Ogham characters, the Irish academy made search and found it.

It has been thought impossible for a language to remain unchanged for so great a length of time, and this objection has been urged with much vehemence, as an unanswerable argument against the antiquity of Gaëlic poetry. In the second Chapter of the first volume, some of the causes

[b] Smith's Gallic Antiquities.

[c] From Colgan's Life of Saint Patrick, we find he had a convert called Ossian, which circumstance has led to some confusion.

affecting language are noticed. By these causes, that of the Scotish mountaineers has not been altered in any great degree these 2000 years, but that no change has taken place would be a rash assertion. From the publication of the original poems which James Mac Pherson first translated, it is manifest, that certain changes have been produced, by the introduction of Christianity and the altered state of society; but the number of words now obsolete are very few, and, to the studious, may be easily understood from etymological solution. A Life of Saint Patrick, written in verse, in the sixth century, is still perfectly intelligible to an Irishman,[d] and the Ossianic remains are, with trifling exceptions, still understood in the language in which the bard composed them.

Finally, if the poems of Ossian are an imposture, Mac Pherson is not the only one implicated.[*] Smith and others have been equally skilful in the deception, and a whole nation have been the abettors of an imposition. But no rational being can now, it is believed, entertain any doubt that these poems have existed in Highland tradition through successive centuries, and been the solace of the aged, and the means of virtuous excitement to the young. The bard of Caledonia "is one of the most transcendant geniuses that ever adorned the history of poetry, or that ever graced the annals of valour and glory—let such as do not like to name him Ossian, call him Orpheus: doubts may be entertained whether Fingal was

---

[d] Dr. Smith.

[*] The authenticity of "Ossian" is still a vexed question, nor is the controversy ever likely to be satisfactorily settled either way. The best and most recent contributions to the subject are Dr. Clerk's "Dissertation" prefixed to his translation of Ossian's poems, and J. F. Campbell of Islay's "Heather na Feinne," Introduction *et passim*. Clerk is all in favour of the "Celtic Homer;" Campbell dead against him. ED.

his father, but no one will say that he is not the son of Apollo."◦*

"Upon the construction of the old Celtic poetry we want much information."‡ The chief aim of the poet was to compose his pieces in short, simple, and forcible sentences or stanzas, so that they might be easily learned and retained in the memory, and that they succeeded in their object is abundantly proved. The language, from its simplicity, was admirably calculated to assist recollection, and the ingenuity of the poets added infinitely to the effect. In Mac Pherson's Dissertation on the era of Ossian, are these remarks: "Each verse was so connected with those which preceded or followed it, that if one line had been remembered in a stanza, it was almost impossible to forget the rest. The cadences followed in so natural a gradation, and the words were so adapted to the common turn of the voice, after it is raised to a certain key, that it was almost impossible, from a similarity of sound, to substitute one word for another. This excellence is peculiar to the Celtic tongue, and perhaps is to be met with in no other language. Nor does this choice of words clog the sense or weaken the expression. The numerous flections of consonants, and variation in declension, make the language very copious."

The genius of the people, naturally musical and poetical, materially assisted in the preservation of oral compositions, and inclined them to afford that encouragement to the order of bards which fostered their talents, and enabled them to devote the years of probation which the profession required,

---

◦ The Abbe Cesarotti's Dissertation.

* Two objections among others have been urged against the authenticity of the Ossianic poems; (1) that there is no reference to anything like religious worship to be found in them; nor (2) any mention of the Clan system.

Dr. Clerk in his notes has called attention to the fact that both are, not once and again, but frequently referred to. ED.

‡ Pinkerton's Enquiry, ii. 145.

with undivided attention to its duties. The length of time which students were obliged to spend in qualifying themselves for the dignified station of bard, demonstrates the importance in which it was held.

Among the ancient Irish, the Fileacht was a mental composition for the exercise and improvement of poesy, which took place at stated times. This people retained their esteem for the bards, while they preserved their primitive manners, and Spenser ceased to wonder at their attachment to old customs when he understood the nature of their poetry, and witnessed their respect for the reciters. This writer, an accomplished poet himself, says the native compositions, were "of sweet wit and good invention, sprinkled with pretty flowers of their natural device." The importance of national poetry, nowhere more influential than among the Celts, is acknowledged by those who have most deeply studied the history of man. "Songs are more operative than statutes, and it matters little who are the legislators of a country compared with the writers of its popular ballads." It would appear from Hume and Barnet, that the misfortunes of James II. were chiefly owing to the effect of the Irish song or ballad called Lilli burlero.

According to Ælian, Homer's poems were at first detached pieces, called Rhapsodies. The rhapsodists of Greece bear a strong resemblance to the Celtic bards. The name is derived from $\rho\alpha\beta\delta\sigma$, a rod, or branch, and $\omega\delta\eta$, a song or poem, because the person always held a bunch of laurel while reciting the poems. The order, like that of the bards, having began to abuse the liberty of their profession, the term came to be applied contemptuously, and a rhapsody signified a vile performance, the meaning which it still retains, although it was originally used in quite another sense.[g]

[g] Larcher, note on Herodotus.

The first efforts of the muses in all countries are melancholy themes. Ossian never stoops from his sublimity, for wit or levity did not accord with his feelings. The Leudus of the Celts was a sort of ode, and the term survives in the Gaëlic Laoidh, applied to a hymn. Carthon, one of the Ossianic poems, is called in the original, Duan na' n laoi, or the poem of the hymns, probably from the celebrated address to the sun, and Fingal's pathetic "song of mourning," which it contains.

Dan is the Gaëlic name of a song. The bards distinguished those compositions in which the narration is often interrupted by odes and apostrophes, by the name of Duan, but since the extinction or disuse of the order, it has become a general name for all compositions in verse. The Duans always finished with the opening words. The bards were sometimes styled history-men, or tell-talers, and repeated a short argument before commencing. This traditional tale, which accompanied a poem, and sometimes has survived it, is called Sgeulachd, and, considering that much art was required to reduce the language to measure, they may be supposed to have preceded the poetical version. Of the various sorts of versification, I confess myself at a loss to form a complete list, especially of those in ancient use. In the Irish uiraiceacht na neagir, or rules for poets, there are upwards of one hundred different kinds described.[b] Doctor Molloy assures us that the construction and variety of Irish metre is the most difficult he had ever seen or heard of. In its composition these things are required—number, quartans, number of syllables, concords, correspondence, termination, union, and caput, the sub-divisions of all which are minute and perplexing. The rules respecting the division, conjunction, affinity, mutability, eclipses, and power of conso-

[b] Walker's Memoirs of the Irish bards, who refers to Vallancey and O'Molloy for specimens.

nants were to be understood, and the long and short quantity of vowels in the beginning, middle, and end.

The Welsh system is described as comprehending twenty four classes of verse or elementary principles. These, with their sub-divisions, say the authors of the Myvyrian Archæology, "include every species of verse that has ever yet, in any age, or amongst any people, been produced, besides a prodigious number of originals, entirely and exclusively our own, all which had been discovered and brought into general practice about the close of the second period," commencing about the beginning of the twelfth century, and continuing to the fourteenth. Those who are interested in Cumraeg poetry and literature may consult the above work, which contains numerous specimens, unfortunately, by not having a translation, sealed up from all who are ignorant of the language. The antiquaries of the Principality, who account for the origin of almost everything, tells us that Gwyddon Ganhebon was the first poet. The oldest sort of rhyme is called, in Rhys's Grammar, Englyn Milur.

We find the pupil of a learned Scot master of no fewer than one hundred different kinds of verse, with the musical modulation of words and syllables, which included letters, figures, poetic feet, tones, and time.[1]

The warlike propensity of the Celts afforded ample scope for the employment of the bards, who chaunted stimulating poems at the commencement and during the heat of a battle. The subject of those songs, which animated the Celtic warrior, was chiefly "the valorous deeds of worthy men composed in heroic verse."[2] Tacitus says, that, when the Germans advanced to battle, they extolled Hercules in their songs. Among the Gaël these spirit-

[1] Anglia sacra, ii. p. 2—7. Among the Northern nations, who seem to have despised simple versification, there were no less than one hundred and thirty-six different kinds of measure.—Olaus Wormius.

[2] Amm. Marc. xv. 9.

stirring odes were styled Prosnachadh cath, or the incentives to battle; to which the Irish Rosga cath, martial odes, and the Welsh Arymes prydain and Cerdd valiant, or songs of praise, were analogous.[k] There was also a sort that may be called the recruiting song, or incentive to rise.

"The song of battle" had an astonishing effect on the Celtic warriors, and its powers of animation was not less remarkable among the Scotish Gaël, than it was among the ancient Gauls. "Support," cries Fingal. "the yielding fight with song, for song enlivens the war."

The war song of Gaul Mac Morn is given in the first volume, page 163. Those compositions were in a short measure, and were repeated in an animated, rapid style; and so well adapted were the verses to the subject and the tune in which they were chaunted, which was again expressive of the feeling, that the sound partook of the tone of whatever passion the poet was at the time inspired with. Of this admirable adaptation of language to the expression of feeling, a thousand striking instances might be produced. The following may suffice:

> "The hoarse roaring of a wave against a rock.
> Stairirich measg charraige cruaidh a garraich."

The song of victory was chaunted by the bards, who preceded the army on its return from a successful expedition.

The Cumhadh, or Lament, otherwise called the Coronach,* was an elegy composed on the death or misfortunes of any celebrated individual. It partook, in some degree, of the

---

[k] The Greek orthia and pæan must have been more than a huzza. A war song, probably resembling the Prosnachadh, appears to have been so termed.

* The difference between the *Cumha'* and *Corranach* seems to be that the latter—the *Corranach*—was a loud and excited lament at the moment of death or immediately afterwards; the *Cumha'* was a melancholy and more subdued lament, which might be composed and sung years after the death of the person commemorated. ED.

song of praise, for it extolled the virtues of the individual; and in pathetic verse, to which the most plaintive wild notes were adapted, the bard gave vent to his own grief and excited that of his hearers. These compositions were anciently repeated at funerals, but they have given way to the music of the bag-pipe, the tune only being now played during the impressive ceremony. The Irish caoine, or cine, is still retained in secluded parts of the island, and is religiously adhered to by some even in London. The wife, or other near relations, commonly assisted by mercenary mourners, occasionally get up whilst the corpse is *waking*, and, in an extempore effusion, accompanied with tears and the most doleful cries, celebrate the merits of the deceased. The same conduct was formerly continued while the corpse was on its way to its last resting place. An ancient and affecting lamentation over Cuchullin, has fortunately been preserved, and shews the nature of this sort of composition, one characteristic of which is, that every stanza closes with some remarkable title of the person to whom it refers.

The ancient poems were repeated at entertainments, and in those, where a dialogue occurs, the characters were represented by different bards, or other individuals. In the poem of Carric thura, the parts of Vinvela and Shilric were represented by Cronnan and Minona.

Sir John Sinclair sketches, from the first book of Fingal, a dramatic scene, which, he believes, was acted by different persons. Clarke, who refuted the attack of Shaw, on the authenticity of the poems, declares that he went with Mac Pherson to late wakes in Badenoch, where they were so acted or represented. "The Highlanders, at their festivals and other public meetings, acted the poems of Ossian. Rude and simple as their manner of acting was, yet any brave or generous action, any injury or distress exhibited in the representation, had a surprising effect towards raising in them corresponding passions and sentiments."[1]

When the Highlanders met to watch the corpse of their friends, most part of the night was spent in repeating their ancient poems, and talking of the times of Fingal. On these occasions they often laid wagers who should repeat the greatest number of verses; and to have acquired a great store of this oral knowledge was reckoned an enviable acquisition. Dr. Mac Leod says, he knew old men who valued themselves much for having gained some of these wagers. The Prosnachadh fairge, already noticed, contains upwards of 800 lines, the Lament of the Women of Mull about 250, and Mac Intyre's Beindoran is about 1000 lines, or nearly as long as any of Ossian's compositions, yet the people learn every word of these long poems. Even in the Low Country the people delighted in lengthened recitations, as witness the poem on Flodden Field, on the Battle of Harlaw, 62 verses, the Battle of Glenlivat, 82, &c., &c.

Most of the Highland amusements were connected with poetry, and some of those diversions in which they took greatest delight were, in fact, poetical exercises. The obligation laid on every one who partook of the Drom-uinn to recite an extempore verse has been noticed. Dr. Johnson describes an amusement in the hall of a laird, where a person, dressed in the skin of a beast, makes his appearance, and is immediately attacked, but ultimately the assailants, as if frightened and overpowered, run out. The door is then shut; and when admission is solicited, for the honour of poetry, it is not to be obtained but by repeating a verse; this is called Beannachadh Bhaird.*

[1] Rev. Donald Mac Leod writing to Dr. Blair, 1763.

* *Beannachadh Bàird* is also applied to a chant—a sort of epithalamium—with which the bard of a family or of a district greeted the young bride on the morning after her marriage. ED.

A curious method of composition was, by connecting three lines or sentiments, of which sort are the famous Welsh Triads, first committed to writing, it is thought, about 1200 years ago. Cormac, king of Ireland, about 260, wrote De Triadibus, and Camden mentions a Welsh work, Triadum Liber. Some of the Triads of the celebrated Fingal are still preserved in oral record.

In Gaëlic poetry, the rhythm sometimes consists in the similiarity of the last words of the first and third, and second and fourth lines, as in English composition, thus—

> Measg aoibhneis an talla nam fear
> Mar so thog crònan am fonn
> Dh'eirich maduinn a, soills' o'n ear
> Bughorm air an lear, an tonn.
> *Carraig Thura*, ver. 195.

In the stanza which immediately follows this, the rhymes are in the last syllables, but the final consonants are not alike, the harmony depending on the concord of the vowels.

> Ghairm an righ a shinil gu crānn;
> Thanig gaoth a nall o'n Chrunaich;
> Dh'eirich Innis-Thore gu māll.
> Is Carraig Thùra iul nan stuadh.

Here the correspondence is in the *a* in the first and third lines, and in the *ua* in the second and fourth.

Sometimes the conformity between the last word of a line and some word or part of a word about the middle of the following line, constituted the rhyme: as

> 'Snigneach m' aigne 'n uaimh mo bhroīn;
> 'Smor mo leōn fo laimh na h'aois.
> Ossag 'tha gastar o Thuath
> Na dean tuasaid ruim 'smi lag.
> *Morduth.*

The above three sorts of rhyme are often found in one

composition, intermixed with couplets rhyming as softly and perfectly as in modern Italian; for example—

> Soilsichibh Srad air Druim feinne
> 'Sthig mo laoich o ghruaigh gach beinne.
> *Morduth.*

Some of the most beautiful passages in old Gaëlic poetry are, however, a sort of blank verse, having no rhyme. It appears that the bards sought in this case no more than to render every line perfect, without any dependance on the next, of which the above poem affords an example.

> Dhaluich a gealach a ceann;
> Bha cadal reultan air chul neoil.
> Cabhag ghaoth is cuan o chian;
> Bu gharbh an cath bha eadar stuaidh
> Is sileadh gailbheach nan speur.

The Prosnachadh cath Gariach, a specimen of which is given in Vol. i. p. 164, is a curious example of ingenious alliteration, each stanza being composed of epithets, the initial letter of which is always the same. The ease with which the language is rendered harmonious is the cause that there are so few bad verses in Gaëlic. Many of the sweetest lyrics have no other rhyme than the frequent sound of a single vowel or diphthong running throughout the stanza, with hardly any regularity of situation.

> A nighean donn na buaile
> Gam bheil an gluasad farusda
> Gun tug mi gaol co buan duit
> 'Snach gluais è air an Earrach so
> Mheall thu mi le d' shughradh,
> Le d' bhriodal a's le d' chuine
> Lub thu mi mar fhiuran
> 'Scha duchas domh bhi fallain uaith. *Anon.*

In singing or playing these compositions, the rhyming vowels are apparent, and prove the harmony of the measure. "The Aged Bard's Wish" is probably older than the introduction of Christianity among the Gaël, for he displays his belief in the ancient Celtic theology, and anticipates the joys that await him in the elysium of the bards—in the hall of Ossian, and of Daol. It shews that at a very early period, harmony of numbers was sedulously studied. There is a beautiful poetical translation of this piece by Mrs. Grant; for the literal version of the stanzas quoted I am indebted to the author of Melodies from the Gaëlic.

THE AGED BARD'S WISH.

Ocairibh mi ri taobh nan allt
A shiubhlas mall le ccumaibh ciuin.
Fo sgail a bharraich leag mo cheann
'S bith thus a ghrian ro chair deil rium.

Gu socair sin 's an fheur mo thaobh
Air bruaich na'n dithean 'snan gaoth tla,
Mo chos ga slioba sa bhraon mhaoth,
Se luba thairis caoin tren bhlar.

Biodh sòbhrach bhàn is ailli snuadh
M'an cuairt do m' thulaich, suain fo dhriuchd,
'San neonain bheag 's mo lamh air chluain
'San calbhuigh mo chluas gu cur.[m]

---

[m] O lay me by the streams that glide,
With gentle murmurs soft and slow,
Let spreading bows my temples hide;
Thou sun, thy kindest beams bestow.

And be a bank of flow'rs my bed,
My feet laved by a wandering rill:
Ye winds, breathe gently round my head,
Bear balm from wood, and vale, and hill.

Thou primrose pale, with modest air,
Thou daisy white, of grateful hue,
With other flow'rs, as sweet and fair,
Around me smile through amber dew.

Lyrical compositions are, without comparison, the most numerous in the Highlands, the first-mentioned measures being chiefly confined to those called Ossianic and other ancient poems. Of lyric poems, thousands might be collected, some of considerable antiquity, and many of great beauty, and the measures are nearly as numerous as the airs to which they are sung.

There is an ode, the stanzas of which consist of two lines and a repetition of the last. In this, the word upon which the cesural pause falls, rhymes with the final word, and with some other word about the middle of the second line; thus—

> Lochluinneach threun toiseach bhur sgeil
> Sliochd solta bhair treamh Mhànais
> Sliochd solta bhair freamh Mhanais.

In the ode of three lines, with the stanza twice repeated, the antepenults of the first and second lines rhyme with a syllable at the middle of the third line.

> Gam biodh faram air thàilisg,
> Agus fuiam air a chlàrsaich,
> Mar a bhuineadh do shar Mhac Mhic Leod.[a]
> Gam biodh, &c.
> Gur e b'eachdraidh na dheigh sin
> Greis air ursgeul na Feìne
> 'S air a chuideachda cheir-ghil na' n crochd.
> Gur e b', &c.

---

[a] The game of chess,
And the music of the harp,
The history of the feats of the Fingalians,
With the relations of the pleasures of the chase,
Were what the good son of Mac Leod loved.

The ode of six lines of four syllables, and a seventh of six syllables, has the first six lines rhyming at the end, and with the antepenult of the seventh—

>Leansa 'sna treig
>Cleachdadh as beus
>Taitim gu leir,
>Macanta seamh,
>Pailt ri luchd theud
>Gaisgail am feim
>Neartmhor an deigh toirachd.

These three sorts of measures are by the celebrated poetess Mary Mac Leod, and she appears to have invented them, for I do not think they occur in the works of any other.

There are stanzas of four lines, each of the three first having a double rhyme, and the rhyming word of the last line of every stanza answers to that of the fourth line of each of the first stanza, as seen by this specimen.

>Thuair mi sgeula moch dicedin
>Air laimh fheuma bha gu creuchdach,
>'Sleor a gheurad ann san leumsa
>Anal ou treud bha buaghar.

>O Dhun Garanach ur Allail
>Na'u trup meara 's na 'u steud seanga,
>Na'u gleus glana s'ceutach sealladh,
>Beichdail allaidh uaibhreach.

A stanza of eight lines, of six and eight syllables, where the final syllables of the second, fourth, sixth, and eighth lines rhyme, is common. In another also of eight lines of seven and five syllables, the last words of the second fourth, sixth, and eighth lines rhyme, and cesural and penult, and cesural and final rhymes occur irregularly throughout the other lines.

Si so'n aimsir an dearbhar
An taiganach dhiunn;
'S bras meinmnach fir Albin
Fon armaibh air thus;
'Nuair dh eireas gach reun-laoch
Na'n cididh ghlan ur
Le run feirg agus gairge
Gu seirbhis a chruin.º

That Gaëlic poetry may be regularly scanned, is shewn by Mr. Armstrong in his excellent Dictionary.

Gaëlic poetry seems to have had its classical as well as its declining period. There are many ancient poems of great beauty that cannot have been composed later than the first, second, or third century at least, but from the fall of the Pictish kingdom until the thirteenth century there is hardly anything to be found of historical poetry. Whatever destruction may have been occasioned by Edward I. to the other historical documents, he could never carry away the productions of Mac Alpin's bard and succeeding professors; they must have come down to our times like those of Ossian and Ullin, had they ever existed, or been at all worthy of preservation. The dark age of poetry and learning in the Highlands continued nearly 500 years.ᵖ

Some Highlanders have heard a song repeated on the battle of Perth, 1396, which bore evidence of its having been composed about the period of that event. Lachlan Mòr Mac Mhuirich Albinnich, bard to the Lords of the Isles, was probably born about the middle of the fourteenth

---

º John Lom Mac Donald's Address and Invitation to the Clans, in 1714, to take up arms.

ᵖ Poetry flourished in Wales until the time of Elizabeth, when it declined, until revived by the encouragement of late institutions.—*Myvyrian Archæology.*

century. He composed that curious Prosnachadh, to animate the troops at the battle of Gariach in 1411, since which time everything memorable in Highland history is recorded in poetry.

Mary Mac Leod, better known by the appellation of Nighean Alastair Ruadh, or the daughter of Red Alexander, was born about 1570. Many of her compositions are of great beauty.

Shelah Mac Donald, of the house of Keppoch, a family that may be termed hereditary poets, who lived from the reign of Charles II. to that of George I., wrote many patriotic and moral odes of great merit.

Mr. Alexander Mac Donald, whose admirable Prosnachadh Fairge has been partially translated, in a previous chapter, was an excellent poet, and strongly imbued with the spirit of Ossian. He lived from the latter end of the seventeenth until the middle of the eighteenth century, and was a good scholar and musician. His first song, "Banarach Dhonn a Chruidh," is still very popular, and the air to which it is sung made so strong an impression on Burns, that he wrote the words of "the Banks of the Devon" to it. Mac Donald's "Praise of Morag" is equally popular, and appears to have been the first poem adapted to a Piobrachd. It has three parts, the first being quick, the second quick, quick, and the third quick, quick, quick, and is the same measure as that in which Mac Intyre composed his celebrated descriptive poem of "Beinn Dorain," and Mac Kenzie that of "the Ship."

John Lom Mac Donald was born in the reign of James the First of England, and, I believe, died either in the reign of Queen Anne, or that of her successor, at a very great age. He accompanied Montrose in all his wars, being named poet laureate to the king, and contributed to the support of the royal cause, probably as much by his songs as the marquis did by his sword. He celebrated in verse the notable victory at Kilsyth, which he attributes to Montrose, and that at Inverlochy, which he thinks was achieved by Alexander Mac Donald, commonly called Mac Coll, or Colcitach. This last poem he composed on the top of the castle of Inverlochy, to which he had retired to view the battle; and being reproached by Montrose for not taking the field, he asked the hero, who would have commemorated his valour had the bard been in the fight? He laments, in pathetic verse, the murder of the king and of Montrose, but his indignation does not lead him to abuse Cromwell. He sung the murder of the children of Keppoch, and having obtained a commission to apprehend the murderers dead or alive, he ceased not to pursue his object, until he carried their heads to the lords of council. He was an eccentric character, warm and ardent in his friendship, bitter and unrelenting in his hatred, the greatest share of which fell to the Campbells. It is related, that dining one day with the Earl of Argyle, his host asked him why he kept always gnawing at his clan; when John, presuming on the bardic privilege, promptly expressed his regret that he could not swallow them.

From the time of John Lom, there is an uninterrupted succession of good poets. Mr. Mac Pherson, of Strathmasie, who was born about 1720, and died in the latter end of the last century, was a gentleman and a scholar, equal to the best Gaëlic bards in every respect, and superior to them all in one particular—humour. His poems have not been published in a collected form, and some of them have never been committed to the press, but a good many of them are to be met with in the collections of Stewart, Macfarlane, and Turner. Alastair Mac Aonais composed a Prosnachadh do na Gaël in 1745, and other pieces.

The celebrated John Roy Stewart, who was both a good

soldier and a good poet, must not be forgotten. In a poem on the battle of Culloden, he finds an opportunity to inveigh against Lord George Murray, whose proceedings during the progress of the rebellion he often disapproved of. He directly charges his lordship with treachery. His Lament for Lady Mac Intosh, who may be called his *sister* in arms, from having joined the rising in 1745, is pathetic and elegant.

William Ross, Robert Donn, and Duncan Mac Intyre, possess superior excellence. Ross may be called the Gaëlic Anacreon, Donn the Juvenal, while Mac Intyre combines the descriptive powers of Thomson with the versatile genius of Burns. The works of Robert Donn, who was a native of Sutherland, were published in one volume, 1829. Mac Intyre was a native of Glenurchy, and served in the Argyle Militia at the battle of Falkirk, where he lost his sword, which was a favourite weapon of the chieftain of the Fletchers. His Apologetic Poem on this misfortune is humorous, and shews that he was not sorry at the defeat of the royal forces. When after the rebellion in 1745, the wise ministry of George II. thought the Highlanders could be made loyal by being compelled to wear a foreign, and to them very inconvenient dress, Mac Intyre wrote his poem of "The Grey Breeches," in which he flatly accuses parliament and the ministry of injustice in imposing such a garb on the loyal as well as disloyal clans, insinuating that it would make the next rising more general: for this he was imprisoned. His poems were published in 1768, and that on Bein Dorain is said to excel everything of the kind.

Dugald Buchannan, a schoolmaster at Rannoch, published a volume of poems in 1770; and Kenneth Mac Kenzie, originally a sailor, and afterwards an officer in the army, who is perhaps still alive, published in 1796 a volume of poems of some merit. John Mac Gregor, of Glenlyon, published his poetical works in 1801. Those of Allan Mac Dougall, the blind bard of the late Glengarry, were first published in 1800, and their popularity is attested by many subsequent editions. This man was blind from his infancy, but Apollo, to compensate for the loss of sight, made him not only one of the best poets, but also of musicians.*

Among the modern poets of Caledonia, the late Mr. Ewen Mac Lachlan, master of the Grammar School of Old Aberdeen, makes a conspicuous figure. He translated, from the Greek, the third book of Homer's Illiad, and various excerpts from the same poet. He also wrote "The Seasons" in four songs, and a variety of other pieces; but what is remarkable is, that although his English and classical writings are good, they are not at all equal to his Gaëlic poetry, a proof, perhaps, of the superior fitness of that language for the service of the muses.†

Alexander and Donald Stewart published a large collection of the works of the bards who flourished within the last 400 years, and Turner, himself an aspirant for poetic

---

* It is incorrect to say that "Ailean Dall" was "blind from his infancy." We have it on the direct authority of his son, a musician and teacher of dancing, who only died a few years ago, that his father was grown to man's estate before he lost his eyesight. He was teasing a fellow-workman, who in play thrust at him with his needle, which, accidentally piercing one of his eyes, so wounded it that loss of sight ensued. In less than a year the other eye, as if in sympathy, became weak and clouded, and finally sightless as its companion.

He was neither one of the best of poets nor of musicians. He composed two or three good songs which are deservedly popular, and some other poems of fair merit. As a musician he was no more than a fair performer on the violin. We believe he sang his own and other Gaelic songs admirably, as he had an excellent voice and a correct ear. ED.

† MacLachlan's finest poem is his "Lament for Dr. Beattie," the author of "The Minstrel." He was MacLachlan's patron and friend for many years. ED.

fame, in addition to his first work, obtained a numerous subscription for a collection of the Gaëlic Jacobite songs, translated into English.

Music is either the mother or daughter of poetry. It is probably the former. The manner of the Gaëlic bards seems to have been to make the tune or melody first, and then to adapt words to it. The original poem was often lost, but the air, if a good one, seldom shared the same fate, because a tune is easier learned than a song. Many, however, could make a song who could not compose a tune, and, consequently, many were adapted to the same air. The poetry, which was composed by the Celts for the service of religion, was chaunted to appropriate music, and to the sweet melody of harps. The bards, who were of the Druidical order, sung the deeds of worthy men, celebrating the virtues of the good, and denouncing the vices of the reprobate. The practice of advancing to battle with songs of incitement and defiance was truly Celtic. The Gauls attacked Hannibal at the Rhone, crying and singing after their custom.[q] The bards conducted the music, and, by different modulations and changes in the air, the troops were led to advance or retreat, a fierce and harsh tone of defiance, according to Tacitus, being chiefly studied, with an unequal murmur, sometimes produced by applying the shields to the mouth, to swell the notes. To Pythagoras, from whom the Druids did not much differ, if he did not form his opinions from their maxims, the world is said to be indebted for the discovery of the principles of music, and he introduced the system of seven planets from the seven tones.[r] The ancients esteemed a knowledge of music an indispensable accomplishment. The Arcadians, a people resembling the Scots' Highlanders, reckoned it infamous

[q] Polybius, iii.   [r] Dion. Cassius, ap. Beloc on Herodotus.

to be ignorant of so agreeable an art. The youth were carefully taught to sing until they were thirty years of age, and their favourite songs were in celebration of the angels of birth, the gods and virtuous men, affording in this a remarkable resemblance to the Celts. Whether the melody of the human voice preceded or followed instrumental music, it was much cultivated by the primitive Celts, and their descendants in the different races have evinced a strong attachment to it. It is probable that music was seldom heard in ancient times, without being accompanied by the recitation of poetry, the harper being also a vocal performer. The song of the Druids, engraved in the following plates, is well known in the Highlands, where it is revered like a sacred hymn. The chaunting of the Druidical precepts in times of paganism was imitated by the early Christians, who were passionately fond of music. Adomnan is represented as having taken much delight in hearing Cronan, a famous poet, sing his native melodies. The clergy did not confine their talents to the voice, and it was not surprising that they should excel in performing on instruments where the qualification was so common. Bede says, that at entertainments the harp was handed from one to another, and if any one could not play, he felt so ashamed of his deficiency, that he took the first opportunity to slink off.[*] The bishops continued to carry this instrument along with them in the time of Cambrensis, and, indeed, the clergy were often excellent bards. Donchadh O'Daly, Abbot of Boyle in 1250, excelled all the bards of his time. The members of the Scots' Church brought sacred music to great perfection, and rendered it celebrated throughout Europe in very early ages, and left many treatises on it. When Neville Abbey, in France, was founded, the queen

[*] Lib. iv. c. 24.

of Pepin sent for Scots' musicians and choristers to serve in it. Mungret Abbey, near Limerick, is celebrated by monkish writers for its religious melody, having no fewer than five hundred, who served continually in the choir.[1] Coradh, from cor or cur, music, is applied to a proficient in the art, from which Dr. O'Connor thinks the name of curetes among the primæval Celts was derived.

The ancient Gaël were fond of singing, whether in a sad or cheerful frame of mind. Bacon justly remarks, that music feedeth that disposition which it findeth: it was a sure sign of brewing mischief when a Caledonian warrior was heard to "hum his surly song." This race, in all their labours, used appropriate songs, and accompanied their harps with their voices. At harvest the reapers kept time by singing; at sea the boatmen did the same; and while the women were graddaning, performing the luaghadh, or at other rural labour, they enlivened their work by certain airs called luineags. When milking, they sung a certain plaintive melody, to which the animals listened with calm attention. The attachment which the nations of Celtic origin have to their music is strengthened by its intimate connection with the national songs. The influence of both on the Scots' character is confessedly great—the pictures of heroism, love, and happiness exhibited in their songs are indelibly impressed on the memory, and elevate the mind of the humblest peasant. The songs united with their appropriate music affect the sons of Scotia, particularly when far distant from their native glens and majestic mountains, with indescribable feelings, and excite a spirit of the most romantic adventure. In this respect the Swiss, who inhabit a country

---

[1] Archdall's Monasticon, Hib. The English Church appears to have been a contrast. Prinn, in 1663, compares the music to the bleating of brute beasts. Histrio mastix. See Ledwich's Observations on the Gregorian and Ambrosian chaunts, in Walker's Bards.

of like character, and who resemble the Highlanders in many particulars, experience similar emotions. On hearing the national Ranz de vache, their bowels yearn to revisit the ever dear scenes of their youth. So powerfully is the amor patriæ awakened by this celebrated air, that it was found necessary to prohibit its being played under pain of death among the troops, who would burst into tears on hearing it, desert their colours, and even die.

No songs could be more happily constructed for singing during labour than those of the Highlanders, every person being able to join in them, sufficient intervals being allowed for breathing time. In a certain part of the song, the leader stops to take breath, when all the others strike in and complete the air with a chorus of words and syllables, generally without signification, but admirably adapted to give effect to the time. In singing during a social meeting, the company reach their plaids or handkerchiefs from one to another, and swaying them gently in their hands, from side to side, take part in the chorus as above. A large company thus connected, and see-sawing in regular time, has a curious effect; sometimes the bonnet is mutually grasped over the table. The Low Country manner is, to cross arms and shake each other's hands to the air of "auld lang syne" or any other popular and commemorative melody. Fhir a bhata, or the boatmen, the music of which is annexed, is sung in the above manner, by the Highlanders with much effect. It is the song of a girl whose lover is at sea, whose safety she prays for, and whose return she anxiously expects. The greater proportion of Gaëlic songs, whether sung in the person of males or females, celebrate the valour and heroism, or other manly qualifications, of the clans.

We are not precisely informed of the method by which the bards taught the music. In the college of choristers, we are told, it was taught in the drochaidh, or circle of melody. Brompton says, those of Ireland were instructed in secret, their lessons being committed to memory; and it is believed, that they had not in ancient times the art of communicating their melodies by notation, circumstances to which must, in a great measure, be attributed our imperfect knowledge of ancient Celtic music. Although the principle which led the Celts to teach by memory long existed, some remains of musical notation are yet to be found. A curious specimen, not older, however, than the time of Queen Elizabeth, is given by Walker. An air, called the tune of David the Prophet, a production of the eleventh century, was deciphered from an ancie:t Welsh MS., and Mr. Turner mentions another MS. of British music in existence, of which the notation cannot now be explained; being disregarded while it could be understood, it is thus lost for ever.[u] An Irish MS. of the fifteenth century contains the native musical terms. Car was a line of poetry, marked, and the characters; annal was a breathing, and ceol was the sound, which also signified the middle tone, or pitch of the voice. Ard ceol was a third higher, and bas ceol was a depression, one-third lower than the pitch. Cir ceol denoted the turning, or modulation, and semitones were left to the musician's ear. There were three names for harp notes, signifying the single, the great, and the little harmony.

Celtic music, like the poetry, is generally of a grave and plaintive character, although cheerful and animating airs are by no means wanting. "The Welsh, the Scots, and the Irish, have all melodies of a simple sort, which, as they are connected together by cognate marks, evince at once their relationship and antiquity."[v] The Manx have but a few national airs that much resemble the Irish. The

[u] Preface to his History of the Anglo Saxons.   [v] Caledonia, i. 476.

Golltraidheacht of the Irish was the martial music.— This sort seems adapted to the Prosnachadh Cath of the Gaël, which is in a short, rapid, spirit-stirring measure, of which many curious specimens might be given. This species of music being introduced at entertainments, is also called the festive. The Gentraidheacht is the sorrowful, of which sort the Caledonians are very fond. The Suantraidheacht is the reposing, or that which was calculated to quiet the mind and dispose the person hearing it to sleep. We perceive in the works of the old bards melodies for war, for love, and for sorrow, but in later times we shall find other classes that seem to have emanated from the pipers. The song of peace was raised in the field of battle at the termination of a conflict, and the song of victory was sung by the bards before the king after the gaining of a battle. In the poem of Cath Loda is an invocation to the harp of Cona, with its three voices, to come "with that which kindles the past." Fingal had a particular tune that appears to have been well known; it is called "that song which he hears at night when the dreams of his rest descend."

The love songs compose the chief part of the national poetry of Ireland and Scotland. Of the former country, it has been said, that its poetry seems considered as designed for love only, an opinion for which there is some reason. The amatory effusions of the Scots' bards exhibit great knowledge of the human heart and delicacy of sentiment, with a spirit of affection, and romantic tenderness and devotion, not surpassed, if equalled, by any other people, either ancient or modern. The passion of love is excited by the sensibility and tenderness of the music; and, stimulated by its influence, the Gaël indulge a spirit of the most romantic attachment and adventure which the peasantry of, perhaps, no other country exhibit.

It is well known that the Scots' music is composed on a peculiar scale. Caledonia has indeed to boast of the most ancient melodies, and, perhaps, the only national melody in Europe; the Irish rank next to her; and the Welsh must be permitted to follow in the possession of their corresponding styles.

The Scotish scale consists of six notes, having, in the key of C, c, d, e, g, a, c, corresponding to the black keys of the pianoforte; a scale, from its natural simplicity, singularly well adapted for the composition of an air. This is the enharmonic scale, used by the Egyptians, and other Eastern nations, and similar to that of the ancient Greeks. Whether, from the possession of this system, or peculiar organization, the Celts were proverbially musical; and the music of the Scotish Lowlanders which they think their own, being genuine Gaëlic, they probably have preserved from the time when they retained the same language and manners as their brethren in the mountains. Those who believe that Pictish invasions rendered the Eastern Scots a Gothic people, and altered their language, are obliged to confess that the music underwent no such change. The diatonic scale used by the Gothic nations produces melodies of a character completely different from that of the Celts.

Cambrensis contrasts the slow modulation in Britain with the rapid notes of the Irish. He says the Welsh did not sing in unison, but had as many parts as there were performers, and that they all terminated in B flat; the treble part also began soft, and produced, at last, a wild melody; and, speaking of the natives of Cumberland, he says, they sung in parts, in unisons, and octaves.

Although the Welsh were not previously ignorant of music, it is related that Gryffith ap Cynan, or Conan, being educated in Ireland, brought its music, musicians, and instruments to his own country about 1100, and having summoned a congress of the harpers of both countries to revise the music, the twenty-four canons were established. It is difficult to account for the fact, that the Welsh music, some of it of considerable antiquity too, differs from the Gaëlic airs, being composed in the diatonic or perfect scale. This modern style predominates, although not to the exclusion of the ancient, but the circumstance proves that the Welsh have materially swerved from their ancient simplicity. In a small degree, this has been the case with the Irish also, but that which is considered their proper harp music is of the Scotish character. Musicians and antiquaries seem to have found a bone of contention in the subject of these airs, some maintaining, that in the Highlands there are no harp melodies, while others assert that the luineags, or singing tunes, are composed for the harp only, and are unfit for the pipes. I am not a sufficient musician, perhaps, to discuss this subject with due ability, but I venture to say that both opinions are erroneous. Harp music is abundant in the Highlands, although not generally of the refined sort now so termed, and the old vocal melodies can certainly, with only a few exceptions, be performed on the pipe. The old harpers, who performed airs in the diatonic scale, appear to have tuned the instruments without knowing on what principle.

It has excited the wonder of some, that the ancient Scots' airs are usually in the minor mode; some are not in it, because the flat series is never constituted as a key note by means of its sharp 7th, as it invariably is in modern music.*

The most ancient vocal tunes had only one measure, and by attending to this, perhaps, one could form a tolerably

---

* Essay on the Influence of Poetry and Music upon the Highlanders, in the Preface to Mac Donald's Collection of Gaëlic Airs.

accurate collection of genuine melodies, for it is my opinion, that the fiddlers added 2nd, 3rd, and sometimes 4th parts to the original strain, which additions may be detected by being above the compass of the pipe chanter. Thus the beautiful Strathspey, for instance, called Callum Brogach, given as a specimen of this delightful music, is admirably adapted, in the first part, for the bagpipes. From this practice, however highly we esteem the merits of the individuals, we must regret the vitiation of some of our ancient pieces by Gow, Mac Intosh, and others. The simple harmonies, as given by Clarke, Fraser, and Mac Donald, are preferable to those put forth in characters unsuitable to the Celtic, and dressed up to please corrupted tastes; the airs are altered indeed, but they can scarcely be said to be improved, and the collection cannot claim to be one of genuine Scots melodies, or aid in assisting to preserve these interesting relics in purity.

There is another remarkable feature in the Gaëlic school, and a criterion by which to judge of the age of tunes: the old airs, however slow and plaintive, are generally, with good effect, convertible into a quick, or dancing measure, and vice versâ. Of this conversion, the dancing airs of modern times do not admit, at least, with any propriety.

The appogiaturas in modern music, are usually the next in degree to the chief note, and any great departure from this rule is accounted a barbarism. In Scots music they are some degree distant, and appear very graceful. This is most remarkable in pipe tunes, to which instrument they are indispensable.

There are certain differences very perceptible to a musical ear, in the style and character of the music of certain districts. The Caithness and Sutherland people are noted for playing in quick time, and the people of Strathspey, or rather the part of Scotland in which that valley is situated, are celebrated for their partiality to slow time, and the perfection in which they have composed and play the airs, which are known by the name of the place where they originated. The Strathspey is in simple common time, and it has been described as being to the common reel what a Spanish fandango is to a French cotillion.[x] Many assert that Strathspeys are so essentially different from reels that they can never be transposed: to me, it is evident that Strathspeys can be played in reel time with perfect facility, if not always with good effect, although I shall not say that reels can be made Strathspeys. The people of this district liked their music of a slower turn than others, and produced that style now so much and so justly admired.

Of the first composers or performers of Strathspeys, there appears to be no certain accounts. According to tradition, the first who played them were the Browns of Kincardine, to whom several of the ancient tunes are ascribed. After these, the Cummings of Freuchie, now Castle Grant, were the most celebrated. Of these musicians there were a hereditary succession, the last of whom, John Roy Cumming, who was very famous, died between 1750 and 1760. His descendants in London inherited the musical genius of their ancestors, and are known by many ingenious works in mechanics.[x]

The Reel of Tulloch, given as a specimen, is a popular tune among pipers, from whom it receives the appellation Righ na m Porst, or king of airs. It is stated by Mac Donald, that this reel was composed at Tulloch, in Aberdeenshire, a tradition that I have often heard repeated, detailing the particular circumstances connected with its production; but in Mac Gregor's Collection of poems, where the song is

---

[x] Newte.

Cogadh na Sith.

A Piobrachd.

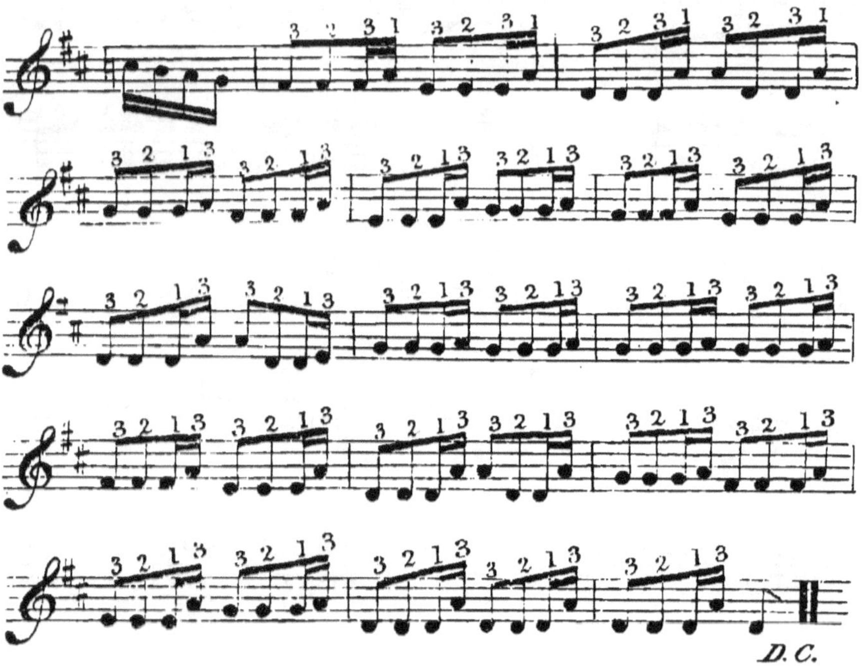

D.C.

CUILFHIONN.

A Slow March.

No II.

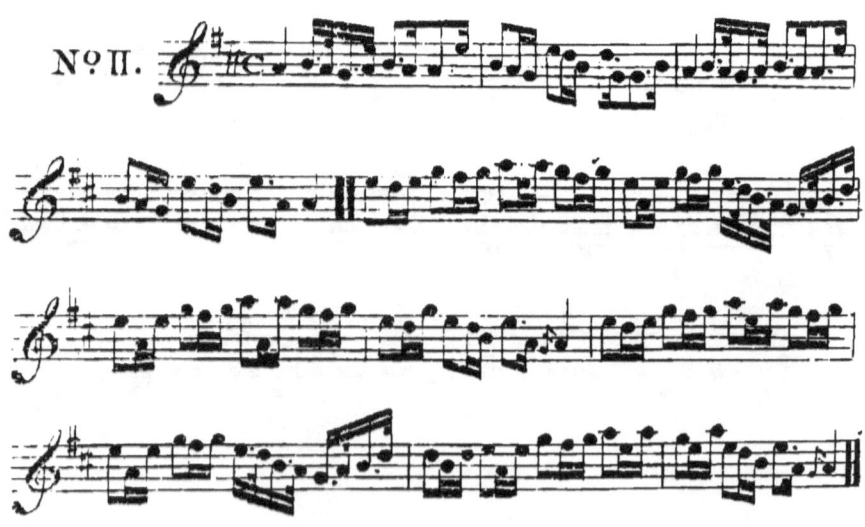

CALLUM BROGACH.

A Strathspey.

Ruighle Thulaichean.

Lively.   A Reel.

Cro nan Gobhar.

Sprightly.   A Jig.

FHIR A BHÀTA.

An Iorram.

Slow

Nº VI.

GU MO SLÀN A CHÌ MI MO CHALLIN DÌLEAS DONN.

A Pastoral Melody.

Tenderly.

Nº VII.

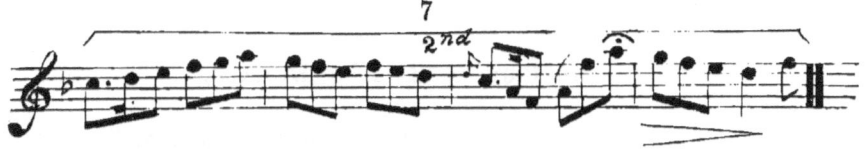

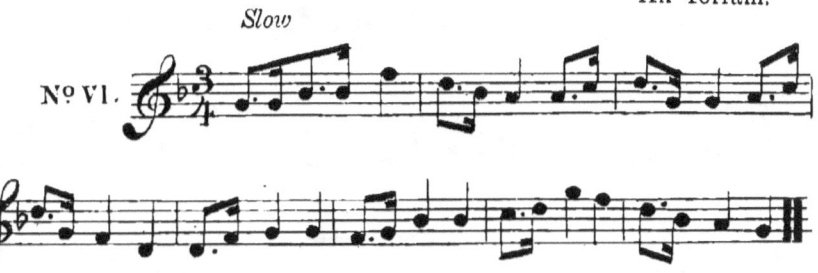

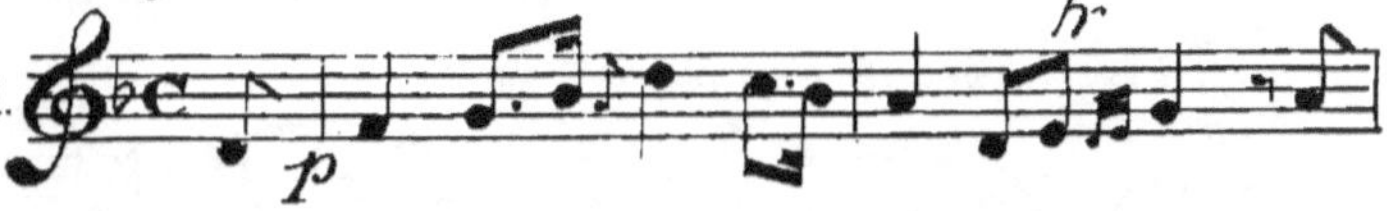

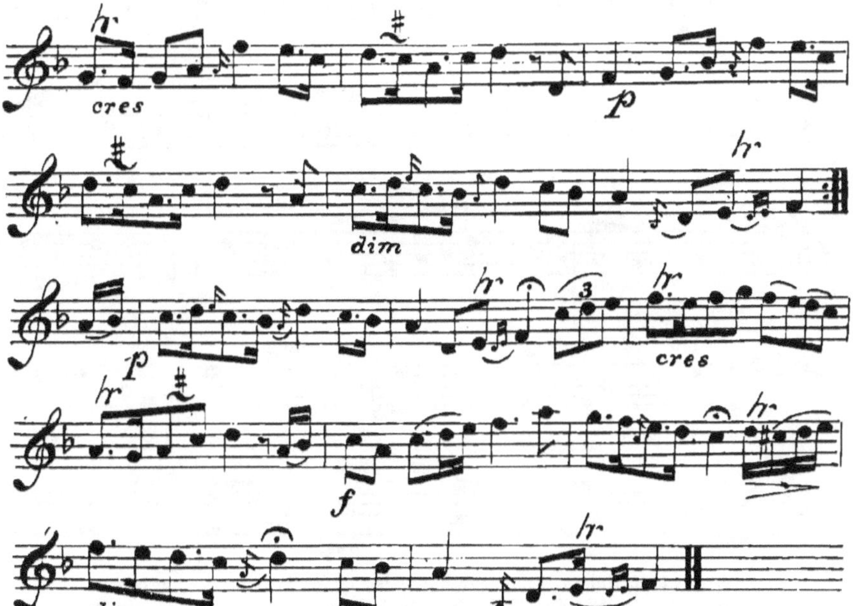

Mac Mo Righ 'Se 'Dol Fo' E'ideadh.

A Song of the Druids.

Cumhadh Fhinn.*

Ossian's Lament for his Father.

*A very beautiful air, which the Editor has no hesitation in saying is the original of "Oran an Fhéidh," so popular in Lochaber and the surrounding districts. Ed.

given, it is confidently asserted to be the composition of John Dubh Gear, a Mac Gregor of Glenlyon.

Some affect to discover a striking difference between Scots and Irish Jig tunes. I confess I cannot so easily perceive it, although I am aware that each have their characteristic style. A frequent distinction, though by no means a general rule, is, that the first is most frequently in 6, 8 time, the last 9, 8. The specimen given is a lively Highland air, but if sung or performed slowly, it is a very beautiful melody.

Of the Pastoral Melodies many others might have been selected, perhaps superior to the one given, but amid so great a variety of beautiful airs, it is not easy to fix on one that will be admired by all. In looking over Fraser's Collection, I hesitated whether I should substitute "Nighean donn na Gobhair," The Maid that tends the Goats; Bhanarach dhonn a chruidh," The Dairy Maid; or others of the same character. The Lament of Ossian may not be received by the sceptical as the production of that bard, but it must be allowed to be, like the Druid's song, a fragment of merit, which bears undoubted marks of great antiquity.

The MUSICAL INSTRUMENTS of the ancient Celts were simple; that of which we read most is the harp, but they also had others. When the Gauls sacked Rome they had trumpets with which they sounded the charge,[r] and which were employed to assemble their council; they made a most horrid noise, and were at times blown to terrify the enemy.[r] The horn of battle was used by the old Caledonians to call the army together, and sounded for a retreat; "The horn of Fingal" was, probably, his attendant trumpet. The Cornu was blown by the Druids, and their Christian successors appear to have retained the practice. St. Patrick is represented as carrying one. The wind

[r] Diodorus.

instruments of this sort in use among the ancient Irish, were the Stuic, a brazen tube, used as a speaking trumpet. The Corna, in its rudest form, was a cow's horn, and was sometimes sufficiently powerful to be heard at a distance of six miles. The Dudag is not certainly known, but is believed to have been a semi-circular horn. Some of them were found near Armagh, and are engraved in the Transactions of the Royal Irish Society;[x] when blown they are said to have made a tremendous noise. The Buabhal, Beann, and Adhare, are not precisely known, but are conjectured to be only different names for cornua. O'Connor says, that particular clans had horns of peculiar tones, and Froissart describes the Scots at Otterburn as blowing them in different notes. The Irish also speak of Gall trompa, the stranger's trumpet, and the Blaosg, or concha marina, resembling the buccinum of the Latins. The Cibbual, or corabas, was composed of several small plates of brass, or shingles of wood, fastened with a thong, being held in one hand while it was struck with the palm of the other. The Corabasnas consisted of two circular plates of brass, connected by a twisted wire, which, on being struck, produced a jingling sound, and was used to mark time. The Corna'n, or crona'n, was named from cor, music, and anan, base, an instrument to which the Iachdar channus was similar. The readan, fideog, or lonloingean, are supposed to have been a sort of flutes.[a]

The HARP, that most ancient and esteemed of stringed instruments, was a favourite of the Celtic nations, and was retained in the British Islands when it had become almost unknown on the continent. The Hyperboreans, who are believed to have been the Aborigines of Britain, were celebrated performers on it, accompanying their hymns with its music, and carrying their offerings to Delos with both flutes and harps.

[x] Vol. viii.   [a] Walker's Irish Bards.

The Irish have, in all ages, been noted for their excellence in harp music, and many proofs could be adduced of their proficiency. It is related of the King of Munster, so early as 489, that he had the best band of harpers of any in his time, who accompanied their music with singing;[b] but the most flattering testimonial to the national merit is paid by Geraldus Cambrensis, who resided in Ireland for some time in the latter part of the twelfth century. His eulogium is certainly high, and its justice is confirmed by his countrymen, who acknowledge, that to the Irish they owe not only the improvement of the harp, but that of their music also.[c] Powell, in his History of Cambria, says, that in 1078, "Gryffith ap Cynan, or Conan, brought from Ireland cunning musicians, that devised in a manner all the instrumental music now used, as appears by the names of the tunes and measures." That their harp may have been improved by the Irish is probable, but it was used by them from the remotest ages. The harper was a distinguished member of the royal household; none were permitted by their laws to play on this instrument except freemen; and it was reckoned disgraceful for a gentleman not to have a harp and be able to play on it. Buchannan is adduced as testifying that the harpers in Scotland were all Irishmen, but as the passage refers to a king, whose existence is denied, it is unfair to press it into the service, or lay any weight on it. Ireland at one time does appear to have obtained a superior reputation for skill in harp music; but Giraldus, who extols them so highly, says, when he had made himself better informed, that it was the opinion of many that the Scots far surpassed the Irish in musical science, and that Scotland had become the resort of those who were desirous of perfecting themselves in it.

[b] Life of St. Kieran.   [c] Caradoc, ap. Wynne, Walker, &c.

Although there is not, I believe, at present in the Highlands any professional harper, and although it had been so long disused, that its former existence in these parts was doubted, it is easily proved, from other authorities than the above, to have been common to the Gaël. Buchannan speaks of their delightful playing on it; and Major tells us James I., who died in 1437, excelled all the Irish and Scots' Highlanders, who were the best of all harpers. In short, harpers were hereditary attendants on the Scots kings and the Highland chiefs, from whom they had certain lands and perquisites; and this is confirmed by a hundred names of places throughout the Highlands, and by numerous traditions.

One instance, apparently the latest, of a harper attending a Highland army occurs in the case of that sent against the catholic lords, Errol, Huntly, and Angus, in 1594, on which occasion, Argyle carried with him his harper to animate his troops, unfortunately without effect. The prophecy of a witch, whom he also took with him, that it should be played at the Castle of Slanes, the Earl of Errol's seat, on a certain day, may have been literally true, for it could have been there sounded at the time foretold, but the Campbells had previously suffered a total defeat.

A harp key, that had been time immemorial in the family of Lord Mac Donald, and that bore marks of antiquity, being ornamented with gold and silver, and a precious stone, making its value eighty or one hundred guineas, was presented by his lordship to the celebrated O'Kane. But the harps of Lude, that have been preserved so long by the Robertsons of that house, are now in possession of the Highland Society, and remain valuable relics in themselves, and evidence that this instrument held the same place in Scotland that it did in Wales and Ireland. One of these harps was brought from Argyle by the daughter of the Laird of Lamont, who married into the family about 1460, and is supposed to be some centuries older than that time; the other was presented by Queen Mary, when on a hunting excursion, to Beatrix Gardyn, daughter to the Laird of Banchory, near Aberdeen, who was married to Findla Mhor, an ancestor of the Farquharsons of Invercauld, from whom both families are descended,[d] and such a present shews that to play on the harp was at that time an accomplishment of the ladies of Scotland, at least of the Highlands, for it is not to be supposed the Queen would have bestowed this instrument on one who did not understand it.

Mr. Bowles, the ingenious author of Hermes Britannicus, believes the form of the Celtic harp is represented in the figures on an ancient monument in Egypt, where it is seen exactly to resemble that of the moderns.

There appears to have been four sorts of harps among the ancient Irish. The common sort, or clarsach, the ceirnine, a smaller sort, the creamthine cruit, and the cionar cruit. The harp proper was called clar, or clarsach, by the Scots and Irish, and was sometimes termed sitearn, a word now obsolete. The Welsh call the harp telin, which seems to be a pronunciation of teud luin, an appellation borrowed from the Gael, who frequently term it poetically, teud ciuil, strings of melody.

The Cruit, or croith, as some Irish will have it, is often confounded with the harp, but they were evidently different; "*am bu lconmhar cruit is clar*," there were many a cruit and harp, says an old poem. The name, which is Latinized Crotta, is derived by etymologists from crith, a shaking. It is the crwth of the Welsh, and the parent of the violin, from which, in old English, a fiddler was denominated a

[d] Trans. of Highland Soc. iii. p. 39. Introd.

crowther.* This instrument was once much esteemed in Scotland, but has been so long disused in that country, that the Welsh think it their own.ᵉ

The Creamthine cruit had six strings, and was used at carousals; the Cionar cruit, used by the bards, had ten strings, and was played by a bow, answering, it is thought, to the canora cythara of the Romans, and the modern guitar.

From some ancient sculpture, the Gaëlic harp appears to have been of the same form as it is still. That which is believed, apparently with truth, to have belonged to Brian Boroimh, king of Ireland, slain in 1014, is preserved in Trinity College, Dublin, and has been engraved in several works. It bears an exact resemblance to the clarsach Lumanach, as the Lamont's harp is called, and that of Queen Mary, in the number of strings and general appearance, being only one inch higher than the latter, which is thirty-one inches in extreme height, and the breadth of the lowest part of the sounding board, which rises towards the middle, while that of the other is flat, is only eleven inches and a half. This harp has twenty-eight string-holes, and the like number of pins or keys, to which the strings are fixed. The holes are quite plain, unlike those of the other, which have brass escutcheons of neat workmanship fixed in the sound board. In front of the upper arm were the Queen's portrait, and the arms of Scotland, both in gold, and on each side was placed a jewel, surrounded by minute inlaid work, as represented, but of those valuables it was despoiled in the troubles of 1745. Queen Mary's harp is altogether a more neat and compact instrument than the

---

* "I never heard the old song of Percie and Douglas (Chevy Chase) that I found not my heart moved more than with the sound of a trumpet; and yet it is sung but by some blind CROWDER, with no rougher voice than rude style."—Sir Philip Sidney. ED.

ᵉ Evans.

other, being little more than half its weight. The Caledonian harp has thirty strings, and has this peculiarity, that the front arm is not perpendicular to the sounding board, but is turned considerably towards the left, to afford a greater opening for the voice of the performer, and this construction shows that the accompaniment of the voice was a chief province of the harper.[f] Giraldus describes the harp as containing twenty-eight strings, but they were afterwards increased to thirty-three, and Mysut, a Jesuit, is said to have introduced double strings in the fifteenth century. The old Welsh harp is said to have had nine strings, and that of the Caledonians only four. An account is given by Martin of a man who travelled about as a harper, with an instrument containing only four strings, and ornamented with two hart's horns in front. It was first intended to string the above two harps with brass wire, according to the old Scots and Irish manner, but as it would have been necessary, in order to bring out the proper sound, for one to allow the finger nails to grow to a certain length, that method was abandoned. A fine clear tone was produced by the finger nails from the wire, and it is related of O'Kane, the Irish harper, who frequented the Highlands about thirty years ago, that, inheriting a bardic spirit of arrogance, he was often punished by being turned from the houses of his patrons with his nails cut. The strings were also sometimes struck by a plectrum, or bit of crooked iron. Both Highlanders, Irish, and Welsh, held their harp on the left side, and a remarkable peculiarity in the construction of the Caledonian one, as represented by Gunn, is, that it is bent to accommodate the arm.

Buchanan describes the Scots harp as sometimes strung with wire, and sometimes with gut. The Welsh now use

---

[f] Gunn's Enquiry respecting the Performance of the Harp.

strings of the latter, but formerly they appear to have used hair; hence Borde speaks of his harp, which was

"made of a good mare's skyn,
The strynges be of horse hair, it maketh a good dyn."

There is this distinction made by the Chronicle of 1597, that the clarishoe (clarsach) had brass wire, and the harp sinew strings.

The Highlanders took great pains to decorate their harps. Buchanan said their only ambition seemed to be to deck them with silver and precious stones; the poor, who could afford nothing better, using crystals and brass.

Roderick Morrison, usually called Rory Dall, or the blind, was one of the last native harpers. He served in that capacity to the laird of Mac Leod, but on the death of his master, Dunvegan castle and its establishment being abandoned, he began an itinerant life. About 1650, he accompanied the Marquis of Huntly on a visit to Robertson of Lude, on which occasion he composed a porst or air, which, with other pieces, are yet preserved, called Suipar, chiurn na Leod, or Lude's Supper.* There is a proverb in Gaëlic, referring to this man, implying that "one may tire of the best tune that Roderick ever played."

Mr. Robertson was an eminent performer himself; and Mac Intosh, the compiler of the Gaëlic Proverbs, relates the following anecdote, which he received from his father: "One night, my father, James Mac Intosh, said to Lude, that he would be happy to hear him play upon the harp, which, at that time, began to give place to the violin. After supper, Lude and he retired to another room, in which there were a couple of harps, one of which belonged to Queen Mary. James, said Lude, here are two harps; the largest one is the loudest, but the small one is the

* *Suipear chuirm an Leòid*, a very fine air admirably played on the violin by Tom Allan of Forfar. ED.

sweetest, which do you wish to hear played? James answered, the small one, which Lude took up and played upon till daylight."

John Garbh Mac Lean, of Coll, who lived in the latter end of the reign of King James VI., and first of Charles, was a composer of music and a performer on the harp. Caoineadh Rioghail, the Royal Lament, and Toum Murran, two of his compositions, are yet preserved. This anecdote has been handed down concerning him: the captain of an English vessel, which had been wrecked on the island, went to the Castle of Coll, where, seeing the laird sitting with a bible in one hand, and a harp placed by his side, he was struck by the venerable appearance of the old gentleman and his occupation, and exclaimed with admiration, "Is this King David restored again to the earth?"

Murdoch Macdonald, who was brought up in this family, was, perhaps, the last harper. He studied with Rory Dall. in Sky, and afterwards in Ireland, and remained with Mac Lean, as harper, until 1734, as appears from an account of payments still remaining, soon after which he appears to have retired to Quinish, in Mull, where he died. He is still spoken of as Murdoch Clarsair, and his son was distinguished as Eoin Mac Mhurchaidh Clarsair. The Mac Niels, a celebrated race of bards, were the hereditary harpers of the Mac Leans, of Dowart.

When Alexander III. met Edward I. at Westminster, he was attended by harpers and minstrels, and Elye, the chief performer, in the first class received more than either the trumpeter or minstrel.

Harps were a sort of heirlooms, and were sometimes very old. The Caledonian harp before described, carries evidence in its shattered state, of its antiquity and ill usage. Mr. Gunn, in his "Enquiry," has the following passage on this subject:—" I have been favoured with a copy of an ancient Gaëlic poem, together with the music to which it is still sung in the Highlands, in which the poet personifies and addresses a very old harp, by asking what had become of its former lustre? The harp replies, that it had belonged to a king of Ireland, and had been present at many a royal banquet; that it had afterwards been successively in the possession of Dargo, son of the Druid of Baal, of Gaul, of Fillan, of Oscar, of O'Duine, of Diarmid, of a physician, of a bard, and lastly of a priest, 'who, in a secluded corner, was meditating on a white book.'"

The PIPE is a most ancient instrument of music. It was well known to the Trojans and Greeks, among whom there were different sorts for Dorian, Lydian, and Phrygian measures; but the addition of a bag and accompanying drones or burdens, must have been an invention of subsequent times. Theocritus, who flourished 385 A. C., mentions it in his Pastorals, and Procopius describes it as having both the skin and the wood extremely fine. Pronomus, the Theban, is said, by Pausanias, to have been the first that played the different measures at once on one pipe.

There is at Rome, a fine Greek sculpture, in basso relievo, representing a piper playing on an instrument bearing a close resemblance to the Highland bagpipe. The Greeks, unwilling as they were to surrender to others the merit of useful inventions, acknowledge, that to the barbarians, i. e. the Celts, they owed much of their music, and many of its instruments. The Romans, who, no doubt, borrowed the bagpipe from the Greeks, used it as a martial instrument among their infantry.[g] It is represented on several coins, marbles, &c.; but from rudeness of execution, or decay of the materials, it is difficult to ascertain its exact form. On the reverse of a coin of the Emperor Nero, who thought

[g] Varro calls it Pythaula, a word of Greek derivation, and not dissimilar o the Celtic piob-mhala, pronounced piovala.

himself an admirable performer on it, and who publicly displayed his abilities, the bagpipe is represented. An ancient figure, supposed to be playing on it, has been represented, and particularly described by Signor Macari, of Cortona, and is engraved in Walker's History of the Irish Bards, but it does not, in my opinion, appear to be a piper. A small bronze figure, found at Richborough, in Kent, and conjectured to have been an ornament of horse furniture, is not much more distinct. Mr. King, who has engraved three views of it, and others, believe it to represent a bagpiper, to which it has certainly more resemblance than to "a person drinking out of a leathern bottle."

The bagpipe, of a rude and discordant construction, is in common use throughout the East, and that it continues the popular instrument of the Italian peasant is well known. In this country it is the medium through which the good Catholics show their devotion to the Virgin Mother, who receives their adoration in the lengthened strains of the sonorous Piva. It is a singular but faithful tradition of the church, that the shepherds who first saw the infant Jesus in the barn, expressed their gladness by playing on their bagpipes. That this is probable and natural will not be denied, but the illuminator of a Dutch missal, in the library of King's College, Old Aberdeen, surely indulged his fancy when he represented one of the appearing angels likewise playing a salute on this curious instrument. The Italian shepherds religiously adhere to the laudable practice of their ancestors; and, in visiting Rome and other places to celebrate the advent of our Saviour, they carry the pipes along with them, and their favourite tune is the Sicilian mariners, often sung in Protestant churches.

"It is a popular opinion that the Virgin Mary is very fond, and is an excellent judge of music. I received this information on Christmas morning, when I was looking at two poor Calabrian pipers, doing their utmost to please her and the infant in her arms. They played for a full hour to one of her images, which stands at the corner of a street. All the other statues of the Virgin, which are placed in the streets, are serenaded in the same manner every Christmas morning. On my inquiring into the meaning of that ceremony, I was told the above-mentioned circumstance of her character, which, though you have always thought highly probable, perhaps you never before knew for certain. My informer was a pilgrim, who stood listening with great devotion to the pipers. He told me, at the same time, that the Virgin's taste was too refined to have much satisfaction in the performances of these poor Calabrians, which was chiefly intended for the infant, and he desired me to remark, that the tunes were plain, simple, and such as might naturally be supposed agreeable to the ear of a child of his time of life."[h]

Some writers suppose the Highlanders derived the bagpipe from the Romans, while others think it was received from the Northern nations. Giraldus Cambrensis does not appear to have found it among the Scots, except he means it by the chorus, an instrument of the Welsh also. The term may be used to express a chord of pipes, a conjecture that is supported by the inability of antiquaries to tell us what else it can be. The chord at any rate is not mentioned by him as an instrument of the Irish, but the writers of that country think the bagpipe was known very anciently. The Cuisley ciuil is believed to have been a simple sort, but Walker and others acknowledge that the bagpipe was introduced from Scotland.

It seems impossible to trace its origin among the Scots, but it is undoubtedly of great antiquity. Without deduc-

---

[h] Moore's View of Society and Manners in Italy. Letter 52.

ing it from other nations, we may reasonably presume that in a country to which it has been so long peculiar, it was from its primitive simplicity, gradually brought to its present perfection: that the chanter was an improvement of the simple pastoral reed, to which the drones, a happy accompaniment, were subsequently added. The great Highland pipe is, perhaps, the only national instrument in Europe; every other may be found common to many countries, but this is used in Scotland alone. "In halls of joy, and in scenes of mourning, it has prevailed; it has animated her warriors in battle, and welcomed them back after their toils, to the homes of their love and the hills of their nativity. Its strains were the first sounded on the ears of infancy, and they are the last to be forgotten in the wanderings of age. Even Highlanders will allow that it is not the gentlest of instruments; but when far from their mountain homes, what sounds, however melodious, could thrill round their heart like one burst of their own wild native pipe? The feelings which other instruments awaken, are general and undefined, because they talk alike to Frenchmen, Spaniards, Germans, and Highlanders, for they are common to all; but the bagpipe is sacred to Scotland, and speaks a language which Scotsmen only feel. It talks to them of home and all the past, and brings before them, on the burning shores of India, the wild hills and oft frequented streams of Caledonia, the friends that are thinking of them, and the sweethearts and wives that are weeping for them there! and need it be told here, to how many fields of danger and victory its proud strains have led! There is not a battle that is honourable to Britain in which its war blast has not sounded. When every other instrument has been hushed by the confusion and carnage of the scene, it has been borne into the thick of battle, and, far in the advance, its bleeding but devoted bearer, sinking on the earth, has sounded at once encouragement to his countrymen and his own coronach."[1]

How many anecdotes might be given of the effects of this instrument on the hardy sons of Caledonia! In the war in India, a piper in Lord Mac Leod's regiment, seeing the British army giving way before superior numbers, played, in his best style, the well known Cogadh na Sith, which filled the Highlanders with such spirit, that, immediately rallying, they cut through their enemies. For this fortunate circumstance, Sir Eyre Coote, filled with admiration, and appreciating the value of such music, presented the regiment with fifty pounds, to buy a stand of pipes. At the battle of Quebec, in 1760, the troops were retreating in disorder, and the general complained to a field officer in Fraser's regiment of the bad conduct of his corps. "Sir," said the officer, with a degree of warmth, "you did very wrong in forbidding the pipers to play; nothing inspirits the Highlanders so much, even now they would be of some use." "Let them blow in God's name, then," said the general: and the order being given, the pipers with alacrity sounded the Cruinneachadh, on which the Gaël formed in the rear, and bravely returned to the charge. George Clark, now piper to the Highland Society of London, was piper to the 71st regiment at the battle of Vimiera, where he was wounded in the leg by a musquet ball as he boldly advanced. Finding himself disabled, he sat down on the ground, and, putting his pipes in order, called out, "Weel, lads, I am sorry I can gae nae farther wi' you, bit deel hae my saul if ye sall want music;" and struck up a favourite warlike air, with the utmost unconcern for anything, but the unspeakable delight of sending his comrades to battle with the animating sound of the piobrachd.

[1] Preface to Mac Donald's Ancient Martial Music of Caledonia.

It is a popular tradition, that the enemy anxiously level at the pipers, aware of the power of their music; and a story is related of one, who, at the battle of Waterloo, received a shot in the bag before he had time to make a fair beginning, which so roused his Highland blood, that, dashing his pipes on the ground, he drew his broadsword, and wreaked his vengeance on his foes with the fury of a lion, until his career was stopped by death from numerous wounds. It is related of the pipe major of the 92nd, on the same occasion, that, placing himself on an eminence where the shot was flying like hail, regardless of his danger, he proudly sounded the battle air to animate his noble companions. On one occasion, during the Peninsular war, the same regiment came suddenly on the French army, and the intimation of their approach was as suddenly given by the pipers bursting out their gathering. The effect was instantaneous; the enemy fled, and the Highlanders pursued.

The use of the bagpipe in war is very ancient among the Highlanders. Its fitness for the tumult of battle must have given it an early preference over the harp, and led, from the military state in which the Gaël were so long placed, to the disuse of the latter.[j] Robertson, in his Enquiry into the Fine Arts, says, that pipe music is the voice of uproar and misrule, and that the airs calculated for it seem to be those of real nature and of rude passion. Its correspondence with the feelings may have increased the influence of pipe music over the Highlanders, but their partiality does not depend on this; for although its use in inspiring courage in battle was unparalleled and held indispensable, yet it was equally in request for the exhilaration of wedding and other parties, expressing sorrow on occasion

[j] The Athenians rejected the use of pipes, as they were not only a hindrance to discourse but to hearing. Major represents the Scots at Bannockburn as using tubæ, litui, and cornua.

of death or misfortune, and amusing the shepherd in the solitude of his avocations. At all rural occupations in the Highlands it has been observed that labour is accompanied by singing. Where music can be had, it is preferred. A piper is often regularly engaged in harvest to animate the reapers, and he generally keeps behind the slowest worker.

The effect is not confined to the mountaineers, for the inhabitants of the Low Country are equally partial to it; and even those of the Southern parts of the island are not unmoved by the tones of a well-played Highland bagpipe. When the Margrave of Anspach was on a visit to Duff House, he was entertained by this instrument, and on being asked how he liked the piobrachd, he confessed the effect of the bold, rapid, and intricate measures, by placing his hand on his heart, and intimating the emotion which he experienced.

The piobrachd, as its name implies, is properly a pipe tune, and is usually the Cruinneachadh, or gathering of a clan, being a long piece of music composed on occasion of some victory, or other fortunate circumstance in the history of a tribe, which, when played, is a warning for the troops to turn out. There are, however, other classes of this sort of music, which generally pass by the same name, but which in reality are, or ought to be, used for particular purposes. Some of these had their origin in similar events to the cuairt piobrachd, or regular gathering, and are of the same character, but are properly a cumhadh, coronach, or lament, and a failte, salute, or welcome. The first has been composed on the death of some celebrated chief, and is played at the funeral of his successors and others of the clan, and the second has been composed on the birth of a chief, or gentleman of a clan, his baptism, arrival at age, marriage, or other happy event, and was played on like occasions to his successors, and when the chief, or colonel of a clan, came on the field of muster. Although their characters are much alike, with the exception of the coronach, which is, of course, particularly slow, plaintive, and expressive, little or no attention is now paid to the distinctions, and so much has propriety been disregarded, that these pieces of music are frequently called " marches." Now the pipers may and do play piobrachd when a regiment is on the march, but it is not adapted for regularity, because the time varies in its different parts. A piobrachd may be described as an extended piece of music adapted for the bagpipe, composed in celebration of a battle where the clan was successful, or composed, before the conflict commenced, to excite the warriors to heroism, or it was first played even in the midst of a battle, from a sort of inspiration produced by enthusiasm; which pieces of music become, in particular clans, consecrated to all succeeding enterprises of war and occasions of festive enjoyment, when it is desirable to enliven the company by recalling the deeds of other years. But although clan gatherings are now all more or less old, pipers continued to compose similar music until recently. Several originated in the year 1745, as one by the piper of Cluny, who composed a piobrachd during the battle of Falkirk, which is yet well known; and later instances may not be wanting, but the old gatherings retained their place, which they certainly deserve, from the true expression and genuine character of their music. Indeed, the composition of salutes and other piobrachds is now, perhaps, oftener attempted than success can warrant; and pipe musicians would acquire greater credit by paying more attention to the inimitable works of their ancestors than to their own rhapsodies. It is alleged, by those who are competent to form a correct opinion, that the present pipers are inferior to their ancestors, and are getting worse. There are certainly many exceptions to this assertion where a musical car is assisted by knowledge, which the old pipers did not possess. The lists of competitors at Edinburgh shew numerous names of clever pipers; and in London, Mr. Mac Kay, piper to his Royal Highness the Duke of Sussex, and Mr. Clark, who officiates in the same capacity, to the Highland Society, are excellent; but we must regret that the same cause which led to the decay of oral recitation, impaired our modern list of ancient Gaëlic music; for the former celebrated seminaries being no more, a considerable portion of pipe music, from having never been noted down, is already lost. "In less than twenty years," says Mac Donald, in his excellent Preface to his Gaëlic Melodies, "it would be in vain to attempt a collection of Highland music."

The piper, who was hereditary, held an important place in the establishment of a chief. He had lands for his support, and was of superior rank to the other members of the "tail," had a gilli, or servant, who carried his pipes, and was esteemed, as his profession entitled him, to the appellation of a gentleman. He accompanied the chief wherever he went, and with the harper had a right to appear in all public meetings. He promenaded in front of the castle while the laird was dressing, at an early hour in the morning, and enlivened the meals either in the same way, or at the end of the hall.[k]

A striking proof of the respect paid to this class, resembling the veneration in which the bards were held, occurred on the defeat of the Mac Leods at Inverury, in

---

[k] In some towns a practice exists, derived, in all probability, from the duties of these musicians. In Perth, I believe, there is still a piper who plays through the streets at five o'clock in the morning and seven at night. The death of one of these performers some time since was much regretted at the time, the music having an effect in the morning "inexpressibly soothing and delightful."—Memorabilia of Perth, p. 13. In Keith, an inland town of Banffshire, the same custom is retained.

Aberdeenshire, by the rebels in 1745. Mac Rimmon, the chief's piper, and master of the celebrated college, was, after a stout resistance, made prisoner. Next morning none of the pipers in the victorious army played through the town, as usual, and being asked the reason of this extraordinary conduct, they answered, that while Mac Rimmon was in captivity their instruments would not sound; and it was only upon the release of the respected prisoner that the musicians returned to their duty.

Being held in so much estimation, it was to be expected that they should become aware of their own importance, and be tenacious of their honour and privileges. Many instances might be recorded of their nice feeling upon this point.

The captain of one of the companies of the Black Watch had received orders to add a drum to his bagpipe, which could not be dispensed with, as the Highlanders could not be made to march without it. The drummer was accordingly procured, between whom and the original musician a bitter contest arose about the post of honour. The contention at last grew extremely warm, and came to the ears of the captain, who called the parties before him to adjust their difference, and decided the matter in favour of the drummer, notwithstanding the warm remonstrances and forcible reasoning of the piper. "The devil, sir," says he, "and shall a little rascal that beats upon a sheepskin take the right hand of me, who am a musician?"

Perhaps this is the first instance of a drummer being placed in a Highland regiment; formerly they had none, and, although they were used in 1745, the pipers outnumbered them beyond comparison, for, wherever they found one who could perform on this instrument, they compelled him to follow them, and Prince Charles is said to have been entertained by thirty-two, who marched before his tent during meals. Some of the unfortunate pipers who were taken on the suppression of the rebellion, thought they could effectually plead that, being only pipers, they had not carried arms against his Majesty, but it was decided that their pipe was an instrument of war. Mac Donnel, the famous Irish piper, lived in great style, keeping servants, horses, &c. In the "Recollections" of O'Keefe, the following anecdote is given: "One day that I and a very large party dined with Mr. Thomas Grant, at Cork, Mac Donnel was sent for to play for the company during dinner. A table and chair were placed for him on the landing ouside the room, a bottle of claret and glass on the table, and a servant waiting behind the chair designed for him, the door being left wide open. He made his appearance, took a rapid survey of the preparation for him, filled his glass, stepped to the dancing room door, looked full into the room, said 'Mr. Grant, your health, and company!' drank it off, threw half-a-crown on his little table, saying to the servant, 'there, my lad, is two shillings for my bottle of wine, and sixpence for yourself.' He ran out of the house, mounted his hunter, and galloped off, followed by his groom!" This was a remarkable case; all pipers, though comfortable enough, had not quite so much of the good things of this life.* I recollect an eccentric but respectable minstrel, who perambulated Aberdeen, Banff, Moray, Kincardine, and adjoining counties, delighting the families he visited by his melodies, and gratifying them by his amusing compositions, for he wooed the muses. Poor Clark, although aware of his abilities, was not so independent as Mac Donnel, who would play and rhyme *con amore* to his friends for a lee lang day, and good humouredly tell his entertainers, at the close of a panegyric,

> "I maun gang hame, the nicht's growin' dark,
> Your humble servant, Kennedy Clark."

Whilst other professions, with the exception of the bard, might be adopted at pleasure, the piper was obliged to serve a regular apprenticeship. The most celebrated seminary for instruction was kept in the Isle of Sky by the Mac Rimmons, hereditary pipers to the chiefs of Mac Leod. They held certain lands, from time immemorial, for the duty of attending the chief and his clan, and increased their income by pupils, who spent seven years in perfecting themselves for pipers, and the masters never admitted a student, it is said, who had not an ear for music. In the Highlands, however, such an individual was not likely to be met with.

The Mac Rimmons have long since ceased to play for their chief, or give instructions to youth. Captain Mac Rimmon died lately in Essex, at an advanced age, and the descendant of those celebrated pipers is now, I believe, a respectable farmer in Kent.

The Mac Carters were the hereditary pipers of the Mac Donalds of the Isles, and a descendant was long established in Edinburgh as a professor of that branch of music, and was attended by several scholars.

There was a branch of the Mac Gregors established in Rannach who were celebrated musicians, and afforded instruction to the chief part of the pipers of the central Highlands, as those of the house of Mac Pherson, of Cluny, &c. This tribe, from their extensive knowledge of history, were termed Clan an sgeulaich, or tellers of tales, which proves that pipers were anciently qualified in that part of the bardic duties.

The care of the Highland Societies of London and Scotland, to encourage the preservation and perfection of pipe music by periodical competitions, and the award of various prizes of considerable value, has done much to revive the popularity of the bagpipe. The interesting performances, which are held at the theatre, are numerously attended, and the audience are transported with feelings of enthusiasm when the performers, in all the imposing effect of costume and thrilling war notes, are on the stage. The plan is, to intersperse dancing with the music, and may be thus shortly described. The exhibition is divided into acts, and commences with a salute to the Society, by its piper, which is followed by a Highland dance. Then three or more of the competitors play each a piobrachd, when another dance leads to the performance of two or three piobrachds, by as many pipers. The second act is also three or four piobrachds, a dance, two or three piobrachds, and a dance; and the third act is similar, the only difference being in the dancing, which is sometimes Strathspey, sometimes Reel, &c. The judges then retire to determine the prizes, which are also given for dress, during which time the audience are entertained by a salute. The prizes, being determined, are delivered by the president, when a dance forms the conclusion. Ten or fifteen other Highlanders usually appear, who are rewarded by a share of the money received by the sale of tickets.

Every piper must give a list of not fewer than twelve piobrachds which he can play, from which the committee select one. At the competition in 1829, there appeared twenty-five pipers, whose twelve tunes would amount to three hundred, but there were only one hundred and three different, which is certainly a small proportion, but perhaps not so surprising when the length of these pieces are taken into consideration, the few that have ever been noted in musical characters, and the small time that can now be devoted to the acquirement of music taught only by the ear.

A piobrachd will be understood by those to whom "The Battle of Prague," and similar pieces of that class of music, are familiar. It opens with a certain measure called the urlar, subject, or groundwork of the piece, and by variations of this air, sometimes extending to great length, the piece is completed. The different parts are meant to express the various feelings according with the transaction, such as the rising to battle, the tumultuous collision of the combatants, the cries of the wounded, and wailing of their relations; and, finally, the exultation for victory, or lamentation for defeat. After each part is gone through, the opening strain is repeated, and invariably concludes the piece. This, which is observable in poetry, is allied to the "pugnavibus ensibus," which introduces every stanza in the celebrated song of Regner Lodbrog, and would seem intended to recall the mind to a certain stage in the enterprise on which it can rest with unalloyed satisfaction.

This sort of music cannot, however, be appreciated by many, who erroneously imagine it to be a mere voluntary, played as the taste and fancy of the performer may dictate. The late Duke of Gordon used to relate an anecdote, with much humour, which came under his own observation. In a town, in the north of England, a piper played a piobrachd which wonderfully excited the attention of his hearers, who seemed equally astonished at its length, and the wildness and apparent disconnection of the parts. Unable to understand it, yet desirous of gratifying their curiosity, one of the spectators, at the conclusion of the performance, anxiously entreated the piper to "play it in English."

When the urlar, which most generally is in common time, is played, the siubhal, or variation, first succeeds, of which there is most usually a doubling, and often a trebling, the time quickening, and the last, being generally termed taorluidh, or fast movement; the urlar, like a chorus, is then repeated, and variation second commences. I shall finish the description from " Cean na drochait bige," or the Clans' Gathering, a piobrachd composed at the battle fought by

Montrose at Inverlochy, in 1645. The second variation has both doubling and trebling, after which is the urlar, and then the third variation, with its doubling, trebling, and closing strain. The fourth variation has only a doubling, and the repetition of the urlar leads to the crunluath, or round, quick, and yielding movement, which has its doubling, trebling, and quadrupling, the latter part, in $\frac{2}{8}$ time, being in the style of music known in Gaëlic by the term cliathluath, which is the "quickest of all runnings," and extends through sixty-four bars, the piece closing with the opening strain additional.

It is to be observed, in explanation of the musical terms applicable to the bagpipe, that the taorluidh is $\frac{2}{8}$ time; the crunluath is also of that time, but the crunluath fosgilt, "an open running," and crunluath breabich, "a smart and starting running," are in common time, while the cliathluath may be either in $\frac{2}{4}$, $\frac{2}{8}$, or $\frac{6}{8}$.[1]

A short list of some well known piobrachds and porsts, or airs, with an account of their origin, may not be unacceptable.

CRUINNEACHADH, OR GATHERINGS.[m]

Of Cogadh no sith, "peace or war," the history appears to be unknown, but it is supposed to indicate a determination either to obtain honourable peace, or engage in immediate war, and is peculiar to no clan.

Piobrachd Mhic Dhonuil dhubh was the war tune of Black Donald Balloch of the Isles, when preparing for the battle of Inverlochy, in 1427, and Cean na drochaite mōra was composed during the battle.

---

[1] Mac Donald's Martial Music of Caledonia.
[m] Called also Porst tiannal. It is to be regretted that we are never likely to see the historical accounts promised by Mr. Mac Donald, his son, who was to superintend the work, being unfortunately dead.

Ruaig Ghlinn Bhruin* was composed on the rout of the Colquhons, by the Mac Gregors, in 1602.

Cill Chriosde was played by Glengarry's piper, when, in revenge of the murder of Aonghas a Choile, by the men of Culloden,† a number who had taken refuge from the exasperated Mac Donalds in a place of worship called Cill Chriosde, or Christ's church, were burned.

Craig elachadh, the Grant's Gathering, a fine piobrachd, derives its name from their war cry, or place of rendezvous: a rock near Aviemore, in Strathspey.

Creag dubh is, for a similar reason, the gathering of the clan Chattan; but Cluny's piper, at the battle of Falkirk, in 1745, composed a piobrachd which is very popular among the clan.

The Cruinneachadh Clan Ranuil excited the Mac Donalds of Clan Ranald to the rising in 1715, and subsequent battle of Dumblane, or Sherrifmuir, where the chief was slain.

Bodaich na m briogas, "the fellows with the breeches," commemorates a battle in which the men of Braidalban defeated the Sinclairs of Caithness at Wick.

Blar Druim Thalasgair was composed on the battle of Waternish, in the Isle of Sky.

Thogail nam bò, "We come through drift to drive the prey," is the Mac Farlane Gathering.

Spaidseareachd, and Birlinn thighearna Chilla, are those of the Mac Leans, of Coll; and Spaidseareachd Siosalaich Strathglais, is that of Chisholm, of Strathglas.

The Forbes' Gathering is now known by the local words, which begin "Ca' Glenernan, gather Glennochty," and seems the air which has been appropriated to the "Locheil's

---

* *Vide* Scott's *Boat Song* in the "Lady of the Lake." ED.
† By the MacKenzies of Kintail. ED.

Warning" of Campbell. There is another tune, called Glenernan, having every characteristic of a piobrachd.

FAILTE, OR SALUTES.

Failte Phrionsa was composed by John Mac Intyre, piper to Menzies, of Menzies, on the landing of King James in 1715. There was also a welcome of Prince Charles to the Isle of Sky, and a salute on his landing at Moidart in 1745.*

Ghlas mheur is an ancient piobrachd, composed by Raonull Mac Ailean oig, a Mac Donald of Morar, to which there is a wild traditional account attached.

Moladh Mari, or Mary's Praise, is an animated piece throughout. It was composed by the Mac Lachlan family piper, and is the clan salute.

The Mac Donalds of Boisdale have a salute composed when Alastair More, the first of the title, took possession of his estate.

The Menzies, the Mac Kenzies, the Mac Donalds of Clan Rannald, the Mac Gregors, the Mac Kays, the Frasers, &c., &c., have also their appropriate salutes.

An Groatha was composed on the baptism of Rory More, son of Mac Leod of Dunvegan, and another salute was composed at the birth of a son of the same family in 1715.

Leannan Donald Gruamaich, "Grim Donald's Sweetheart," is also a salute of very ancient origin.†

CUMHADH, OR LAMENTS.

Siubhal Shemis was composed on the departure of King James in 1688. There is also a lament for Prince Charles.

---

* To the air of this very fine "salute" *Rob Donn*, the celebrated Sutherlandshire bard composed his "Iscabail Nic Aoidh," worthy to rank with Duncan Bàn Mac Intyre's "Beinn-Dòrain" as a masterpiece in this curious and very difficult style of composition. ED.

† "Craig-an-Sgairbh" or "Failte Mhic Iain Stiubhart," Stewart of Appin's Salute is a very old and much admired "piobaireachd." ED.

Cumhadh mhic a' Arisaig, or Mac Intosh's Lament, is extremely plaintive and expressive.

Mac Leod of Mac Leod, had not only a peculiar Cumhadh, but the family piper composed one which is still very popular, on his own situation after the battle of Sherrifmuir, where he was left on the field stripped of all his clothes. The unfortunate bard entitles it, "Too long in this condition." Pipers, as was becoming, were honoured with long and very affecting funeral dirges, one of which is on the last mentioned, who was designated "Great Patrick." There is a "Doleful Lament" on the death of Samuel, a celebrated piper, and another very beautiful one for John Donn, who was a poet.

Donald Gruamach, of Slate, laments in woeful and protracted strains the death of his brother, and the before-mentioned Mac Donald, of Morar, is commemorated in a well known plaintive and popular coronach.

The Sister's Lament for her Brothers, one being the chief of the house of Keppoch, who were barbarously murdered, and whom she did not survive many hours, may be supposed of a very melancholy cast, but it is not long.

There is a Lament for a Duke of Hamilton, and another for one Brian O'Duff, and Cumhadh Chlaidheamh is the aged warrior's regret that he was no longer able to wield his sword. This last of only two parts, is accounted a piobrachd, and, contrary to the opinion of some pipers, I believe that many tunes that are not admitted to this class ought to be so ranked. Some of the parts may be lost.

Fhuair mi pòg 'o laimh an Righ, composed on having had the honour to kiss hands with the king, is presumed to be a salute; but can Colda mo run,* played to warn the

---

* "Cholla mo rùin," a very fine "piobaireachd." It is usually classed with the "Salutes." It was composed to Kolkitoch (Colla-Ciotach, Cole the Left-handed), father of Alexander Mac Donald Montrose, Major-General, so distinguished for his loyalty and bravery. ED.

piper's master from the danger he was in of falling into the hands of his enemies, be called a salute, or a lament? They are piobrachds of great length and considerable merit.

There is an ancient slow air of one measure, called A mhic Iain mhic Sheumis, celebrating a battle between the Mac Donalds and the Mac Leods, and another composed on Blar léinne, or the shirt battle, fought at Kinloch Lochy, between the Frasers of Lovat, and Mac Donalds of Clan Rannald, and so called from the parties having stripped to their shirts. There is a fine lament, called "The Chieftains," to which words are sung on the unfortunate death of the colonel of Glengarry's regiment, who fell in the streets of Falkirk after the victory, by the accidental discharge of the gun of one of Clan Rannald's men. The horrid murder of the Keppoch family was lamented, besides the piobrachd, in a slow and pathetic song of three unequal measures, called Keppach na fasich, or "Desolate."

"The Spreith of the Lowlands now graze in the Glen" must have been sung with joy on the celebration of many a successful descent, and "The Fiery Cross" was admirably expressive of the effects of its appearance.

Of Ossianic music, several pieces are attributed to the bard, or bear his name, and have been sung to the poems and native songs time immemorial. Dàn Ossian; Ossian an deigh nam Fion; Dàn Fhraoich; Tha Sgeul beag agam air Fion; Dargo; Bas Dhiarmid a 'Duine; Maol Donaidh; Oscar's Ghost; Manus, and others, may be enumerated; many of which were collected between 1715 and 1745, by Mac Donald, Fraser, and others.

The following is a list of the piobrachds and other military music of the Mac Kenzies, still preserved and entered, I am assured, in the orderly book of the 72nd regiment, the first that was raised from the clan:—

Day Break	Surachan.
Cruinneachadh, gathering, or turn out	Tulloch Ard.
Salute when the Chief comes on the field	Failte mhic Coinnich.
Slow March	An Cuilfhionn,
Quick March	Caisteal Donnan.
The Charge	Caber Fèidh.
While Engaged	Blar Strom.
Coronach played when burying the Dead	Cumhadh mhic Coinnich.
Sunset	Siubhal clann Choinnich.
Tattoo	Ceann drochait Aclin.
Warning half an hour before Dinner	Blar ghlinn Seille.
When Dinner is on the Table	Cath sleibh an t' Shiora.

It is remarkable that the Gaël of Ireland have no music of the description of piobrachd. That singular piece called Mac Allisdrum's March, which has latterly been connected with Cath Eachroma, or the battle of Aghrim, has been deemed a genuine Irish piobrachd; but the intelligent Mr. Croker, in his "Researches," has shown that it is a Scots composition. Alexander Mac Donald, or Allisdrum, commanded a party of Highlanders in the Irish service under Lord Taafe, at the engagement with the Parliament army, near Mallow, 13th Nov., 1647, where they fought manfully, but were all cut to pieces, or, as some say, murdered in cold blood, their skulls and bones being yet to be seen piled up in the ruins of a neighbouring abbey. This composition is still popular, and may be partially seen in the works of Walker and Croker. After the urlar, or air, is played, the four provincial cries are performed: the Gair Chonnachtach, Gair Muimhneach, Gair Olltach, and Gair Laighneach; after which the Gall na mnà' san àr, lamentations of the women while searching the field for their husbands and relations, succeed, the whole concluding with a loud shout, as supposed from the auditors. The Irish certainly used our national instrument in war, at least in Derrick's time, who says that when the pipers perceived defeat inevitable, they sounded a retreat, and in another passage we find that "the bagpipe then insteade of tromp, did lull the backe retreate." The Scots had, however, so much to do in the then affairs of Ireland, that he may in this case be speaking of them. Other airs of great antiquity and beauty they possess in sufficient number, among which may be mentioned Cumh' leinn, Ailein a rùin, Gràmachree Molly, &c., and in those called Speic, or humours, they excel.

The Welsh are also destitute of this peculiar style of music, although they have military airs of high antiquity and interest:—the "Monk's March," and "Come to Battle," are powerful. Besides warlike melodies and Coronachs, they have much of a peculiar cast, and their Penyllion singing with the harp seems peculiarly their own. The Gorleg yr Halen, or "Prelude of the Salt," played to the renowned King Arthur, is yet performed in the Welsh School, Gray's-inn-road.

The Scots have been from the beginning of history celebrated for musical genius, and of that sort which Geminiani declared could not be otherwise found on this side the Alps, and as poetry and music are inseparably connected, they were consequently renowned for both. The knowledge which the bards possessed of these sister arts was cultivated by the Christian priests, and a reference to Bale, Leland, Dempster, and others, will shew the very great numbers of those who excelled. The whole nation was in fact declared to be musical, and the Scots minstrels were much superior to English writers, there being not one poem which can with certainty be ascribed to an English poet previous to the time of Chaucer.[a] An old author declares with much naïvete, that a great many of both

[a] Ellis's Metrical Romances, i. 130.

sexes in the Highlands had a gift of poesy, and could form a panegyric or satire extempore, without anything stronger than water to raise their fancies.* They had certainly a strong propensity to turn everything into rhyme, which they could as easily adapt to music, as has been before shewn: many tunes, and even long pieces of music having been composed in a short space of time, and under unpropitious circumstances. The harpers were so noted for this faculty, that it passed into a proverb:—" Where would be the melodies the harper could not find?" A piper of St. Kilda composed a tune of the notes of a bird called the Gawlin, which was reckoned a very fine piece of music,† and we have the swan's mournful ditty:—

> Luineag na h Ealui'
> Gui eug i, gui eug o,
> Sgeula' mo dhunach,
>   Gui eug i
> Rinn mo liere,
>   Gui eug o, &c.‡

---

* This extraordinary "gift of poesy" is a fact. In every hamlet you will find individuals, often perfectly illiterate, who will with but very slight premeditation knock off an epigram or a verse of rhymed satire or panegyric of surprising point and pith. ED.

† The words of this curious ornithological composition will be found in a small volume of poems by the late Rev. Mr. MacCallum of Arisaig, a Gaelic scholar and poet of some note. ED.

‡ The first verse of the Swan's "mournful ditty" is more correctly as follows:—

> " Guileag i, guileag ò,
> Sgeula mo dhunaigh,
>   Guileag i,
> 'Rinn mo leire'
>   Guileag ò,
> Mo chasan dubh,
>   Guileag i,
> 'Smi féin glé-gheal
>   Guileag ò," &c.

The air is strangely wild and plaintive.

We have even the mermaid's song, and perhaps those of other syrens have been composed, with the fisherman's song for attracting seals, &c. Music has at times produced effects on the Highlanders, in some degree, like the lyre of Orpheus. The celebrated Mac Pherson, who has been mentioned in the first volume, composed his "Farewell," and played it, when proceeding to the place of execution; and some other Highlanders have requested, as a last favour, permission to play their pipes. When old Lovat was taken by Captain Campbell, of Achacrosan, it is said that, unaffected by his situation, it afforded him the highest delight to hear the pipers playing his family march as he was conveyed across the country. The bagpipes seem to charm even the brute creation. Deer will be arrested by their sound, and stand listening with evident pleasure; and cattle that are otherwise unmanageable, will be rendered calm by a spring on the shepherd's pipe. The story of the piper of Hamelin, whose instrument had such power, is well known; on one occasion he charmed an immense number of rats into a river, where they were drowned, but not receiving the stipulated reward, he speedily collected as many and carried them to the same place.

About the beginning of the sixteenth century, Mac Lean, of Coll, had been carried off by Allan Mac Lean, who received the appellation of na Sop, or "of the wisp," in allusion to his burnings. Coll was a poet and musician, and when in prison he composed a tune, still, I believe,

---

An English version by the Editor of an old and very beautiful "Mermaid's Song," appeared in the *Inverness Courier* some two or three years ago.

The "Fisherman's Song for attracting Seals" was not properly a song at all, but a wild, wordless chant, an extraordinary melody with which bursts of loud whistling were frequently introduced. The Editor has often heard it in his boyhood. Ed.

preserved, under the name of "Allan na Sop's March," which having sung with much grace, his stern enemy was so moved that he immediately gave him his liberty.

The following "Ode to Scotish Music," by a poet who is now almost forgotten, but whose merit deserves commemoration,° displays, in beautiful lines, the effect of the national melodies :—

> "What words, my Laura, can express,
> That power unknown, that magic spell,
> Thy lovely native airs possess,
> When warbled from thy lips so well,
> Such nameless feelings to impart,
> As melt in bliss the raptur'd heart.
>
> No stroke of art their texture bears,
> No cadence wrought with learned skill;
> And though long worn by rolling years,
> Yet, unimpair'd, they please us still;
> While thousand strains of mystic lore
> Have perish'd, and are heard no more.
>
> Wild, as the desert stream they flow,
> Wand'ring along its mazy bed;
> Now, scarcely moving, deep and slow,
> Now, in a swifter current led:
> And now along the level lawn,
> With charming murmurs, softly drawn.
>
> Ah! what enchanting scenes arise,
> Still as thou breath'st the heart-felt strain!
> How swift exulting fancy flies
> O'er all the varied Sylvan reign!
> And how thy voice, blest maid, can move
> The rapture and the woe of love!
>
> There, on a bank by Flora drest,
> Where flocks disport beneath the shade,
> By Tweed's soft murmurs lull'd to rest,
> A lovely nymph asleep is laid;
> Her shepherd, trembling, all in bliss,
> Steals, unobserv'd, a balmy kiss!

° Mac Donald, better known as Matthew Bramble, the author of Vimonda, &c.

Here, by the banks and groves so green,
Where Yarrow's waters warbling roll,
The love-sick swain, unheard, unseen,
Pours to the stream his secret soul;
Sings his bright charmer, and, by turns,
Despairs, and hopes, and fears, and burns.

There, night her silent sable wears,
And gloom invests the vaulted skies;
No star amid the void appears,
Yet see fair Nelly blushing rise;
And, lightly stepping, move unseen
To let her panting lover in.

But far remov'd on happier plains,
With harps to love for ever strung,
Methinks I see the favour'd swains
Who first those deathless measures sung;
For, sure, I ween no courtly wight
Those deathless measures could indite.

No! from the pastoral cot and shade
Thy favourite airs, my Laura, came,
By some obscure Corelli made,
Or Handel, never known to fame!
And hence their notes, from nature warm,
Like Nature's self, must ever charm.

Ye sp'rits of fire, for ever gone,
Soft as your strains, O be your sleep!
And, if your sacred graves were known,
We there should hallow'd vigils keep,
Where, Laura, thou should'st raise the lay,
And bear our souls to heaven away!

The PIOB-MHOR, or great Highland bagpipe, is different from the common sharp pipes of the Low country, and both are very unlike the Irish or flat pipes. The first, which is accurately represented in the frontispiece, is by far the most noble and warlike instrument, and produces the most clear and ear-piercing notes. The various pipes are separately inserted in the bag, and the drones or burdens are connected by ribands of different colours. When the bag is inflated, they are steadily supported over the shoulder, and the tallest displays a flag, on which is richly embroidered the arms of the chief, colonel of a regiment, gentleman, or society, in whose service the piper may be. In the figure introduced for illustration in the frontispiece, the arms of Scotland are the insignia.

These arms have been alluded to in Vol. i. p. 298, and the Lion is there shewn to have been a general badge of the Celtic nations. It is asserted by all heralds and historians of authority, that the tressure of fleur-de-lis was added to the arms of Scotland by Charlemagne, to indicate his regard for the nation; but when the Unicorns were adopted as supporters, is not ascertained. They bear up the royal banner, and that of St. Andrew, and stand, as here shewn, on a compartment, and not on an escrol, as often represented. For the "lacesset" in the motto, I have the authority of Sir George Mac Kenzie and other competent antiquaries, and the difference from lacessit is certainly of some importance in this very nicely regulated science. The Scots, as is well known, paid great attention to heraldry, and the whole achievement, as a specimen of their skill, must be allowed to have a good effect, even pictorially. The ensign of Scotland, that is, a thistle of gold imperially crowned, is represented on the title-page. The Highland Society of London have a pipe flag of beautiful workmanship and rich effect. Those who have no flag usually display party-coloured ribbons, which have a very pretty appearance streaming in the wind. They are often presented by the musician's sweetheart, and are of course exhibited with becoming pride.

Several pipers carry their instruments on the right side, and some are of opinion that it is necessary for those who have to play with others because it would neither look well, nor be convenient, on a march, for pipers to have their drones all over the same shoulder. Surely, if otherwise, it would look as awkward as if the soldiers carried their musquets on opposite sides. We do not know the rule which prevailed in Sky, but a learner would most assuredly be taught to use his right hand in tuning.

The pipe through which the wind is conveyed is also kept in its position by the tension of the bag, but the performer does not allow it to slip from his mouth, but retains it in an easy manner, the end being tipped with horn to prevent its being injured by the teeth. It has a joint, and is provided with a leather valve, which prevents the egress of air. The Chanter, or pipe on which the tune is performed, is like the others fixed in a head stock, which is sufficiently large to contain the reed. This is formed of two thin slips of common reed or cane, fixed with much nicety to a small metal tube, and produce the sound by vibration. Those of the other pipes are formed of a joint of the reed, one end close, the other open, with an oblong slit for the passage of the air, as here shewn.

GOTH.

REFEID.

The sharp Lowland pipes have the same tone as the Highland, but are less sonorous, and are blown by a bellows, put in motion by the arm opposite to that under which the bag is held. This is the manner of giving wind to the Irish pipes, like which they also have the three drones fixed in one stock, and not borne over the shoulder, but laid horizontally over the arm. The Union pipes, that have been called the Irish organ, are the sweetest of musical instruments; the formation of the reeds, and the length of the pipes, increased by brass tubes, produce the most delightful and soothing melody, while by the

DESCRIPTION OF THE BAGPIPE. 305

addition of many keys, and the capability of the chanter, any tune may be performed.

One George Mackay was the reformer of the Scots Lowland pipes, but I cannot precisely tell the nature of his improvements; he, however, studied seven years at the college in Sky.

There is a miniature sort of bagpipe, called the Northumberland, the advantage of which is that they are conveniently portable, and are much less noisy than the others. None of these sorts resemble the rude instruments of the same kind used on the Continent.

The pipes are commonly formed of black ebony or lignum vitæ; but woods less valuable, and less excellent for the purpose, are sometimes employed. The joints are handsomely tipped with ivory or bone, and silver ornaments and precious gems are often placed on the headstock of the chanter. Northumberland pipes are often wholly formed of ivory, and richly ornamented with silver. The bag is covered with cloth or tartan, sometimes fringed, and otherwise adorned.

A stand,[p] or set, of Highland pipes sometimes cost a considerable sum,[*] especially if made by a celebrated tradesman, of which there are several in Edinburgh, Glasgow, Perth, Aberdeen, and Inverness.

The drones are tuned by means of the movable joints to the E of the chanter, the two small ones being a fifth below, and the larger an eighth; and this preparation, called the Ludh, is what often needlessly occupies so much time, giving rise to that saying in the Low Country applied to one who procrastinates in a small affair: "You

[p] The absurd term, "pair of pipes," perhaps arose from many of the poorer sort having formerly but two drones. It may be observed, pipers often have but two that are furnished with reeds.

[*] The price at the present day is from £8 to £40, according to the "mounting." Ed.

are langer o' tuning your pipes nor playing your spring." To be sure, the pipes must be put in tune; but it is the piper's duty to have them in as good order as possible before he is called to perform, and thereby avoid that monotonous noise and unmeaning rhapsody of notes which many feel so unpleasant. I am afraid some pipers think there is a deal of grace in those flourishes called "preludes of tuning,"[q] forms of which are actually taught; but I can say, that although Scotsmen may bear with them, to Englishmen they have no charms.

On the chanter are nine notes, G, A, B, C, D, E, F, G, A, and a B may also be produced by "pinching," that is, striking the thumb nail in a peculiar manner in the hole of the upper note A; but Highland pipers do not admit this addition, but despise its assistance as much as they do the keys and other attempted improvements. They seem inspired with the same feeling which led the Spartans to banish Timotheus for presuming to add to the strings of the lyre; and amusing anecdotes are told of their concern to think that the pipes should be taught by notes, or that they should be fettered in learning by book rules.

The C and F in the chanter scale are sharp; and if they were omitted it would be the ancient Scotish scale of C major, agreeing with that of the black keys of the piano, but these sharps are not noticed by the performer. Although the pipe can imitate different keys, they are not real, as in other instruments.

As the tone of the bagpipes is continuous, the monotony is broken, and the notes divided by warbling, beating, or battering, as I have heard some call it, which is done by a sudden movement of the fingers on certain other notes. Thus, in running up the scale, the effect is given to low G by smartly striking the hole under No. 1, or the fore-finger

[q] Deachin Ghleust.

of the upper hand, and on sounding A the third finger counting downwards performs the same office. This will explain the figures inserted, according to the plan of Capt. Menzies, in his Pipe Preceptor, to shew the warbling of Cogadh na sith, a sort of expression peculiar to the bagpipe, and productive of that indescribable thrilling in the performance of a good piobrachd, or of many of the other pipe tunes.

There is an ancient and celebrated pipe in the possession of the chief of Clan Chattan, known as the Feadhan dubh, or black chanter, concerning which various curious particulars are recorded.

It is believed to possess some charm or supernatural virtue, which ensures prosperity to its owners and their connections. It is this instrument which Sir Walter Scott mentions as having fallen from the clouds during the conflict on the North Inch of Perth in 1396. It appears to have been taken from the vanquished party at that fiercely contended battle.

Three Mac Donalds, of Glencoe, had, on one occasion, taken a creagh from Strathspey, but were overtaken by a strong party of the Grants near Aviemore, when they thought themselves out of danger; and while asleep the two elder Mac Donalds were surprised and bound, but the younger escaped to the woods. The Grants, on their return home, stopped about two miles from the place, and while they were refreshing and enjoying themselves in apparent security, the three dauntless heroes, who had recovered themselves and come together, attacked their enemies, sword in hand, with such daring and resolution, that they drove them clean off with confusion and slaughter, killing seven and wounding sixteen, and rescued the whole of the cattle! The cry of the two elder Mac Donalds was, "A mhic, a mhic, luathich do laimh 's cruadhich do bhuille," i. e., My son, my son, quicken and harden thy blows.

The Laird of Grant, vexed in the highest degree at the shameful conduct of his men, compelled the delinquents, for three successive Sundays, to walk round the church in presence of all the rest of the clan, carrying wooden swords suspended by straw ropes, exclaiming, "We are the cowards that disgracefully ran away." The whole clan were disheartened by this affair, and to re-animate them, the chief sent to Cluny for the loan of the Feadhan dubh, the notes of which could infallibly rouse every latent spark of valour. Cluny is said to have lent it without hesitation, saying his men stood in no need of it. How long it remained with them at this time does not appear; but after it had been restored, the Grants again received it, and it remained with them until 1822, when Grant of Glenmorriston presented it to Ewen Mac Pherson, Esq., of Cluny, the present worthy chief.[a] It is probable that the first loan of this wonderful chanter was made to the Grants of Glenmorriston, who had no doubt observed the happy effects of its possession among their brethren in Strathspey. This clan, had, however, an opinion of their own prowess, that would seem to render it improbable they should require such aid, and had, besides, some particular charm by which they rendered themselves invulnerable; in which belief they fearlessly engaged in war, and, in truth, acted like heroes; although the writer of a MS. history of the clan, which I have seen in the King's Library, sneeringly says, they prevented their charm from working at the battle of Sherrifmuir, by making a speedy retreat.

The Mac Phersons assuredly, whether in consequence of their fortunate talisman or their own bravery, have never been in a battle which was lost, at least where the chief was present. Before the battle of Culloden, an old witch, or second seer, told the Duke of Cumberland, that

[a] His letter to the author.

if he waited until the bratach uaine, or green banner, came up, he would be defeated.

The cultivation and practice of poetry and music are chief amusements of the Gaël, and connected with both is DANCING. If the Scots excel in the former, they certainly of all nations are pre-eminent in partiality to the latter. Their passion for this pleasing and healthy exercise is indeed so strong, that it seems part of their nature. The art of dancing, which a person without a musical ear can never attain, is a harmonious adaptation of the bodily powers to time and measure, accompanied with grace, ease, expression, position, &c.; yet the Scots have been said to be "entirely without grace" in their dances. Their agility may surprise, without pleasing, those who do not understand the national system, but that a person should be able to execute the most intricate and complex steps with the utmost ease, keeping the justest time, without "a particle of grace," is surely impossible. Grace, in dancing, is described as "fitness of parts and good attitude," and that the Highlanders possess these necessary qualifications cannot be denied; indeed, their aptitude for music is not more striking than their fondness for the national reel.

Dancing has been practised by almost every people; it formed, in fact, part of the religious ceremonies of almost all nations, and the gods are not only said to have been pleased, but were themselves emulous in the dance. Pindar represents Silenus as

> "Strenuous in the dance to beat
> Tuneful measures with his feet."

It was also encouraged as a useful and elegant amusement, and the Athenians reckoned those unpolite who refused to dance at a proper time.' Its importance as an innocent and healthful recreation rendered it an object of attention

' Note in Beloe's Herodotus, vi.

to the legislator. Lycurgus instituted dancing from a conviction of its utility in making the youth strong, agile, and expert in the use of their weapons, and in the evolutions of warfare. This particular sort was accompanied with the singing of certain heroic verses, and was performed by the old men, the youth, and children. Homer mentions the art as a diversion at entertainments; and Merion, one of his heroes, was known among the Grecian chiefs by a graceful carriage and superior agility, acquired from his long practice of dancing.

The effect of dancing and music in a moral point of view, is certainly considerable. Polybius attributes the hospitality and piety of the Arcadians to the care with which these two arts were cultivated, the youth being instructed in them at the public expense; and this influence he proves from contrasting those happy people with the Cynæthians, a neighbouring nation, that neglected so salutary regulations. Dancing promotes health, cheerfulness, and the kindly affections between the sexes, and Locke says it ought always to be taught to children, as it gives graceful motions to all their actions, and, above all things, manliness and a becoming confidence; for this effect he cannot account, but his good opinion entirely coincides with that of the wisest of the ancients. Socrates became so sensible of the good effects of this exercise, that in his old age he sedulously practised it; and Lucian, Plato, Aristotle, Athæneus, Xenophon, Plutarch, and others, have written in praise of it. Some of the ancient philosophers were excellent dancers, and thought it not unbecoming to perform in public; Lucian even goes so far as to say that dancing works all the wonders ascribed to the caduceus of Mercury, being able at the same time to soothe and animate the soul. Among the Jews, it was a solemn religious discipline; and, as an exercise of divine worship, was of no less importance among the Greeks and Romans. Nor was the performance confined to the men; when Moses had conducted the Israelites across the Red Sea, he and his sister Miriam performed a grand chorus and accompanying dance. Pliny calls the sacred dances "mediatorial."

Of the ancient Celtic dancing we find some curious particulars. The Lusitani, says Diodorus, have a light and airy dance which they practise in peace, and which requires great dexterity and nimbleness of legs and thighs. In war, they march, observing time and measure, and sing their triumphal songs when they are ready to charge the enemy.

The passion for dancing was strong in all the Celtic race, and it was employed in the services of religion, some remains of which practice long continued among the Welsh, who were accustomed to dance in the church-yard. Rincefada, or field dance in Irish, shews its relation to Rincadoir, a musician. This was performed to the Cuisley Ciuil, a simple sort of bagpipe before described, and used to conclude all balls. When James II. landed at Kinsale, his friends received him with the rincefada, by which he was much gratified. The manner of its execution was thus:— three persons abreast, holding the ends of a white handkerchief, moved forward a few paces to the sound of slow music, the rest of the dancers following in couples, and holding also a white handkerchief between them. The music then changing to a quicker tune, the dance began, the performers passing successively under the handkerchiefs of the three in front, and then wheeling round in semi-circles, they formed a variety of pleasing evolutions, interspersed with occasional entrechats, finally uniting and resuming their original places. The Manx are much addicted to dancing jigs and reels, in which four or five couple join to the music of a fiddle. English country dances are unknown among them.

We are told that the military dances of the old Irish were conducted by the Curinky, or dancing-master, a surname that yet exists in many families.

The ancient Caledonians had a sort of Pyrrhic dance over swords, which is not yet entirely unknown, but the Gilli-Callum, which generally terminates a ball, is supposed to have but a faint resemblance to the ancient sword-dance. The same observation may be applied to the dirk-dance. Both of them are, indeed, still executed by a few, and were exhibited in London some years ago by one Mac Glassan; but a gentleman informed me that he knew a person who, at the age of 106, saw the dirk-dance performed, and declared it was not at all like that which he had formerly known. Besides these, it is evident from the words of an old Isle of Sky dancing song, Bualidh mi u ann sa cheann, "I will break your head,"* that the parties in the performance went through the evolutions of attack and defence. The chief art in the modern sword-dance consists in the dexterity with which the dancer escapes touching one or more swords or sticks crossed on the ground, the tune to which it was performed being called Gilli-Callum, and that appropriate to the dirk, Phadric Mac Combish. There was a dance called Rungmor, of which little is now known; from the only description I could get of it, the dancer appeared in some manner to touch the ground with his thighs, without losing his balance.

In Lochaber there was formerly a gymnasium for teaching all sorts of athletic exercises and graceful accomplishments, the scholars eating at a common table, being allowed a certain time for their meals, and submitting to other regulations; but, without tuition, the Highlanders excel in dancing. A perfect judge thus expresses him-

---

* "Buailidh mi thu anns a cheann." I will strike you on the head. ED.

self: "This pleasing propensity, one would think, was born with them, from the early indications we sometimes see their children shew for this exercise. I have seen children of theirs, of five or six years of age, attempt, nay, even execute, some of their steps so well, as almost to surpass belief. I once had the pleasure of seeing, in a remote part of the country, a reel danced by a herd boy and two young girls, who surprised me much, especially the boy, who appeared to be about twelve years of age. He had a variety of well chosen steps, and executed them with so much justness and ease, as if he meant to set criticism at defiance;" and, speaking of the colleges of Aberdeen, where he was long established as an elegant and accomplished teacher of dancing, he adds, "they draw hither, every year, a number of students from the Western Isles, as well as from the Highlands, and the greater part of them excel in the dance; some of them indeed, in so superior a degree, that I myself have thought them worthy of imitation."

After the toils of a long day, young men and women will walk many miles to enjoy a dance, which seems to have the effect of banishing fatigue, and, instead of adding to the sensation of weariness, it becomes really a recreation. This delight in dancing is diffused throughout Scotland, and the strongest efforts of the kirk to put down "promiscuous dancing," with the bitter reproofs of the more rigid covenanters, have failed in repressing the "ungodly" exercise.

The reel and strathspey are the dances common to all the Scots, and those of which they are most passionately fond. They are either a quartette or trio, "a foursome or a threesome reel;" and those who are ignorant of this species of dance will find the principal steps used in it plainly described by Peacock,[*] the intelligent writer already men-

[*] Francis Peacock, Dancing-Master in Aberdeen, author of "Sketches relative to the History and Theory, but more especially to the Practice of

tioned. It will be observed that the difference in time between the two sorts of music produces a corresponding difference in the steps or evolutions.

I shall here present the reader with a list of those most in use by the Highlanders.

Ceum-siubhail, pronounced kemshoole, the forward step, is the common step for the promenade or figure. Ceum-coisiche, or kemkossey, is the setting or footing step, and is divided into three sorts: first, where one step is equal to a bar; second, where two steps are required to a bar; and third, where two bars are required to a step. Leum-trasd, or cross springs, are a series of Sissonnes. Siabadh-trasd, chasing steps or cross slips, is like the balotte. Aiseag-trasd, or cross passes, is a favourite step in the Highlands. Ceum-Badenach is another step much used, and requiring considerable agility. Fosgladh, or open step, and Cuartag, or turning step, are also very becoming movements. All these, and many more, are combined in one dance, and the association depends on the taste of the party. That called the back step, in which the feet are each alternately slipped behind, and reach the ground on, or close to, the spot occupied by the one just removed, is of difficult acquirement, and severely exerts the muscles of the calves of the legs. So much dexterity can some persons display in this, that they will go through the setting time of the music without moving beyond a space marked by the circumference of their bonnet.

SEAN TRIUS, or old trowsers, from the name of the accompanying air, is the native Highland hornpipe, and is danced with much grace.

I have seen two brothers of the name of Grant, who were good violin players, exhibit feats of great agility.

Dancing," 1805. 1 vol. 8vo. pp. 224. Aberdeen: Angus & Son; London: Longman; Edinburgh: Constable. ED.

Part of their performance consisted of dancing the Highland fling, in that style called the Marquis of Huntly's, Strathspeys over a rope, and Gilli-Callum over a fiddle bow; and one of them danced a Strathspey, played the fiddle, played bass on the bagpipe, smoked, spoke Gaëlic, and explained it in question and answer at the same time!

Dancing, among the Gaël, does not depend on the presence of musical instruments. They reel and set to their own vocal music, or to the songs of those who are near; people, whose hearts are light and responsive to their native melodies, will find their limbs move in consonance to its music, however produced.

SINGLE STICK, or cudgel play, was formerly taught the youth from an early age, as a necessary preparation for the management of the broadsword, and they used in certain dances to exhibit their dexterity. They are still partial to this amusement; in the higher parts of Aberdeenshire "the young farmers," says the Rev. Skene Keith, "like their fathers, are very expert in dancing and managing a cudgel without a master."

The delight which the Gaël had in the recitation of their traditional history was extreme. The duty of preserving and relating their legends was properly the province of the bards, who were supported for the purpose, but the whole population were accustomed to acquire the sgeulachds, or historical narrations, and when there was no bard, the teller of tales, sometimes called the rhymer, a character much respected, supplied his place.

The Irish had their cleasamhneagh, or jesters, and druith righeadh, or royal mimics.* We find there were in the Scots' army, in 1138, buffoons and jesters, both male and female. A curious amusement is described in p. 248, and

* Coll. reb. Hibernica.

it has been stated elsewhere that little dramas and ludicrous interludes from the ancient poems, were often performed.

An idle people are naturally prone to gaming. Tacitus, speaking of the Germans, says they were passionately given to play at games of chance, at which they continued not only until their whole substance was gone, but would even stake their lives, and, if they lost, would patiently suffer themselves to be sold, calling it honour! The brotherhood of Carrows, a sort of common gamblers in Ireland, resembled these Germans. They did nothing else but play cards all the year round, staking their mantles, shirts, and every thing to the bare skin, when they trussed themselves in straw or leaves, and in that state would wait on the highways with unabated desire, and invite passengers to play on the green. "For defaulte of other stuffe, they pawn portions of their glibe, the nails of their fingers and toes," and other members of their body, which they lose or redeem, at the courtesy of the winner.[1] One of the Irish games, called "short castle," is played by two persons, with three counters or pebbles on a board marked by a cross and two diagonals, the game being won by getting the three on a straight line. Chess and drafts were favourite amusements of the Highlanders. A passage from a poem of Mary Mac Leod, given in p. 252, mentions the delight which her chief took in these games. Martin describes a set of "table men," carved with different figures, which he saw, that were made of a blue sort of stone found in Lewis, and relates a curious occurrence of second sight that happened when Sir Norman Mac Leod and some others were playing at a game of tables called Falmer-more, where three of a side cast dice in turn, for the disposition of the pieces.

Hunting, which has been already described, was a favorite diversion of the Celts; their other amusements were chiefly

[1] Campion. Riche, p. 38.

of a martial character, and on several occasions there have been opportunities of showing their propensity to display their courage and address in single combat. The amusement described in Volume i. p. 122, so popular among the Germans, strikingly shews the military character of that people. The rude Celts had no taste for the refined pleasures of other nations, their only enjoyment being in those manly sports which cherished their warlike and independent spirit. For this purpose, chariot racing and other sports were apparently enjoined as a religious duty, and to inspire the people with due ardour, the services of the bards were consecrated. Some Frisian ambassadors, it is related, having visited Rome, they were taken to the theatres, as the most attractive exhibitions, but, to the astonishment of the Romans, those men took not the smallest interest in the amusements. The Caledonians practised a sort of tournament, which is spoken of in old poems as "the honour of the spear," and in their encounter, they only asked cothrum na Feinne, "the equal combat of the Fingalians." Athletic exercises were the delight of the Gaël, and from the chief to the lowest clansman, they vied with each other in generous contention, the highest individual being often the strongest and most accomplished in feats of prowess. An anecdote is related of a wrestler, who, presuming on his great strength and skill, had insulted a whole clan, none of whom would venture to encounter him, except the chief, who accepted his challenge, and succeeded in vanquishing him, but in the exertion he burst a blood-vessel, and shortly afterwards died. Besides Gleachd, or wrestling, the Highlanders contend for a short stick or rachd, which they endeavour to wrench out of each other's grasp. They also, sitting on the ground, feet to feet, and mutually holding a stick, endeavour each by main strength to force his opponent from the ground.

The Clach-neart, literally stone of strength, or the putting stone, is a favourite and ancient amusement, and consists in projecting a large round stone to the greatest possible distance. It was formerly the custom to have one of these lying at the gate of every chieftain's house, and on the arrival of a stranger, he was asked as a compliment to throw. Indeed, when chiefs or gentlemen called on each other, their followers always diverted themselves in wrestling, fencing, putting, running, &c., and sometimes resorted to the more serious amusement of breaking each other's heads in good earnest. The throwing of the stone requires both strength and skill, to which practice alone can give effect.

Clach cuid fir is lifting a large stone two hundred pounds or more from the ground, and placing it on the top of another about four feet high. A youth that can do this is forthwith reckoned a man, whence the name of the amusement, and may then wear a bonnet.

Throwing a heavy sledge hammer is a popular trial of strength, which often leads the blacksmith and his customers to forget their business for some time. A fine trial of strength is by endeavouring to turn a heavy bar of iron fairly over, by placing the foot under it.

Swiftness of foot was reckoned a very considerable accomplishment, and was often of much importance in their military transactions. We have seen the Highlanders able to contend with cavalry in running, and their ability in this way had a double advantage—if they put the enemy to flight, it was not possible to escape their pursuit, and if themselves routed, it was scarcely possible to molest their retreat. The Geal ruith, or racing game, which comprehended the running leap, to the Highlanders so useful an accomplishment, was sedulously practised, and the gilli ruith, or running footman, was capable of performing astonishing feats of pedestrianism, both in distance and velocity.

Boat racing, and Geall-snamh, or contests in swimming, were also popular, and a native of Isla was not reckoned a man if he could not catch a seal when in the water.*

A truly Highland sport is Cluich-bhall, or Camanachd, called in the Low Country hurling or shinny, and in Ireland bandy. Great numbers collect on a plain, chiefly about Christmas, and dividing into parties of twelve and upwards on a side, endeavour, by means of sticks, crooked at the lower end, to drive a ball to a certain goal. This is a very animated game, and is enlivened by numerous spectators, plenty of whisky, and by the presence of pipers. The balls in Argyleshire are often of wood; in Badenach they are formed of hair, hard and firmly twisted.

The Golf, called Cluich-dhesog, is a Highland game, but is more simple than as played in the Lowlands. Two or more persons, by means of clubs of a certain form, strike a small hard ball, the contest being to decide either who shall reach a distant spot, or put the ball into a hole with the fewest strokes.

Two parties kicking a ball with the feet in opposite directions is another game, where much agility is required. Grand matches were formerly played in the Northern counties on Fasten's Even, and other festivals. "The Christmas ba'in' of Monymusk," in Aberdeenshire, has been described in a poem by the Rev. John Skinner, 1739, which is worthy of comparison with the "Christ's Kirk on the Green," of King James I., or the productions of Allan Ramsay.

As a humorous description of this popular diversion, which at the above place was formerly held in the church-

* An utter impossibility!—as well say that he was not reckoned a man until he could catch an eagle on the wing. The hunting of the seal was in long past times a matter of no small importance throughout the Hebrides, and he who could not trap or spear, or otherwise "circumvent" and kill his seal, was not reckoned a man. ED.

yard, and, as a specimen of the singular dialect of that part of Scotland, which, to most readers, will require a glossary to be understood, a few verses, taken at random from the poem, may be thought worthy of insertion.

>Has ne'er in a' this country been
>Sic shouderin' an' sic fa'in',
>As happen'd twa three days sin' seen,
>Here at the Christmas ba'in'.
>At even syne the fellows keen
>Drank till the neist days dawin';
>Sae snell that some tint baith their een,
>An' could na' pay their lawin'
>   For a' that day.

>Rob Roy, I wat he was na' dull,
>He first leit at the ba',
>An' wi' a rap, clash'd Geordy's skull
>Hard to the steeple wa'.
>Wha was aside but auld Tam Tull,
>His frien's mischance he saw,
>He briend like ony baited bull,
>An' wi' aye thud dang twa
>   To the yird that day.

>In cam' the inset Dominie,
>Just riftin' frae his dinner,
>A young mess John, as ane could see,
>Was neither saint nor sinner.
>A brattlin' band unhappilee,
>Drave by him wi' a binner,
>An' heels-o'er-gowdy couped he,
>An' rave his gued horn penner
>   In twa that day.

>A stalwart stirk in tartan claise,
>Sware mony a sturdy aith,
>To bear the ba' thro' a' his faes,
>An' nae kape muckle skaith.
>Rob Roy heard the frisksome fraise,
>Well browden'd in his graith,
>Gowph'd him alang his shins a blaise,
>An' gart him tine baith faith
>   An' feet that day.

The prior's man, a chiel as stirk
Amaist as giant could be,
He kent afore o' this day's wark,
For certain that it would be.
He ween'd to drive it o'er the park,
An' ilk ane thought it should be;
What way it was he miss'd the mark,
I canna' tell, but fon't be,
     He fell that day.

Ere he wan out o' that foul lair,
That black mischance had gi'en him,
There tumbled an unlucky pair
O' mawtent loons aboon him.
It would hae made your heart fu' sair,
Gin ye had only seen him;
An't hadna' been for Davy Mair,
The rascals had outdeen him,
     Belyve that day.

When Sawney saw the Sutor slain,
He was his ain half brither,
I wot mysel he was right brain,
An' how could he be ither?
He ran to help wi' might an' main,
Twa buckled wi' him thegither,
Wi' a firm yowph ne fell'd the tane,
An' wi' a gowph the tither,
     Fell'd him that day.

The Strath-fillan Society, lately established by Lord Gwydir, on his Drummond estate, in Perthshire, is for the purpose of encouraging all sorts of games and amusements peculiar to the Highlands.* The annual meetings are held in a romantic spot, and are attended by numerous noblemen, gentlemen, and ladies, with a large assemblage of Highlanders. The effect of their gaudy costume, the bagpipes, and the various sports exhibited amid highly picturesque scenery, is extremely fine. A beautiful lake affords the pleasure of a boat race, and a recital of

* These games are now held at Bridge of Tilt, and are largely attended. Similar games are held at the "Northern Meeting," at Inverness, every autumn. At the annual "gathering" of the "Gaelic Society," too, in July, dancing, and violin and bagpipe music are patronised. ED.

Gaëlic compositions relieves the fatigue of the athletic exercises, while prizes of bagpipes, dirks, suits of tartans, snuff mulls, &c., send the competitors home in high delight.

Two of the Druidical order are shewn at the commencement of this chapter. As the poets and musicians of the Celts, they occupy an appropriate place; and as a highly interesting specimen of the peculiar instrument which belonged to the order, the harp of Mary Queen of Scots is here introduced.

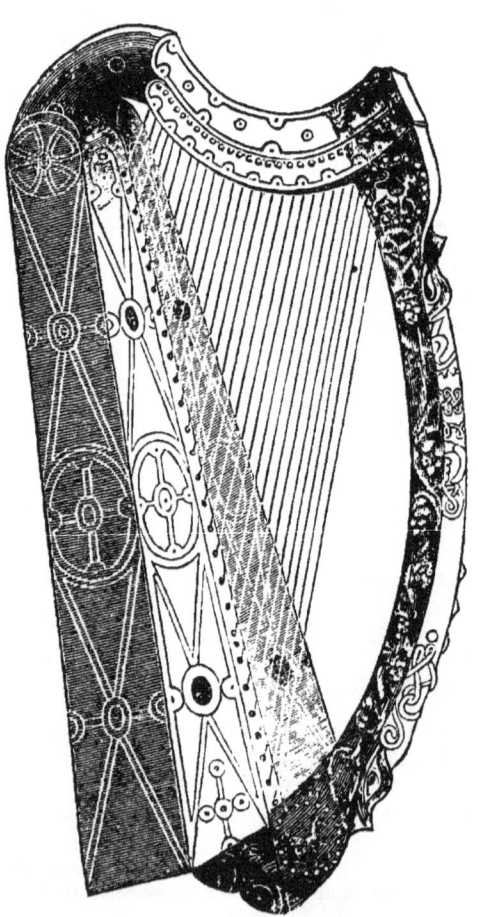

HARP OF MARY QUEEN OF SCOTS.

STONEHENGE, p. 330, (Restored).

CHAPTER VII.

RELIGION, MARRIAGE CEREMONIES, AND FUNERAL RITES.

DRUIDISM is one of the most ancient systems of religion. It is supposed by many to have been derived from Pythagoras, but is certainly of much more remote origin. According to Clemens Alexandrinus, Pythagoras was but an auditor of the Gauls. Valerius Maximus asserts that his opinions were those of the Celts, and Iamblichus says he heard that his learning consisted of the Gallic and Iberian mysteries. Druidism must be a more ancient system than the time of this philosopher, who appears to have borrowed his tenets from it. He was, perhaps, a reformer of a religion that had begun to lose its original simplicity, but it must be borne in mind that there was a near resemblance among ancient systems of religion, as there was an affinity of language and similarity of manners. Eumolpus, the

Thracian, introduced the Eleusinian mysteries to the Greeks, who subsequently revered them so deeply. At this period the Athenians were beginning to distinguish themselves from their neighbours, and their fertile genius soon produced, from the simple dogmas of their ancestors, a peculiar system of theology; hence Lucian thought it strange that the barbarians, who introduced those mysteries, should be afterwards excluded from them.

The religious connections which the Greeks had in the most distant ages formed with the Hyperborei, proves that the primitive mythology was at first universally respected. Those people, who are believed to have been the inhabitants of Britain, were in the practice, from a period before all record, to transmit their first fruits to Delos. Eratosthenes relates that Apollo deposited the Arrow with which he slew the Cyclops, with the Hyperborei; that their high priest Abaris carried it to Greece, and at last presented it to Pythagoras. This story is too mysterious for elucidation; it is probably allegorical, but it shews the veneration which was in those ages paid to one religion.

The secresy with which the mysteries of ancient religion were preserved is remarkable. The priests and other members concealed their knowledge from the uninitiated with the most scrupulous care, which, in most cases arose from feelings of real piety. Those who did not value their oaths of secresy must have been deterred from divulging their secrets by the fear of detection and consequent execration and punishment. The dark allusions to the mysteries of Pagan theology occasion a regret that they are now unknown. "I shall not relate what I know," says Pausanias, "from the mysteries of the mother of the gods, concerning Mercury and the Ram;" again, "who the Cabiri are, and what the ceremonies performed in honour of them and the mother of the gods, I must beg those who are desirous of hearing such particulars to suffer me to pass over in silence; farther he adds, Ceres deposited something with Prometheus, one of the Cabiri. What this deposit was, and the circumstances respecting it, piety forbids me to disclose.* It was the invariable practice of the ancient priests and philosophers to teach by enigmas, lest strangers should be able to understand them.

The Druids committed none of their theological secrets to writing, a principle which has involved their system in peculiar obscurity. The singular practice of committing their doctrinal learning to memory was a severe and tedious probation for a student, but it was well calculated, in the particular state of Celtic society, to preserve in purity their ancient traditions. The care with which this race cultivated the memory has been shewn in the previous chapter. The youth spent twenty years in acquiring the knowledge necessary to the Druidic profession, and, it is said, stored their minds with no less than 60,000 verses.

It seems strange that the extensive prevalence of this religion should be denied. It has been inferred from Cæsar, that it was confined to a limited portion of Gaul, but it has been remarked by a zealous antiquary, that, although Cæsar says of the Germans, that they had no Druids, he does not say they were without religion or priests. He mentions some of the gods they revered, and those were the same as the Gauls worshipped. Tacitus also does not appear to have found Druids among the Germans, but he mentions their gods, their sacred groves and altars, their songs and their ceremonies, all which resembled those of the Gauls. The religion of both people was, therefore, alike Druidism, although its ministers may have had different appellations, and its mysteries been somewhat differently solemnized. Druidism is said to have been only partially cultivated in

* Lib. ix. c. 25.

part of South Britain, and perfectly unknown in Ireland: these assertions are certainly rash and unwarrantable. This system of religion was cherished in Britain as its most ancient and hallowed seat, and should the remarkable passage in Diodorus, concerning "the round temple in an island of the Hyperboreans,—opposite Celtica,—where was a magnificent grove, and where the people were harpers," be considered inapplicable to Albion, yet the fact is evident from the express testimony of Cæsar, corroborated by Pliny, that the youth of Gaul resorted to Britain for instruction in the sacred religion, that they spent twenty years in its acquirement, and that it was believed to have originated there. Mela, indeed, describes the Irish as extremely barbarous, and devoid of all religion; but this is too improbable to be credited, especially when he allows them to have had those he calls magicians, whom Ware considers Druids. That they could be no other is evident, for dry is the Gaëlic term for a magician, a philosopher, and prophet; and Alfric, in his Saxon glossary, said magi were so called even by the Angles.[b] On the conversion of Edwin, king of Northumberland, he summoned all his councillors, among whom appeared the high priest Coefi. There is a proverb still in use by the Highlanders, which extols a person as being "as dexterous as Coefi, the Arch Druid;" and Doctor Mac Pherson observes, that coifi-dry, is well known to mean a person of extraordinary sense and cunning. Druidh is still used in Gaëlic for wise men, from which is Druithnich or Drui, servants of truth, and the Teutonic Druid or Druthin.[c] The usual etymon of this word is attended with some difficulty. It is derived from δρυς, an oak, in Welsh derw, in Gaëlic darach, &c. It is improbable that the Celts should have distinguished their magi by a

[b] Waldron's History of the Isle of Man.
[c] Doctors Smith and Mac Pherson.

Greek word, and the Gaëlic derivation is not very plain. Menage believes it came from the old British word drus, a magician, and Keysler says draoi is a magician or enchanter. Mr. Grant, of Corrimony, will have the name Draothian, which shews the root of a series of words. Draoneach is an improver of the soil, and this being the first way in which man exerted his ingenuity, it came to signify an artist or clever person, in which sense the Irish still use it. The rational belief is, therefore, that the name of this celebrated order imported their abilities, and is one of that class of words formed on the D and R, which seem to have conveyed the idea of dexterity and superior qualifications.

The Druidic religion does not appear to have been either "a late invention, or confined to the South of Britain and North of Gaul," but is maintained to have been observed and taught throughout the Island, contrary to the assertion of Pinkerton, who charges those who say there were Druids in Scotland, with speaking "utter nonsense."

The Druids taught their disciples, and performed their religious rites in the deep recesses of woods and in caves. The Germans consecrated whole groves and woods, which were named from the gods, and amid the gloom and quiet of this seclusion, they contemplated their divinities in deep reverence.[d] Within these groves, which were generally on conspicuous situations, were raised their rude but impressive temples, where, on festivals, the people met in great numbers.[e] The practice of surrounding places of worship with trees was usual among all Pagan nations, hence the Jews were particularly enjoined not to plant a grove of any kind near unto the altar of the Lord.[f] In 2nd Kings we find mention of the "women who wove hangings for the groves." They were the places where the statues of the

---

[d] Tacitus   [e] Florus, iii. 10.   [f] Deuter. xvi. 21.

gods were set up. Pausanius mentions the sacred grove of Apollo, called Carneus, and many others; part of which were inclosed by a bulwark of stones, being the most sacred spot where the statues of the divinities were placed, and which is always distinguished from the "uncovered part." There was a grove and temple at Pergamos; and that of Jupiter Ammon was surrounded by trees.[g]

There seems to have prevailed among all rude nations a predilection for circular formed temples, and it is difficult to say whether the upright stones which composed them were simply viewed as the boundary of the sacred precinct, or were considered representations of gods. From the following observation of Pausanias, and other passages in ancient authors, it would appear that there was a peculiar sanctity attached to them. "Near Pharæ are thirty quadrangular stones, which the Pharenses venerate." It was anciently held unbecoming by the Celts to represent the gods under any other form than that of a rude and shapeless obelisk, and this feeling was common to the early Grecians, it being formerly the custom with all the Greeks to reverence rude stones, in place of statues of the gods. The Thespians preserved an ancient statue of Love, that was but a rude block.[h] A square unpolished stone was also a symbol of Bacchus, and a round one that of the earth.[i]

The Celts did not presume to represent any of their deities under the human form, but typified them by various articles. The images of wild beasts and other animals, as well as inanimate objects, the symbols of their gods, they were accustomed to bring from their sacred groves, and use as insignia during war. After their subjugation to Rome, they apparently imitated their conquerors, and allowed

[g] Diod. xvii. 5.   [h] Pausanias, lib. vii. 22, ix. 27.   [i] Beloe.

their gods to be represented under terrestrial forms;—those Gallic and other statues that have been discovered being referable to an era subsequent to that event. Gildas speaks of some of the statues of the British deities being to be seen in the sixth century, when he wrote. That of Isis, the tutelary goddess of Paris, remained in the Abbey of St. Germain des Priz until 1514, when it was removed by the order of the Bishop of Meaux.[k]

The circular form of the Celtic temples was probably typical of eternity, and of the deity. It was religiously adhered to as the general plan, and has given rise to names by which places of worship have been distinguished even to our own times. The Gaëlic cearcal is evidently the origin of the Latin circus, the old English church, and the Scotish kirk,[*] which is spelt according to its pronunciation. In like manner, as the primitive temple was composed of large stones, it was termed clachan by the Gaël, from which the Latin ecclesia is apparently derived; and the Highlanders to this day use the expression, calling the church "the stones!"

The most astonishing temple, in point of magnitude, in Britain, is that of ABURY, or Avebury, in Wiltshire. The area of this astonishing work contained upwards of 28 acres, and was surrounded by a wide and deep ditch, and rampart, measuring about 70 feet in height from the bottom. One hundred stones of amazing size formed an outer circle, within which were two others not concentric, formed of double rows of stones. Of these the outer contained thirty, and the inner twelve. In the centre of one were

[k] Religion des Gauls.

[*] *Church* and *Kirk* come into our language from the Greek, after having been first adopted and disguised elsewhere. Anglo-Saxon, *Circ;* Danish, *Kirke;* Scottish, *Kirk*—all contracted from the Greek, *Kyriake*, the Lord's (House.) ED.

three stones, and in the other was a single obelisk which measured twenty-one feet in length, and eight feet nine inches in breadth. Besides the circles, which we thus see contained the number of 188 stones, there were two extended avenues which are supposed to have contained 462 more, making a total of 650!

STONEHENGE, in the same county, must yield in magnificence to Abury, but if much less in size, it is greatly superior in the architectural science which it displays. This wonderful structure, as shewn in the vignette, where it is represented as it is supposed to have appeared when in its pristine grandeur, was circular, but much smaller, and of much more ingenious construction, than Abury. A consideration of this has given rise to an opinion first, I believe, expressed by Mr. Warner, that the latter being the rudest and apparently the most ancient, was the grand temple of the original Celts, whilst Stonehenge was erected by the Belgians, when they obtained possession of the Southern parts of the Island, and was intended as a rival to the other; the deep ditch called Wansdike, supposed to be the line of demarcation between the two people, passing between these two astonishing monuments. This is very ingenious, but it is of course entirely supposititious. We do not find that the Belgians were better able to raise such a temple than the Celts, and we do not find that the two people had different forms of their places of worship. It is, besides, conjectured, with much probability, that Stonehenge was reared at different periods, the outward circle and the inner oval of trilithons being one erection, and the smaller circle and oval of inferior stones being another. This opinion is borne out by the fact that the latter are granite whilst the others are not; but antiquaries have come to opposite conclusions respecting the priority of erection, some believing that the outward circle was the original work, and others that the inner, and most simple design, must have been the first formed. This last idea appears reasonable; and although the granite stones must have been brought from a considerable distance, with such a people it was no obstacle to their adoption at any era. It is against the hypothesis of Stonehenge having been erected by a nation in hostility with the Celts, that the outward stones must have been brought from the Northern part of the country, beyond the frontier line of the Belgian territory.

When the light of history fails us, we may indulge our fancies, and form plausible and delightful conjectures, but as there is an illimitable field for the imagination to wander, it is evident that it may run sometimes into the wildest conceits. The state in which Stonehenge is found, and in which it has remained with apparently little alteration from time immemorial, has left ample room for antiquaries to exert their ingenuity in endeavouring to determine its original plan and appearance.

The restoration of this wonderful pile is according to Waltire, an enthusiastic old philosopher, who actually encamped and remained on the ground beside this temple for several months, to satisfy his curiosity and complete his investigations concerning its appropriation. It is much to be regretted that the papers of this deep-thinking and veracious antiquary were lost after his death. Some account of his opinions concerning it may be seen in Mr. Higgins' work; it need only be here observed that the view gives an idea of this work which could not be done in words. According to Waltire's plan, the outer range of uprights consists of thirty. The inner trilithons, according to all, were five, to which he adds six smaller stones, as a continuation towards the entrance. The intermediate circle consists of thirty-eight, and the semi-circular range inside he makes nineteen. Thus with the altar, and reckoning the imposts,* the whole number is one hundred and thirty-nine.¹ The height of the outward stones is in the highest about thirteen feet, and six or seven in breadth, and, contrary to what we find in similar erections, the stones have been formed by the tool, the imposts being secured by tenons, and one stone is found formed with a rib, or moulding.

The most remarkable character of Stonehenge consists of the imposts, no similar structure in Britain appearing to have ever been erected in this way, and except a circle at Drenthiem, and another on a mountain near Helmstad, represented in Keysler's work on Northern Antiquities, there is perhaps no other instance of the trilithon style. In these examples the incumbent stones appear heavy, partaking more of the character of cromleachs, and the temples are by no means equal to Stonehenge either in design or execution.

The remarkable temple at Callernish, in the Isle of Lewis, is represented at the end of this Chapter. This singular monument is placed north and south, and consists of an avenue five hundred and fifty-eight feet long, eight feet wide, and composed of thirty-nine stones, generally six or seven feet high, with one at the entrance, no less than thirteen. At the south end of this walk is a circle of sixty-three feet diameter, that appears to have been com-

---

* Gilbert White, of Selborne, in writing about the Jackdaw (*Corvus Monedula*) observes:—"Another very unlikely spot is made use of by daws as a place to breed in, and that is *Stonehenge*. These birds deposit their nests in the interstices between the upright and the impost stones of that amazing work of antiquity, which circumstance alone speaks *the prodigious height of the upright stones*, that they should be tall enough to secure those nests from the annoyance of shepherd boys, who are always idling round the place." ED.

¹ Plan in the "Celtic Druids."

posed of either thirteen or fifteen stones, six to eight feet in height, the centre being occupied by an obelisk thirteen feet high, and shaped somewhat like a chair. Beyond the circle several stones are carried in right lines, producing a cruciform appearance. The length of this cross part is two hundred and four feet, and the total of stones appears to have been sixty-eight or seventy. Borlase, it may be noticed, makes them fifty-two, and Mac Culloch forty-seven. The magnitude and singularity of this work has led several antiquaries to believe that it is the very Hyperborean temple spoken of by the ancients. Conjecture seems to lie between Abury, Stonehenge, and Callernish, except we think with D'Alton, the late writer on Irish History, that the round temple of the Hyperborei means the round towers of Ireland. It is remarkable that Eratosthenes says, Apollo hid his arrow where there was a winged temple. The cross parts, resembling the transepts of a cathedral, are, I believe, peculiar to Callernish, and may very well bear the appellation of wings.

The plain of Clava, a mile eastward of Culloden, in Inverness-shire, is remarkable for being full of circles, surrounded by "rows of immense slabs of sandstone." Some account of remarkable objects of this sort, with original drawings made to the Society of Antiquaries of London by the author, have been thought worthy of being engraved and printed in the twenty-second volume of the Transactions of that learned body.* There are many other curious monuments of the same kind scattered throughout Scotland, Ireland, and England; but all Celtic monuments

---

* The opinion long prevalent that these and similar structures were temples for Druidical worship has of recent years been less positively entertained, because unquestionable proofs of the sepulchral character of many of them have been discovered. That some of them, however, were designed as religious edifices seems equally certain. ED.

now in existence must yield to that stupendous work at Carnac, in Britany. This truly astonishing memorial of a distant race, exhibits a tract of not less than five or six miles, on which are placed, at distances of 18, 20, or 25 feet, eleven rows of stones, chiefly planted on the smallest end, forming ten avenues or walks, of 12, 24, 18½, 18½, 30, 30, 36, 36, 30½, and 36 feet in width respectively, the whole resembling a huge serpent, as shewn in a plan engraved in the above volume. This vast assemblage of stones is so astonishing that many have considered it impossible for human hands to arrange them, and believe it to be the effects of some convulsion of nature; but however much we may be amazed at the magnitude of Carnac, it is assuredly an artificial erection. The reason for a departure from the usual circular form it seems impossible to discover, but the hypotheses of Cambray, Penhouet, and others, are ingenious. The authors of the "Celtic Druids" and "Hermes Britannicus" suggest the idea that the number of stones indicated the years which, according to the Druids, had passed from the creation. The number of stones now remaining being about 4000, is found to agree very nearly with the age of the world, but it must be observed that in its original state they are believed to have equalled 10,000. Whatever credit may be attached to it, the tradition is, that a stone was added every year at midsummer, on which occasion the whole pile was illuminated, a practice that points to the worship of Belus. That it was consecrated to this deity also may be inferred from the tradition that it was the work of the Crions, surely a name derived from Grianus, the Celtic term for the sun. On this subject the opinion of Olaus Magnus may be stated, which appears to savour too much of fancy. If stones are arranged in a circle, they denote a family burial-place; if in a right line, the battle of heroes; in a square, troops of warriors were represented; and in a wedge form, they imported that on or near the spot, armies of horse or foot were victorious.

That the Celts worshipped in circular temples formed of rude stones is indisputable; because we find the circular inclosures used until late times for courts of law as well as places of worship, and although the time when some of them were actually built be known, we are not, therefore, justified in denying their original appropriation. As the Celtic priests were legislators, the temple was the place whence they promulgated their laws, and on the abolition of Paganism, although discouraged, the use of the circle for this purpose, and for worship, was long retained. Christianity did not at first deny the use of the place of worship for judicial purposes; but, gaining ground, an express canon of the Scotish church prohibited courts from being held in churches, for they were usually erected on the sites of temples; and I am convinced that when the Christian edifice ceased to be the place where civil matters were decided, as had been the practice in Pagan times, the laws or moot-hills were substituted, and hence it is that these mounts are so generally found in the close vicinity of churches. Where, however, zeal for Christianity did not lead to the destruction of circles and their condemnation as places of meeting, they continued to be used as courts, especially by the Northern nations, until very late times; and from the circumstance of surrounding the circle, after the meeting had assembled, the term of "fencing a court," in all probability, is derived. One of the latest instances of this appropriation of the " standing stones " occurs in 1380, when Alexander Stewart, Lord of Badenach, held a court at those of the Rath of Kingusie.

The chief seat of Druidism on the continent, Cæsar tells us, was in the country of the Carnutes, supposed to have been where the city of Chartres now stands.

It appears to me that the principal Celtic deity was the sun, Belus, Belenus, or Baal. Herodian[m] says, the Aquileians worshipped this god, whom they considered the same as Apollo, whence we see why the Hyperborei especially venerated him, for he was the personification of that luminary. The Caledonians worshipped this deity under the name of Baal, or Beil, and to his honour they lighted fires on Midsummer-day, or the 1st of May. This festival, which is not even yet discontinued, was called Baal-tein, or Beltain, signifying the fire of Baal, and was formerly commemorated so generally that it became a term in Scots law, which is yet in use. This practice of lighting fires on Midsummer, arose from the circumstance of the Druids having at that time caused all fires to be extinguished, to be re-kindled from the sacred fire that was never allowed to expire. It is surprising that this sacred flame, like that in the temple of Vesta, should be preserved for ages after the extinction of the religion, by Christian priests. It was no earlier than 1220, that Loundres, Archbishop of Dublin, extinguished the perpetual fire, which was kept in a small cell near the church of Kildare; but so firmly rooted was the veneration for this fire, that it was relighted in a few years, and actually kept burning until the suppression of monasteries![n] This fire was attended by virgins, often women of quality, called Inghean an Dagha, daughters of fire, and Breochnidh, or the fire-keepers, from which they have been confounded with the nuns of St. Brigid. A writer in the Gentleman's Magazine, 1795, says, being in Ireland the day before Midsummer, he was told that in the evening he should see "the lighting of the fires in honour of the sun" at midnight; and Riche describes the preparation for the festival

---

[m] Lib. viii.   [n] Archdall's Mon. Hib. ap. Anth. Hib. iii. 240.

in these words: "What watching, what rattling, what tinkling upon pannes and candlesticks, what strewing of hearbes, what clamors, and other ceremonies are used," and all this apparently in Dublin itself. Spenser says, on kindling a fire, the Irish always made a prayer. A practice of the cooks at Newcastle, who light bonfires on Midsummer-day, may be derived from the Beltain rites; and the chimney-sweeps of London and other parts who go in procession and dance in grotesque dresses, appear to represent the ancient fire worshippers at their holiday amusements.

Graine, Grein, or Grannus, was a term for this god among the Caledonians, and an inscription to him was found in the ruins of Antonine's wall.° The word is gre-thein, the *t* being quiescent, and it signifies the essence or natural source of fire. Camden says, Grannus is of similar import with Gruagach, a supernatural being, latterly distinguished among the Scots as Brownie; and he quotes Isodore to shew that the long hair of the Goths was called granni, which it is apparent is neither more nor less than the Gaëlic word. The sun, distinguished as the source of fire, became known by a natural change, as the yellow, or golden haired, and the libations of milk were always offered on the granni, or gruagach stone, of which there was one in every village, on days consecrated to the sun. The singular method of raising the tein-egin, or needfire, has been described, and the virtues which it is supposed to possess, in page 68. The Highlanders passed through the fire to Baal, as the ancient Gentiles did; and they thought it a religious duty to walk round their fields and flocks with burning matter in their right hands, a practice once universal throughout the country. The Northern nations had an equal veneration for fire, preserving it continually on their altars.

° Mac Pherson's Diss. xvii.

Piorun was the chief god of the Poles, and two places where he was worshipped are known. At Walna, where one of them was situated, the altar is still preserved in the cathedral; and it is related that his image stood under an oak with a fire constantly burning before it. The Poles became Christians only in the end of the fourteenth century.[p]

It appears to have been in imitation of the sun's course that the Gaël religiously observed, in their rites and common occupations, to make the deisal, or turn to the right hand. Pliny, it is to be observed, says that the Gauls, in worshipping, contrary to the practice of other nations, always turned to the left, but Possidonius and others expressly say to the right, a reconciliation of which apparent inconsistency is attempted by D. Martin, in his Religion des Gauls.

Between Badenach and Strathspey is Slia-grannus, the heath of grannus, called by the inhabitants griantachd,[*] which has undoubtedly been a magh-aoraidh, or field where Druidical worship was performed. The sun was believed to be propitious to the high minded warrior. In the work of Dr. Smith, Grian is thus addressed: "Thou delightest to shed thy beams on the clouds which enrobe the brave, and to spread thy rays around the tombs of the valiant." It was also a belief that the world should be consumed by this deity: and la bhrath, the day of burning,[†]

---

[p] Letters from Poland.

[*] The original, probably, of the name of Clan *Grant*. In Gaelic *Grann daich*. Ed.

[†] *La bhràth*—the day of burning; the day of judgment. *Gu bràth*—for ever; literally, till the *burning*. The phrase is probably no older than the early Christian age, and seems to be founded on the well known and terribly grand verse in the Second Epistle of Peter, ch. 3. v. 10—"But the day of the Lord will come as a thief in the night; in the which the heavens shall pass away with a great noise, and the elements shall melt

now understood of the last judgment, came, from the improbability or remoteness of the catastrophe, to be translated "never." Connected with this belief seems the clachan bhrath, a globular stone, still viewed with superstitious feelings in the Islands of Iona and Garveloch.

with fervent heat; the earth also, and the works that are therein shall be burnt up." This passage also suggested the fine old Latin hymn, the "Dies Irae."

> Dies irae, dies illa
> Solvet saeclum in favilla,
> Jeste David cum Sybilla.
>
> . . .
>
> Confutatis maledictis,
> Flammis acribus addictis,
> Voca me cum benedictis.
> Oro supplex et inclinis,
> Cor contritum quasi cinis,
> Gere curam mei finis.

> The day of wrath, that dreadful Day,
> Shall the whole age in ashes lay,
> As David and the Sybil say.
>
> . . .
>
> When the condemned are put to shame,
> And cast to the devouring flame,
> Oh! with the blessèd call my name.
> With prostrate soul my head I bend,
> My broken heart before Thee rend,
> Be Thine the care to guard my end!

Scott's magnificent hymn—finer even than the Latin one, must be familiar to most of our readers.

> "That day of wrath, that dreadful day,
> When heaven and earth shall pass away,
> What power shall be the sinner's stay?
> How shall he meet that dreadful day?
> When shrivelling like a parched scroll,
> The flaming heavens together roll,
> While louder yet, and yet more dread,
> Swells the high trump that wakes the dead!
> Oh! on that day, that wrathful day,
> When man to judgment wakes from clay,
> *Be Thou* the trembling sinner's stay,
> Though heaven and earth shall pass away.
>   ("Lay of the Last Minstrel.") ED.

A fire having originated among the Iuhones, and consumed the woods to the walls of Cologne, the people collected and attacked the devouring element, first with stones at a distance, which appearing to check its rage, they ventured closer, and, using clubs, they ultimately repulsed and subdued it. Finally, we are told, they smothered it entirely by means of their clothes. All this apparent madness must have arisen from their belief that they were contending with supernatural beings, and it is not more absurd than many actions of the old Highlanders.

Cæsar has said that the Gauls paid their highest veneration to Mercury; to which opinion he may have been led by having a better opportunity of observing his worship, or his attributes being numerous, he must have had many devotees, as the Virgin Mary, among the ignorant catholics, receives often more attention than the Saviour himself. The god whom Cæsar calls Mercury, was Teut, or Theuth, Dhu taith, or Teutates, i. e., the god Taute, who was no other than the Taatus of the Phœnicians. The word bears a strong resemblance to the Armoric Tad, or Tat, a father. The Gallo-Belgic name for Teutates, Schœpflin says, was Wodan, who was worshipped by the Saxons. They also adored Hermes, or Mercury, under the name of Irmin, or Ermensul, a statue of whom was found at Eresburg, by Charlemagne.

The Gauls derived their origin from Dis, a god that has been assimilated with Pluto, but who is with more reason believed to have been the earth, or its elements, and the same being as the German Tuisto, or Tuitos, from whom that people alleged themselves to be sprung.

We learn from Tacitus, that the Aviones, Angles, Varinians, Eudoses, &c., universally worshipped Herthum, Hertæ, or Mother Earth; believing she visited countries, and interposed in human affairs. In an island of the ocean was the wood Castum, where was a chariot dedicated to the goddess, covered with a curtain, and not permitted to be touched but by the priest, who watched the time when she entered the car, which was always drawn by cows, and with profound veneration attended its motions. In all places which she deigned to visit were great feasts and rejoicings, and every warlike instrument was then carefully put out of the way, and peace and repose were then proclaimed. When tired of conversation with mortals, the same priests reconducted her to the temple. Then the chariot and the curtains, and even the deity herself, if you believe it, adds the historian, were washed and purified in a secret lake. In this office slaves officiated, who were doomed to be afterwards swallowed up in the same lake; hence all men were possessed with a mysterious terror, as well as with a holy ignorance, what that must be which none see but such as are immediately to perish. "The Truce of God," so often and so effectually proclaimed by the clergy about the eleventh century, was an obvious imitation of the procession of the goddess Earth, which in Pagan times took place in the territories of present Mecklenburg. The appeal to Hertha was made by passing under a strip of green sod, as described in the first volume.

Mannus was celebrated among the Germans as one of their founders, being the son of Tuisto. Mannus, according to Clarke, is the same as Manes, which Menage on Laertius says was used by the Greeks for a servant.

The Æstii, says Tacitus, worship the mother of the gods; and, as the characteristic of their superstition, they wear the images of wild boars, by which every worshipper of the goddess is secured from danger even amid his foes. The Germans also wore, in veneration of their gods, a shackle round their leg.[q] Of the Suevi we are told the

[q] Neu. Brit. p. 41.

Semnones reckoned themselves most noble and ancient, and the belief of their antiquity was confirmed by religious mysteries. At a certain time of the year, all the people descended from the same stock, assembled by their deputies in a wood consecrated by their fathers, and by superstitious awe in times of old, and began there their worship by sacrificing a man. To this grove another sort of veneration was paid; no one entered it unless bound; from that circumstance evincing his own subordination and meanness, and the power of the deity. If any one fell down he was not permitted to rise or be lifted up, but grovelled along on the ground. They believed that in that place God resided, that from this place they drew their origin, and that all things are subject to the deity.

Mars is placed by Cæsar the third in the list of five gods, which, he says, the Gauls adored. This god, to whom the Scyths paid the highest honour, is believed to be the Esus, or Hesus, of the Gauls, mentioned by Lucan, who was called, according to Leibnitz, Erich by the Germans; and a sculpture of whom was to be seen in the cathedral of Paris in 1711. The Britons called this being Belatucadro, or, according to Richard of Cirencester, Vitucadrus. The first appellation is derived from Beladuw, the god, Cadwyr, of wars. There was also Maleen, the goddess of war. Before a battle, the spoils of an enemy were devoted to the gods of destruction;' and Porevith was the German god of spoils. On one occasion the Gauls vowed to Mars a chain made of the plunder of the Romans.* To this deity they devoutly offered up the cattle and other spoils which were deposited in consecrated places throughout their provinces, where might be seen vast stores piled up, for no one concealed any part of the plunder, or presumed to touch

---

' Tacitus' Annals, xii. 57.   * Florus, ii. 4.

that which was thus disposed of. Those temples were at last rifled by Cæsar.

The Gauls worshipped Taran, or Tanar, who was the god of thunder, and corresponds to the Jupiter Tonans of the Romans. Torran signifies, among the present Highlanders, the low murmur of distant thunder; tarninach is applied to the loudest peals; and torneonach is an uncommon noise. Doctor Mac Pherson thinks the name may be Nd' air neonach,* or wrathful father. In Cheshire an altar was found inscribed D.O.M. TANARO, to the great Jupiter Tanarus.

The British god of justice was called Andraste, according to Richard of Cirencester, who tells us he had his information from a dux Romanorum; but he seems to make two gods out of one, when he says that Andates was victory. This last was the Andate, or Andraste of Dio, to whom four places of worship were consecrated in the Isle of Sky.†

Nehelania, supposed to have been the new moon, was a goddess worshipped by Gauls and Germans, and at Brittenburg, near the Rhine, a stone was found, dedicated to Nehelania Creta, which would make it appear that she presided over agriculture, in which case, Nehelenia of Marl would correspond to the Ann of the Irish, and Anactis of the Scots, to whose immediate care the productions of the earth and waters were confided.

Mona, or Mena, who was worshipped by the Sequani, was the moon. The Gaël blessed the beams of this luminary that saved them from the danger of precipices, &c.

* '*N d' Athair neonach*, which is just a bit of as pure etymological nonsense as ever was perpetrated. The Gaelic *Torrunn*, *Tàrnach*, *Tarnaineach*, &c., are all closely allied to the Latin *tonitru*, *tonitrus*, *tonitruum*, noise, loud noise, thunder. ED.

† Dr. Mac Queen.

St. Augustine says, that the Gallic peasants invoked Mena for the welfare of their women. The influence which this luminary is supposed to have over the human destiny is a remarkable relic of Pagan superstition. The old Germans, who thought when the moon was in eclipse, it had become angry with them, were little less credulous than the Scots, who, in some parts, will neither marry nor engage in any undertaking of importance until that planet is full.

The special god of waters was called Neithe, an appellation derived from a word signifying to wash or purify with water. The Celts venerated lakes, rivers, and fountains, into which they were accustomed to throw offerings of gold and silver." The Britons entertained the same superstitious feelings concerning water; and Adomnan mentions it among the Picts. It is well known that it prevailed among the Highlanders and Scots in general, until very lately, and the common people yet retain some peculiar notions of this element quite unconnected with Christianity. The people of Lewis anciently sacrificed to a sea god called Shony. In Strathspey is Loch nan Spioridan, or the Lake of Spirits, being the residence of two, namely, the horse and water-bull, which sometimes make their appearance.* The mermaid is seen before floods, and the Marcach sine, or rider of the storm, blows the waters of a river or lake into violent waves or whirling eddies.* Well-worship is a superstition that is not yet entirely eradicated, it being customary to visit certain fountains on particular days, and leave on the margin or adjoining bushes bits of party coloured rags, pebbles, or pins, the representatives of

---

" Religion des Gauls, i. 128.

* The water-horse and water-bull superstition is common all over the Highlands, and in the Hebrides. ED.

' Stat. Account, xiii.

the more valuable offerings of more distant times.* The same superstition exists in Ireland; and statutes expressly prohibiting the practice were passed by Edgar, by Canute, and even by Anselm at London, in 1102. The dedication of fountains to saints, after the introduction of Christianity, perpetuated the veneration instilled by the Druids, who certainly employed water in their ceremonies. Pope Gregory writes to Boniface, the German apostle, that those who had received the Pagan baptism only should be rebaptised." The rock basins seem very probably designed for the performance of this rite. A fountain was often found near a circle, as it afterwards was in the vicinity of a Christian church; and the noise of a distant river was desirable.

What is related of some of the Celts, who are represented as rushing into the floods and attacking the billows sword in hand, must be referred to their peculiar mythological notions. From this must be deduced the ordeal, to which malefactors were subjected, by being committed to the water, there to be judged by the presiding deity, who, if guilty, would refuse to receive them, but if otherwise, would, by allowing them to sink, show that they were accepted by the god.

Is it not to be wondered that divine honour should be paid to woods, when the temples were surrounded with them as a sacred precinct. Certain beings called Dusii, were supposed by the Celts to have the dominion of certain forests; the partiality of this race to hunting, for success in which they

---

* The Editor has seen a well of this kind beside a mountain path leading from Dunkeld to Kirchmichael in Strathardle, Perthshire, in which were many small coins, pins, brooches, &c., the offerings of those who resorted to it to be cured of certain ailments, for which its waters are held in high estimation. This was in 1842. ED.

" Keysler, Ant. de Celt, p. 313.

sacrificed to Diana, and the uses of trees as a system of letters, also increased their veneration to forests. The Britons appear to have had some consecrated to victory. The Gauls reverenced the winds, and gave thanks when Circius, or the N.N.W. blew.[x] In an island called Sena, opposite to the Loire, are the wives, says Strabo, of the Samnitæ, possessed with Bacchic fury, who sell the winds which they can raise by songs, to mariners.[y] The deep and melancholy sound, well known by the inhabitants of a high country, that precedes a storm, is called by the bards "the spirit of the mountain;" and it was customary for a Highlander, when roused by a sudden blast of wind, to search it with his sword, and he sometimes imagined he discovered the corpse or spirit of a relation just dead.

From the annals of Tacitus we find, that among the Naharvali, a sacred and extremely ancient grove was shewn, where a priest habited like a woman presided. The deity which was there worshipped was called Alcis, and as the followers of this being addressed themselves to young men and to brothers, the Romans believed that they worshipped Castor and Pollux.

Hercules, or Ogmius, was worshipped by the Gauls, who had a singular opinion of his attributes, which will be spoken of presently. He was reckoned the founder of the city of Alise, now Arras, and to this day, says Diodorus, the Celtæ have a great respect for it on that account. Tacitus says, the Germans, believing he had been in their country, chiefly extolled him when they were singing the *Barditus*, or chant with which they advanced to battle; a decisive proof, by the by, I apprehend, of the identity of their religion with that of the Gauls. Vulcan is also said

[x] Seneca, v. 17.
[y] Mela, iii. 6. The Druids and Druidesses of this island were burnt by Conan, Duke of Bretagne.—Rojoux' Ducs des Bretagne, i. 135.

to have been worshipped by the Celts, and the names of several other gods and goddesses may be seen in Montfaucon's Antiquities and elsewhere. On a hill at Framont, near Lorraine, there seems to have been a sort of Gaulish pantheon, from the number of statues and other singular antiquities that are from time to time discovered.

It is probable that the different nations had their tutelary deities, for the Celts, although originally possessing a pure religion adoring one supreme god, appear in time to have brought it to as much complexity as their neighbours of Greece and Rome. Adomnan speaks of the Picts as having their own gods and magi, or priests, and it is not unlikely that each people placed themselves under the protection of certain beings, as nations afterwards adopted their different saints, champions, and mediators.

Besides the circular temples, the Celts had Cromleachs, that is, huge stones raised on several others, one of which is represented at the commencement of Chapter III. Vol. I. These sometimes form a rude sort of cell, as at Maen Cetti, or Kit's Cotty house, in Kent, and the superincumbent block is sometimes of very large dimensions. One at Plas Newydd, in Anglesea, measures twelve feet by thirteen feet two inches where broadest, its greatest depth being five feet; so that it cannot weigh less than thirty tons seven cwt. Constantine Tolmæn, in Cornwall, contains at least 75 tons. Tolmæn is usually applied to a stone that is perforated, the object of which does not seem to be well known. Cromleach is said to be a punic word, signifying the bed of death, by others it is believed to signify sloping or bending stone.* It is said to have been originally called Botal, the house of God; and Bethel, a name of similar import, was the very term applied by Jacob to the

* That is, the stone at which the worshipper *bent* in the performance of religious rites. ED.

pillar which he set up. Ponderous rocking stones, masses that are either naturally or artificially poised on so small a point that a slight effort will make them vibrate, are considered druidical works, and it is not improbable that they were; but a mind heated with bardic enthusiasm, will refer everything curious of this kind to the Celtic priesthood. The Druids were unfortunate in not having met with historians to hand down to posterity their singular manners. The measures they took have been too successful in preventing their secrets from being divulged. Large and rude obelisks, sometimes single, and sometimes several together, may have been erected by them.

The religious order among the Celts was divided into three classes; namely, the Druids, the Bards, and the Ovates, Vates or Faidhs. The first were the chief priests, and the second were those to whom the compilation and preservation of the oral chronicles of the nation were especially committed, and whose duty as poets and musicians have been already dilated upon. The third class, sometimes called Eubages, were prophets, and had the immediate care of the sacrifices. They contemplated the nature of things, as the ancients expressed themselves, and were highly respected by the people, who universally resorted to them for information on all subjects. It was not lawful to sacrifice without one of these philosophers, and it was devoutly believed, that through those who were acquainted with the nature of the deity, all supplications and thanksgiving should be offered.[z] The Archdruid, called Ard-dhruid in Gaëlic, who had a casting vote in all questions, was chosen by the others, but rivals sometimes contended for pre-eminence in arms.

The Celts, according to Justin, were skilled in augury above any other people, and the Germans are represented

[z] Diodorus.

by Tacitus as equally prone to it. Their method of divining by lots was simple; they cut a twig from a fruit-tree, and divided it into two pieces, which they distinguished by marks, and threw them at random upon a white garment. If the affair was of a public nature, a priest, or if private, the father of a family, having solemnly invoked the gods with uplifted eyes, took up each of the pieces thrice, and formed a judgment according to the marks. If the conclusion was unfavourable, they consulted no more that day; when favourable, they confirmed the appearances by auguries. They also divined events from the flight and notes of birds, and it was peculiar to the Germans to draw presages from horses, which were kept in uncontrolled freedom, in the sacred woods and groves, at public expense. They were milk white, and were yoked in a holy chariot, attended by the priest and chief, who carefully marked their actions and neighing. This was the augury in which most faith was reposed by the nobles and people, for they thought the animals privy to the will of the gods.

Pliny says the Gauls made much use of vervain in divination. When the Celts were to consult concerning any important matter, they sacrificed a man, by striking him with a sword across his breast, and judged of the event by the manner in which he fell, the convulsion of his members, and the flow of blood; in all which they had great faith, from ancient practice and observation. In Sena, now L'Isle de Sain, opposite Brest, was a celebrated oracle, with nine priests, called Senæ, or Samnitæ, who professed celibacy.

In the Silures, or Silina, the Dumnonii worshipped the gods, and had a knowledge of futurity,[a] and a British Druidess foretold the fate of Diocletian. On Bonduca's revolt, women, transported with oracular fury, chanted

[a] Solinus.

denunciations. One method of divination is recorded which was practised by this heroine. At the conclusion of her harangue, she let slip a hare which she had concealed, and from its course having drawn a favourable presage, the whole army shouted for joy. The religion of the Britons did not permit them to eat either a hen, a goose, or this animal, and it was reckoned unlucky if one of the last should cross one's path.

Fingal is celebrated, among other qualifications, for his knowledge of futurity. The Highlanders had several methods of consulting the fates, some of which are not yet disused. One of the most remarkable was when a number of men retired to a lonely and secluded spot, where one of the number was, with the exception of the head, enveloped in a cow's hide, and left alone for the night. Certain invisible beings then came, and answering the question which he put to them, relieved him. Martin tells us of one Erach, who had been a night in this situation in North Uist, and declared that he felt and heard such terrible things as could not be expressed, that the terror he was in had disordered his mind, and that "for a thousand worlds he would never again be concerned in the like performance." The Taghairm nan caht was another method of seeking for information, and consisted in putting a live cat on a spit, and roasting it until other cats made their appearance, and answering the question, in Gaëlic of course, obtained the release of the unfortunate animal.* In order to get oracles, the Celts would pass whole nights at the tombs of brave men,[b] a frequent practice of the old Caledonians.

* See a very remarkakle instance of the *Taigh-ghairm* or *Tigh-gairm* in the Appendix to Dr. Clerk's (of Kilmallie) most interesting "Memoir of Col. John Cameron, Fassiefern." Glasgow: Thomas Murray & Son, 1859. ED.

[b] Nicander. Tertullian.

The Taibhsearachd, or second sight, is a faculty in some Highlanders that has excited the surprise and the doubts of the learned. A person, without any previous warning, sees something that is to happen, both at a distance of time and place, and consequently can foretel death or accident, and many other circumstances. That the Gaël have been and still are subject to this impression, is too well ascertained to be denied; and it has been attempted to account for it without admitting supernatural agency. To suppose that the seers are imposters, and the people deluded, is rather too much, for no gain is derived from it, but, on the contrary, the second sight is, by the persons who possess it, considered a misfortune, and the people cannot consult them as they would fortune tellers. The presages also are usually unfortunate, and the prophets are found to be temperate and well living. That this faculty can be communicated to another, as a correspondent informed Aubrey, is not true, neither is it hereditary, but affects those of all classes and ages. Dr. Johnson could not satisfy himself that the Highlanders were deceived in this impression; and so many instances of well authenticated foresights are recorded[c] as appear sufficient to silence the sceptical. The second sight is not indeed so prevalent as formerly, which, according to a writer in some work which now escapes my memory, who attempts to account for it on rational grounds, may arise from the altered state of society in the Highlands, the people not being obliged to lead that solitary life which they formerly did, when the imagination was affected by the loneliness, the wildness, and seclusion of the country. A German predicted the good fortune of Agrippa from observing an owl perched on a tree on which he leaned, affirming that should he see it again he had but five days to live.[d] A

[c] See Martin's Western Isles, p. 300, &c.
[d] Josephus' Antiquities, xviii. 6, 7.

female Druid foretold, in her native language, the death of Alexander Severus; and a story is related by Vopiscus, of a Druidess who predicted that Diocletian, while a private, should become Emperor, after killing a boar, which happened to prove true by his slaying Aper, who had killed Numeranius. This is thought by Rowland, in his Mona Antiqua, to be an instance of second sight. The Manx possess this faculty; and a story is related by Sacheverel, of a magistrate of Belfast, who had been wrecked, and was told by the natives, who could not of themselves have known the fact, that he had lost thirteen men. Waldron, the historian of that island, says he could not bring himself to believe the inhabitants could see funerals, &c., until he had on several occasions, when he visited families, found the table spread, and the people prepared to receive him, having had this supernatural warning that he would come. Martin also relates, that in some of the isles which he visited, they had made preparation for his company, telling him they had been informed by appearances that he was to visit them.

Fauchet remarks, that all the ancients agree that the Gauls were religiously inclined. With whatever ceremonies the Druidical religion was accompanied, or however the doctrines of its professors were disguised under superstitious and, in some cases, very objectionable practices, adapted for the gratification of the vulgar, it appears to have been really a belief in one supreme being. The purity of this religion, when stripped of its mysteries and unmeaning observances, is acknowledged. The Druids, besides teaching all sorts of useful knowledge, disputed of morals, of which justice, says Strabo, was the chief sentiment; and it has been shown in another place, that Celtic society was regulated under their government with the strictest regard to equality and independence, both personal and national.

The grand doctrine of the immortality of the soul was taught by this people, and it was one of the strongest incitements to the practice of virtue. This is expressly said by Diodorus to be the Pythagorean system; a proof of the identity, or at least strong resemblance, of both religions; and a refinement of the doctrine of metempsychosis, or transmigration of the souls of human beings into the bodies of other animals. The Celts are said not to have had an evil principle, which the Scandinavians admitted.* By the Edda this people had a fixed elysium and a hell; and the dead were believed to carry their bodies into bliss, but the Celtæ held that the deceased were unsubstantial, although they continued to be inspired with the same feelings which animated them on earth: they were as immaterial as the clouds on which they were borne, and were subject to the same impression of the wind; "often has the blast whirled his limbs together, but still he seemed like Curach." The women appear to have been excluded from the Valhalla of the Northern nations, apparently to prevent brawling, except in cases where they voluntarily killed themselves; on the contrary, the Celts admitted them as their most agreeable associates, and believed that in the second state of existence their charms were much increased. The works of the bards abound in beautiful allusions to this belief, which long subsisted among the Gaël. A poem, quoted by Mac Pherson, and supposed to be one thousand years later than Ossian, has these remarkable words. "Hark! the whirlwind is in the wood! a low murmur in the vale! it is the mighty army of the dead returning from the air." *Dreeug** is the meteor on which, says Dr. Smith, the Highlanders yet believe they ascend to heaven.

● Mac Pherson's Introduction to the Hist. of Great Britain.

* *Drèug* or *Drèag* (*Draoidh-eug*) a meteor supposed to portend the recent death of some person of distinction. ED.

A general belief of the Gaël was, that the future state of permanent happiness was in Flath-innis, a remote Island in the West; but they also thought that particular clans had certain hills to which the spirit of their departed friends had a peculiar attachment. Tom-mhor was that appropriated to the house of Garva, a branch of Clan Pherson; and Orc, another hill, was regarded by the house of Crubin, of the same clan, as their place of meeting in a future state, and their summits were supernaturally illuminated when any member of the families died.

It was the opinion formerly, and it is believed at this day, that the souls of the deceased continued to hover round the places they loved to haunt when in this world, and kept near their friends, and sometimes appeared when they were to engage in any important business. The popular belief also was, that the Druids continued to frequent the oak trees, for which they had so much respect when alive. It was no very irrational persuasion, that the spirits of the good should exist in a state of happiness hereafter, should ride on the clouds, and, in addition to the pleasures of their own state, should enjoy the songs of praise which those who were left on earth composed to their memory. Less ferocious than the Scandinavian heroes, they did not place their delight in quaffing wine from the skulls of their foes, but their chief enjoyments were the careful protection of their earthly friends and the refined pursuit of aërial hunting and feasting. There the passions which disturbed the tranquility of a sublunary life were hushed; "side by side," says an ancient bard, "they sit who once mixed in battle their steel." There were, however, bad as well as good spirits, and the distinction which the ancient Scots made between them was, that the latter sometimes appeared by day; and although the place was unusually lonely and unfrequented, it was never in those dismal and gloomy parts where the evil genii presented themselves, and invariably during night.

As teachers of morality, the Druids, by their own example, enforced their precepts; their austerity and contemplative habits inspired the populace with reverence and awe, while enjoying an exemption from war, and immunity of all things, many were brought up to the profession.ᶠ What is related of the Pythagoreans is equally applicable to the professors of Bardism; they were particularly careful to guard against all sorts of intemperance; and to inure themselves to abstinence, they had all sorts of delicacies prepared, as if for a banquet, which they spread out and feasted their eyes with for some time, when, having sufficiently tried their resolution, the whole was cleared away, and they all withdrew without tasting anything.

The attachment of these philosophers to each other was an admirable example of brotherly affection. They often travelled great distances to relieve the distresses of each other, the whole sect being animated with a desire to assist those who had, through misfortune, become reduced; and instances are recorded of their even offering their lives for each other.ᵍ In this there is a striking resemblance to the philanthropy of Freemasons, the traditions of whom, scriptural and oral, are, I apprehend, referable to the institutions of Druidism. The Pythagoreans, like their brethren the Celtic Druids, were fond of an enigmatical way of speaking. Their injunction to refrain from eating beans, involved a command to abstain from unlawful love.ʰ

The Druids were, like the priests of other nations, obliged to clothe religion with ceremonies calculated to excite the wonder and awe of the common people, but the

Cæsar.   ᵍ Diod. Frag. Valesii, vi. sec. 36, 37, &c.
ʰ Beloe, note on Herod. iv. c. 131.

opinions of the better informed were not so gross as the externals of their religion might indicate. The respect which the Druids had for the oak was a characteristic of the profession, and was only exceeded by the veneration which they had for the Misletoe; they had also a mysterious regard for the number 3, and the Pythagoreans knew each other by it. Vallancey has remarked that the misletoe, in its berries and leaves, grows in this number, but it is to be observed that it was that which was found on the oak only, that the Druids considered sacred, and which they gathered with so much ceremony. It seems that this veneration pervaded the Greeks also, and by the Edda it would appear to have been the forbidden fruit. The veneration which the Celts had for vervain and other plants, with the superstitions accompanying their gathering and preparation, have been spoken of in Chap. IV.

The Ovum anguinum, described by Pliny,[1] was thus formed. Innumerable serpents, entwining themselves together, produced an egg, which being forced into the air, was caught in a robe before it reached the ground, and borne off instantly on horse-back, the intervention of a river alone stopping the pursuit of the serpents. Those only which were procured at a certain age of the moon were valued, and their goodness was proved by their swimming against the water, even when bound with gold. This egg was the ensign of a Druid, and the virtues ascribed to it were numerous. I truly, says Pliny, have seen it, about the size of a moderate round apple, with a shell like the claws and arms of a polypus. For success in law suits, and interest with kings, it was wonderfully extolled; and I know that a Roman knight of the Vocontii, was put to death, because, while pleading a cause, he had it in his

Lib. xviii. 3.

bosom. This is the glain nadir of the Welsh, who still regard it with superstitious feelings.

The sacrifices of the Celts, as we have seen in their auguries, were not always bloodless. Hercules and Mars were appeased with beasts, but to Mercury, on certain days, it was lawful to offer even human victims. The shocking practice of immolating human beings is so repugnant to modern feelings, that many have become sceptical as to its existence among the ancient Celts. It certainly was in use by those people on the Continent and in the British Isles, particularly in Anglesea.ʲ

The principle of life for life, may account for the apparent frequency of these horrid rites, for those convicted of crimes were preferred. They kept malefactors and prisoners sometimes five years, and then impaled them on stakes, and presented them as a burnt offering for the honour of the gods. It must, nevertheless, be admitted that guiltless individuals were often doomed to fall as a propitiation to the Celtic deities. The Galatians, when successful in war, sacrificed their prisoners, and we read that they prepared for battle with Antigonus, by sacrificing many of their children and relations.ᵏ Some, we are told, were shot with sacred arrows; but let us not conclude that the Celtæ were more sanguinary and cruel than other nations. Human sacrifices were not abolished in the refined "city of the world" ninety-seven years before the appearance of Christ.ˡ A male and female Gaul, and a Grecian man and woman, we are informed by Livy, were buried alive after the battle of Cannæ, but not by the Roman rites, it is added! a distinction which doubtless altered the case.ᵐ In the time of Cæsar, two men were publicly sacrificed, and human victims were offered to Jupiter Latialis

ʲ Tac. Annals, xiv. ᵏ Justin, xxvi. 2. Strabo, iv. p. 195.
ˡ Pliny, xxxi. ᵐ Dio. xliii. 24.

even in the fourth century. The history of Rome affords a few instances of individuals devoting themselves to death for the purpose of averting an impending evil. The Massilians, or rather the Gauls around them, were accustomed to sacrifice a voluntary victim, who was delicately fed and sumptuously treated for a year previous to his death. He was then dressed in holy garments; and, crowned with a wreath of vervain, he was thrown headlong from a precipice.[n]

The colossal figure, formed of osier and described by Cæsar, was certainly used by the priests of Druidism as the vehicle in which numerous human beings were occasionally immolated. Strabo says that it was chiefly filled with sheep, but it cannot be denied that the sacrifices were not always of so innocent a nature. Dr. Milner, in his History of Winchester, says that at Douay and Dunkirk there is an immemorial 'custom of constructing huge figures of wicker work and canvas, that are filled with men and moved about to represent a giant that was killed by their patron saint. In Paris, there used to be a custom, which is not yet abolished in some small towns, and that seems evidently to derive its origin from the barbarous practice of the Druids. The Mayors, on the eve of St. John, put into a large basket a dozen or two of cats, which are thrown into the bonfires kindled on that festival.[o]

Between the Seine and the Loire, where Chartres now stands, it is believed, was that famous establishment of the Druids, " where rustics pled and private persons decided." At this place all who had controversies met together, and, from an ancient comedy quoted by Ritson, it appears the " sentences of the oak" were here pronounced and written on bones. At a certain time of the year the Druids sat

[n] Petronius.   [o] St. Foix, Essay on Paris.

down in a consecrated grove of Mona, or Anglesea, whither all went to have their disputes settled.[p]

A beautiful description, by Lucan, of a consecrated grove of the Gauls near Marseilles, has been thus translated:

> Not far away, for ages past had stood
> An old, inviolated, sacred wood;
> Whose gloomy boughs, thick interwoven, made
> A chilly, cheerless, everlasting shade:
> There, not the rustic gods, nor satyrs sport,
> Nor fawns and sylvans with the nymphs resort;
> But barb'rous priests some dreadful power adore,
> And lustrate every tree with human gore.
> If mysteries in times of old received,
> And pious ancientry may be believed,
> There not the feather'd songster builds her nest,
> Nor lonely dens conceal the savage beast:
> There no tempestuous winds presume to fly,
> Ev'n lightnings glance aloof, and shoot obliquely by.
> No wanton breezes toss the wanton leaves,
> But shiv'ring horror in the branches heaves.
> Black springs, with pitchy streams, divide the ground,
> And, bubbling, tumble with a sullen sound.
> Old images of forms misshapen stand,
> Rude, and unknowing of the artist's hand;
> With hoary filth begrimed, each ghastly head
> Strikes the astonish'd gazer's soul with dread.
> No gods, who long in common shape appear'd,
> Were e'er with such religious awe rever'd;
> But zealous crowds in ignorance adore,
> And still, the less they know, they fear the more.
> Oft, as fame tells, the earth in sounds of woe,
> Is heard to groan from hollow depths below;
> The baleful yew, though dead, has oft been seen,
> To rise from earth, and spring with dusky green:
> With sparkling flames the trees unburning shine,[q]

---

[p] Richard of Cirencester, b. i. c. 4, § 13.

[q] The Gaëlic Druillin, or Druidhlann, the flame of the Druids, denoted a sudden gleam produced in their ceremonies. They appear to have been the inventors of gunpowder, or something similar.

And round their boles prodigious serpents twine.
The pious worshippers approach not near,
But shun their gods, and kneel with distant fear:
The priest himself, when or the day, or night,
Rolling, have reach'd their full meridian height,
Refrains the gloomy paths with wary feet,
Dreading the dæmon of the grove to meet;
Who, terrible to sight, at that fixed hour
Still treads the round about his dreary bow'r.
This wood, near neighbouring to th' encompass'd town,
Untouch'd by former wars, remain'd alone;
And, since the country round it naked stands,
From whence the Latian chief supplies demands.
But lo! the bolder hands that should have struck,
With some unusual horror, trembling shook;
With silent dread, and reverence they survey'd
The gloom majestic of the sacred shade:
None dares, with impious steel, the bark to rend,
Lest on himself the destined stroke descend.
Cæsar perceived the spreading fear to grow,
Then, eager, caught an axe, and aimed a blow.
Deep sunk, within a violated oak,
The wounding edge, and thus the warrior spoke:—
"Now, let no doubting hand the task decline;
Cut you the wood, and let the guilt be mine."
The trembling bands unwillingly obey'd,
Two various ills were in the balance laid,
And Cæsar's wrath against the gods was weigh'd.
With grief and fear, the groaning Gauls beheld
Their holy grove by impious soldiers fell'd;
While the Massilians, from the encompass'd wall,
Rejoiced to see the sylvan honours fall:
They hope such power can never prosper long,
Nor think the patient gods will bear the wrong.

The two Druids forming the vignette to the last Chapter are from an engraving in Montfaucon's splendid work, who appears to have copied them from Auberi's Antiquites d'Autun. The mace, or sceptre, carried by one is the Druidical ensign of office. The Highlanders retain a traditional knowledge of the slatan drui'achd, which they say was a white wand. The other carries the crescent, or first quarter of the moon, called cornan by the Irish, of which some, formed of gold, have been found in that country. The robe of a Druid was pure white, indicating holiness and truth. The Pythagoreans held it improper to sacrifice to the gods in gaudy habits, but only in white and clean robes, for they maintained that those so engaged should not only bring bodies free from gross and outward wickedness, but pure and undefiled souls.[r] The bards wore a robe of sky blue colour, the emblem of peace and sincerity. The robe of the ovydd, or ovate, was a bright green, the emblem of true learning, as being the uniform clothing of nature. Strabo describes the Druidesses as clothed in white linen cloaks fastened by clasps and girdles of brass work.[s]

The knowledge of the Druids was profound. They taught, says Cæsar, of the stars and their motion, the magnitude of countries, the nature of things, and the power of the gods. Talliesin, a Welsh bard of the sixth century, said, he knew the names of the stars from north to south; and his opinions, which must have been those of the order to which he belonged, were, that there are seven elements—fire, earth, water, air, mist, atoms, and the animating wind; that there were seven sources of ideas— perception, volition, and the five senses, coinciding in this with Locke. He also says, there were seven spheres, with seven real planets, and three that are aqueous. The planets were Sol, Luna, Marcarucia, Venerus, Severus, and Saturnus; and he describes five zones, two of which were uninhabited, one from excessive cold, the other from excessive heat.[t]

[r] The Irish say that, by the Brehon laws, a Druid had six colours in his robe; a remarkable difference from the Britons.
[s] Douglas's Nen. Brit. p. 40.   [t] Roberts's Early History of the Cumri.

The Druids reckoned by nights and not by days, and held thirty years an age. The Gaël call the spring ceituin, or ceuduin, literally the first season, or May, the Druidical year commencing at that time, an expression that corresponds with the French printems and Italian primavera. The civic or artificial year began the 25th of December, on which occasion the Iul feast, in honour of the sun, was held; and when it became a Christian festival the heathen fires were permitted, it being a practice, but lately discontinued, even in England, to burn the Christmas log.

The Highlanders call the year Bheil-aine, the circle of Bel, or the Sun. The days of the week are thus named:

Sunday	Dies Solis	Di Sol.
Monday	Dies Lunæ	Di Luain.
Tuesday	Dies Martis	Di Mairt.
Wednesday	Dies Mercurii	Di Ciadoin.
Thursday	Dies Jovis	Di Taran.
Friday	Dies Veneris	Di Haoine.
Saturday	Dies Saturni	Di Sathuirne.

The affinity of the English, Latin, and Gaëlic is here plain, and corroborative of the observations in former pages.

The knowledge which the Druids possessed of mathematics must have been great. The erection of their astonishing temples is, alone, proof of their skill, but the mode in which those immense stones were brought together, and piled up, cannot well be conceived, unless we admit the use of machinery. A traveller in Greece, whose work I recently read, gives an account of a very ingenious manner of detaching large masses of stone from the native rock. In Bakewell's Travels, when speaking of the dissolution of the Alpine rocks by Hannibal, the writer supposes that the expansive power of vapour might be the means adopted. Count Rumford ascertained that a drachm of water, inclosed in a mass of iron the size of a solid 24-pounder, was sufficient to burst it, with a violent explosion, by the application of heat; and freezing, as is well known, will split the hardest rocks. It is, however, said that Hannibal used vinegar, a story that could scarcely have originated without some foundation in fact. The vinegar of the ancients, which could dissolve pearls, as in the case of Cleopatra, must have been very different from any kind now known. Whether the Druids used the above methods, or by what other means they procured the enormous blocks which they used, we cannot ascertain. It is no less difficult to conceive how they could have been poised on their ends. The natural supposition, which is, indeed, corroborated by the description of an ancient author, is, that they were placed in the proper position by means of an inclined plane of earth, up which they were rolled, and at the highest end were slipped into their place. They were set on so true a perpendicular that, although some of the largest are not deeper in the ground than $1\frac{1}{2}$ or 2 feet, they have never swerved from the upright. Considering the trouble with which they must have been procured, it can scarcely be supposed their height would have been needlessly lessened. It is a tradition among the Highlanders, that the Druids worked at night and rested during the day.

The Druids were physicians, and their medical knowledge, which was by no means small, has elsewhere been spoken of. The Feryllt of Talliesin was skilled in every thing requiring the operation of fire, and this comprising botany, from the duty of selecting plants for the mystical cauldron, the name in time came to signify chemists.

It is not surprising that a religion so venerated and universal should be long ere it finally gave way to the establishment of Christianity. "Under the specious pretext of abolishing human sacrifices, the Emperors Tiberius and Claudius suppressed the dangerous power of the Druids;

but the priests themselves, their gods, and their altars, subsisted in peaceful obscurity till the final destruction of Paganism."[u] The latest mention of the Gallic Druids appears to be by Ammianus Marcellinus, who flourished in the latter end of the fourth century; in Britain the religion certainly remained to a period considerably later.

Talliesin, who lived in the sixth century, was initiated in the mysteries of Druidism; nay, Prince Hywell, who died in 1171, thus invokes the deity, "Attend thou my worship in the mystical grove, and whilst I adore thee, maintain thy own jurisdiction." A manuscript of the twelfth or thirteenth century, which contains a life of Columba, relates that the Saint, going to Bruidhi Mac Milcon, King of the Picts, his son Maelchu, with his Druid, argued keenly against Columba in support of Paganism.[v]

A curious dialogue is preserved, in which Ossian and St. Patrick dispute, concerning the merits of their respective religions. The bard contrasts the pitiful songs of the apostle with his own poems, and extols the virtues of Fingal, in reward for which he believed he was then enjoying the delights of the aërial existence; but the saint assures him that, notwithstanding the worth of Fingal, being a Pagan he was assuredly at that time roasting in hell. The choler of the honest Caledonian rising at this, he passionately exclaims, "If the children of Morni and the many tribes of the clan Ovi were alive, we would force brave Fingal out of hell, or the habitation should be our own."

Druidism was so powerfully assailed in the Southern parts of the Island, that its votaries took refuge in the North, and the Island of Iona became its most sacred retreat, to which the Welsh are said to have made frequent

[u] Gibbon, from Suetonius. Pliny, xxx. 1, &c.
[v] Report of the Highland Society on the Poems of Ossian, App. 311.

pilgrimage. So well settled did it become in these parts, that Gwenddollen, the Ard-dhruid, is represented by Merddyn or Merlin, his priest, as "gathering his contributions from every extremity of the land;" but it was not maintained without difficulty, and in other parts it was more vigorously attacked, and its votaries bitterly persecuted. Merddyn deplores that the rites of his religion dared not be practised in "raised circles," for "the gray stones they even removed."

When Colan, or Columba, established himself in Ii, or Iona, it was the death blow to Druidism in Scotland. He had, however, according to tradition, a great respect for the order, although he opposed their doctrines and burnt their books, and did actually, with King Aidan, intercede for the Irish bards at the council of Drumceat, and procured a modification of their punishment, the profession not being abolished, but restricted to Ulster and Dalriada. On the suppression of Druidism in Iona, it is said that the Welsh carried away many of the mystical instruments, which a partial revival of the system in their own country enabled them for several centuries to use.

This singular religion influenced, in no small degree, the early Christians, who mixed a great deal of the ancient superstition with the ceremonies of the church. By a council of Lateran in 452, the adoration of stones in woods and places now decayed, was forbidden; and Gregory of Tours, a writer of the sixth century, shows that woods, waters, birds, beasts, and stones, were still worshipped.* Pope Gregory III., about 740, prohibits the Germans from sacrifices or auguries beside sacred groves and fountains. So difficult is it to wean people from the religion of their fathers, and that which has been long venerated, that the first Christians were obliged to conciliate their proselytes

* Keysler, p. 63.

by tolerating some of their prejudices; perhaps they themselves were somewhat affected by a respect for ancient usages. When Ethelred, as Malmesbury informs us, was to hear Augustine preach, he refused to enter a house with him, but sat in the open air, actuated, it is probable, by the persuasion that the deity should not be worshipped under cover.

Various enactments were passed against practices that must have originated in the times of Druidism, without effecting their abolition. One observance, that of decking houses and churches with evergreens and misletoe, under which, in presumed imitation of the Druids, it is customary to kiss the maids, has survived in England to the present day. At the close of the tenth century, stones were revered in Ireland; but this is not very remarkable, since they are even yet looked upon by the Gaël with a degree of awe. James Shaw, bard to Campbell of Lochnell, reproaches one Finlay for destroying these venerable monuments; he supposes a Druid appears, and charges him to convey his displeasure to the sacrilegious offender, who, being a merchant, is told that his unhallowed work is a more serious affair that cheating the Glasgow traders. It has been carefully noted, that none who ever meddled with the Druids' stones prospered in this world.*

Turgot, confessor to Queen Margaret, says that the Scots celebrated mass with barbarous rites; and Scaliger remarks that the Popery of Ireland was mixed with much Paganism. More has been shown in preceding pages of

---

* It is pleasant to have to record that during the year 1875 a bill was introduced into Parliament by Sir John Lubbock and others, the object of which is the preservation of our "Ancient Monuments." It passed the second reading by a considerable majority, notwithstanding the opposition of the Government, and there is no doubt that some legislation in the desired direction will result. ED.

the mixture of ancient superstition with Christianity among the Gaël of both countries. The Culdee clergy succeeded the Druidical order.

It has been remarked that the Highlanders seldom or ever meddle with religion, and the late General Stewart has some very sensible remarks on their tolerant spirit, mixed, however, with regret that sectaries should have been able to infuse among them a spirit of cavilling and dispute on religious topics. He deplores that, instead of the contented, plain, Christian-like satisfaction formerly to be found among them, they occupy themselves too frequently in "disputes of interminable length."* The example of the chief was formerly almost sufficient authority for the religion which the clan professed. Mac Lean of Coll converted his tenants in Mull from Popery, by meeting them when going to chapel, and driving them into a barn where the Presbyterian clergyman was to preach; and having on this occasion used a gold-headed cane, it passed into a saying that their religion was that of the yellow-headed stick. The Highlanders were, however, too liberal to molest any on account of their religious principles; and Martin mentions a person who alone professed the Catholic religion in a populous island of Protestants.

It must be allowed that the Highlanders have, until lately, been extremely ill supplied with spiritual instruction, some of the parishes being of incredible size. It is related that a Lowland clergyman at the General Assembly urged his necessity for an augmentation of stipend, on account of the largeness of his parish. He was asked its size, when he

---

* Within recent years this evil has largely increased, and one is sorry to be obliged to confess that in many parts of the Highlands fanaticism and religious rancour and bitterness have taken the place of that love and "good will toward men" which are the characteristics of genuine Christianity. ED.

said eight miles in breadth; on which a member immediately replied that his was more than ten; mine is twenty, says another; mine is thirty; forty, said a third and fourth; and others could have proved their parochial districts considerably larger. Missionaries, or assistants, have now been established in suitable places, it is to be hoped, with much advantage to the people: the morality and former happiness of the Highlanders reflect credit on themselves and on their spiritual teachers, who laboured with such success in so extended a field.

MARRIAGE CEREMONIES.

In Chapter V. of the first Volume, some remarks have been offered on the intercourse of the sexes, when speaking of the mercheta mulierum. The Celts, it has been there said, are charged with a neglect of their women, and a disregard to the proper regulation of the married state, that could but ill accord with the condition of a people in any degree civilized. Ten or twelve Britons, it is said, espoused a virgin each, and taking up their abode together, they lived in promiscuous cohabitation, but the children of each woman was considered as belonging to the man who had originally married the mother. The custom which continued until lately in some parts, and yet subsists among a few of the rudest, who sleep all together on straw or rushes, according to the general ancient practice, there is reason to believe, led to the aspersion cast on the British and Irish tribes. How natural it must have been for a casual observer to suppose, from seeing men and women reposing in the same place, that the marriage rites were not in force. To judge of the ancient inhabitants by the rudest of the present Highlanders and Irish, who often sleep in the same apartment, and are sometimes exposed to each other in a state of semi-nudity, we should not come to a conclusion unfavourable to their morality, for this mode of life is not productive of that conjugal infidelity which St. Jerome and others insinuate as prevalent among the old Scots. Solinus, indeed, says the women in Thule were common, the king having a free choice; and Dio says the Caledonians had wives in common: yet these assertions may well be disputed. Strabo describes the Irish as extremely gross in this matter; O'Connor says polygamy was permitted; and Derrick tells us they exchanged wives once or twice a-year; while Campion says they only married for a year and day, sending their wives home again for any slight offence; but notwithstanding the attempt of Sir William Temple to shew the advantages of such loose connection, it is reasonable to believe that it did not exist, at least to the extent represented. Nations that are even in a savage state are sometimes found more sensitive on that point of honour than nations more advanced in civilization; and all, perhaps, that can be admitted is, that certain formalities may have been practised by the Britons, from which the bundling of the Welsh, and the hand-fisting in some parts of Scotland, are derived. The conversation which took place between the Empress Julia and the wife of a Caledonian chief, as related by Xiphilin, certainly evinces a grossness and indelicacy in the amours of the British ladies, if true; but it appears to be a reply where wit and reproof were more aimed at than truth. The case of the Empress Cartismandua shews the nice feeling of the Britons as to the propriety of female conduct. The respect of the Germans for their females, and the severity with which they visited a deviation from virtue, have been described; and the farther testimony of Tacitus may be adduced, who says that but very few of the greatest dignity chose to have more than one wife, and when they did, it was merely for the honour of alliance. It may here be stated that the Gaël have no word to express cuckold, and that prostitutes were, by Scots law, like that of the ancient Germans, thrown into deep wells; and a woman was not permitted to complain of an assault if she allowed more than one night to elapse before the accusation.

The Gauls, according to Cæsar, had no sexual intercourse before twenty. The Germans were equally long before they partook of connubial happiness; they married in the prime of life, and the parties were matched in stature as well as disposition, and this was not only with a view to their own happiness, but to insure a fine family.

The ceremonies of courtship and marriage among the Celts were not tedious, but the latter was never consummated without consulting the Druidess and her purin, which was five stones thrown up and caught on the back of the hand, called, says Vallancey, by the Irish, Seic seona, now corrupted into jackstones.[x] The ancient Irish presented their lovers with bracelets of women's hair. Duchomar, a Caledonian hero, recommends his suit to Morna, by saying he had slain a stately deer for her. The Gauls brought a portion equal to that of the women, and the united product was reserved for the survivor.[y] Among the Germans the husband gave the wife a dowery—oxen, and a horse accoutred, a shield, with a sword and javelin; and the parents attended to approve of these presents, by whose acceptance the damsel was espoused. The oxen in the same yoke, we are told, indicated that the wife was henceforth to be a partner with the husband in his hazards and fatigues. The arms which she received, with certain others which she also, it appears, brought to her husband,

---

[x] Brande's Pop. Ant. xlviii.   [y] Bello Gall. vi. 17.

she preserved for her sons, whose wives might again receive them.[z] The father of a bride among the old Highlanders gave his arms to his son-in-law. Spelman remarks that the Irish dowers were bestowed exactly in the manner of the old Germans.

The Highlanders gave dowers according to their means, cattle, provisions, farmstocking, &c.; and where the parents are unable to provide sufficiently, it is customary in Scotland for a newly-married couple to "thig," or collect grain, &c., from their neighbours, by which means they procure as much as will serve for the first year, and often more. The portion of a bride is called a tocher. The wedding feasts are scenes of great mirth and hospitality. It is often the case that they are "siller bridals:" otherwise, those in which the parties are paid for the entertainment, which is sometimes resorted to as a means of raising a few pounds to begin the world with; but the feasts are generally free, and consist of an abundance of everything. In the Highlands the company occasionally get breakfast, dinner, and supper, and there is sometimes so numerous an attendance that many sheep are killed for their entertainment. A Mull wedding feast is thus described:—A long table is placed in a barn or outhouse, on which is set, at convenient distances, meat with eggs, oatbread, and potatoes, and near every third person a whole cheese and a lump of butter; the whisky, or other liquor, is provided by the bridegroom, but the rest of the entertainment is furnished by the parents of the bride. In Tiri, another of the Western Isles, a respectable marriage feast was provided with a profusion of mutton, turkeys, geese, ducks, fowls, custards, puddings, vegetables, butter, cheese, oatbread, milk, and whisky, all provided by the parents of the

[z] Tacitus.

bride, except she has only a mother, in which case the bridegroom is thought bound to bear the expense.[a]

In the Isle of Man, the relations always bring something to a marriage feast. On one platter you may sometimes see a dozen capons, on another six or eight fat geese—sheep and hogs are roasted whole, and oxen cut up in quarters.[b]

Dr. Henry says, that within twenty or thirty years, when a party in Orkney agreed to marry, they went to the temple of the moon, which was semi-circular, and there the woman fell on her knees and invoked Woden, a singular relict of superstition. The ring was a badge of the married state among the Celts, and was worn both in Gaul and Briton on the middle finger. That used among the Northern nations seems to have been nearly as large as to admit the whole hand.

A marriage company, among the Galatians, all drank out of the same cup. When the German bride entered in the morning she was clothed in a white robe, and was crowned with herbs and flowers, particularly vervain, which was sacred to Venus. A Lusitanian woman was taken into the house with a sort of violence, her husband dragging her from the arms of her brother, and she was preceded to her new residence by a person who implored the favour of Hymen to the happy couple.

A very ancient custom of carrying off a wife by force, remains in some parts of Ireland to this day. In 1767, a girl was carried off in the county of Kilkenny, but was rescued and married to another party. The disappointed lover raised his friends, and, provided with arms, they besieged the house, in order to recover the prize, and although they were beaten off, it was not before lives were lost.

---

[a] Mrs. Murray's Guide. On this subject "the Bridal of Caolchairn," by Mr. Hay, will be read with interest.

[b] Waldron's Hist. p. 169.

A Scotish bride was expected to show a reluctance, and require a certain degree of violence, which was neither thought unbecoming in the man, nor a hardship to the woman; many instances being found of happy unions, accompanied with apparent force and cruelty. The practice was, sometimes, however, carried too far, and the real violence which was used constituted the raptus, or forcible abduction of women, of which so many instances occur in the legal history of the country. The unfortunate Lovat was accused of this crime, in having married, without the lady's consent, and actually cut her dress from her person with a dirk! An old north country song, entitled "Lord Saltoun and Achanachie," alludes to a similar act of deforcement:

> "When she was married she would na' ly down,
> But they took out a knife and cut off her gown."

One of the sons of the celebrated Rob Roy was hanged for carrying off the heiress of Balfron, more, however, apparently against her friends' consent than her own, for she lived some time contentedly with him in the Highlands.

In the pastoral districts of Ireland the parents and mutual friends meet on a hill side, usually midway between their respective dwellings, and there drink "the agreement bottle" of whisky. This settled, the father, or next of kin to the bride, sends round to his neighbours and friends, and every one gives his cow or heifer, by which means the portion is soon raised. Caution is, however, taken of the bridegroom on the day of delivery for restitution of the cattle, should the bride die childless, in which case, within a stipulated time, each receives back his own; care being thus taken that no man get rich by frequent marriage. On the day of "home bringing," the bridegroom and his friends ride out to the place of treaty, where they meet the bride, and the custom of old was to cast short darts at the bride's company, but at such a distance as seldom to occasion any wounds; "yet it is not out of the memory of man that the Lord Hoath on such an occasion lost an eye. This custom is now obsolete."[e]

The following observances at a wedding in Wales, if not entirely disused, are fast dying away. Some weeks previous, a person well known in the parish, went round inviting all, without limitation or distinction, to attend. The company assembled the evening previous to the ceremony at the bride's father's, the bridegroom arriving accompanied by music. The bride and her retinue were then shut up in a room, and the house doors being locked, the company made loud demands for admittance until the bride's maid opened a window and assisted the bridegroom to enter, after which the doors were opened and the party admitted. After a few hours dancing and a refreshment of oatcake and spiced ale, the bride's maid and company retired: the bridegroom returning early next day with all his friends, preceded by a harper playing "Come haste to the wedding." They were joined by the bride at her father's, who, along with her brother or other male relation, took their station behind the bridegroom, with their retinue of friends, and all proceeded to church. On leaving the church the harper played "Joy to the bridegroom," and the bride and her maid having changed partners, they all went to a part of the churchyard, if such there was, unappropriated for interment, and there danced to the tunes of "The beginning of the world," and "My wife shall have her way." They then adjourned home, where various sorts of bread, ale, and cheese, were prepared, and a collection

[e] This is about 1682. Sir H. Pier's Description of Westmeath, ap. Vallancey's Coll. i. p. 122.

for the bride was made, a benevolence which was not always in money; sometimes the friends and neighbours went the night before, carrying presents of grain, meal, cheese, &c. It is a practice among the better sort in these days for the bride to remain with her parents for some weeks, and when she goes to her husband, the furniture which she has provided, and which is called starald, is removed with much ceremony, every article being moved in succession, according to fixed rules. The next day the young couple are attended by the younger part of their friends, and this is called a turmant.[d] When parties separated in this country, by Hwyel's laws, the property was equally divided.

There are several other observances that are to be refered to the original Britons, such as the cake broken over the head of the Scots bride, on her first entering her future residence. It is a curious practice of newly married women to commence spinning and preparing linen for their shroud. The bard who attended a marriage was entitled to the bridegroom's plaid and bonnet.

Many superstitious movements and notions were occasioned by a woman's confinement, that are not worth observance. In some parts of the Highlands, we learn from Mrs. Murray, when near her time, a large knife and a spade were laid under the bedstead, and beneath the pillow was placed the Bible, while salt was plentifully strewed about the doors to avert the fairies. These unearthly creatures derive the Gaëlic name, sithich, from sith, a sudden attempt to grasp, which accords with their known propensity to carry off children. They lived under little green mounts, called sith dhuin, which are still approached by the Highlanders with veneration, certainly from the supposed residence of these beings, and not from their being "hills of peace," as Dr. Smith thinks.

[d] A. B. Table Book, ii. 793.

The Gallic women delighted in a numerous family.*
The mode of rearing children has been described. They
were inured to hardship and brought up in military virtue,
and rude, but imposing, simplicity of manners. No rights
of primogeniture, or undue partiality, engendered feelings
of discord and contention—they were alike excluded from
mixing in society, or even appearing before their parents
in public, until they were able to bear arms. The children
of the Germans were held in the same estimation by their
mother's brother as by their father, which, says Tacitus,
was an inviolable tie.

Baptism, it has been shown, was a heathen rite; with
the Christian ceremony the Celts retained many superstitious practices. Handing the infant over the fire, sometimes in a basket, in which bread and cheese were placed,
which the Highlanders, I believe, yet perform in christen-
ing their offspring, is believed to counteract the power of
spirits. It certainly originated in some of the druidical
services to Baal, and is perhaps the "passing through the
fire to Moloch," which the Scriptures notice as a Gentile
custom. The Irish hung about children's necks a crooked
nail, a horse-shoe, or a piece of wolves' skin, not forgetting
a bit of St. John's Gospel, and both it and the mother, or
nurse, were girt with belts of women's hair, finely plaited.ᶠ
In the Highlands it has been said they sometimes baptised
a child over a broad sword. It was a notion until lately,
that faint voices of children who had not received this mark
of consecration were heard in the woods bewailing.

FUNERAL RITES.

The Druids, elevating their minds to the most sublime
conceptions, boldly asserted the immortality of the soul.

---

* The Thracian women laid their new born children on the earth and wept over them. Les diff. Mœurs, &c., 1670.

ᶠ Memorable things noted in a Description of the World.

This belief inspired the Celts with that contempt of death which led to those deeds of heroism by which they signalized themselves. The sublime doctrines of one supreme God, and a state of blessed existence hereafter, must have had wonderful effects on this race, naturally of a sanguine temperament. The belief that a place of happiness awaited them in another world, led them often to seek it by self-destruction, when pressed by the adversities of fortune. The Celtic mothers would kill their children to prevent their falling into the hands of the enemy, and the children would without compunction destroy their parents.

Boiscalus, the high-minded but unfortunate chief of the Ansibarians, who were obliged to fight for their very existence, which their utmost efforts could not at last preserve, piously addressing the Sun, appealed to his enemies whether, the heavens being the residence of the gods, as the earth was that of the children of men, such portion of it as none possessed should be free to the destitute, but his unhappy situation and earnest supplication only produced an offer from Avitus, the Roman general, of ample lands for himself, if he would betray his people. "A place to live in," replied our hero, "we may want, but a place to die we cannot," and they perished to the last man.[g]

The Gauls who lived at the foot of the Alps, being attacked by the Romans, surrounded and unable to escape, killed their wives and children and threw themselves into the flames. Some who were surprised and made prisoners, afterwards committed suicide, some with iron, some by strangulation, and some by refusing all food.[h] The Japides, also, to prevent anything of theirs from falling into the hands of Cæsar, slew themselves, their wives, and children, and a few who were taken alive speedily put an end to

---

[g] Tacitus' Annals, xiii.   Orosius, v. 15.

their captivity by voluntary deaths.[j] The Gallo-Grecian prisoners attempted to gnaw asunder their iron chains, and offered their throats to be strangled by each other.[j] The Gauls, believing that they should rejoin their friends in another state of existence, did not hesitate to accompany them across that bourne, which even Christians think of with doubt and anxiety. The confidence of the Celt in his future existence was full, and he would write letters to those friends who had gone before, and transmit them at the obsequies of the deceased.[k] The Gallic prisoners in Hannibal's army fought by lot, and the survivors, with bitter regret, complained of their hard fate in not having fallen.[l] The wives of the Teutons, after their defeat, offered to surrender on condition that, with their children, they should be received as the slaves of the Vestals, who served that deity which themselves revered, but their request being denied, they escaped the vengeance and insult of their enemies by mutual destruction. Innumerable instances are recorded of the suicide of individuals after defeat or disappointment. Cativulcus, king of the Eburones, poisoned himself with an extract of yew. Brennus, on his discomfiture at Delphos, either ran himself through with a sword or drank wine until he died. Ancroeste and Drasses, two other chiefs, destroyed themselves by starvation, and the heroic Bonduca put an end to her existence by poison, and was sumptuously buried by her sorrowing followers. Many of the Caledonians, on their defeat at the Grampians, relieved their minds from the dread of witnessing their wives and children exposed to the outrage of the Roman soldiery, by laying violent hands on them.

The ancient Celts sometimes burned the bodies of their

---

[i] Dio. xlix. p. 403. [j] Florus, ii. 11. [k] Diodorus, v.
[l] Polybius, iii. 139.

deceased friends, and sometimes interred them without that ceremony. It is probable that the latter practice was in use by the poor, yet in the same sepulchre there have been found entire skeletons as well as urns containing the ashes of those bodies that had been submitted to cremation. The Irish, according to Ware, who quotes an ancient authority, "preserved that cleanly custom" long after the introduction of Christianity. The Picts in Columba's time did not burn their dead, but Sturleson says, the practice was more ancient among the Northern nations than that of burial. This is, however, improbable; the most obvious method to dispose of the dead is by simple interment. Even the Romans at first buried the dead, and only began the practice of burning the bodies in consequence of hearing that those slain in war were often disinterred, and the practice was not universally adopted; many refused to have their bodies consumed by fire, and preferred plain burial, like Varro, who, dying at an advanced age, ordered his corpse to be decked with shrubs and flowers.[m] The Gauls had numerous lights at their funerals,[n] and we find that the Christians did not object to carrying torches on these occasions, as it was an innocent practice.

At the funerals of the Germans, says Tacitus, this is carefully observed; with the bodies of eminent men certain woods are burned. On the funeral pile they put neither apparel nor perfumes, but throw into the fire the arms of the deceased, and sometimes also his horse. In Gaul, those slaves who had been most loved by their masters sacrificed themselves at their funerals. It was usual among this people to burn bonds and accounts, from a belief that the person would require them in the other world;[o] and persons would lend money to deceased friends

[m] Pliny, vii. 54, xxxv. 12.   [n] Durand, de Ritibus.   [o] Mela, iii. 2.

relying on its repayment when they met in the state of future existence. It is a reasonable conjecture, that the articles which were used in life by the parties were buried with them, that they might have them to use hereafter. A stone hammer has often been found in Celtic graves, and on monuments presumed to belong to that people, this instrument, formed like 1 and 2 in the plate, Vol. I., is often represented either by itself or in the hand of a figure. The body of a stout man was found interred at Wilsford, in Wiltshire, at whose feet a massy stone hammer was placed, and the remains of the ancient inhabitants of Scotland are often discovered with the same implement beside them. It was, indeed, a Celtic practice to deposit in the grave whatever had been particularly esteemed by its tenant when alive, or was deemed necessary for use in the next world, and certain articles indicated the rank of the deceased.[p]

Different methods of interment are found to have been practised; and antiquaries seem agreed that a most ancient position is that in which the limbs are drawn up to the body. It is likely, that the wishes of individuals respecting their mode of sepulture occasioned that diversity which is discovered. At Largo, in Fifeshire, a stone coffin, found beneath a cairn, contained a skeleton, of which the legs and arms had been carefully severed from the trunk, and laid across it.[q] The bodies are also found lying in various positions.

At Evreux, in 1685, sixteen or eighteen interments were discovered, the bodies in which were placed side by side, their faces turned to the mid-day sun, the arms down by their sides, and every one had a stone under the head. A stone hatchet was placed beside each, and one was formed of a precious stone. There were also arrow heads of the

[p] Val. Max. ii. 6.   [q] Stat. Account, iv. 538.

same materials, and bones, apparently of horses, sharpened for spear heads, and a piece of deer's horn was fitted to receive one of the axes. There were also urns, and near them a great quantity of half-burnt bones, and a vase full of charcoal resting on a heap of stones and covered by a layer of ashes 1½ feet thick. A large stone almost round, on which were three smaller ones, was also found in this very curious sepulchre. The bodies were of the common stature, and one of the skulls had been fractured in two places, but had been subsequently cured.[r] Another place of interment was discovered in 1685, at Cocherell, in France, where eight skeletons were found side by side, each with a flint stone under the head, and several stone hammers. On the summit of the hill on which the tomb was found, were two stones about five feet in length.

It appears to have been an almost universal custom to deposit arms in the grave of a deceased warrior. Quintus Curtius relates that when Alexander the Great caused the sepulchre of Cyrus to be opened, there were found a shield, two bows, and a battle-axe. This practice was characteristic of a military nation, and the belief that warlike-deeds were peculiarly acceptable to the gods, was strong in the Celtic race. In the mythology of the Northern nations, it was thought that to fall in battle was a sure passport to the hall of Odin, and the arms of a warrior, especially his sword, were carefully placed in the grave with his remains.[s] That the Gauls deposited arms with the dead is shown by numerous discoveries. In the grave of Childeric, and other kings of France, their swords, javelins, and other weapons, have been found, and in Britain the fact is still oftener proved.

The mode of interment among the ancient Scots was

---

[r] Montfaucon's Antiq. Expliq. x. 195.   [s] Keysler.

thus: A grave, six or eight feet deep, was made, the bottom of which was lined with fine clay, and on this the body was placed, along with the sword, if the person had signalized himself in war, and if a high character, the heads of twelve arrows. Above the body another stratum of clay was laid, in which a deer's horn, as the symbol of hunting,* with the favourite dog, were placed, and the whole was finished by a covering of fine mould. Lord Auchinleck writes, in 1764, to Dr. Blair, in proof of the veracity of description in Ossian's poems, that several tumuli had been opened near the kirk of Alves, in Badenach, which contained each a skeleton, with the horn of a deer placed at right angles with it. A sepulchral mound at Everley, in Wiltshire, which was opened by Sir Richard Hoare, discovered three feet from the top, the skeleton of

---

* In a *cairn* opened some years ago in the editor's parish, an urn of the usual type was found, beside which lay ten immense stags' antlers, and a large bison or wild ox horn, with about ten inches of the top cut off, so that it could be blown through. It was probably a hunting-horn.

In "Fingal," Duan iv. 241, Ossian enjoins Oscar, his son,

"Cuimhnich, 'Oscair, cuir mo lann,
M' inbhar càm 'us croc an fhéidh,
Ri taobh cloich ghlais a tha ri ceann
Caol, thall, a chùirn gun leus."

Lines from internal evidence unquestionably of great antiquity. Clerk has translated them correctly thus:—

"Remember, Oscar, lay my sword,
My bended yew, and antler of the stag,
Beside the grey stone at the head
Of the far-off, narrow, darksome cairn."

"In "Temora," i. 376, Oscar, mortally wounded, entreats his father to "raise stones on the Ben," to his "renown," and continues:—

"Cuir Cabar an ruaidh rium féin,
Lann thana nam beum ri m' thaobh."

That is—

"Close by me lay the antler of the stag,
And the sharp cleaving blade by my side."   Ed.

a dog, and at the depth of five feet, in the bottom of the grave, were the bones and ashes of a human being. They were piled up in a small heap, which was surrounded by a circular wreath of horns of the red deer, and amid the ashes were five beautiful arrow heads of flint, with a small red pebble. In that ancient and beautiful poem called the "Aged Bard's Wish," he requests his harp, a shell of liquor, and his ancestor's shield, to be buried with him. In Umad's Lament on Gorban, a white hound, of which he was extremely fond, he tells the animal that they should again meet on the clouds of their rest.[t]

Nature seems to have implanted in the human heart a desire to honour the dead by raising some sort of memorial over their remains. Herodotus says, the Scythians laboured to raise as high a mound as they could, over the grave of a departed hero. Heaps of earth or stones were always raised over the graves of the Celts; the latter, from the abundance of the materials, being chiefly used by the Scots, Welsh, and Irish. They are denominated Cairns by the Gaël, and are sometimes of prodigious size, the effect being often increased by their position on hills. Some are 300 or 400 feet in circumference at the base, and 20, 30, or 40 feet in perpendicular height. The quantity of stones composing these artificial mountains is astonishing; some of them have served as quarries, whence neighbouring farmers have supplied themselves with materials for building and inclosing for years, without entirely removing them. Many have, indeed, been swept away in the progress of improvement, but they are still numerous in Scotland, and continue "to speak to other years" of unknown transactions. "Grey stones, a mound of earth, shall send my name to other times," says the bard of ancient

---

[t] Manos, in Smith's Gallic Ant. p. 255.

days; but, alas! neither the size of the cairn, the careful formation of the barrow, nor the impressive "stone of fame," has been able to transmit a knowledge of the persons to whose memory they were reared. Tradition has, with few exceptions, failed to preserve the name or the history of "the dark dwellers of the tomb." Cairns were sometimes surrounded by an inclosure of stones, and sometimes they were surrounded by a rude obelisk. There is a particular sort in some of the Western Isles, called barpinin, a Norwegian word, according to Dr. Mac Pherson.

The well known practice among the Highlanders of throwing a stone to a cairn, on passing, is connected with two different feelings. In the one case, it arose from the respect which was had for the deceased, whose memory they wished to prolong by increasing the size of his funeral mount, and hence arose a saying, intended to gratify a person while alive, that the speaker should not fail to add stones to the cairn. It would appear that the soul was considered much pleased with this attention, and with the honour of a great monument, in which respect the old Germans seem to have differed from the Celts, for they raised sods of earth only above the grave, conceiving that large monuments were grievous to the deceased. The other motive for throwing stones to augment a cairn, was to mark with execration the burial-place of a criminal, the practice, according to Dr. Smith, having been instituted by the Druids. It is curious that the same method should be adopted with views so different; yet the fact is so, and the author has often, in his youth, passed the grave of a suicide, on which, according to custom, he never failed to fling a stone. The true motive in this case seems to have been to appease the spirit which, by the Celtic mythology, was doomed to hover beside the unhallowed sepulchre.

On the death of a respected individual, his followers assisted in raising a suitable cairn; and, cherishing his memory, the whole clan met on certain days and repaired or augmented it. The sepulchral tumuli in England are termed barrows. The appellation is very similar to the Hebrew Kebera, used by Abraham for a burying place, and is allied to the German barke, the Saxon beorgen, to hide, the English burrow, bury, &c.

The barrow was formed with much nicety, and varied in size and in shape. The plain of Salisbury, that interesting field of ancient sepulture, contains the most beautiful specimens of all the sorts which antiquaries appear to have yet discovered. They are the long barrow, the bell, the bowl, the Druid, the pond, the twin, the cone, and the broad barrows, all of which are described by Sir Richard Hoare.

The simple tumulus seems the most ancient sepulchral monument. It was raised by Greeks and Trojans, and was common to Romans, Gauls, Germans, and other European nations 2000 years ago. Charlemagne, wishing to put a stop to heathen practices, decreed that Christians should have gravestones, and not Pagan tumuli. The Celts certainly on one occasion evinced a shocking carelessness of the last duty. After the desperate battle of Thermopylæ, they asked no truce to bury their dead; for which brutality, Pausanias can suggest no excuse, but that they may have intended to strike terror into the Greeks, by displaying a savage indifference to the usages of all other people.

Both in cairns and barrows are found the kistvaens, or rude stone receptacles for the body, usually formed of a flat slab at the bottom, one or more at each side or end, and another placed on the top. If Mac Pherson's translation of a passage in the "Songs of Selm" is correct, these stones were raised above the grave. "Narrow is thy dwelling now! dark the place of thine abode! with three steps I compass thy grave, O thou who wast so great before! four stones with their heads of moss are the only memorials of thee, a tree with scarce a leaf." Various interments are often found in one place, indicating that tumuli were a sort of family burial places; they may, however, have been used at distant periods by different people.

Besides the barrow, or cairn, the British tribes erected either a single large stone, or several of lesser size, to mark a place of burial. Fingal's supposed place of interment, near Loch Tay, is indicated by six "grey stones," and in Glenamon stood Clach Ossian, a block seven feet high and two broad, which, coming in the line of the military road, Marshal Wade overturned it by machinery, when the remains of the bard and hero were found, accompanied with twelve arrow heads. So great respect had the Highlanders for this rude, but impressive monument, that they burned with indignation at the ruthless deed. All they could do they did—the relics of Ossian were carefully collected, and borne off by a large party of Highlanders, to a place where they were thought secure from farther disturbance. The stone is said still to remain with four smaller, surrounded by an inclosure, and retains its appellation of Cairn na Huseoig, or Cairn of the Lark, apparently from the sweet singing of the bard. The veneration of the Scots for the graves of their ancestors is becoming; the Welsh seem to have less of this feeling, the grave of Talliesin, their renowned bard, having been violated, and the stones carried off for servile uses. In some work which now escapes my memory, it is said, that three stones usually composed the tomb of a male person, two indicating that of a female. It seems to have been an ancient practice, but perhaps of Christian origin, to bury the males and females apart. In Iona the custom was retained within these sixty years.

Among the Caledonians, a fir tree appears to have been often planted on or near the tomb of a warrior:—"A tree stands alone on a hill and marks the slumbering Connal." The taxus, or yew, the Romans accounted "tristis ac dira," but the picea, or pitch tree, called padcs by the Gauls, may have been that which was the symbol of death; Pliny says it was commonly seen at burial places in Italy,[a] and a branch of it was stuck at the doors of houses containing a corpse. By the ancient Welsh laws, a consecrated or holy yew was valued at a pound.

On occasion of a death all fires are extinguished, and the Highlanders put a wooden or other platter, with salt and earth unmixed, on the breasts of the dead, the earth being an emblem of the body, and the salt of the spirit. Watching a corpse has, perhaps, been used from the infancy of time. A tourist describes the manner in which the old Highlanders performed this. Having met, with a bagpipe or fiddle, the nearest and elderly relations, for the young people were not so lugubrious, opened a melancholy ball, dancing and weeping till day-light. At these meetings, which are termed lyke or late wakes, dramas from the poems of Ossian were performed. Throughout Scotland at this day young and old collect to sit up with a corpse, but the night is spent in singing psalms and taking refreshments. The Irish, on the death of any one, take the straw of the bed, and, burning it before the door, set up the death howl, as a signal to the neighbours, who, especially in Connaught, send beef, ale, bread, &c., to assist in entertaining the company. The Welsh called this wyl nos, lamentation night, and if the parties were poor, the visitors took bread, meat, and drink, with them. The arvel, or arthel dinner, given on the day of interment among this people, is so called from a British word, arddelw, to avouch,

[a] Lib. xvi. 10, xvii. 40.

because the heir and others then showed that no violence had been used to the dead. By the ancient laws of this people, a corpse was insulted in three ways:—to stab it, to expose it, and to ask whose it was, or who thrust a spear in it. For the two last a third of the fine was abated, as the actions were less disgrace to the dead than the living.

The anxiety of the Scots of all classes to be respectably buried is strong. The reporter in the Statistical Account of Kincardine, in Ross, says, that all who can by any means afforded it, lay up £2 to insure a decent funeral. The soldiers of the Black Watch wore silver buttons, that in case of death there might be wherewithal to lay them in the ground with decency. I have heard an old woman, who was reduced to the necessity of living on the benevolence of her neighbours, express the strongest dread at the idea of being interred in that part of the churchyard appropriated to strangers and the poor. The desire of the Scots to rest with the bodies of their ancestors is extreme; and a corpse is often conveyed a great distance to accomplish this object. It is a feeling that cannot be condemned, although attended sometimes with inconvenience; the expense is lessened by the willingness of neighbours to assist in carrying the corpse, and providing refreshment. In numerous instances the churches of the North of Scotland have of late been rebuilt on sites considerably distant from their former positions, and the burial ground has, consequently, been left in a retired situation. In this there may be no impropriety; but it has happened that an heritor, wishing to improve his property, has inclosed the old churchyard by shrubberries, and stopped the road which formerly enabled the public to approach it; and the consequence has been, that parishioners, determined to fulfil the wish of their deceased relatives, have, in proceeding to their ancient place of sepulture, become trespassers on the laird's grounds, and suffered the most vexatious litigations. In General Stewart's "Sketches," some remarkable instances of the attachment of the Highlanders to their family resting places are given. Dr. Mac Culloch relates an anecdote to illustrate the pugnacity of the Highlanders, but from which we may draw another inference. A desperate fight took place in a churchyard respecting the right of one party to a certain burial place in it.

At burials, which is the name given by the Scots to funerals, the nearest of kin preside at the ceremonial, and etiquette usually obliged even the widow to lead the festivities, however painful her loss. Mrs. Murray was surprised at an account she heard of a funeral preparation in the Isles. The deceased had been a respectable laird, but not very rich, yet there were six cooks for a week at the house preparing the feast, towards which meat, fowls, fish, and game of all sorts, had been sent by the friends and relations. A funeral in the olden time was well managed if it cost less than £100 Scots. A lady, lamenting the inconvenient and needless expense, requested her husband, should she die first, to omit the custom, but he positively refused to do that which would bring on him the obloquy of being not only covetous, but unfeeling, and devoid of that affection which he had for her.

The Highlanders had no feasts nor rejoicings at a birth, but a funeral was conducted with all the display which the parties could make. All the clan, and numerous neighbours, were invited and entertained with a profusion of everything. The male part of the procession was regularly arranged according to rank, and, instead of laying aside their weapons, they were all well armed and equipped on such an occasion. The statistical account of the parish of Tongue, in Sutherland, informs us that a funeral procession there was regulated with military exactness by an old soldier, a person easily found in these parts. If the coffin is borne on a bier, he, every five minutes, or at such time as may be thought convenient, draws up the company, rank and file, and gives the word "relief," when four fresh bearers take place of the others. There are some particular observances in Highland families, such as that of the Campbells of Melfort, Duntroon, and Dunstaffnage, who being descended from a Duke of Argyle, took the following method of cementing their friendship : when the head of either family died, the chief mourners were always to be the two other lairds. This was the case on occasion of the death of the late Archibald Campbell of Melfort. The coffin was usually borne in a sort of litter between two horses, called carbad, a term which is now often applied to the coffin itself. Carbad seems to have been originally applied to such vehicles, and, when restricted to those used for funeral purposes, became synonymous with the shell in which the body was deposited. The Gaëlic Cobhain, the origin of coffin, in its primary sense, meant a box, or any hollow vessel of wood. The desire to be interred in the sacred Isle of Iona appears to be as old as the era of Druidism. The Druidical cemetery is still seen separate from the others, and has never been used as a Christian burial place. In the poem of Cuthon, as translated by Dr. Smith, it is said that Dargo, who is called Mac Drui' Bheil, son of the Druid of Bel, was buried in the Green Isle, an epithet given to Iona, where his fathers rested. In this Isle forty-eight kings of Scotland, four of Ireland, and eight of Norway are buried, besides numerous individuals of note. There are certain cairns on the lines of road along which funerals passed, both in Ireland and Scotland, on which the body was rested; and some villages, particularly one at the entrance of Locheil from the muir of Lochaber, are called corpach, from the circumstance of the coffin being laid down there on the halt of the company; corp, in Gaëlic, being a body. Durand says that the Gauls used black in mourning. The Highlanders, have, I presume, ever done the same, but, except by the wearing of crape, I know not how they evinced the loss of their relatives.

In the minutes of the Society of Antiquaries, July 1725, an account, by a Mr. Anderson, appears of a Highland chief's funeral. The nearest relations dug the grave, which was marked out by the neighbours; and while this was performing, women, who had been hired for the purpose, continued to sing, setting forth the genealogy of the deceased, his honourable connections, and noble exploits. After the last rites had been performed, 100 black cattle, and 200 or 300 sheep, were killed for the entertainment of the company." The feast must necessarily have been great, where nearly the whole clan had attended, besides all neighbouring gentlemen, for it was not always deemed necessary to make a formal invitation, attendance being often given as a mark of respect. In the Isle of Man the company is not invited, but all who had known the deceased voluntarily accompanied the funeral; and Waldron says he has seen 100 horsemen and 200 on foot in one procession. The dinners or entertainments were often in the churchyard; in England they were sometimes in the church itself; and in many cases the deceased left money to be expended in drinking for the weal of the soul.

An account of a curious circumstance that happened at a Highland funeral, was thus related in a Scots publication some years ago: "The inhabitants of the village of Glenurchy, in Argyleshire, had, some time ago, occasion to attend the funeral of Peter Fletcher, a respectable old man, who had attained the age of 102. Auchallander, the place of

---

ᵛ Brande's Pop. Ant. ii. 151.

interment, is distant from the village about seven miles, and stands on a lonely spot on the confines of Glenurchy forest, and singular, as being almost exclusively appropriated to persons of the name of Fletcher. Having proceeded to the spot, and paid the last duties to all that remained of their friend, the nearest connections of the deceased, according to the custom of the Highlanders, brought forth refreshments for the company. These were spread out on clean linen, and consisted of ample store of bread and cheese, with a due allowance of something stronger than water to wash them down. This part of the ceremony having been brought to a conclusion, all began to move away in different directions towards their homes. The friends of the deceased were the last to quit the spot; and before gathering up the remains of the feast, they wandered a few yards from the place, to bid farewell to their acquaintances. In this way the fragments of the bread and cheese were left unprotected. What was the astonishment of the company when they beheld three wild deer issue from the adjoining forest, and actually commence an attack on what remained of the bread and cheese. On no occasion are the Highlanders more liable to be impressed with all the superstitions of their country, than whilst engaged about their dead. The party at once concluded that the singular appearance of the deer betokened that the feast of mourning had been prematurely closed. Each anxious to remove the portending evil far from himself, looked eagerly round to see if he could read in the countenance of his companions a forerunner of the impending disaster. Such prognostications, it may be presumed, are sometimes fulfilled by the very feelings they excite. That such was the case in the present instance we shall not say, but what followed was ill calculated to remove the impressions which had been entertained. John Fletcher, brother to the man whom they had just buried, hale and active, though ninety-nine years of age, was drowned, a few hours after, in the river Urchy, whilst on his way homewards.

A superstition once strong, still exists, it being believed that the ghost of the last buried person is obliged to perform the Faire-chloidh, or keep watch, in the churchyard until another corpse is brought, whose spirit relieves the former, and waits for the next interment.*

The practice of chaunting at funerals is very ancient, and was apparently universal. Macrobius says the heathens sang on such occasions, because they believed the souls of the deceased returned to the original of musical sweetness, which is heaven. Lamentations and howling at the grave were common to the Phœnicians, Greeks, Romans, and Celts; but with the latter it did not consist merely of notes of woe—it was an opportunity for the bards to celebrate the virtues of the deceased, and rehearse his noble descent, thereby improving the occasion by setting before others the advantages of a well spent life. The Goths conducted their funerals in the same manner,—Theodoric, Jornandes tells us, was buried amid songs of praise. The expression of sorrow by the relations was manly and becoming. Of the Germans, it is said, "Wailings they soon dismiss, their affliction and woe they long retain. In women it is reckoned becoming to deplore their loss—in men to remember it." This was the feeling of the Highlanders, who left the duty of mourning to the females, thinking it unmanly, whatever they felt, to betray their sorrow by shedding tears, or show a want of fortitude by the indulgence of excessive grief. They were, however, far from not displaying a becoming sorrow. "Three days" the Caledonians

---

* An interesting discussion on the curious old superstition of *Faire-chlaidh* appeared in the *Inverness Courier* in the summer of 1874. ED.

"mourned above Carthon," and for some much respected individuals, annual commemorations were appointed. The Gaël of more recent times have shown extreme grief at the death of some of their chiefs; it is related, even of the rude inhabitants of St. Kilda, that, on one occasion when they heard of the death of Mac Leod, they abandoned their houses and spent two days sorrowing in the fields.

The Celts, who were so partial to music, thought it indispensable on occasion of death. The bards always attended at the raising of a tomb, besides singing the praises of the dead in the circles; and the poem, or rather both it and the music, was called the coronach. Without its due performance, the soul was supposed to wander forlorn about its earthly remains; but although the practice of repeating it continued so lately, if it is indeed entirely exploded among the present Scots, religion formed no part of the subject. The ancient custom of addressing a dead body in broken and extemporary, but forcible verses, is believed to have been given up in the Highlands and Isles for more than half a century; but the lament is still performed, and the coronach, or expressions of woe, that may be so termed, are, in some remote districts, still to be heard at funerals. The coronach was, for the most part, a voluntary effusion, repeated on the way to the churchyard, in which the good deeds of the deceased and glories of his ancestry were extolled. At intervals, numerous females of the clan, who followed near the coffin, burst into paroxysms of grief, tearing their hair, beating their breasts, and making the most woeful lamentations. It resembled the cine,* or keen, of the Irish, which is still performed in their native land, and may occasionally be heard when the body is waked, in London. This wild and

---

* Cina, in Hebrew, is a lamentation. Kuyn, in Welsh, is a complaint.

melancholy dirge has been termed "the howl," and gave rise to the expression among the English of "weeping Irish." It is an extempore composition, descanting on the virtues and respectability of the deceased. At the end of each stanza, a chorus of women and girls swell the notes into a loud plaintive cry, which is occasionally used without the song. These ciners are women, and many officiate professionally. At one of their wakes, where I was present, the widow was the leader, and was assisted by one or two who had been hired. Others, however, occasionally took part, and the excessive grief displayed by them as they stood wringing their hands over the inanimate body, and exhibiting other symptoms of bitter sorrow, had an impressive effect. The Irish in remote parts, before the last howl, expostulate with the dead body, and reproached it for having died, notwithstanding he had a good wife and a milch cow, several fine children, and a competency of potatoes. One of the Gordon Highlanders told me, that having, when in Ireland, gone with some others to a wake, the widow spoke with displeasure to the body of her husband, because he would not take notice of those who had come even from Scotland to see him! In the Philosophical Survey of the South of Ireland, we find that the elegy which the bards wrote, enumerating his riches and other happiness, the burden was always, "Oh! why did he die?"

The vocal lamentations in the Highlands are now almost confined to the act of sepulture. The Statistical Account of Avoch, in Ross-shire, says, "the lamentations of the women, in some cases, on seeing a beloved relation put in the grave, would almost pierce a heart of stone.

The practice of singing at a funeral was retained by the Christians, who substituted their psalms and hymns for the Celtic laments, and it was usual on some occasions to employ a whole choir, who preceded the corpse. Waldron says the

Manx funerals are met about a quarter of a mile from the church by the clergyman, who walks before, singing a psalm, and in every churchyard is a cross, round which the company pass three times. The Welsh played the Owdle barnat before a corpse on its way to the churchyard.

The singing of the coronach appears to have given place to the playing of the bagpipes among the Highlanders, but it would seem that both were used for some time. The bagpipes were more suitable to the military character of the people, and well adapted to produce those wailing notes, according with the solemnity of the occasion, and adding so much to the effect of the scene. The Cumhadh, or lament, as already shown, is a family tune of a most plaintive character, and often very ancient, and its performance is in sympathy with the emotions of the company. General Stewart says that the funeral of Rob Roy was the last in Perthshire at which a piper was employed. In Lochaber and some other parts, these musicians, I believe, are occasionally engaged; in the Highlands of Aberdeenshire, the most inland district in Scotland, I can assert that the employment of pipers is by no means uncommon. I, of course, speak of the continuance of the ancient practice, not of its revival by the influence of individuals or societies. The funeral of the late Sir Eneas Mac Intosh, of Mac Intosh, who died at a patriarchal age, was attended by six bagpipers, who preceded the body, which was followed by a numerous cavalcade, playing the affecting lament of the clan.*

† Within the last fifteen years the editor has attended two funerals at which the pipes were played in the old fashion. The first was the funeral of Mrs. MacDonald, of Achtriachtan, daughter of the last of the old Glenavis Camerons. The other was the funeral of the late Sir Duncan Cameron, Bart., of Fassiefern and Callart. The effect of the music was solemn and striking. ED.

BURIAL PLACES. 397

The Scots gentry have usually family burial places on their own lands, and often in the vicinity of the mansion. That of the Laird of Mac Nab, near Killin, in Braidalban, is, like most others, embosomed in wood, and in a situation from its seclusion and natural gloom, in fine accordance with the melancholy scene—the conclusion of life's eventful drama.

Plan of the Stone Temple of Callernis, in Lewis.

OBELISK IN THE CHURCHYARD AT DYCE, ABERDEENSHIRE,—p. 405.

CHAPTER VIII.

OF THE KNOWLEDGE OF LETTERS AMONG THE CELTS.

THAT the Celts, at least the Druids, were acquainted with the use of letters is certain. The roll found in the camp of the Helvetii, containing the number of men, women, and children who composed the expedition, is a sufficient proof that they could write, were we possessed of no other. The principles and practice of the Druidical priesthood were adverse to literature as the medium of instruction, and they did not trust their mysteries to writing; but is it to be inferred that so learned a body were ignorant of this most useful art? The signs or hieroglyphics which priests and philosophers of all ancient nations used, were of themselves a sort of language, and must have led to the formation of a regular system, by which a mutual communication was established. The Celts, however, had the use of letters at a very early period; the Turdetani, a people of Spain, according to Strabo, declared that they could produce not only traditional poems, but written documents of 6000 years' antiquity.

Lhuyd asserts that the Britons had letters long before the time of Tacitus, which they imparted to the Irish; and Leland, Pits, and Bale, give accounts of many learned men who flourished and wrote about the era of redemption and even before; but the early use of writing does not altogether rest on the biographies of the above authors, whose authority, I am aware, is often doubtful. The Leccan record of Irish history say, that Saint Patrick burnt no less than one hundred and eighty Druidical tracts, and a uniform tradition has been preserved among the bards, that Colan, or Columba, on his establishment in Iona, burnt a heap of books written by the Britons.' Their historians affirm that a large colony, who had taken refuge in Britany on the Saxon invasion, carried with them the archives that had escaped the ravages of those illiterate rovers, which circumstance Gildas, who wrote in the sixth century, alludes to with regret.

' Davies' Celtic Researches. Conla, a Brehon, or Judge, of Connaught, is said to have written a book against the Druids.

That national annals and other records did exist, is undeniable. Nennius, writing in the middle of the ninth century, says he compiled his work, among other documents, from the writings of the Scots and English, which, however, had in frequent wars suffered great mutilation. Gaimar, a Frenchman, who wrote on the Saxon kings, refers to a work on British history now lost;[a] but, in the prefatory chapter, the use of letters and cultivation of literature by the ancient Celtic inhabitants of these islands, has been satisfactorily shown.

The Helvetian roll is said to have been written in Greek characters, from which it would appear that the Celts understood that language. The same authority,[a] however, informs us, that on one occasion he engaged a Gallic horseman by promise of great rewards, to convey a letter to Cicero, which letter was written in Greek, lest, if it fell into the hands of the enemy, it might be intelligible, which is so directly in point, that there is no getting over it.[b] We can only suppose that the characters resembled those used by the Grecians, for that the Gauls did not know Greek, and but few of them Latin, is very certain. Divitiac, the Æduan, for whom Cæsar had a particular friendship, could not converse with him, but by the assistance of an interpreter. Those Gauls who lived near Massilia learned the Greek letters from that colony, but this is a particular case.[c] Few, or perhaps no remains, it is to be observed, of the Celtic language, either on monuments or elsewhere, remain to prove what characters they did use. Origen, in his answer to Celsus, said it was uncertain whether any writings of either Gauls or Getes then existed.

[a] Ellis's Specimens of Metrical Romances, i.   [a] Cæsar.
[b] Ib. et. Dio. Yet Greek inscriptions were reported to exist in Germany, (Tacitus,) and even in Britain.
[c] Strabo, iv. p. 181.

Lucian gives the following curious account of the Gallic Hercules:—The Gauls, in their language, call him Ogmius, and they represent him as a decrepid old man, bald, with a beard extremely grey, and a wrinkled, sun-burnt, swarthy skin. But what is most strange is, that he draws after him a multitude of men all tied by the ears, the cords by which he does this being five chains, artificially made of gold and electrum, like most beautiful bracelets; and though the men are drawn by such slender bonds, yet none of them think of breaking loose, but cheerfully follow. The right hand being occupied with a club, and the left with a bow, the painter has fixed the chains in a hole in the tip of the god's tongue, who turns about smiling on those he leads. I looked upon these things a great while, but a certain Gaul who stood by, and who, I believe, was one of the philosophers (Druids) speaking Greek in perfection, said, "I will explain to you, O stranger, the enigma of this picture. We, Gauls, do not suppose, as you Greeks, that Mercury is speech, or eloquence, but we attribute it to Hercules, because he is so far superior in strength. Do not wonder that he is represented as an old man, for speech alone loves to show its vigour in old age, if your own poets speak true; and, finally, as for us, we are of opinion that Hercules accomplished all his achievements by speech; and that, having been a wise man, he conquered mostly by persuasion. We think his arrows were keen reasons, penetrating the souls of men, whence, among yourselves, is the expression 'winged words.'" Thus spoke the Gaul.

Ogmius is here a Celtic word, pronounced and spelt by a Roman, yet it is sufficiently pure to show its relationship with ogham, or ogum, the name of that secret alphabet which was used by the Druids and learned Celts. The Ogham characters were represented by twigs of various trees, and the figures resembled those called Runic. The

Ogham bobeleth, and Ogham craobh letters, are well known to the student of Irish history. In the sister island, as well as in Britain, inscriptions on stones have been discovered in these characters, which Vallancey was able to decipher, particularly on one monument, which he says is mentioned in Scotish Chronicles, as in "the grove of Aongus." It informs us that there was the sepulchre of that hero. It is not unreasonable to suppose that different characters were adopted, the knowledge of which it may have been intended to confine to certain classes. There is a stone at a place called the Vicar's Cairn, in Armagh, on which are certain characters, consisting of perpendicular lines of unequal length, that do not appear to be Ogham letters. In the isle of Arran, one of the Hebrides, are several caves, well lighted, which contain places apparently for cooking, &c., and that have rude lines cut in the wall. In different parts of Scotland, and particularly in a certain part of Galloway, are found numbers of stones, many of inconsiderable size, which are marked with various figures. Specimens of these stones have been submitted to the Society of Antiquaries, but their import, I believe, has never been discovered. A remarkable inscription is seen on a stone at Newton, in Aberdeenshire, which is represented in Vol. I. p. 73. The characters here used are more conformable to the Gaëlic than to the Ogham; but they are so rude, and apparently so ancient, that it is impossible to decipher the inscription, or assign it a recent date. Vallancey procured a drawing of this obelisk, and conjectured that the two first words are Gylf Gommara, Prince Gommara, but this appears to be mere conjecture. The author, through a respected friend, transmitted a drawing to the Society of Antiquaries at Paris, by some of whose learned members the inscription may be elucidated. The stone is beside another of nearly similar size, on which are represented a serpent, circles, and those other figures, which will be presently described, and hence it appears referable to a remote and unknown era. The inscription is unique,[d] and the characters are different from those of the Tree system. Concerning this system we have, indeed, but dark and mysterious intimations, yet sufficiently plain to enable us, I trust, to explain the origin of certain figures introduced in the sculpture of distant ages, and preserved in the ornaments of later times.

The Gaëlic alphabet consists of eighteen letters, as here shown:—

A.	Ailm, the elm tree.[e]	L.	Luis, the quicken.
B.	Beithe, the birch.	M.	Muin, the Vine.[g]
C.	Coll, the hazel.	N.	Nuin, the ash.
D.	Duir, the oak.	O.	Oir, the broom.
E.	Eadha, the aspen.	P.	Peit or pethbhog, dwarf elder.[h]
F.	Fearna, the alder.	R.	Ruis, the elder.
G.	Gort, the Ivy.	S.	Suil, the willow.
H.	Uath, the white thorn.[f]	T.	Teine, the furze.
I.	Iodha, the yew.	U.	Uir, the heath.

These letters are chiefly according to the Irish pronunciation and acceptation. We here see that they are all named after trees, but some of the appellations are now obsolete, as the last, which is consequently thought to be the iuthar, or yew. Had the Celts derived their alphabet from the

---

[d] At Fordun, in the county of Kincardine, a stone was discovered under the pulpit of the church, inscribed with characters somewhat resembling the above.—Trans. of Scots Antiquaries, ii. pl. 5. Among other sculptures, on the stones of a corridor at Morbihan, in Britany, are some unknown letters.

[e] Vallancey calls it the palm; O'Flaherty, the fir.

[f] Dr. Molloy does not admit this letter into the original alphabet, and shows that its introduction was sufficient to alter the dialect. Instead of H, a T was used, as in tulloch, a hillock, talla, a hall.

[g] Originally the blackberry bush.

[h] Sometimes called B soft, or rather Beith-beag, little b.

Romans, or from any other people, the names would certainly have been the same, and the same order would have been preserved, which is not the case in the Irish Beth-luis-nion alphabet, which, it may be observed, is presumed to be according to the ancient and proper arrangement, and is so termed from its three first letters. It stands thus—B, L, N, F, S, H, D, T, C, M, G, P, R, A, O, U, E, I.

The word aos in Irish, which at first signified a tree, was applied to a learned person; and feadha, woods, or trees, became the term applied to prophets or wise men, undoubtedly from their knowledge of the alphabet, or sylvan characters, which were used.[1]

The "Researches" of Mr. Davies have thrown much light on Celtic antiquities, and in his pages will be found several passages from bardic compositions, which elucidate the tree system of learning. It is well known that various trees and shrubs have been symbolical, or used as tokens, but the learning of the sprigs consisted in arranging, tying, and intertwining them in various ways, thereby altering their expression or import. There is a work which Mr. Davies quotes, in which the author says "he loves the sprigs with their woven tops, tied with a hundred knots, after the manner of the Celts, with the artists employed about their mystery." Small branches of different trees were fastened together, and being "placed in the tablet of devices, they were read by sages who were versed in science." The art of tying the sprigs in numerous and intricate knots was an important part of the mystical studies of the druidical order, and appears to have been known by few. Taliesin, who gloried in belonging to the profession, boasts of this part of his knowledge; his acquaintance with every

---

[1] The Hebrew az, or es, has precisely the same acceptations.

sprig, and the meaning of the trees, he calls "understanding his institute." We thus see that the Celts had a method of conveying their knowledge to the initiated by a sort of hieroglyphic, or symbolical characters, produced by twigs, or branches of various trees, and the characters which afterwards formed an alphabet, represented those branches and retained the names of different trees. I shall now draw the reader's attention to the representations in ancient sculpture of these intricate, but, at one time, significant combinations and interlacings, from whence, I conceive, is to be deduced a style of ornament that was long retained, not only by the Gaël, but by others, without knowing to what origin it was to be referred.

The curious obelisk represented at the beginning of this Chapter is situated in the churchyard of Dyce, a parish in the county of Aberdeen. Its position, near a churchyard, will indicate that the Christian edifice has been planted on a spot previously respected, the appearance of the cross being no certain proof of a Christian origin, inasmuch as it is known to have been a Pagan symbol, introduced even on sepulchral monuments.[j]

The cross appears formed of, or filled with, a tracery produced by the interlacing of twigs, and this sort of work is common to all such stones, and appears also, but with more taste, in the monuments known to be Christian, and denominated, with propriety, stone crosses. This ornament has been, by some writers, considered an imitation of the Roman fret work, to which it certainly bears little resemblance. The late Professor Stuart, of Marischal College, Aberdeen, speaking of the singular sculpture on these stones, properly observes that the figures "were not employed merely as

Keysler, &c. A large cross is formed on the face of a hill, in Buckinghamshire, by removing the soil from the chalk, in the same manner as the white horses of Wilts and Berks are represented.

ornaments, but to express some latent meaning, at that time, probably, well known, though, in the lapse of ages, now totally lost and forgotten."[k] The bards understood the meaning of these figures, as we learn from their poetical remains, where repeated allusion is made to the " knowledge of the trees," although the secresy with which their mysteries were preserved, has left us in ignorance of the science.

Talliesin, in his enthusiasm for a profession, then subjected to ridicule and persecution, in figurative language exclaims, " I know the intent of the trees, I know which was decreed praise or disgrace, by the intention of the memorial trees of the sages,"[l] and celebrates " the engagement of the sprigs of the trees, or of devices, and their battle with the learned." He could " delineate the elementary trees and reeds," and tells us when the sprigs " were marked in the small tablet of devices they uttered their voice." He does not, however, divulge the secret of their meaning, but speaks of " the Alders at the end of the line beginning the arrangement." Trees are to this day used symbolically by the Welsh and Gaël, as, for instance, coll, the hazel wood, being indicative of loss and misfortune, is presented to a forsaken lover, &c., whence appears to have arisen the saying that " painful is the smoke of the hazel."[m] Merddyn, or Merlin, the Caledonian, not less devoted to his religion than the Cambrian bard, laments that " the authority of the sprigs" was beginning to be disregarded. The powers of this vegetable alphabet, or symbolic system, were fated to yield to those of a different character. This race, in disusing the trees, as the secret means of preserving a medium of communicating knowledge, left the ancient system, with as little elucidation as the hieroglyphics of Egypt, and

[k] Trans. of Scots Ant. ii. [l] Welsh Archæo. i. 34.
[m] Owen's Welsh Dict.

preserved the recollection of its former existence by little more than the names which they gave to the letters. The stones of Gwiddon Ganhebon, on which the arts and sciences of the world were to be read, are mentioned in the Triads, and are supposed to have been inscribed in the Ogham character, and Gwydion ap Don, an astronomer was buried in Caernarvon under a stone of enigmas. Whatever these sculptures may have been, it is singular that in Wales no stones are found similar to those that are to be seen in so many parts of Scotland, on which are various figures, like those on the stone at Dyce, as well as some other singular devices elsewhere introduced. In the Principality, we, however, do find some monuments on which is seen the intricate fret-work which I have every reason to believe, if not the actual resemblance of some of the mysterious knots of sprigs, is derived from that singular practice. The interlacing of the rods in the cross had certainly some meaning. The same ornament is often seen by itself, and seems to have been retained when all knowledge of its signification had been lost. Let the reader compare this tracery with that on the handle of the bidag, Vol. I. p. 337, with the ornaments on the leathern target, on the brooch, and indeed with everything susceptible of embellishment by the old Highlanders; and it will be impossible from such a similarity, not to perceive that their taste was at first influenced by some cause. I not only think that their peculiar style of ornament is to be deduced from the art of twisting the sprigs into significant forms, but that, as the Celts, who were certainly the most learned people, after the establishment of Christianity, gave to the letters of their alphabet the names of the trees, they retained a vestige of their intricate combination by their ancestors, in the fanciful capitals, which illuminators of manuscripts never failed to introduce. A specimen of these from a manuscript version of the poems of Ossian, written in the eighth century, and now in possession of the Highland Society, is introduced at the termination of this Chapter;* but it must be observed that it bears less resemblance to the Celtic tracery than may be seen in many other examples. The tree system in this particular seems to have influenced the writers of all European countries.

The crescent was sacred to Ceredwen, the Welsh Ceres, who hence appears to have been metaphorically called "the lady of the white bow." This figure was also the symbol of the moon. The reason of its being surmounted by the two implements resembling arrows, or javelins, as shewn on the stone, cannot be guessed at, except we believe they were also sprigs. The zig-zag figure is evidently the same article under a different form; and both these are frequent on such obelisks, as well as the figure on which they are placed, the purport of which is equally unknown. The small object appears to be part of the latter, and is also often introduced. Sometimes, indeed, it consists of a greater and lesser circle, or globe, attached to each other. in which case it precisely resembles an article which a figure, supposed to be a Druid, on a Gallic monument, carries in his hand.[b] There are occasionally some other figures seen on these obelisks, but one of the most usual and most remarkable is here shown.

* Is there such "a manuscript version of the poems of Ossian" of the eighth century in existence? Surely not, otherwise the Ossianic controversy were easily settled. Ed.

[b] Montfaucon, iii. pl. 51.

This is, by Pennant, supposed to represent the musimon, an animal now extinct, and other writers have indulged their various conjectures as to what it is intended for. The Ceres of the Britons was represented under the figure of "a proud, crested mare," and also as "a crested hen," in which form it appears on coins, brooches, &c. If the reader will turn to page 198, this favourite symbol of the Britons will be seen on one of their coins, and it will be remarked that the legs have a very singular termination, both there and in the figure above shown. This goddess was regarded, as it were, in an amphibious character, and, perhaps, the state of the arts, or certain rules, did not permit a nearer representation of this mystical character. Some Eastern relics have a resemblance to this figure in the circular formation, or ornament of the legs; and even in St. Nicholas's Church, Ipswich, is a figure of an animal, the upper parts of the haunches of which are finished in spirals. The white bull was much venerated, and where we can only conjecture, it is worth observation, that the moon was called bull-horned, in the Orphic hymns, from its crescent form, and the ancient priests of Ceres termed this planet a bull.[o] One of the Celtic fragments at Notre Dame, Paris, represents a beast like a bull in a wood, in which are also birds. This very much resembles some of the sculptured stones in Scotland that may have had allusion to hunting, concerning which many curious bardic traditions exist. It has been observed in a criticism on a slight essay of mine, published by the Society of Antiquaries of London, that such figures are indicative "of the acts, habits, or character of the person commemorated." This I will readily admit, but the explanation of the symbols from Olaus Wormius, I conceive, does not apply here. The wolf is an apt

---

[o] Note on Pausanius, from Porphyry.

hieroglyphic of tyranny, and the lamb of gentleness and innocence, &c., but how will the above singular figures be explained? The intimations of the bards, dark enough, I allow, afford us the only light by which we can venture to attempt any solution of the mystery, and as they appear in some cases tolerably satisfactory, there may still be an agreement, for it is probable that if sepulchral, the tracery, rods, and other insignia, point out the grave of one initiated in the mysterious tree system learning of the Celtic priesthood.

That stones were erected to mark the burial places of celebrated men is not to be disputed, and instances have already been noticed. It was an ancient practice, and yet survives in the churchyard tombstones. A circular column, six feet high, but supposed when entire to have been twelve, at Llangollen, in Wales, was raised in memory of Conceum, who was defeated at the battle of Chester in 607, as Lluyd found by an inscription. Stones were also placed in commemoration of remarkable events, even to late ages. A rude pillar indicates the place where the battle of Pentland was fought; and a great block, raised by the Highlanders, marks the spot where the brave Viscount Dundee fell in the conflict at Reuruari.

The ceremony observed in raising a stone of memorial is thus described in the poem of Colna-dona. "Beneath the voice of the king we moved to Crona . . . three bards attended with songs. Three bossy shields were borne before us: for we were to rear the stone in memory of the past. By Crona's mossy course Fingal had scattered his foes . . . I took a stone from the stream amid the song of bards . . . beneath I placed at intervals, three bosses from the shields of foes, as rose or fell the sound of Ullin's nightly song. Toscar laid a dagger in the earth, a mail of sounding steel. We raised the mould around the stone, and bade it speak to other years."*

To conclude: the race, especially in the British Isles, were remarkable for their learning, and, to use the words of a popular writer, for "the cultivation of letters, that power of imagination which seems in them a trace of their

---

* The passage, which is an exceedingly interesting one, is translated by Clerk as follows:—

"Three bards, with music by our side,
Three bossy bucklers (borne) before—
We went to rear on high the stones
Which memorise the glory of the brave.
By Crona's winding, mossy stream,
Fingal, high-chief, discomfited the foe;
Fled strangers from his sword in utter rout,
Like stormy sea that's dashed upon the shore.
We reached the field of his renown;
Night came down beyond the cairns:
Tore I an oak from a crumbling bank,
And kindled a flame mid mists of the hills.
My mighty ancestors, look down,
Look down from halls which are your own;
When glory wakes your sons anew,
On the wind shall shine the arm renowned.
From Crona's beach I chose a stone,
Mid songs of bards who sang with power,
To mark the blood of Fingal's conquered foes
On the dark-grey moss of the burns.
Beneath I set, due interval between,
Three bosses from the stranger's shield,
As fell and rose by turns
The song of night from gracious Ullin;
Toscar placed his dagger 'neath the sod,
And a dark-blue mail of tempered steel;
Earth was heaped around the upraised stone,
Calling to renown the years of praise."

"The raising of stone pillars," says the learned translator in a note, "to preserve the memory of important events as here described, appears to be coeval with the history of man. The practice is at least as old as the days

Celtic origin."[p] A most remarkable fact in the history of the Scots is, that from being the most learned people in Europe, they became less noted for their literary acquirements than the other Celtic nations. Yet that they did not entirely neglect literature, is evident from the manuscripts which still remain, and those which we find formerly existed.

There are at present upwards of three millions of people in the British Isles who speak Celtic, viz., about two millions in Ireland, about 400,000 in Scotland, and about 700,000 in Wales. This latter country began very early to pay considerable attention to the printing of books in the native language, and by a catalogue in 1710, there appears to have been then upwards of seventy. Almanacks, magazines, dictionaries, grammars, religious books, and even several scientific works, have been published, and the number is supposed now to exceed 10,000. The first Welsh bible, a black letter folio, was printed in 1568, the first in Ireland, I believe, was in 1609. Bishop Kerswell's

of Joshua, or even of those of Jacob and Laban. It prevailed from Hindostan to the 'Ultima Thule' of the Scottish Isles, and has produced every form and size of monument, from the humble Highland cairn to the great pyramid of Cheops.

"The number of Celtic names for these commemorative stones is remarkable. We have 'càrn,' 'carragh,' 'cromleac,' 'dolben,' 'men hir,' &c. Tradition connects many of the multitude to be seen in the Highlands and Islands with the Druids or the Fingalian heroes. Fingal, Ossian, and Dermid have their 'pillars' in almost every district of the country; and the 'Sculptured stones of Scotland' prove that the practice referred to prevailed in the south and north long before the days of Ossian. In the description before us two peculiarities are mentioned which are worthy of remark—raising the stone in cadence to the music of bards—

'As rose and fell by turns
The song of night from gracious Ullin.'
and placing the armour of friend, as well as foe, beneath it."

Clerk's Ossian—Notes to 'Golnandona.'

[p] Thiery's Norman Conquest.

Liturgy, 1566, appears to have been the first book printed in Gaëlic; the Bible and many other books, among which is not to be forgotten the poems of Ossian, from the original manuscripts, by the Highland Society, have been since published, yet education and literature were certainly less attended to by the Highlanders than their characteristic thirst of knowledge might have led us to expect; but the cause is to be found in the unsettled state of society. Wales is nearly four times richer than Scotland, and supports seven or eight periodicals, while Scotland has only recently established one,* the Teachdaire Gaëlach, or Highland Messenger, which, however, appears to meet with suitable encouragement.

The want of a Gaëlic dictionary was long felt in Scotland, but that of Mr. Armstrong, published in 1825, was hailed with satisfaction; and the labours of the gentlemen employed by the Highland Society have more recently appeared in the "Dictionarium Scoto Celticum," in two large volumes, 4to., which will now preserve this pure and valuable dialect of a language once universal in Europe.† It will also fix the orthography, which was previously so unsettled. The singularity of this, in many instances, the reader must have remarked, and it has not escaped the notice of the learned, who have suggested means of simplifying the spelling, by getting rid of numerous consonants

---

* The publication of the *Teachdaire Gaëlach* has long since ceased; but besides the admirably conducted *Gael*, a monthly periodical, we have *Bratach na Firinn*, the *Highlander*, *Pioneer*, &c. A great deal of interesting Gaelic matter may be found in the annual "Transactions" of the Gaelic Society of Inverness, an excellent Society that has already done wonders. ED.

† In addition to the dictionaries mentioned two others, very useful in their way, have since been published, viz., MacAlpin's, and MacLeod and Dewar's. Monro's excellent grammar should be in the hands of every one interested in the language. ED.

which are retained without being at all sounded. The Celtic Society of Glasgow have this year offered four prizes for the best essays on the subject, but their exertions have come too late, it is to be feared, to produce any effect. The apparently useless consonants are retained to show the root, or primitive, of a word, and thereby prevent confusion.

The Celtic language has been several times the object of legislative severity. In Ireland severe enactments were passed against it, as was the case in Wales, about 1700. Even so late as 1769, a plan was entertained by the bishops to extinguish Cumraeg, by having the church service performed in the English only; a circumstance that but too often occurs, it is to be feared, without such a design. In Scotland, I have often heard it complained, that clergymen were put into a living who were quite unable to preach to the people in their vernacular tongue. It was attempted to root out the Gaëlic, but as might be expected, the design was impracticable. I do not know if the French ever thought of abolishing the Breton language, which, by Lagonidec, is said to be still spoken by upwards of four millions of people;—a trial would have shown that no measures could accomplish this. The case of the Wends, whose language it was attempted to repress, shows the impracticability of forcibly changing the mother tongue of any people. In 1765, it was thought expedient to eradicate the Bohemian language, and the design was long prosecuted, before the impossibility of accomplishing the object was discovered.

The nobility and gentry of Ireland continued to speak their native tongue until the reign of Elizabeth, or James the First. The Highlanders relinquished the practice of writing in Gaëlic before they had acquired any taste for conversation in English. Rory Mor, chief of the Mac

Leods, is said to have been the last of the Gaël who continued to write in the language of his fathers.

Notwithstanding the important assistance which, in acquiring other languages, would be derived from a knowledge of this primitive tongue, there is not a Celtic Professorship in any seminary of learning in the kingdom.*

* This reproach is in a fair way of being removed through the exertions of the editor's learned friend, Professor John Stewart Blackie, of the University of Edinburgh, who has already at an expense of time and trouble that cannot be too highly valued, collected upwards of £5000 of the £10,000 necessary to the endowment of a Celtic Chair in the Metropolitan University. ED.

APPENDIX.

TABLE OF CLAN TARTANS.

THE list here given is an Appendix to what has been said of Tartans in the Sixth Chapter of Vol. I., and contains as many specimens as I could procure and authenticate. I have noticed some variations in the patterns worn by different families of the same name, but I have not inserted any fancy tartan. The plan which is adopted in the following table, in perfecting which I had the valuable assistance of Captain Mac Kenzie of Gruinard, is sufficiently simple. Should any one desire to supply himself with this pattern, by copying the scale, and applying it to the web, the object will be accomplished. In like manner these descriptions are a guide to manufacturers, who will now, it is hoped, produce the true patterns.

A web of tartan is two feet two inches wide, at least within half an inch, more or less, so that the size of the patterns make no difference in the scale. Commencing at the edge of the cloth, the depth of the colours is stated throughout a square, on which the scale must be reversed or gone through again to the commencement. There is, it may be observed, a particular colour in some patterns which can scarcely admit of description, but which is known to the Highlanders, as, for example, the green of the Mac Kay tartan is light. The plaid which the clergy wore is popularly believed to have been used by the Druids and Culdees. The Highland ministers, it has been shown, went armed and generally dressed in the national costume. Martin describes a lay Capuchin, whom he met in Benbecula, clad in the breacan, and several within the memory of man continued to preach in their native garb.

⅛ of an inch.	Colours.	⅛ of an inch.	Colours.	⅛ of an inch.	Colours.	⅛ of an inch.	Colours.
	ABERCROMBIE.	8	blue	8	green	1	black
3½	green	½	red	8	black	1	blue
¼	white	8	black	8	blue	7	black
3½	green	8	green	1	black	½	yellow
3½	black	1½	red	1	blue	11	green
1	blue	½	green	1	black	½	yellow
1	black	½	red	8	blue	7	black
1	blue	4	green	8	black	6	blue
1	black	½	red	8	green	1	black
3½	blue	½	green	1	black	1	blue
		1½	red	2	yellow		
	BUCHANAN.	8	green	1	black		CHISHOLM.
		8	black	8	green		
½	azure	½	red	8	black	2½	red
8	green	8	blue	1	blue	8	green
½	black	1½	red	1	black	2½	red
1	azure	4	blue	1	blue	2	blue
½	black	1	yellow	1	black	1	white
2	yellow			4	blue	2	blue
½	black		CAMPBELL.	This is worn by the Duke of Argyle and the Campbells of Lochaw. The Earl of Braidalban & his clan, wear the following pattern.		11	red
2	yellow					2	blue
½	black	4	blue			1	white
1	azure	1	black			2	blue
½	black	1	blue			2½	red
8	red	1	black			8	green
1	white	1	blue			2½	red
		8	black			1	blue
	CAMERON.	8	green				COLQUHON.
		1	black	2	blue		
½	yellow	2	white	1	black	½	blue
4	blue	1	black	1	blue	1	black
1½	red						

TABLE OF CLAN TARTANS. 419

⅛ of an inch.	Colours.	⅛ of an inch.	Colours.	⅛ of an inch.	Colours.	⅛ of an inch.	Colours.
6	blue	\multicolumn{2}{c	}{Douglas.}	6	blue	½	red
9	black	¼	white	½	red	5	blue
1½	white	4	blue	6	black	\multicolumn{2}{c	}{Gordon.}
7	green	4	green	6	green		
1	red	1	azure	1	black	½	blue
7	green	1	black	6	green	1	black
½	white	1	azure	6	black	5½	blue
9	black	4	green	½	red	6	black
6	blue	4	blue	6	blue	6	green
1	black	½	white	1	green	1	yellow
1	blue					6	green
\multicolumn{2}{c	}{Cummin.}	\multicolumn{2}{c	}{Drummond.}	\multicolumn{2}{c	}{Forbes.}	6	black
		¼	white			1	blue
1	azure	1	azure	1	blue	1	black
1	black	1½	blue	1	black	1	blue
2	azure	4	red	6	blue	1	black
5	black	8	green	6	black	6	blue
½	orange	½	yellow	6	green	1	black
5	green	1½	blue	1	black	1	blue
2	red	½	white	1	white	1	black
½	white	17	red	1	black	1	blue
2	red	½	white	6	green	6	black
½	white	1½	blue	6	black	6	green
2	red	½	yellow	6	blue	1	yellow
5	green	8	green	1	black	6	green
¼	orange	4	red	1	blue	6	black
5	black	1½	blue			5½	blue
2	azure	1	azure	\multicolumn{2}{c	}{Fraser.}	1	black
1	black	½	white			1	blue
2	azure			2½	blue		
				½	red	\multicolumn{2}{c	}{Graham.}
\multicolumn{2}{c	}{Dalzel.}	\multicolumn{2}{c	}{Farquharson.}	½	blue		
				½	red	½	black
6	red	½	red	5	green	6	smalt
¼	white	2	blue	6¼	red	6	black
½	blue	½	black	1	green	½	green
2	red	½	blue	6¼	red	1	azure
13	green	½	black	5	green	8	green
2	red	½	blue	5	blue	1	azure
½	blue	4	black	½	red	½	green
¼	white	4	green	½	blue	6	black
2	red	1	yellow	½	red	6	smalt
3	blue	4	green	5	blue	1	black
2	red	4	black	5	green		
¼	white	4	blue	6¼	red	\multicolumn{2}{c	}{Grant.}
½	blue	½	black	1	green		
13	red	1	red	6¼	red	1	red
1	green			5	green	¼	blue
1½	crimson	\multicolumn{2}{c	}{Ferguson.}	½	red	¼	red
1½	green	½	green	½	blue	18	red

⅛ of an inch	Colours	⅛ of an inch	Colours	⅛ of an inch	Colours	⅛ of an inch	Colours
¼	azure	16½	red	1½	black	½	red
½	red	2	purple	4½	blue	¼	azure
5	blue	¾	red			16	red
1	red	¾	yellow	**LOGAN.**		½	azure
¼	green	2	red	1¼	red	½	red
1	red	15	purple	1½	blue	11	dark green
21	green	¾	red	¾	red	½	red
½	red	15	black	¾	blue	¼	azure
½	blue	¾	white	¾	red	5½	red
2½	red	15	green	7	blue	½	white
½	blue	2	red	5¼	black	¼	red
½	red	¾	yellow	7	green	4	blue
21	green	¾	red	½	red	½	red
1	red	2	green	½	black	¼	white
½	green	16½	red	1	yellow	2½	red
1	red	2	black	½	black	3	dark green
5	blue	1	yellow	½	red	½	light green
½	red	1	red	7	green	2	red
¼	azure	3	black	5¼	black	½	light green
18	red			7	blue	3	dark green
½	blue	**LAMONT.**		¾	red	¾	red
¼	red	2¼	blue	¾	blue	¼	white
¼	blue	1½	black	¼	red	½	red
2½	red	1½	blue	1¼	blue	2½	blue
		1½	black	2¼	red		
GUNN.		1½	blue			**MAC AULAY.**	
½	green	6	black	**MAC ALASTAIR.**		½	black
7	blue	6	green	4	red	9	red
½	green	1½	white	½	light green	3½	green
7	black	6	green	3	dark green	1½	red
7	green	6	black	1	red	5	green
1	red	6	blue	1	azure	½	white
7	green	1½	black	1	red	5	green
7	black	1½	blue	½	white	1½	red
½	green	1½	black	1	red	5	green
7	blue	6	blue	1	azure	½	white
1	green	6	black	1	red	5	green
		6	green	3	dark green	1½	red
HAY. *		1½	white	½	red	3½	green
1½	black	6	green	½	white	9	red
1	red	6	black	6	red	1	black
1	yellow	1½	blue	½	azure		
2	black	1½	black	½	red	**MAC DONALD.** †	
		1½	blue	11	dark green	2½	green

* This rich tartan is claimed by the Leiths.

† There is a white stripe introduced for distinction by the Glengary Clan, and Lord Mac Donald wears a pattern composed of red and green.

⅛ of an inch.	Colours.
½	red
1	green
1½	red
8	green
8	black
½	red
8	blue
1½	red
¾	blue
½	red
5	blue
½	red
¾	blue
1½	red
8	blue
½	red
8	black
8	green
1½	red
1	green
½	red
5	green
MAC DOUGAL.	
3	red
6	green
1	red
½	blue
18	red
2	crimson
18	red
½	blue
1	red
6	green
6	red
6	green
3	crimson
1	red
3	crimson
6	blue
2	red
1	green
2	red
18	green
1	red
1	crimson
MAC DUFF.	
4	red
3	azure
4	black
6½	green
3½	red
1	black
3½	red
1	black
3½	red
6½	green
4	black
3	azure
8	red
MAC FARLANE.	
10½	red
½	black
6	green
1	white
1½	red
½	black
1½	red
1	white
1	green
6	purple
2	black
1½	red
2	white
1½	green
2	white
1½	red
2	black
6	purple
1	green
1	white
1½	red
½	black
1½	red
1	white
6	green
½	black
21	red
MAC GILLIVRAY.	
½	blue
2	red
¼	azure
2	red
9	green
1	red
7	blue
½	red
½	azure
18	red
¼	blue
¼	azure
2	red
¼	azure
¼	blue
18	red
½	azure
½	red
7	blue
1	red
9	green
2	red
¼	azure
2	red
½	blue
MAC GREGOR.	
12	red
6	green
2½	red
3	green
¼	black
1	white
¼	black
3	green
2½	red
6	green
24	red
MAC INTOSH.*	
12	red
6	blue
2½	red
10½	green
4	red
½	blue
4	red
10½	green
2½	red
6	blue
24	red
MAC KAY.	
¾	green
7	corbeau
1	green
7	black
7	green
1½	black
7	green
7	black
1	green
7	corbeau
1½	green
MAC KENZIE.	
3½	blue
1½	black
1½	blue
1½	black
1½	blue
7	black
7	green
1½	black
1½	white
1½	black
7	green
7	black
7	blue
1½	black
1½	red
1½	black
7	blue
7	black
7	green
1½	black
1½	white
1½	black
7	green
7	black
1½	blue
1½	black
1½	blue

* The chief also wears a particular tartan of a very showy pattern.

APPENDIX.

⅛ of an inch	Colours	⅛ of an inch	Colours	½ of an inch	Colours	⅛ of an inch	Colours
1½	black	1	black	6	crimson	2½	black
7	blue	1	red	6	red	¼	yellow
				1	crimson	2½	black
Mac Kinnon.		**Mac Lean.**		6	red	6	green
		½	black	6	crimson	6	black
½	white	1½	red	1	green	6	smalt
1½	red	1	azure	1	crimson	½	white
1	green	11	red	1	green		
1	blue	5	green	1	crimson	**Mac Pherson.** *	
3	red	1	black	6	green		
8	green	1½	white	1	crimson	¼	red
1	red	1	black	1	green	½	black
2	blue	½	yellow	1	crimson	½	white
1	green	2	black	1	green	5½	red
8	red	3½	azure	6	crimson	2	azure
4	green	2	black	6	red	½	black
1	white	½	yellow	1	crimson	½	azure
2	red	1	black	6	red	½	black
1	white	1½	white	6	crimson	2	azure
2	red	1	black	6	green	3	black
1	white	5	green	1	crimson	½	yellow
4	green	11	red			4	green
8	red	1	azure	**Mac Naughton.**		5½	red
1	green	1½	red	¼	black	1	azure
2	blue	1	black	½	azure	5½	red
1	red			8	red	1	azure
8	green	**Mac Leod.**		8	green	5½	red
3	red	1	yellow	6	black	4	green
1	blue	½	black	4½	azure	½	yellow
1	green	6	blue	8	red	3	black
1½	red	6	black	½	azure	2	azure
1	white	6	green	½	black	½	black
		½	black	½	azure	½	azure
Mac Lachlan.		2	red	8	red	½	black
4	red	½	black	4½	azure	2	azure
1	black	6	green	6	black	5½	red
1	red	6	black	8	green	½	white
1	black	6	blue	8	red	½	black
1	red	½	black	½	azure	½	red
8	black	2	yellow	½	black		
8	blue					**Mac Quarrie.**	
1½	green	**Mac Nab.**		**Mac Niel.**		2½	red
8	blue	1	green	1	white	12	blue
8	black	1	crimson	6	smalt	15	red
8	red	6	green	6	black	¼	azure
				6	green	2	red

* The chief has recently dressed in a different pattern, which is said to have been formerly worn by his family.

TABLE OF CLAN TARTANS.

⅛ of an inch.	Colours.	⅛ of an inch.	Colours.	⅛ of an inch.	Colours.	⅛ of an inch.	Colours.
¼	azure	1	black	½	white	2	red
15	red	1	blue	½	blue	½	black
12	blue	1	black	¼	white	1	yellow
5	red	6	blue	3½	red	8½	green
16	green	1	black	¼	white	1	black
7	red	1	blue	½	blue	1¾	green
		1	black	3½	red		
MENZIES.		1	blue	½	black	ROBERTSON.	
12	red	6	black	1	red	½	red
9	green	6	green	½	green	1	green
1	white	2	red	1	yellow	8½	red
3	azure	6	green	1½	green	1	blue
24	red	6	black	½	yellow	1	red
3	azure	6	blue	1½	green	8½	green
1	white	1	black	1	yellow	1	red
9	green	2	blue	3	black	8½	green
				¼	white	1	red
MUNRO.		OGILVIE.		1	blue	1	green
6½	red	1	red	¼	white	8½	red
½	yellow	¼	white	3	black	1	green
½	blue	½	black	2	red	1	red
1½	red	½	yellow	½	white	1	green
13	green	1	purple	2	red	8½	red
1½	red	½	yellow	½	white	1	green
½	blue	1½	green	2	red	1	red
½	yellow	½	yellow	½	black	8½	blue
1¼	red	½	black	½	yellow	1	red
3	blue	½	red	3½	green	8½	green
1½	red	½	black	1	black	1	red
½	yellow	½	red	3½	green	1	blue
½	blue	½	black	1	black	8½	red
13	red	½	red	3½	green	1	green
1½	green	½	black	½	yellow	1	red
1½	red	1	yellow	½	black	1	green
1½	green	2	green	2	red	8½	red
1½	red	1	yellow	½	white	1	blue
1½	green	½	black	2	red	1	red
13	red	2	red	½	white	8½	green
		½	white	2	red	½	red
MURRAY.		2	red	½	black		
1	blue	½	black	½	yellow	ROSE.	
1	black	½	yellow	2	green	½	red
6	blue	2	green	½	white	5	blue
6	black	¼	white	2	green	5	black
6	green	2	green	½	yellow	5	green
2	red	¼	yellow	½	black	½	white
6	green	¼	purple	2	red	2	black
6	black	1	red	½	white	½	white
1	blue	½	black	2	red	5	green
		3½	red	½	white	5	black

APPENDIX.

¼ of an inch.	Colours.	½ of an inch.	Colours.	½ of an inch.	Colours.	½ of an inch.	Colours.
5	blue	\multicolumn{2}{c}{STEWART.}	1	blue	1	red
1	red	¼	white	8	black	8	blue
\multicolumn{2}{c}{Ross.}	1½	red	8	green	8	black
		1	black	1	black	8	green
4½	green	4	red	8	green	1	black
1	red	8	green	8	black	1	green
9	green	1	black	8	blue	\multicolumn{2}{l}{Breacan na'n Cle-}
9	red	1	white	1	black	\multicolumn{2}{l}{rach, or Tartan of}
1	green	1	black	1	blue	\multicolumn{2}{l}{the Clergy.}
2	red	½	yellow	1	black	¼	white
1	green	5	black	8	blue	2½	black
9	red	3	azure	8	black	½	white
9	blue	16	red	8	green	2	grey
1	red	3	azure	1	black	½	white
9	blue	5	black	8	green	5	black
9	red	½	yellow	8	black	2½	grey
½	blue	1	black	1	blue	1	black
½	red	1	white	1	black	2½	grey
1	blue	1	black	1	blue	5	black
½	red	8	green	1	black	½	white
½	blue	4	red	11	blue	13	black
9	red	1	black	\multicolumn{2}{c}{URQUHART.}	½	white
		1½	red			2	grey
\multicolumn{2}{c}{SINCLAIR.}	1	white	4	green	½	white
9	red			1	black	2½	black
10	green	\multicolumn{2}{c}{SUTHERLAND.}	1	green	½	white
2½	black	5½	blue	1	black		
½	white	1	black	1	green		
4	azure	1	blue	8	black		
18	red	1	black	8	blue		

INDEX.

A

ABDUCTION of women, ii. 372.
Aberdeen, old, axes of the guard of, 311.
——— shire, flint arrow heads in, 348.
——— anciently noted for sheep ii. 58.
——— abundance of fish in, ii. 132
Abernethy, palace at, ii. 12, tower at, ii. 22.
Abury, temple described, ii. 329.
Achindoer, earth houses at, ii. 11.
Acts against Highland dress, 278.
——— repealed, 279
Adultress, how punished, 219.
Aeduans, their mode of government, 190.
Agincourt, battle of, 346.
Agriculture, ii. 70—Welsh laws respecting, ii. 78—respect of the Romans for, ii. 78, n.—ancient marks of, ii. 85—in Hebrides, ii. 87.
Agrippina, its siege, 391
Aireach, 145.
Airisaid, an ancient habit, 270.
Alarm, methods of giving, 142.
Albanach, 44, 52.
——— Duan, an ancient poem, ii. 231.
Albani, origin of the name, 4, n.
——— the Scotish war cry, 304.
Albania, 52.
Alce, a singular animal, ii. 32.
Alcis, worship of, ii. 346.
Aldborough, ruins at, ii. 6.
Ale, Pictish, ii. 158—herb, ii. 159.
Alesia, a Celtic town, 377.
Alia, defeat of the Romans at, 118,
Altacholihan, battle of, 328.
Alting, 211.
Alves, discoveries at, ii. 382.
Amber, vessels of, ii. 212.
Amida, heroism of the Celts at, 130.
Amusements of the Highlanders, ii. 252.
Anecdotes of heroism, 127.
——— Anspach, Margrave of, ii 284
——— Argyle, Duke of, 324, ii. 272.
——— Assynt, laird of, ii. 163.
——— Athol, Duke of, ii. 46.
——— Boiscalus, ii. 377.
——— Breusa, William de, 340.
——— Campbell, John, 324.
——— Cameron of Lochiel, ii. 120.
——— Clan Rannald, 195.
——— Clark, George, ii. 283.
Anecdotes of Clark Kennedy, ii. 289.
——— Clovis, King of France, 145.
——— Coote, Sir Eyre, ii. 283.
——— A Frenchman, 199.
——— Dionysius the tyrant, ii. 119.
——— Gordon, Duke of, ii. 293.
——— Mac Bane, Gillies, 128.
——— Mac Codrum, a bard, ii. 231.
——— Mac Donald of the Isles, 154.
——— Captain, 324.
——— of Keppoch, 105, 153, 203.
——— Donald, of Aberarder, ii. 137.
——— Mac Gregor, of Glenstræ, ii. 137.
——— Mac Intosh, James, ii. 276.
——— Mac Kenzie, Roderick, 179.
——— Mac Lean, of Coll, ii. 300.
——— Mac Lean, John Garbh, of Coll, ii. 174.
——— Mac Leod, Donald, 324.
——— Mac Pherson, of Cluny, 325.
——— Ewen, ii. 231.
——— Mac Rimmon, ii. 286.
——— Mar, Earl of, 324.
——— Munro, of Culcairn, 179.
——— Nelan, an Irish bard, ii. 221.
——— Robertson, of Lude, 324.
——— Steuart, 335.
——— Stratherne, Earl of, 281, &c.
Anglesea, its formation, 38.
Angli, painting of their bodies, 225.
Animals, extinct, ii. 30.
Anna clough, mullach, cave at, ii. 10, n.
Annals, preserved by bards, ii. 229.
Ansibarians, their hard fate, 21, ii. 377.
Aonachs, or fairs, ii. 196.
Apple Trees, 83.
Aquitani, 23.
Arable land, how estimated, ii. 78.
Araradh, ii. 104, 120.
Archers, Royal Scotish, 351.
Archery, trial of, between Scots and English, 342—laws to encourage, 344.
Architecture of the Britons, 389, ii. 1.
Ard na sœur, ruins at, ii. 7.
Areopagus, court of, 211.
Argyle, etymology of, ii. 62, n.
Aric, employment at, ii. 63.
Arkel, its peculiar deer, ii. 35.

426   INDEX.

Arms of the Celts; number collected by M. Wade, 371—custom of exchanging, 372—time of fixing, 365—of Scotland, ii. 374—deposited with the dead, ii. 381.
Army, how commanded, 153—how drawn up, 154.
Arrows, a signal of war, 143—sent to assemble a ting, 213—how pointed, 345, 345.
Arthel, or arvel dinner, ii. 386.
Arthur's oven, a curious building, ii. 16.
Artificers, British, their skill, ii. 209.
——————————hereditary, ii. 212.
Arvydd Vardd, a Welsh Herald, ii. 226.
Arymes prydain, Welsh War Song, 163.
Asion, Irish regal cap, 258, n.
Assemblies, their speedy convocation, 141.
Assythments, 214.
Athol, men of, their numbers, 97.
Atticots, 61.
Augury, skill in, ii. 349.
Auris Batavorum, 108.
Anxerre, cave at, ii. 10.
Avaracum, a Celtic town, described, 377—its noble defence, 127, 389.
Azores, 35.

B

Baal, or Bell, the chief god of the Celts, ii. 336—ceremonies respecting, 370.
Baal tein, feast of the sun, ii. 336, 337.
Bachul Murry, 148.
Badenach, a gymnasium at, 324, cave at, ii. 10.
Badges, 205—list of, 302.
Baggage, how disposed of, 152.
Bagpipe, known to Greeks and Romans, ii. 277—origin among Scots, ii. 279. Highland, the only national instrument, ii. 280—its effects, 181 to 284—its use encouraged, ii. 288—used at funerals, ii. 395.
Baking, how performed, ii. 117.
Balearic Isles, 307
Banchory, Laird of, ii. 271.
Band, the hundred, 143.
Banff, the supposed residence of Andrea Ferrara, 323.
Banquet, Highland, account of. ii. 150.
Baptism, a Pagan rite, ii. 344.
Bards, 178—their duties, 100, 161; ii. 221, 222, 225, 347—their portion, ii. 124—education, ii. 220, 228—their compositions, ii. 221—persecuted, ii. 221.
Bark of Trees, a manufacture, 227.
Barmekin, a hill fort, 378.
Barns, used for drying corn, ii. 93, 94.
Barra hill, a Caledonian fort, 378.
Barritus, 157.
Barrows, sepulchral, their varieties, ii. 385.
Bass, of Inverury, 217.
Battle axe, 312.
————— shout, 157, 303.
Bear, a natural product of Britain, ii. 29.
Beaver, once found in Britain, ii. 29.
Beds of the Highlanders, ii. 206—flock, invented by Gauls, ii. 206.
Bees, their culture, ii. 154.
Belgæ, 20—arrival in Britain, 41—possessions, 44—agriculture, ii. 66—dress, 223, 226.

Belt, 337—how ornamented, 267, 338 worn by women, 270.
Ben Nevis, mountain, its height, ii. 15
Beothach, an Fheoir, a singular animal, ii. 37.
Bernera, duns destroyed to build, ii. 15.
Bidag; see Dirk.
Birch, a native tree, ii. 84.
Birlaw men, a rural jury, ii. 80.
Bituriges, their towns burned, 391.
Black, used by Gauls for mourning, ii. 390
Bladair, the chief's spokesman, 180.
Blood, drinking of, 147.
Blue, the favorite colour of the Britons, 234.
Boars, ii. 33—hunting of, ii. 45.
Boat racing, ii. 319.
Bod, hut or cottage so called, ii. 4.
Bodies, burning of, ii. 377.
Boined, 264.
Bonagh, an Irish exaction, 185—beg, do. 187—bur, 181.
Bonnaughts, the pay of Galloglasses, 331.
Bonnet, forms of, 265.
Boots, origin of, 256.
Boundaries, 7, ii. 74.
Bow and arrows, 337—Scotish, 342—when last used, 343—how made, 344.
Braccæ, a vestment, described, 254.
Bræ mar, famed for deer, ii. 35.
Brahan Castle, arms of the Highlanders delivered up at, 371.
Braidalban, men of, their numbers, 97.
Braonan, used as food, ii. 114.
Brass, its manufacture, ii. 201.
Bratach shi, of Mac Leod, 296.
Breacan, 241—a sort of coat armour, 238—feile, described, 249—its usefulness, 276.
Bread, ii. 116.
Brechin, round tower at, ii. 23.
Breeches, derivation of the word, 254—mistake of a Highlander concerning, 263.
Brehon, the Celtic judge, 210.
Breith a nuas, 217.
Brettania, first mention of, 39.
Britain, suppositions, 33, 36—etymology of, 39—first inhabitants, 36, 37, 39, 40—intercourse with the Continent, 41—its products, ii. 198.
Britannia, Romana and barbaria, 50.
British army, its arrangement, 153—horses 351—town described, 376.
Britons, 42—ardent in cause of liberty, 132 corrupted by Roman luxury, 134—defensive armour, 250—offensive do. —their retreats, ii. 2, 6, 7, 10—their grain, ii. 84—manures, ii. 87—cookery ii. 119—deities, ii. 331—statues of do. ii. 325—stature, 99—swiftness of foot, 104—painted their bodies, 228—expert charioteers, 357—their management of the car, 357.
Brog, or shoe, 256.
Brooch, its use, 249—of Bruce, 272—of Glenlyon, 272.
Browns, of Kincardine, musicians, ii. 267.
Brynly's Castle, a British work, 388.
Brython, 43.
Buffaloes, ii. 37.
Builg, the Highland knapsack, 267.
Burkes, the, plundered, ii. 68.
Butter, how made, ii. 114.

C

Cairns, sepulchral, ii 379.
Caledonia, etymology of, 45, 46.
Caledonian ox, ii. 33, 57.
Caledonians, first mention of, 43—their territories, 46—warlike renown, 123, 132—oaths, 147—dress, 226—swords and spears, 313—arrows, 345—cavalry, 351—houses, ii. 2, 7, 6, 22—agriculture ii. 67—food, ii. 105—prejudice to fish, ii. 124—ships, ii. 179, 182—ancient dancing, ii. 309—modern do. 311—tournament, ii. 315.
Calpich, 216.
Camanachd, a game, ii. 319.
Camerons of Lochiel, their numbers, 97.
Campbells, their respect for Duan Diarmid, ii. 238—some funeral observances among, ii. 390.
Cane, 216.
Cannæ, battle of, 252.
Cannibalism, ii. 123.
Canoes, remains of, ii. 186.
Caoine, or Cine, Irish, ii. 246.
Cappeene, 265.
Capercailzie, a mountain bird, ii. 41.
Carnac, temple at, ii. 331.
Carnbre, a British work, 388.
Carriages, ii. 105.
Carrows, Irish gamesters, ii. 315.
Carthaginians, their tents, ii. 2.
Canucate, ii. 81.
Cascrom, an implement of agriculture, ii. 96.
Casdireach, do. ii. 97.
Cashell, round tower at, ii. 21.
Cassiterides, islands of, 34.
Castell Corndochon, a British work, 388.
Castles of the Pictish kings, ii. 12.
Catharn; see Cearnach.
Cath dath, a sort of cloth, 232.
Catherthuns, Caledonian strongholds, 379.
Cathghairm, Highland battle shout, 157.
Cath tei, a fiery dart, 315.
Cats, wild, ii. 36.
Catti, manner of wearing their hair, 109—contend for a salt river, ii. 130.
Cattle, their ancient numbers, ii, 52—folds, ii. 58—diseases, how treated, 340. ii. 62 to 64—spoil of, how divided, ii. 65, —the first article of traffic, ii. 188.
Cavalry, 351—how attacked by the Highlanders, 353—mode of fighting with, 354, 355—Irish, 354.
Caves of the aborigines, ii, 9.
Cearnach, Highland light infantry, 150—their duties, 150, 329.
Celtæ, etymology of, 3, 4—their territories, 20.
Celtiberi, 23—famous sword makers, 320, ii. 201—their drink, ii. 156.
Celto-scyths, 17.
Celts, armies of, their numbers, 96—how raised, 140—how drawn up, 152—personal appearance, 98—dispositions, 113 to 115—exploits, 115, 125 to 130—contempt of death, 130, ii. 376—method of washing and dressing their hair, 111—method of attack, 156—councils, 197—fought naked, 247—treatment of malefactors, 199—pride of dress, 225—splendour of do. 268—armour, 282—ambassadors, their reply to Alexander, 132—chief, how supported, 173 — holdings, 194 — final struggle for independence, 135 — costume, 221—shields, how ornamented, 297—methods of defending and attacking a town, 389, 390—their towns, 374, ii. 8—manner of hunting, ii. 46, 50—prejudice to fish, ii. 43—cookery, ii. 127—aversion to pork, ii. 123—their gods, ii. 327, 333—drank little at meals, ii. 143—recipes, ii. 170—surgical knowledge, ii. 176—their affluence, ii. 200—manufactures, ii. 201, 210, 213.
Celts, stone weapons so called, 310—curious discoveries of, ii. 204.
Cemetery, druidical, at Iona, ii 386.
Cetra, a sort of shield, 287
Chaff, how separated from grain, ii. 102.
Chain mail, a Celtic invention, 282.
Chains, golden, a common ornament, 268.
Chariot, for war, described, 357 to 364—races, 365.
Charioteers, their importance, 357.
Chattan, clan, fight at Perth, 329—their gathering, ii. 295.
Chaunting at funerals, ii. 393.
Cheese, ii. 66, 115.
Chenerotis, a favorite British dish, ii. 124.
Chief, his authority, 141, 145—his body guard, 149—his election in Ireland, 143—duties in war, 143 to 145, 154—inauguration, 197—his name used as an oath, 147.
Children, how reared, 103, ii. 375.
Chirin, clan; see Clan.
Chisholms, the, their strength, 97—gathering, ii. 291.
Christmas ba'ing of Monymusk. ii. 319.
Churches, of wattle, ii. 3—covered with heath, ii. 25.
Churn, invented by the Celts, ii. 114.
Cimbri, their situation, 10—power, 12—their daring exploits, 31—invasion of Italy and defeat, 120.
Cimmerii, their situation 9, 12—lived in caverns, ii. 9.
Cincogish, law of, 173, 208.
Cine, or Keen, Irish funeral lament, ii. 40.
Circus, a place of worship, 212.
Cisalpine, Gaul, a Roman province, 24.
Cities, their numbers in Britain, Gaul, and Spain, 375.
Clachan Ossian, the bard's monumental stone, ii, 239, 380.
Clach cuid-fir, a trial of strength, ii. 318.
Clach neart, a game, ii. 317.
Clans, their numbers, 97 to 99—oaths, 147 Clan na Faiter, 296—Chattan, fight at Perth, 329—Chirin, war cry, 209—Connan, 190—Muntercasduff, 190—Rannald, war cry, 304—chief of, anecdote, 195—his cavalry, 351—gathering, ii. 293—Ricard, war cry, 305.
Clanship, 164.
Classerness, temple at, ii. 333.
Clechda, ii. 79.
Clergy carried arms, 328—dressed in the kilt, ii. 417.
Cliar, or sling, 307.
Clodh, 233.
Cloghadh, or round tower, ii. 20.
Club, a military weapon, 307.

428 INDEX.

Clubbar, an agricultural implement, ii. 106.
Clubbing hair, a mode of dressing it, 118
Cnag, a singular bird, ii. 30
Coals, when first used, ii. 129
Coat armour, origin of, 294, 300
Cockerell, discoveries at, ii. 380
Cœnas, a vestment, 228, 245
Coffin, how carried by the Gaël, ii. 390
Coin of the Britons, ii. 200—Gaëlic name of, ii. 200
Colda mo run, a piobrachd, ii. 295
Colours in cloth, how regulated, 236
Comhairlich, or councillors, 193, ii. 221
Commanders, how elected, 145
Commerce of the Celts, ii. 200
Common holding, its origin, ii. 74, 75—advantages, 76
Common law, of druidic origin, ii. 218
Complexions of Celts, 111
Connan, clan, 190
Cookery, 103
Corn, varieties, ii. 83—how preserved, 100 —ingenious machine for thrashing, 82
Cornwall, ruins in, 388, ii. 7
Coronach, or funeral lament, ii. 247
Coronation stone, of Scotish kings, 200, 201
Corpulence offensive to Celts, ii. 112
Coshering feasts described, ii. 140
Costume of ancient Celts, 245 to 254—of the Highlanders, 276—of the Irish, 232, 274
Cota, a Celtic vestment, 247
Cottages, Highland, ii. 23
Cottars, their situation, ii. 77
Coul castle described, ii. 20
Councils, general, 140—of officers, 145—of elders, 195
Countries, districts so called, 179
Courts transferred to churches, 212—removed, ii. 336
Covinus, a sort of chariot, 350, ii. 301
Crantaraidh described, 142
Creach explained, 206
Crests or badges, 298
Crimes, how compensated, 213, &c.
Cromleach described, ii. 344
Crowns, golden, found in Ireland, ii. 205
Croy, curious sculpture at, 248
Crubban, an agricultural implement, ii. 105
Cruinneachadh, or gathering, ii. 284
Cruit, a musical instrument, ii. 273
Crutheni, Picts so called, 57
Cuaran, a sort of shoe, 256
Cucullus, a sort of cap, 246
Cudgel playing, a favourite Highland game, 316, ii. 315
Cuidolch, a servitude, 215
Cuirtain, a sort of cloth, ii. 236, 274
Culbin hills, discoveries at, 346
Culdees, primitive clergy, ii. 364
Culloden battle, anecdotes of heroism at, 127, &c.
Cults, discovery at, 347
Cumhadh or lament, ii. 246
Cummings slain by the Mac Phersons, ii. 16—of Freuchie, musicians, ii. 268
Cumri, 40
Curach, a Highland boat, ii. 189
Curmi, malt liquor, ii. 158
Curragh of Kildare, 366
Cursus described, 365

D

Daci, where situated, &c. 17—their symbol, 298
Dagger, 331; see Dirk.
Dairy, how managed, ii. 118
Dalmack, ruins at, ii. 8
Dalriada, settlement in, 55
Dalriads, account of, 57
Dancing, ii. 309—Highland steps in, 312
Davach, a measure of land, ii. 80
Days of the week, their Gaëlic names, ii. 302
Dealg, 267
Death, disregard of, ii. 377
Deemsters, law officers in Man, 211
Deer, ii. 35, formerly domesticated, ii. 57
Deities, Celtic, ii. 333
Devana, its site, ii. 8
Diet of the Highlanders, ii. 124
Dining, ancient Irish mode of, ii. 149
Dirk, 332—its usefulness, 334—carried by the 42nd regiment, 336—ornaments of the hilt, 337—dance, 336, ii. 312
Dis, a Celtic god, 2, ii. 338
Dishes, various Scotish, ii. 123 to 131
Divination, modes of, ii. 349
Divisions of territory, 171, 172—ii. 76, 78
Dogs, excellence of the British, 367—of the Scots, ii. 42, 43
Dorlach, the Highland knapsack, 266
Douay, singular custom at, ii. 358
Doune, manufacture of purses at, 267—of pistols, 369
Dower, marriage, ii. 371
Draonaich, name of the Picts, ii. 72—their agriculture, ii. 80
Drenthiem, temple at, ii. 332
Dress, 221—of the Gauls, 225 to 229—Highland, 231, &c.—prohibited, 261—manner of putting on, 240—Irish, 231, &c.—prohibited, 260
Drinking, manner of, in the Highlands, ii. 162 to 165—among the Irish, ii. 163
Drinks of the Celts, Britons, Picts, and Gaël, ii. 154 to 157
Drovers, Highland, ii. 60
Druid dubh, a bird, ii. 41
Druidism, ii. 221, &c.—believed to have originated in Britain, ii. 325—how taught, ii. 326—its chief seat, ii. 325, 358—its abolition, ii. 364—mixed with early Christianity, 365
Druids, their duties, 162, 210—ii. 76, 348—their dress, 231, ii. 361—their physical skill, ii. 171—variety of knowledge, ii. 361, &c.—mode of reckoning, ii. 362—their predictions, ib.,—last mention of, ii. 363
Drumceat, council of, ii. 228, ii. 365
Drumlanrig, wild cattle at, ii. 54
Duan, a sort of poem, ii. 246
Duffhouse, arms at, 327
Duine uasals, an order of society, 176
Dumnonii, their worship, ii. 340
Duns, Celtic forts, 381, ii. 5—dun creich, 383—doruighil, ii. 16—staffnage, ii. 23—deer, 384
Dundee, bonnets made at, 266
Dunvegan Castle, shield at, 290
Dyestuffs, 235 to 238
Dying cloth, perfection of Celts in, 232—234, 277

E

Eagle, ii. 40—mountain, projected order of, 302—feathers of the, badge of Highland nobility, 302
Earl, origin of, 192
Earthen works, 172
Earth houses, ii. 11, 100
Edessa, statues of Celts at, 131
Edgehill, battle of, 307
Edinburgh, axes of the town guard, 313
Edwin's hall, an ancient ruin, ii. 19
Elm, probably indigenous, 82
Eleusis, capital of Thrace, 13
Elf shot, 347
Enach, 215
Ensign staff of Mac Duffaid, 206
Eric, 215
Esseda, a chariot so called, 358
Essie, discovery of arrow heads at, 347
Esus, or Hesus, a Gaulish god, ii. 340
Everley, discovery at, ii. 382
Evreux, discovery at, ii. 380
Eye-brows, small, esteemed beautiful, 112
Eyes, colour of, 113

F

Failter, clan na, their duty, 296
Fairies, ii. 375
Fala, Scots army at, 342
Falkirk, battle of, 126
Fane, ruins at, ii. 20
Farquharsons, their strength, 97, 98—war cry, 305
Fascines, use of in battle, 152
Fast-brotherhood, 147
Farms, management of, ii. 105
Feadhan dubh, or black chanter, ii. 304
Feasts of the Celts, ii. 134—how conducted, ii. 149—at Highland huntings, ii. 142—at funerals, ii. 142, 375—in Wales, how regulated, ii. 142—of the old Irish, ii. 147
Felt, a Gaulish manufacture, 223
Females, their beauty, 111—condition, 218—respect paid to, 161, 182, 223, 229—ii. 367, &c.—dress, 269
Fenns, their manner of life, ii. 2
Ferlaoi, a hymnist, ii. 225
Feudal tenures, origin of, 202
Fibulæ, 271
Fighting, Celtic manner of, 182
Fileas, an order among the Irish, ii. 225
Fir, a native tree, 80—marked a burial place, ii. 387
Firbog, an appellation of the Belgæ, 339
Fire, a signal of danger, 141—its place in houses, ii. 224—how formed, 119—sacred, ii. 70—preserved at Kildare, ii. 336.
Fire-arms, 367 to 370
Fish, Celtic dislike to, ii. 130 to 137
Flail, used by the Celts, ii. 98
Flathinnis, island of, 38—the supposed residence of the blessed, ii. 354
Flaughter spade, ii. 95
Fletchers, repeaters of Ossian's poems, ii. 236
Flint, weapons of, 346
Flour, how made, ii. 100
Fogs, curious phenomena of, 91
Fold, "the old man's," ii. 91
Food, ii. 107.

Foot ball, game of, ii. 319
Forbes's, their gathering, ii. 297
Forests of Britain, 79 to 84—their productions, 80, &c.—causes of their decay, 80
Forester, his duties and perquisites, ii. 53
Forts, vitrified, 376
Fosterage, 176
Foxes, ii. 34
Framont, singular field of antiquities, 222, ii. 346
Franks, admiration of the Gallic habit, 223
Frasers, their military strength, 97, 98—revolt of, 141—punished for mounting their badge, 300—effects of the pipes on, ii. 282
French, their war-cry, 304
Frenchman, anecdote of, 199
Funeral rites, ii. 380
Funeral monuments, ii. 382
Funerals of the Gauls, ii. 379—Highland, ii. 383, &c.—remarkable circumstance at one, ii. 391
Furniture of houses, ii. 210

G

Gaesi, lance bearers, 315
Gaël, inhabitants of Scotland, 44 to 46—their curious arts, 277, ii. 177, 214, &c.
Gaëlic MSS. ii. 237, 239
Gallatians, or Gallogrecks, 3
Gallerus, ruins at, ii. 20
Galli, or Celtæ, 1, &c.—see Gauls—crests of, 298
Galloglach, a sort of military, 331—axe of, 312
Gallovie, sheep farm, its extent, ii. 80
Galwegians, 65—their adherence to tanaist law, 191
Games, Highland, ii. 316—Irish, ii. 316
Garters, 258
Gatherings of clans, ii. 287—of sheep, ii. 57
Gauir conrigh, an Irish fort, 380
Gauls, their invasion of Italy, 118—military renown, 123, 125, 132, &c.—how ordered for battle, 142—their oaths, 140—conduct previous to an engagement, 156—despised defensive armour 281—their arms, 283—their hunting, ii. 44—their delight in fine cattle, ii. 56, 60—their longevity, ii. 170—were religious, ii. 351
Gavel kind, law of, 193—abolished in Wales, 194—in Ireland, ib.
Geese, not eaten by the Britons, ii. 40
Gentleman, Welsh, indispensibles of, 188
Geone, a Pictish cohort, 155
Gergovia, a Celtic town, 377
Germania, its ancient extent, 23
Germanni, 20, 22
Germans, mode of colouring hair, 110, ii.—their stature, 120—their only public diversion, 122—never laid aside their arms, 140—methods of recruitting armies, 142—their oaths, 143—arms, 281—houses, ii. 8, 9—agriculture, ii. 75—respect for their females, ii. 369—their funerals, ii. 379
Getæ, or Goths, 15, 18
Gilli-casfluich, comh strathainn, coise, more, piobaire, ruithe, trusarneis, 180 callum, ii. 311, 314

Glacach, a disease, 170
Glaslig, a supernatural being, ii. 84, n
Glastum, a dye, 223
Glenelg, duns in, ii. 14
Glenlivet, war-cry of, 304—battle of, ii. 272
Glenlyon, brooch of, 272—famous for archers, 343
Glibes, manner of dressing hair, 110
Goats, ii. 38, 57
Gode, or godordsman, 213
Gods of the Celts, ii. 336 to 347—of the Gaël, ii. 345
Golden ornaments, Celts loaded with, 267
Golf, game of, ii. 319
Golspie, subterraneous buildings at, ii. 12
Goths, 15, 17, 42, 43
Graddaning, ii. 101
Grain, ii. 83—how separated from the straw, ii. 100—reduced to flour, ii. 101
Graine, a Gaëlic god, ii. 336
Grampians, battle of, 135
Granaries of the Britons, ii. 99, 100
Grants, their force, 97—of Moynes, defeat the Camerons, 206—their gathering, ii. 296—agility of two, ii. 314—defeated by the Mac Donalds, ii. 304—of Glenmorriston, their charm, ii. 306
Greek inscriptions in Scotland, 37
Grenestede, wooden church at, ii. 4
Grove, sacred, ii. 326—near Massylia, described, ii. 358
Guanacum, a garment of the Britons, 230
Guns, 367—Earl of Mar's, 368
Guinneach cath, an order of battle, 155

H

Hair of the Celts, its colour, 166—modes of wearing, 107 to 111—garments of, 230
Halbert, a Scot's weapon, 318
Halidown Hill, battle of, 342
Hamden Hill, discoveries at, 359
Hamelin, piper of, ii. 301
Hammers deposited in Celtic graves, 312 ii. 379
Hardihood of the Celts, 108, 136, 275, &c.
Hare, not eaten by the Britons, ii. 38— used in divination, ii. 346
Harp, ii. 271—Irish, ii. 271—Welsh, ii. 272, 266—Caledonian, ii. 272 to 275—of Queen Mary, ii. 264—of Brian Boroimh, ii. 275—key of, ii. 272—curious history of one, ii. 277
Harper, last Highland, ii. 272
Harvest, its management in the Highlands ii. 98
Hats, beaver, used by the ancient Welsh, 264—adopted by the Highlanders, 265
Hawking, ii. 53
Hawks, master of, his duties and perquisites in Wales, ii. 54
Hawthorn den, caves at, ii. 10
Hebudæ islands, king of, 173, 186
Helmets, 283
Helvetii, 21—their forces, 94—law of, 185 —their muster roll, ii. 398
Hens, not eaten by the Britons, ii. 40
Herald, anecdote of one, 295
Herbs, their imputed virtues, ii. 174
Herefordshire beacon, a British strength, 378
Herrings, how cured in Sky, ii. 133

Hertha, a deity, worship of, 147—ii. 338
Hiberni, or Hyberni, Scots formerly so called, 54
Hibernia, the ancient name of Scotland, 48
Highland companies, their degeneracy, 137 —knights errant, 204—regiments, their uniform, 250—garb described, 251, &c. nobleman, portrait of, 288—club of Edinburgh, 370—farm described, ii. 76, 78—tenantry, former state of, ii. 107—banquet, ii. 151
Highlanders, their native denomination, 44—personal appearance, 103—hardihood, 105, 137, 275, &c.—conduct in 1745, 136—order of march, 155—manner of fighting, 247—dress restrained, 278—restored, 279—armour, 280 fought with clubs, 307—their onset, 325—attack with fire arms, 369, 371— at the battle of the Standard, 153— their horses, 353—disarmed, 278, 371 —dexterity in hunting, ii. 48—mode of pasturage, ii. 64—agriculture, ii. 87 to 93—superstitions respecting, ii. 92—contempt for delicacies, ii. 110— hospitality, ii. 133—temperance, ii. 164—longevity, ii. 182—manufactures, ii. 204 to 214—talent for rhyming, ii. 298—excel in dancing, ii. 312—modes of divination, ii. 347—their religious feelings, ii. 366—anxiety for a descent interment, ii. 387
Highlands, favourable to fruit trees, 85
History, preserved in verse, ii. 220, 227
Hobblers, Irish horsemen, 354
Honey drink of the Gaël, ii. 155
Horse soldiers of Inverness and Moray, 96 —Celtic, their dress, 355—racing introduced from Scotland, 366
Horses, method of breaking, 353—wild, ii. 44
Hospitality, Celts remarkable for, ii. 133
Houses, Highland, ii. 3, 4—of the Britons, ii. 25
Hunting, ii. 28 to 54—Highland, 46, 48, 49, 51—Welsh, laws respecting, ii. 47— Scots do. ib.—of King James V. ii. 49 —royal, ii. 51
Hybrasil, island of, 38
Hyperborei, 8—their island, 36, ii.
Hubbub, Welsh, 143

I

Iarflath, a title of honour, 192
Ictis, island of, 35
Iern, ancient name of Ireland, 49
Implements of husbandry, ii. 93
Inheritance, modes of, 193
Interment, modes of, ii. 380 to 385
Inverlochy, castle of, ii. 23
Inverness, large ship built at, ii, 191
Iona, first church at, ii. 3—the retreat of the Druids, ii. 366
Ireland, its ancient name, 49—Gaëlic of, its supposed introduction to Scotland, 71—woods, 78—subterraneous buildings in, ii. 11, stone do. ii. 19
Irish, their stature, 104—glibes, 110—order of marching, 155—bond of friendship, 147—wore hair garments, 232— war cries. 303—dress, 269, 276—prohibited, 277—armour, 280—dexterous

INDEX. 431

stone throwers, 213—archery, 389—pride in horses, 354, 361—cannibalism, ii. 115—mode of living, ii. 106—music, ii. 208—dancing, ii. 311—jesters, ii. 315—manner of espousal, ii. 370—waking the dead, 394
Iron, chains and plates of, worn by the Picts and Caledonians, 268—manufacture of in the Highlands, ii. 203
Isis, goddess of Paris, her statue, ii. 329
Isla, celebrated for manufacture of sword-hilts, 323
Islands, formed by inundations, 38
Italy, its inhabitants, 24
Iuhones, singular conduct of the, ii. 338

J

Jacket, how made, 242
Jedworth staff, 307
Jigs, Scots and Irish described, ii. 271
Judge, Celtic, 211
Jurah, cottages in, ii. 4

K

Kale, or Cole, first used by the Grants, ii. 117
Kent, its peculiar customs, 193
Keppoch, family murdered, ii. 256—lament for, ii. 297
Kern, 150, 329: see Cearnach
Keys, civil officers in Man, 211
Kildrummie, eird houses at, ii. 11, 94
Killicrankie, battle of, 334
Killin, a remarkable plain, ii. 82
Kilmarnock, famed for manufacture of bonnets, 266
Kimmeridge coal money, ii. 198
Kincogish, law of, 175, 208
Kineigh, singular tower at, ii. 22, n.
Kingusie, rath of, ii. 335
Kinkynell, law of, 191
Kismul, island, castle in, 392
Knife and fork, 323, ii. 150
Knighthood, its origin, 204
Knockferrel, a vitrified fort, 385

L

Lachdan, a sort of cloth, 231, 239
Ladies, Highland, their dress, 269—German, do. 275
La mas ubhal, feast of, ii. 146
Laments, Gaëlic, ii. 296
Languages, 24 to 30—British, Scottish, Saxon, &c. 66 to 73—Gaëlic, to what extent changed, ii. 341—its adaptation to poetry, ii. 248
Lankai, a lance, 314
Largo, singular interment at, ii. 380
Largs, battle of, 307, 338, 366
Larignum, siege of, 382
Launceston Castle, a British work, 387
Laws, 209—codes of, 210—of colours, 236—preserved in oral rhyme, ii. 218
Lead, its manufacture, ii. 201—balls of, used for missiles, 307
Leaders of armies, how chosen, 143—controuled by their troops, 145.
Lenicroich, or saffron shirt, 274

Leslie among the Lieths, origin of the tune of, 333
Leudus, a Celtic hymn, ii. 243
Lewis, inhabitants, celebrated for archery, 343
Lights of the Gaël, ii. 150, 156
Linen, a Celtic manufacture, 275
Lint, its management in the Highlands, ii. 97
Lion, the badge of the Celts, 291, ii. 302—laughable mistake concerning, 295
Liturgy, Gaëlic, ii. 190, 412
Loarn, a division of Argyle, 57
Lochaber, gymnasium in, ii. 312 - axe, 313
Lochenlour, ancient iron works at, 320
Lochow, garters made at, 239
Locks, wooden, of the Highlanders, ii. 216
Logan, moss of, discovery in, 87
Lon-dubh, a singular animal, ii. 31.
Lords of the Isles, manner of crowning, 199—mode of conveying lands, 204
Lothian, where situated, 70
Luathadh described, 233
Luchdtachk, 149, 180
Lusitani, their military ardour, 150—dancing, ii. 311—marriages, ii. 371
Lychlyn, the ancient name of the Baltic, 23, n.
Lyric compositions prevail in the Highlands, ii. 252

M

Macaladh cattle, 178
Mac Carters, pipers to the lords of the isles, ii. 290
Mac Donalds, their strength, 96, 97—led the right wing of an army, 153—of Slate, their strength, 97—of Glengary, do. 97—of Keppoch, do. 97—of Moidart, do. 97
Mac Dulothes, their strength, 96
Mac Euens, their strength, 97
Mac Farlane's, gathering of the, ii. 294
Mac Gregors, clan na sgeulachd, ii. 290—their piobrachd, ii. 293
Machœra, a sort of sword, 338
Mac Intoshes, their strength, 97—their descent, 190
Mac Kenzies, their strength, 96—crest, 141—punished for mounting their badge, 300—military music, ii. 296
Mac Leans of Coll, their gathering, ii. 284
Mac Leods, their strength, 96
Mac Niels of Barra, 187
Mac Niels, harpers to the Mac Leans of Duart, ii. 278
Mac Phersons, their strength, 96 —their military success, ii. 307
Mac Swineys, famed for hospitality, ii. 142
Magistrates, their election, 197
Magnentius, Celtic legions, their daring exploits, 130
Malefactors, how punished, 217
Manchester, ruins at, ii. 6
Mannus, a German god, ii. 342
Mantle, the Irish, 359
Manufactures, ii. 200 to 206—adaptation of the Highlands for, 297; see Costume
Manures, ii. 86
Manx, their laws, 211—dances, ii. 311—funerals, ii. 300
March; see Boundary

Marl, ii. 86
Matadh achalaise, a dagger, 338
Meals of the Highlanders, ii. 145
Meatæ, 62
Medical knowledge, ii. 172
Medicines, ancient MS. on, ii. 179
Merched mulierum, 219
Metal, manufacture of, ii. 202
Mhona liath, its famous deer, ii. 85
Mictis, island of, 35
Milk, substances for curdling, ii. 64—how used, ii. 156
Mill, hand, ii. 100—horizontal, ii. 101
Minstrels, superiority of the Scots, ii. 298
Miri-cath, 165, 180
Mirrors, metal, ii. 204
Misletoe, veneration for, ii. 356
Moars, officers in the Isle of Man, 213
Mona or Mena, a deity, ii. 343
Mona, the retreat of the Druids, ii. 358
Moniegaff, discoveries at, 311
Moose deer, ii. 31—garment formed of the skin, 232
Moothills, their origin, 217, ii. 336
Mousa, burg of, ii. 17
Muc, a military machine, 391
Multures, ii. 102
Mungret Abbey, its celebrated choir, ii. 262
Munroes, their force, 97—overthrow the Mac Intoshes, 209
Murrain, how averted, ii. 65, 66
Music, its origin and progress, ii. 250, &c.—its use in religion, ii. 260—how taught, ii. 262—terms in, ii. 263—Irish, ii. 264—Welsh, ii. 266—Military of the Mac Kenzies, ii. 297—Scotish, its peculiar scale, ii. 265
Musical instruments, ii. 269

N

Naharvali, their singular worship, ii. 344
Nations of Europe, their origin, 7—northern, 142
Neckcloths, 268
Needfire, how produced, ii. 66
Nehelania, a Celtic goddess, ii. 342
Nervii, their force, 95—their cities, 375—their fortifications, 376—manner of fortifying a camp, 378—their temperance, ii. 161
Nightingale, its Gaëlic appellation, ii. 42
Nobility, indicated by the number of vassals, 160
Nomades, 14
Notation, musical, ii. 263
Noth, a vitrified fort, 384

O

Oak, a native of Scotland, 81
Oatcakes, Scotish soldiers' method of making, ii. 119
Oaths, Celtic, 147—Highland, 148
Obelisks, sepulchral, ii. 384
O'Calinanes, famous physicians, ii. 167
Ocean, its encroachment, 75
Oigthierna, a title, 192
Ollamh, his course of study, ii. 221—qualification and value, 220
Oral record, veneration for, ii. 216—history committed to, ii. 226
Order, in assemblies, singular mode of preserving, 197—observed in Highland armies, 181—of the mountain eagle, 302—of the thistle, 302, n.
Ossan, 258—preasach, 272
Ossianic music, ii. 296—poetry, ii. 248
Ovates, a religious order, ii. 346
Oxgate, its extent, ii. 81

P

Painting the body, 221, 225—prohibited, 225
Parishes, size of, in Scotland, ii. 366
Pastoral state, ii. 54—melodies, ii. 271
Pasturage, ii. 62
Patterns of tartan, how given, 239, ii. 414
Paupers in the Highlands, ii. 140
Pearls, British, ii. 209
Peltæ, a shield, 257
Pen pits, singular excavations, ii. 99
Personal appearance, 101
Perth, battle of, 327, ii. 304
——— Gaëlic poem on, ii. 255
Pharmacy, ii. 180
Phœnicians, the supposed discoverers of Britain, 33
Physicians, Scots, hereditary, ii. 179—their prescriptions, ii. 181
Picardy, excavation at, ii. 10
Picts, 57—their native appellation, ii. 7—identity with Scots, 57—last mention of, 65—their houses, ii. 7—ale, ii. 160—gods, ii. 348
Piobmhor, ii. 302 to 304
Piobrachd, ii. 285 to 291—list of, ii. 293
Pipe, ii. 279—lowland, ii. 304—Irish, ib.—Northumberland, ii. 305—scale of, ii. 306—how performed on, ii. 306, 307
Piper, his duties, ii. 288—of Mac Leod, ii. 290—of Mac Donald, ib.
Pipers, competition of, ii. 291
Pistols, 368
Plaid, how worn, 249—by women, 272
Plough, Gaëlic, ii. 94—Scots, &c. 96
Poems, their antiquity, ii. 230—how preserved, ii. 238
Poetic history, of what extent, ii. 256
Poetry and music, ii. 219
Poetry, its influence, ii. 220 to 225—its construction, ii. 242 to 246—Gaëlic specimens, ii. 249 to 254—manner of composing, ii. 250
Pope, his ambassador hunts in Athol, ii. 50—observation on his entertainment, ii. 153
Poplar tree, a native of Scotland, 83
Population, causes affecting, 91—of Britain, 92—of Wales, ii. 409—of Scotland, 96—favoured by the patriarchal state, 97
Pork, antipathy to, ii. 62
Pots, &c. of the Highlanders, ii. 128
Potter, art of, among the Britons, ii. 210
Prescriptions, medical, ii. 179
Prosnachadh cath, 157, 164—its effects, ii. 245—gariach, 164, ii. 250—fairge, ii. 183
Purse, 266
Pythagoreans, their cultivation of the memory, ii. 218—their tenets, ii. 350, 359

Q

Quarter-master, Highland, ii. 8, 120
Quern, or hand mill, ii. 101
Quivers, how formed, 350

R

Rabbits, ii. 37
Rallying shout, its effect, anecdote, 306
Ranz des vaches, tune of, its effect, ii. 261
Rapparee, his house, ii. 4
Raths, 213
Rats, unknown in some parts, ii. 37
Rawdikes, a race course, 306
Rechailach, ii. 108
Recitation, now almost unknown, ii. 236, 218, 315
Recipes, Celtic, ii. 172—Highland, ii. 180
Red shanks, 256
Reels, of the Scots, described, ii. 267, 313
Regiments, Highland, their dress, 239—Royal Scots, carried bow and arrows, 343
Religion, Druidical, ii. 346, 350 to 355
Rents, how paid, ii. 81, 82
Residence, places of, their names, ii. 5
Rhapsodies, ii. 230
Rhapsodists, ii. 244
Rhi, a royal title, 191
Rince-fada, an Irish dance, ii. 311
Rings, Highlanders set stones in, ii. 213
Roasting, manner of, ii. 125
Robertsons, of Struan, their force, 97
Roses, of Kilravock, their force, 96
Rosses, their force, 97—of Balnagowan, their force, 96
Rother, river, ancient vessel discovered in, ii. 191
Round towers, ii. 20—opinions concerning, ii. 332
Roxburgh, conduct of Highlanders at, 124
Royal race of Picts and Welsh, 185
Rulers of the car, 145
Running, contentions in, ii. 313
Rungmor, a Highland dance, ii. 312
Ruthven, the rendezvous of the Highlanders after Culloden, 136

S

Sacrifices, human, ii. 357
Saddles not in use by Irish or Welsh, 354
Sagum, 227, 245, 269
St. Andrew's, English archers worsted at, 343
Salisbury plain, massacre at, 382—antiquities on, ii. 330, 384
Salt, superstitions concerning, ii. 131, 132
Salute, sword, 325
Salute, or failte, ii. 294
Saxons, their dress, 247, 277—imitation of Celtic manufactures, 230
Scilly islands, 35
Scotland, its original inhabitants, 44—formerly called Hibernia, 51—difference of ancient inhabitants accounted for, 66—its former appearance, 72—singular geographical features, 77, 78, ii. 81
Scots, 47, 48 to 65—etymology of, 59, 60—their warlike education, 122—their struggles for liberty, 134—law founded chiefly on Celtic usages, 200—abstemious, ii. 123—their cookery, ii. 127—music, ode to, ii. 300—invented a method of building, ii. 3—excel in poetry and music, ii. 299—mode of interment, ii. 380—burial places, ii. 397
Sculpture, in Glasgow Museum, 332—on obelisks, ii. 402
Scythe, a Gallic invention, ii. 98
Scythian, anecdote of one, 275
Scyths, 13 to 16—their symbol, 298
Seaforth, Highlanders, their tartan, 240
Seal, eaten by the Highlanders, ii. 132
Seanachadh, his duty, ii. 225, 226
Seantrius, the Highland hornpipe, ii. 314
Semnones, their worship, ii. 342
Sena, singular priesthood of, ii. 314, 347
Serpents' egg, the Druidical badge, ii. 354
Services, 215
Sets of tartan, 239, ii. 418
Sheep, ii. 37, 58—shearing, ii. 59—farming, ii. 58
Shepherds, ii. 61
Shields, 282—how used as a signal of war, 142—striking of, 144, 290
Ships of the Celts, ii. 185—of the Britons, ii. 186—ancient, discovered, ii. 191—large one of James IV. ii. 195
Shirts, 273—regulations of, 277
Shoes of the Highlanders, 256—buckles, 267
Shooting, a favourite diversion, 375, ii. 46
Shot pouch, 267
Signals of battle, 165
Singing, Highland manner of, ii. 261
Single stick, a favourite Highland amusement, ii. 315
Skean dubh, 339
Skelig isle, ruins at, ii. 20
Skellater, anecdote of a Highlander at, 335
Skins, used as clothing, 226, exported from Britain, ii. 204
Skull cap, 265—of the Highlanders, 285
Sky, Isle of, ruins in, ii. 7
Skythæ; see Scyths
Slagan, the war cry, 157
Slaves, unknown in the Highlands, 183—Irish trade in, ii. 206
Slia-grannus, a place of worship, ii. 337
Sliga crechan, ii. 145
Slings, 307
Snuff, partiality of Scots to, ii. 167—an ancient manufacture, ii. 168—horn described, ii. 169
Soap, a Gallic invention, 111, ii. 208
Soldurii, Celtic soldiers, 149, 178
Souls, their supposed state, 38, ii. 354
Spanish swords preferred by the Highlanders, 323
Spear, 312—how denoting war, 143—ditto peace, 152—length of the Scotish, 316
Spoil, its division, 145
Staff, St. Murran's, 149
Stalking deer, ii. 53
Standard, battle of, 153
Standards, of Fingal, 165—of the British tribes, 295—of Mac Leod, 296—of Mac Pherson of Cluny, ii. 307
Stature, causes affecting, 100
Stewarts of Appin, their force, 97
Stirling, celebrated for manufacture of tartan, 244
Stockings, 253
Stonehenge, temple of, ii. 329
Stones, thrown by hand, 307—weapons formed of, 309—rude, first symbols of the gods, ii. 327

VOL II. 2 E

Stranraer, ancient vessel discovered at, ii. 190
Strath-Connan, famous for archers, 343—Fillan, society of, ii. 322
Strathspey tunes, ii. 268—dances, ii. 313
Suessiones, their cities, 375
Suevi, manner of dressing their hair, 108—of agriculture, ii. 74
Sun, worship of, ii. 336
Swearing; see Oaths
Swine, ii. 61
Sword, 318—of the Britons, 319—basket hilt, 320—exercise, 322—anecdotes of Highland expertness in, 323—dance, 326, ii. 325—two-handed, 327—of silver, lands held by, 331—names of, 373

T

Tabhal, 307
Tacksmen, 175
Taibhsearachd, ii. 351
Tail of a chief, 150, 180
Tain-bo, a most ancient poem, ii. 231
Taini, persons so styled, 197
Taixaili, their capital, ii. 8
Talisker, sword preserved at, 328
Tanaist, 140—law of, 180—revenue, 193
Taran, the god of thunder, ii. 342
Target, Highland, 285, 287—manner of fighting with, 289
Tartan, its antiquity, 234—its manufacture, 236 to 240—of the 42nd, 78th, 79th, 92nd, and 93rd regiments, 240—worn by His Majesty and Royal Family, 241—by H. R. H. the Duke of Sussex, 241, ii. 414—table of the various clan patterns, ii. 417—etymology of 243
Tartan of the clergy, ii. 424
Tasgal money, 208
Teeth of the Celts, 118
Temples, druidical, ii. 329
Tencteri, their advice, 391
Tenure by the straw, 194
Teut, or Teutates, ii. 340
Teutones, their contempt of death, ii. 378
Thane, 191
Three, respect for the number, ii. 356
Thirlage, ii. 104
Thracians, where situated, 18
Thule, island of, 37
Tighearna, a title of honour, 192
Timber markets, ii. 216
Tin, isles of, 34—its manufacture, ii. 201
Tings, 212
Tinning, invented by the Celts, ii. 207
Tinwald of Man, 202, 212
Tokens of the kings of Man, 212
Tolmen, ii. 346
Tongue, subterraneous work at, ii. 11
Tonnag, a Highland garment, 270
Toscheodarach, 193
Toshich, a title of honour, 191
Towns, Celtic, 375 to 377, ii. 8
Tracery, a favourite ornament, 294, ii. 38
Triads, ii. 252
Tribes, ancient Scotish, 47
Tricastines, their order of battle, 154
Triughas, or trius, 254, 259, 262
Troddan Castle, ii. 14
Tuisto, a god, 2, n. ii. 341
Tunic, 247, 269
Turf, how cut, ii. 126

Turnips, used by the Gauls, ii. 112
Tyrebachar, circle at, 212

U

Udal, inheritance, 194
Uist, horse races at, 367
Umbrians, 24
Urquhart, fortalice of, 378—glen, ruins in, ii. 7
Utensils, household, ii. 206 to 209, ossier, ii. 215

V

Vaccæi, their agriculture, ii. 75
Vegetables, 105 to 109
Veneti, their shipping, ii. 191
Verse, its importance, ii. 225—varieties of, ii. 249
Vervain, its properties, &c. ii. 175
Vessel, ancient, discovered at Stranraer, ii. 295
Vessels, drinking, ii. 162
Vitrifications, 382
Voice, 113

W

Waking a corpse, ii. 385
Wales, its ancient buildings, ii. 6—the royal palace of, ii. 9
Wansdike, 172—its design, ii 330
War, customs in, 141, &c.
War cries, 303
War song, 164
Water mill, its invention, ii. 104
Waulking cloth, 233
Weapons, 306—legal, by Welsh law, 320
Weddings, ii. 360
Welsh—their struggles for liberty, 135—hubbub, 143—royal attendants, 181 ii. 145—their arms, 281—their archery, anecdotes, 341—their mode of life, ii. 117—agriculture, ii. 95—temperance, ii. 145—system of versification, ii. 245 military airs, ii. 297—their weddings, ii. 373—funerals, ii. 387
Whales, used as food, ii. 131, 132
Wheat, ii. 84
Whisky, ii. 158—varieties of, ii. 159
Wife, Welsh laws respecting the, 219
Wilsford, discoveries at, ii. 380
Winds reverenced, ii. 345
Wine, ii. 160—berry of the Gaël, ii. 161
Wolf dogs, ii. 32
Wolves, ii. 33
Women, Gallic, 112—how affected by tanaist law, 180—Highland, head dress, 260—occupations, ii. 110
Wood, its use in architecture, ii. 2, 3
Woods of Britain, 73—venerated, ii. 346, 364
Wool, Celtic, 228
Woollen, manufacture, 227, 235
Wrestling, 156, ii. 317

Y

Yeast, how preserved, ii. 160

Z

Zythus, a malt liquor, ii. 157

INDEX OF NAMES.

A

ABARIS, priest of the Hyperborei, 230, ii. 324
Abercrombie, tartan, ii. 418
Achadh, or Achaius, Scots king, 60, 65
Adams, Mr. and family, destroyed by wolves, ii. 33
Adcantuan, his followers, 149
Adomnan, 210—his life of Columba, *Introd.*
Æmilius, defeats the Gauls, 93
Agamemnon, his arms, 298
Alastair, ruadh, na cairnach, ii. 85, *n.*
Albany, Duke of, his Highlanders, 240
Alcuin, *Introd.*
Alexander the Great, anecdote of, and the Celts, 131
—————— his method of avoiding the chariot attack, 364
Alexander I., 252, 354
Alexander II., his forces, 96
Alfred, his laws, 208, 210—his songs, ii. 221
Ambiorix, his stronghold, 376
Anacharsis, the Scyth, 15
Anne, Queen, 342
Auspach, Margrave of, ii. 284
Aodh, his laws, 210
Aonghas a choile, his murder, ii. 293
Argachacoxus, or argentocoxus, 224
Argyle, Duke of, his followers, 97
—————— anecdote of, 324
—————— defeated in Glenlivat, 328, ii. 272
—————— his barns, ii. 98
—————— his hunting, ii. 47
—————— his harper and witch, ii. 272
Arianmes, his liberality, ii. 136
Arnot, David, his archery, ii. 346
Arthur, his prelude of the salt, ii. 129
Ashburton, Lord, ii. 184
Assynt, Laird of, ii. 167
Athol, Duke of, 218, ii. 48—his hunting, ii. 49, 50—his banquet to James V. ii. 156
Attila, his bards, ii. 221
Aurinia, a German heroine, 161

B

Baillie, Alexander, his archery, 343
Baird, Lady, her remarkable cure, ii. 174
Balloch, black Donald of the isles, his piobrachd, ii. 296
Barwick, his defence of gunnery, 344
Beaton, Neil, a physician, ii. 181
Beli, a construction of roads, ii. 206
Belovesus, his expedition, 5
Berkeley, Lord, ii. 89
Bissel, a pistol maker, 370
Boadicea, or Bonduca, her army, 94, 391—ditto, how drawn up, 153—her defeat, 182—her dress, 226, 247, 266—her influence, 161—her death, ii. 378
Boiscalus, his heroism, ii. 376
Boroimh, Brian, his diadem, ii. 206—harp, ii. 276
Bothwell, Earl, 367
Boulle, Marquis de, 370
Bourke, war cry of, 305
Braidalban, Lord, his gathering, ii. 296
—————— tartan, ii. 418
Brennus, invades Italy, 6, 117—his forces, 93—his body guards, 148
Breusa, William de, 340
Brinno, 145
Britannia, first mention of, 39—how represented, 222, 288—Romana and Barbaria, 50
Bruce, King Robert, 196—his coronation, 202—his brooch, 270—his badge, 299
Brunswick, hereditary prince of, 369
Buchanan, badge of, 300
—————— war cry, 304
—————— tartan ii. 418
—————— Dugald, a bard, ii. 259
Burnet, Sir Robert, of Crathes, ii. 53
Butler, war cry of, 305

C

Caddel, Thomas, pistol maker, 369
Cæsar, his invasion of Britain, 41, 132—dread of the chariot attack, 364
Cairbro Riada, settles in Argyle, 57
Caligula, fury of his Celtic guards, 121
Cameron, the chief, anecdote of, 105, 204 ii. 122
—————— badge of, 300
—————— tartan, ii. 418
—————— Sir Ewen, killed the last wolf in Scotland, ii. 32
—————— Hugh, his great age, ii. 182

436 INDEX OF NAMES.

Camillus, repulses the Celts, 6, 118
Campbell, Sir Archibald of Clunes, his followers, 97
——— of Glenlyon, his brooch, 271
——— badge of, 300
——— war cry, 304
——— tartan, ii. 418
——— John, his bravery, 324
——— pistol maker, 369
——— Alexander, his great age, ii. 185
——— Archibald, of Melfort, ii. 386
Caol-mhal, a female name, 113
Caracalla, whence derived, 246
Caractacus, or Caradoc, his military fame, 139, 153—his spoils, 269—his fortifications, 377
Carrick, Earl of, charter of, 191
——— Roland de, charter to, 191
Cartismandua, a British princess, 192
Cassivelaunus, number of his cars, 364
Casswalon, ii. 229
Cathmor, his shield, 291
Ceraint ap Grediawl, ii. 6
Chandos, Duke of, purchases Gaëlic MSS. ii. 180
Charlemagne, his dress, 248, 277—laws respecting archery, 340, 351—league with, 53, *Introd.*—his collection of songs, ii. 222—his law concerning tombstones, ii. 386
Charles the Bald, his dress, 249
Charles Stewart, Prince, 153—his welcome and salute, ii. 294
Chevalier, his muster-roll, 98
Childeric, King of France, his grave, 377
Chisholm, badge of, 300
——— tartan, ii. 418
Chonodomarius, his dress, 283
Civillis, a German prince, his exploits, 109, 137
Clan Ronald, Lord of, his prosnachadh fairge, ii. 192
Clark, badge of, 301
——— George, anecdote of, ii. 284
——— Kennedy, a piper, ii. 289
Claudia Rufina, a British lady, her beauty, 112
Clovis, anecdote of, 145
Coefi, a Druid, ii. 320
Coel, ii. 104
Coll ap coll frewi, ii, 86
Colquhoun, badge of, 300
——— tartan, ii. 418
Columba, his curach, ii. 188—his altercation with the Pictish king, ii. 263—burns Druidical writings, ii. 264, *Introd.*
Comontoire, a Gallic king, 121
Conan, his grave discovered by a bardic song, ii. 242
Conceun, ii. 410
Conlach, a famous warrior, 317
Coote, Sir Eyre, anecdote, ii. 284
Correus, his bravery. 129
Cornac, Saint, his voyage, ii. 188
Cranston, war cry of, 304
Cristeed, Sir Richard, his account of the Irish kings, ii. 149
Cromarty, Lord, 241
Cromwell, his opinion of the Scotish soldiers, ii. 124
Cronan, a bard, ii. 260
Crother, his hall, ii. 4
Cuchullin, or Cuthullin, tradition respecting, 314—his chariot, 360

Cumberland, Duke of, 369
Cummin, badge of, 300
——— tartan, ii. 419
Cumming, John Roy, a musician, ii. 260

D

Dall, Rory, a harper, ii. 278
Dalrumpil, Duncan, grant to, 193
Dalrymple, Sir John, his opinion of the Highlanders, 137
Dalzel, tartan, ii. 419
Darius, his expedition, 15
Darthula, a female name, 113
David I. his gardening, 85—judged for the poor, 212
Davidson, badge of, 301
Davy, Sir Humphry, on destruction of forests, 85
Dempster, George, letter on vitrification, 383
Derby, Earl of, 195
Desmond, Earl of, attachment of his followers, 148
——— his rent, 187
——— war cry, 305
Divitiacus, a Celtic chief, 41
Donald of the Isles, at siege of Roxburgh, 125
——— order of battle at Harlaw, 155
——— his bards, 164, ii. 236—his form of charter, 204
——— Gruamach, of Slate, his lament, ii. 295
Donn, John, a bard, lament for, ii. 295 -
Robert, a bard, ii, 256
Douglas, Earl of, 257
——— war cry of, 303
——— tartan, ii. 419
Drummond, badge of, 301
——— tartan, ii. 419
——— H. Home, ii. 57
Dumnorix, his horsemen, 357
Dunbar, ii 9
Dunwallo, an agriculturist, ii. 92
Dyonisius, his Gallic mercenaries, anecdotes of, 120, ii. 121

E

Edgar, Atheling, his alliance with Scotland, 70
Edi, laws of, 210
Edward I. his devastation of Scotland, 82, 88
——— carries off the "fatal stone," 208
Elder, badge of, 302
Elizabeth, warrant of, in favour of archery, 344
Eltud, an agriculturist, ii. 69, 92
Erach, his adventure, ii. 349
Erectheus, 18
Errol, Earl of, fights at Glenlivat, 328
Etas, killed in a tumult, 141
Ethfin, the laws of, 210
Eumolpus, his treaty with Erectheus, 18

F

Farquharson, of Invercauld, his opinion of the fir tree, 81

INDEX OF NAMES. 437

Farquharson, badge of, 301
——— war cry, 305
——— tartan, ii. 419
——— Mr. his Gaëlic MSS. ii. 238
——— Findlamhor, ii. 2
Ferara, Andrea, celebrated sword maker, 323
Ferdinand, Prince of Brunswick, 369
Fergus Mac Eirc, King of Argyle, 57
Ferguson, badge of, 301
——— tartan, ii. 419
Ferus, his belt, 338
Fife, Earl of, his armoury, 327—his deer forest, ii. 35
Fin Mac Coul, his dress, 233
Finan, Bishop of Lindisfarne, his manner of building, ii. 3
Fingal, his dogs, ii. 41, 47—his hunters, ii. 44—his sonorous voice, 144—his shield 292—his standard, 296—his sword, 304 —his medical cup, ii. 172—his remark on drinking, ii. 164
Finlay, ii. 363
Fitz Maurice, war cry of, 305
Flanders, Count of, war cry, 304
Fleming, war cry of, 306
Fletcher, John, his singular death, ii. 394
——— Peter, his funeral, ii. 393
Forbes, badge of, 301
——— war cry, 304
——— tartan, ii. 419
——— Sir Charles, curious sword, *Introd.*
——— of Culloden, his followers, 97
——— his hospitality, ii. 146
——— of Brux, anecdote of, 334
Forgeson, James, his mission, 341
Fraoch, his sword, 321
Fraser, badge of, 301
——— war cry, 304
——— tartan, ii. 419
——— Mrs. of Culbokie, her Gaëlic MSS. ii. 236

G

Gardyn, Beatrix, ii. her harp, 273
Gairden, Peter, anecdote, 318—his great age, ii. 184
Galba, a Celtic prince, 144
Galgacus, a Caledonian prince, 147
Gallus, killed in a tumult, 141
Gaul, his war song, 163—his banner, 297— his war cry, 305
——— a physician, ii. 175
Geraldine, Lord Thomas, incited to rebellion by a bardic song, ii. 221
Gibbon, his opinion of Ossian's poems, ii. 231
Gildas, Albanius, his learning, 210
Gilderoy, a cearnach, 150
Gillescop, his ravages, ii. 3
Gillespie More, his tenure, 332
Gillo, Tancoulard Mac Tuathal, Gaëlic MS. of, 123, *n.*
Gordon, Duke of, his woods—81, his followers, 96, 97—anecdote of, ii. 282
——— badge of, 301
——— war cry, 303
——— tartan, ii. 419
——— Lord Lewis, his troops, anecdotes of, 156, ii. 283
——— of Bucky, his sword, 323
——— Cuthbert, his dyestuffs, 238, ii. 216
——— Alexander, a wizard, ii. 85, *n.*

Graham, badge of, 301
——— tartan, ii. 419
Grant, badge of, 301
——— war cry, 304
——— tartan, ii. 419
——— Laird of, his woods, 81
——— of Balindalish, his followers, 96
——— John, of Freuchie, charter to, 377
——— John, his great age, ii. 183
Gregory the Great, his death, 385
Gryffyth ap Cynan, a Welsh translator. 186 —regulates the bards, ii. 225—introduced Irish music to Wales, ii. 264—270
Gunn, badge of, 302
——— tartan, ii. 420
Gwendollen, a Caledonian Druid, ii. 364

H

Halkston of Rathillet, anecdote, ii. 121
Hamilton, Duke of, lament for, ii. 295
Hannibal, his usage of the Celts, 115, 124 deference to, 115, 356—dissolution of rocks, ii. 362
Hay, badge of, 301
——— tartan, ii. 420
Henry II., his observations respecting the Welsh, 135—entertainment at Dublin, ii. 3
Hepburn, war cry of, 304
Herod, his Celtic guards, 122
Hertha, her worship, 147
Hiffernan, war cry of, 305
Hill, a translator of Ossian's poems, ii. 233
Hoath, Lord, his accident, ii. 373
Howard, Lord, his company defeated, 342
Hungus, a Pictish king, 65
Huntly, Earl of, defeats Earl of Argyle, 328—hunts with the king, ii. 50
Hussey, war cry of, 305
Hwyell, Prince, his invocation, ii. 361

I

Ida, King of Northumberland, invades Scotland, 70
Innes, Margaret, her great age, ii. 186
Irvine of Drum, his arms, 298

J

James I., an excellent Harper, ii. 272
James III., his use of tartan, 235
James IV., his immense ship, ii. 196
James V., his hunting, ii. 50
James VII., his reception in Ireland, ii. 311—his misfortunes produced by a song, ii. 245—his salute, ii. 296
Jean Petit, a pistol maker, 370
John, Pope, letter from the Scots to, 136
——— Bishop of Glasgow, disbursement for tartan, 235
Johnstone, war cry of, 303
Josephus, his opinion of the Celts, 120
Julia, Empress, ii.

K

Kennedy, James, charter to, 191
Kerry, knight of, war cry, 304

INDEX OF NAMES.

Kianan, St., his domliag, ii. 19
Kildare, Earls of, war cry, 304
King, Mr., his opinions respecting architecture, 387

L

Lachlanson, John, grant of, 192
Lamont, badge of, 301
—— tartan, ii. 420
—— Laird of, his harp, ii. 272, 274
—— of Cowal, anecdote, ii. 137
Leeth, Robert, his survey of Ireland, ii. 181
Leinster, Duke of, motto, 304
Leitch, Mr., observations on the Highlands, 85
Lenogh, Tirlogh, Lord of Ulster, 261
Lennox, Duke of, his war cry, 303
Loarn, a king of Argyle, 57, 58
Logan, badge of, 300
—— war cry, 303
—— tartan, ii. 420
Loundres, Archbishop, extinguishes the sacred fire, ii. 336
Lovat, Lord, his followers, 97—his purse, 266—his pipe-march, ii. 300—his hospitality, ii. 143—accused of raptus, ii. 372
Lucullus brought cherry trees to Italy, 84
Lumsden, of Clowach, his rent, ii. 82
Luernius, his profession, ii. 136
Luno, son of Leven, description of, ii. 202
Lycurgus, his observation on long hair, 107

M

Mac Ailean Oig, Raonuil, ii. 294—lament for, ii. 295
Mac Alastair, badge of, 301—tartan, ii. 420
Mac Allisdrum, his march, ii. 297
Mac Alpin, ii. 234
—— Kenneth, 63, 201, 210
Mac Aoidh, or Mac Kay, badge of, 301—tartan, ii. 421
Mac Aongais, Alastair, ii. 256
Mac Art, Cormac, ii. 104
Mac Aulay, badge of, 300
—— tartan, ii. 420
Mac Bane, Gillies, his heroism, 128
Mac Bean, badge of, 301
—— John, 335
Mac Beth, Fergus, ii. 178
Mac Carthy, war cry of, 304
Mac Codrum, anecdote of, ii. 232, 238
Mac Connal, Angus, 144
Mac Crain, Gilour, his great age, ii. 182
Mac Donald, badge of, 301, war cry, 303—tartan, ii. 420
—— Sir Alexander, 86
—— of the Isles, 154
—— of Barisdale, 114, 150
—— of Boisdale, his salute, ii. 294
—— of Clan Rannald, 127 n.
—— of Keppoch, anecdotes, 105, 153, 203, ii. 85 n.
—— of Killepheder, ii. 232, 235
—— Alexander, 165, 270, ii. 256, 297
—— Sir, 86
—— Donald, Sir, of Slate, 206

Mac Donald, Donald, of Aberarder, ii. 140
—— Flora, her age, ii. 184
—— Captain, anecdote of, 324
—— Do. of Moy, ii. 140
—— Do. John, ii. 232
—— John, his age, ii. 183
—— John Breac, 128
—— John Lom, 351, ii. 254
—— Murdoch, Clarsair, ii. 277
—— Shelah, ii. 255
Mac Donnell, 331
—— war cry of, 303
—— tartan, ii. 420
—— piobrachd, ii. 292
—— the Irish piper, ii. 286
—— Peter, ii. 237
Mac Dougall, Allan, ii. 28, 256
—— of Lorn, 272
—— badge of, 301—tartan, ii. 421
Mac Druivel, his bratach, 297
Mac Duff, 190, badge of, 301—tartan, ii. 421
Mac Duffaidh, ensign staff, 296
Mac Farlane, badge of, 300—war cry 303 tartan, ii. 421
Mac Gilli Riabhach, ii. 236
Mac Gillivray, badge of, 301—tartan, 421
Mac Gilpatrick, war cry, 304
Mac Glassan, his dancing, ii. 312
Mac Gregor, badge of, 300—war cry 303 —tartan, ii. 421
—— of Glenstræ, ii. 137
—— Captain, 318
—— John, ii. 258
—— John Dubh Gear, ii. 258
—— Rob Roy, 150
Mac Guire, 215
Mac Hardy, Mrs. 327
Mac Intosh, badge of, 301
—— war cry, 303— tartan, ii. 421
—— lament, ii. 295
—— defeated by the Munros, 209
—— by Keppoch, 203
—— James, anecdote, ii. 276
—— Sir Eneas, funeral of, ii. 390
Mac Intyre, Duncan, a bard, ii. 239, 256—299
—— John, a piper, ii. 296
Mac Kay, charter to, 204
—— piper to H. R. H. the Duke of Sussex, ii. 284
—— George, a piper, ii. 302
Mac Kennedy, John, charter to, 191
Mac Kenzie, badge of, 301—war cry, 306— tartan ii. 421
—— Earl of Cromarty, 241
—— John, decd of, 177, n.
—— Kenneth, a bard, ii. 256
—— Lord Seaforth, 241
—— Roderick, his heroism, 179
Mac Kinnon, badge of, 300—tartan, ii. 422
Mac Lachlan, badge of, 300—tartan, ii. 422
—— salute. ii. 296
—— Ewen, ii. 259
Mac Lean, badge of, 301—tartan, ii. 422
—— Laird of, 154
—— of Coll, ii. 300, 367
—— Allan na sohp, ii. 302
—— John Garbh, of Coll, ii. 277, 278
Mac Lennan, 338
Mac Leod, badge of, 301—tartan, ii. 422— salute and lament, ii. 396
—— his ensign, 299
—— Lord, 240

INDEX OF NAMES. 439

Mac Leod, Donald, anecdotes, 324
—————— Rev. 323, ii. 332
—————— Mary, a bard, ii. 253, 258
—————— Sir Norman, deed of, 177, n.
Mac Mhuireach, Lachlan, 164
—————— Niel, ii. 234, 236
Mac Milcon, Bruidhi, ii. 361
Mac Murrogh, his horse, 354
Mac Nab, badge of, 301—tartan, ii. 422
—————— burial place, ii. 397
Mac Naughtan, badge of, 301—tartan, ii. 422
Mac Nessa, Concover, king of Ulster, ii. 224
Mac Nicol, Doncha Rioch, ii. 233
Mac Niel, badge of, 301—tartan, ii. 422
—————— his castle, 392
—————— James, 192
—————— Lachlan, ii. 224
—————— Niel, 192
Mac Pherson, badge of, 301—war cry, 303
—gathering, ii. 296—tartan, ii. 422
Mac Pherson of Cluny, 325, 370
—————————————— his chanter, ii. 308
—————————————— his tartan, ii. 422
—————— of Crathy, 326
—————— Alexander the revengeful, ii. 10
—————— Donald, his sword, 328
—————— letter on clanship, Introd.
—————— Ewen, anecdote, ii. 234
—————— James, 336
—————— his armour, 326
—————— his lament, ii. 304
—————— Malcolm, a bard, ii. 234, 236
—————— of Strathmasie, ii. 256
Mac Quarie, badge of, 300—tartan, ii. 422
Mac Queen, badge of, 301
Mac Rimmon, anecdote, ii. 280
—————— Captain, ii. 290
Mac Ronald, Callum garbh, ii. 194
Mac Ruari, Ailen, ii. 242
—————— Duncan, ii. 245
Mac Swein, war cry of, 305
Mac Tyre, Paul, his Dun, 383
Mac Varas, ii. 195
Malcolm, 174
—————— Ceanmore, 70, 71
Malmutius, a legislator, ii. 72
Mannus, the parent god of the Germans, 20
Manos, a Caledonian, 147
Mar, Earl of, his targe, 293
—————— his gun, 368
—————— anecdote, 324
Margaret, Queen of Scotland, 70
Marius defeats the Celts, 119
Mark, Provost of Banff, 327
Marriage ceremonies, ii. 345
Mary, Queen, her hunting, ii. 52—her harp, ii. 274, 322
Mary, the virgin, partial to the bagpipes, ii. 281
Maud, Queen of Connaught, her procession, ii. 204
Menander, a Scyth, 18, n.
Menelaus, his arms, 293
Menzies, badge of, 301—tartan, ii. 423
—————— Sir Thomas, his pearl, ii. 214
Mercers, their war cry, 303
Merddyn, a Caledonian Druid, ii. 364
Meyrick, Dr. his armoury, 312
Moelmus, a legislator, ii. 72
Moina, 269
Molloy, Dr. hospitality of his ancestor, ii. 142

Montgomery, Arnulph de, ii. 3
Montrose, Duke of, obtains repeal of law against Highland dress, 278
Morddal Gwr Gweilgi, ii. 6
Morrison, Roderick, a harper, ii. 276
Munich, Count, 375
Munro, badge of, 301—war cry, 203—tartan, ii. 423
—————— of Culcairn, anecdote, 179
—————— John, defeats Mac Intoshes, 200
Murdoch, John, 369
Murray, badge of, 301—tartan, ii. 423
—————— Lord, 141, 240
—————— Regent, his portrait, 258
—————— bonnie Earl of, 323
—————— Elizabeth, her longevity, ii. 182

N

Nechtan, his literary correspondence with Ceolfrid, Introd.
Nchelania, a Celtic Deity, ii. 346
Nelan, an Irish bard, anecdote, ii. 223
Nennius, his history, Introd.
Nicholas, his letter to the Bishop of St. Andrews, ii. 214
Nigel, Earl of Carrick, 191

O

O'Brian, war cry of, 304
—————— of Thomond, 196
—————— Murcertach, 215
—————— Murrough, his execution, 177
—————— his horse, 354
O'Carrol, war cry of, 304
O'Daly, Doncha, a bard, ii. 202
O'Duff, Brian, his lament, ii. 297
O'Kane, a harper, ii. 276
Ogilvie, badge of, 301—tartan, ii. 423
Oliphant, badge of, 301
O'Neal, war cry of, 304
—————— his oath, 148
—————— Sir Arthur, plundered, ii. 70
—————— solicits aid to expel Scots, ii. 86
—————— hospitality, ii. 141
—————— his sitting in state, ii. 212
Orgetorix, 186
Oscar, 284, 286
Ossian, his poems, vindicated, ii. 231, et seq.
—————— known to the Lowlanders, ii. 232
—————— performed in dramas, ii. 248
—————— his grave, ii. 240
O'Sullivan, war cry of, 304
Oswy, King of Northumberland, 70

P

Palladius, first bishops of the Scots, 53
Patrick, St., his dispute with Ossian, ii. 364
Perth, Highlanders of, their numbers, 96
Polybius, his observation on the Gallic wars, 120
Porevith, god of spoil, 316
Ptolemy, overthrown by the Celts, 6
Pythia, the discoverer of Britain, 37

R

Ramsay, Alexander, ii. 9
Rea, Lord, 203
Roderch, king of Strathclyde, ii. 50, 213
Reuthamor, 269
Robertson, badge of, 301
———— tartan, ii. 423
———— of Lude, anecdote of, 324
———— harps of, ii. 274, 275
———— Captain, 327
Roderick, last king of Ireland, 327
Rose, badge of, 301
———— tartan, ii. 423
———— of Kilravock, his followers, 97
Ross, badge of, 301
———— tartan, ii. 424
———— William, a bard, ii. 258
Roy, Rob, his funeral, ii. 392—his son hanged for abduction, ii. 372
Ruthven, presumed origin of the name, *Introd.*

S

Samuel, a piper, lament for, ii. 296
"Sam, big," 104
Scot, of Buccleuch, war cry of, 303
Scott, provost of Banff, 327
———— Sir Walter, 318, 319, *Introd.*
———— Michael, a wizard, ii. 80, n.
Scotland, kings of, war cry of, 304
Seaforth, Lord, his followers, 97—his regiment, 241
Shaw, badge of, 301
———— James, a bard, ii. 266
Shiel, pistol maker, 370
Sinclair, badge of, 300—tartan, ii. 424
Sigovesus, a Celtic chief, 5
Sithama, a Druid, his speech, 114, n.
Smyth, Sir John, 241
Stanley, Sir John, his duties as king of Man, 212
Stewart, badge of, 295—tartan, ii. 424
———— General, on the origin of clanship, 171
———— Mary, 191
———— John Roy, a bard, ii. 259
———— Alexander & Donald, their poems, ii. 250
Steuart, in Avenside, anecdote of, 235—of Appin, his followers, 99
Stone, Jerome, a translator of Ossian's poems, ii. 234
Stratherne, Earl of, anecdote of, 281
Sussex, H. R. H. the Duke of, his tartan, 241
Sutherland, badge of, 301
———— tartan, ii. 424
———— Lord, his troops, 97

T

Tabourner, Stephen, his archery, 343
Talliesin, a Welsh bard, ii. 360—his grave, ii. 386
Taylor, his description of a Highland hunting, ii. 49
Theodoric, his funeral, ii. 3
Thompson, John, 343
Titus, his opinion of the Germans, 119
Turner, John, 326—his poems, ii. 269
Tyrconnel, his regiments, 104
Tyrone, his troops, 144, 155—plundered, ii. 70
Tyrtæus, effect of his songs, ii. 220

U

Umad, his lamentation, ii. 40, 382
Urguist, a Pictish princess, 65
Urquhart, badge of, 302
———— tartan, ii. 424

V

Veleda, a heroine, 161, 191—her habitation, ii. 20
Vercingetorix, a Gallic chief, 152
Veremundus, an ancient historian, *Introd.*
Vergasilanus, ditto, 207
Viriathus, curious account of, 150

W

Wade, General, his list of the Highland forces, 96—receives the arms of the Highlanders, 371
Wallace, 201, 205, 322—portrait, 235
Wedderburn, John, his archery, 343
Wemys, David, of that elk, his archery, 343
West, Sir Benjamin, his opinion of tartan, 239, 245
William the Lion, his portrait, 235
Williams, his notice of vitrifications, 382

Y

York, Duke of, his "Own Highlanders," 239

Z

Zamalxis, a learned Scyth, 18, n.